WOMEN IN THE RENAISSANCE

Women in the Renaissance

SELECTIONS FROM

English Literary Renaissance

EDITED BY

Kirby Farrell,

Elizabeth H. Hageman,

AND

Arthur F. Kinney

The University of Massachusetts Press

Amherst

Printed in the United States of America

LC 90–11074

ISBN 0–87023–727–6

Library of Congress Cataloging-in-Publication Data

Women in the Renaissance : selections from English literary Renaissance /

edited by Kirby Farrell, Elizabeth H. Hageman, and Arthur F. Kinney.

   p. cm.

  Includes bibliographical references and index.

  ISBN 0–87023–727–6 (alk. paper)

  1. English literature—Early modern, 1500–1700—History and criticism. 2. English literature—Women authors—History and criticism.
3. Women and literature—England—History—16th century. 4. Women
and literature—England—History—17th century. 5. Women—England—History—Renaissance, 1450–1600. 6. Renaissance—England.
7. Women in literature. I. Farrell, Kirby, 1942– . II. Hageman, Elizabeth. III. Kinney, Arthur F., 1933– . IV. English literary Renaissance.
PR418.W65W66   1990

820.9′9282′09031—dc20   90–11074

                                            CIP

British Library Cataloguing in Publication data are available.

Contents

Recent Studies in Women Writers of the English Renaissance

Preface

KIRBY FARRELL

Did women have a Renaissance? In a way Joan Kelly-Gadol's famous question (1977) is itself part of a remarkable renaissance. Since the 1970s interest in women of the early modern period has produced an inquiry of extraordinary range and intensity. From its inaugural issue in 1970, which included William Ringler's text of *The Nut-Brown Maid,* a version of the Griselda story, *ELR* has been one medium of that inquiry. The present volume brings together important essays from the journal, including some from the two special issues devoted to women in the Renaissance.

As Elizabeth Hageman observed in her preface to *ELR's* second special issue (1988), "our new interest in Renaissance women is in fact a *re*newal of the attention paid to women a generation ago by scholars such as Pearl Hogrefe, Ruth Hughey, Ruth Kelso, Charlotte Kohler, and Louis B. Wright, who recognized that Renaissance ideas about women's nature are significant markers of sixteenth- and seventeenth-century culture." As it gathered momentum in the late 1970s, the renewal expressed the complex and passionate concerns of scholars working at a time when feminism and new modes of historiography were reshaping the intellectual landscape in Europe and America.

By 1984, in the preface to *ELR's* first special women's issue, Kathleen McLuskie registered the "maturity" of the new feminist scholarship. Since then production has if anything accelerated. Every year brings fresh bibliographies of women writers, new editions of authors ranging from Elizabeth Cary and Mary Wroth to Elizabeth I, textbook anthologies such as Katharine M. Wilson's *Women Writers of the Renaissance and Reformation,* analyses of revealing occasional writing such as letters and diaries, and acute reappraisals of the major authors traditionally at the center of literary study. We can now look beyond the salutary recovery of "lost" women writers and the surprising diversity of their work and appreciate also the intellectual

vii

range of feminist studies that has made the recovery possible. Feminist critical methods have proved to be eclectic and adaptive. Some extend familiar practices, from archival research to psychoanalytic and Marxist theories. Others have assimilated a variety of postmodern tenets.

What many of these critical approaches have in common is another quality characteristic of the Renaissance. For just as European imaginations deliberately courted alienation by reaching beyond local reality to reconstruct vanished worlds, so the recovery of women's marginalized voices has come about through the creation of oblique if not contrary perspectives. In Carol Thomas Neely's words, the feminist critique arose "in opposition to the dominant discourse's construction of woman and gender relations" (*ELR* 18.1 [1988], 5). At the same time, however, the feminist critique has flourished as part of a broader revitalization of historical criticism—an effort to reunderstand texts in terms of cultural process—and the interaction has been synergistic. Interest in women has enlivened, and in turn been energized by, a historiography that searches out back lanes and villages as well as palaces, families and laborers as well as bishops and monarchs, the elusive conditions of subjectivity and intimacy as well as the strategic realities of grand diplomacy.

It would be difficult, for example, to overestimate how significantly feminist studies have been changing our conception of historical causality. To appreciate the change it helps to recall the bold and often blunt hypotheses characteristic of some early investigations—such as Juliet Dusinberre's attempt to specify Shakespeare's attitude toward "the nature of women" by reading the plays in terms of English Puritan subculture (1975). Dusinberre's study inspired contravening arguments (compare Lisa Jardine's *Still Harping on Daughters* [1983]) and a host of current work that refines them both.

But the cumulative effect of feminist criticism has not been a field of perfected polemics. Rather, what has emerged is a tacit recognition of the irrational and multiplistic nature of historical causality often minimized in conventional studies. Gabriele Bernhard Jackson's essay on Shakespeare's Joan of Arc, for instance, demonstrates that there is a topical, opportunistic quality in the dramatist's working imagination that resists the familiar new historicist categories of subversion and containment and makes ready classifications of ideology seem crudely schematic. Evoked in multiple perspectives, Shakespeare's "disjunctive" presentation of Joan in *1 Henry VI* reveals a "progressive exploitation of the varied ideological potential inherent in the topically relevant figure of the virago." Like much of Shakespeare's later work, the play "locates itself in areas of ideological discomfort." The essay discovers Elizabethan imaginations playing out discontinuous positions, as much improvisatory as strategic, constituting a marketplace of bargaining opinions rather than a doctrinal edifice. Such a perspective takes us beyond neat polemical answers to Joan Kelly-Gadol's question, "Did women have a Renaissance?"

This sophisticated vision of historical causality results not from hyperactive postmodernist epistemology, but rather from an abundance of new texts and networks of ancillary cultural material which critics have had to master in order to compensate for scanty or intractable historical evidence. As we find out about women and women writers in the early modern period, the wealth of particular new data exposes the limits of existing theory. At the same time the encounter with individual women's voices from the past makes it possible to search out the networks of relationship—the systems of social behavior—that defined and substantiated them.

While early theories of patriarchy and monarchy tended to postulate monolithic institutions dominating social life, for instance, research has gradually uncovered a far less static and melodramatic reality. We can see now in detail how patriarchal doctrine was promulgated during the 1590s, and not only in directly prescriptive polemics. Consider R. J. Fehrenbach's edition of *A Letter sent by the Maydens of London*. *A Letter* indirectly reports on the lives of servant women in the course of refuting a misogynistic attack against them. Yet *A Letter*'s author was presumably male, and his defense of women is strategic in ways that are anything but simple to identify. The document seems to have been part of a highly improvisational process through which English culture defined the limits of freedom for women servants.

But even brutal domination may be more unaccountable than conventional explanations can appreciate. Suzanne Gossett's account of rape on the Jacobean stage shows how contradictory and self-confounding the process of defining gender and power could be. Among other things, plays which assume that rape victims must die may paradoxically "imply a concern and respect for women in general which is missing from the plays which do not automatically condemn the heroine to death" (*ELR* 14.3 [1984]). In a companion article, reprinted here, Gossett shows how ambivalence toward women is figured in the increasing incoherence of Stuart masques and the cultural values they pretend to enact, even as Charles I and Henrietta Maria—that most connubial of couples—ironically presided over the masque's demise.

While Renaissance women clearly faced repression, it took protean forms, from the house arrest of the complexly reckless Lady Arbella Stuart which Sara Jayne Steen recounts, to the resistance met by women writers such as Margaret Tyler, whose translations Tina Krontiris describes, and Lady Mary Wroth, whose frustrations Carolyn Ruth Swift surveys. Yet repression did not always take reliably antagonistic forms. It could be present in a bewildering tangle of social markers, as Sylvia Bowerbank makes clear in her account of Margaret Cavendish, Duchess of Newcastle, who combined aristocratic vanity and self-intoxicating lyric imagination into a maverick intellectual role that brought her into the reluctant company of the Royal Society. Look closely at the interplay of great social power and personal eccentricity in the Duchess' behavior, and the culture she inhabited begins to appear freshly mysterious.

In this context even quotidian conformity can be intriguing. Witness Lady Southwell's defense of poetry in a letter Jean C. Cavanaugh has edited. An amateur poet living in remote, socially ambiguous Ireland, Lady Southwell apologizes for poetry in stock terms that hark back to Sidney. Yet her compulsive idealism and witty appeals to religious authority also have a competitive edge that suggests she is negotiating for status in a social world whose currency is gender-inflected aristocratic righteousness. Likewise poignant are two childhood poems of Katherine Philips which Claudia Limbert has recovered: texts that wishfully define marriage and gender in ways that make mysterious and moving Philips' actual later life as Puritan-turned-Royalist wife to a provincial gentleman—a Parlementarian—nearly four decades her senior.

It is fascinating to compare Katherine Philips' juvenilia to the politically charged poem on marriage by Queen Elizabeth which opens Ellen M. Caldwell's examination of *Gallathea,* the marital advisory Lyly wrote for the Queen (1588). Lyly managed to present to his monarch a harmlessly perfunctory message about love while covertly using imagery of androgyny to dispel anxiety about marriage and the self-division caused by love. Lyly's ingenious codes reflect the complex semiotic struggles over the Queen's identity which obsessed the realm as long as she lived. But in addition, with a mixture of guile and naivete, Lyly's argument exposes some of the buried assumptions about gender and personal autonomy that gave Elizabethan culture its distinctive shape.

A notable feature of all these studies, that is, is their ability to evoke serendipitous insights beyond their immediate aims. In the course of an essay on the virago in *1 Henry VI*, Gabriele Bernhard Jackson unassumingly offers a profound account of Shakespeare's imagination at work: an account of artistic production in the London theater of the 1590s. As Jacqueline DiSalvo explores imagery of witchcraft and psychic boundaries in Milton's poetry, she arrives at fundamental insights into Milton's ambivalence and creativity that also light up the imaginative terrain around him. DiSalvo's analysis makes it possible to reappraise the magisterial Protestant patriarch and to examine conflicts about authority and gender roles that energize his verse in unsuspected ways.

Like much of the criticism in this volume, DiSalvo's essay asks *(NB)* what sort of living earth the cloud-capped towers of art have been built upon. Such arguments implicitly call for further excavation of the existential ground underlying—and obscured by—the traditional literary monuments of Western culture: not to deconstruct a text into a squall of signs or to advertise its unique genius, and not to dispel or to burnish its aura of imperishable authority so that we see our own gratified faces reflected in it, but rather to clarify the peculiar conditions and mortal limits of its creativity—which, in the last decade of the twentieth century, is criticism's closest approximation to beauty and truth.

It goes without saying that a renaissance needs great libraries and keys to their collections—fine examples of the latter are the updated bibliographies compiled by Elizabeth H. Hageman and Josephine A. Roberts. To maximize the usefulness of this volume, Arthur F. Kinney has provided a subject index.

The present volume represents an effort to collect the best of the journal's studies on women under one cover and to make them available to a wider audience. A project of this scope draws many talents into a magic circle. Arthur Kinney and Elizabeth Hageman proposed the first *ELR* special issue on women, and the editorial board of the journal evaluated a wealth of prospective material before selecting the essays from which this collection has been drawn. We are grateful to Julie Ainsworth and Jean Miller of the Folger Shakespeare Library, who provided the photograph on the cover, and to Ruth Mortimer of the Neilson Library at Smith College, who supplied the logo and ornament for the original special issues. In addition, we wish to thank the Graduate School, the dean of the Faculty of Humanities and Fine Arts, and the English Department at the University of Massachusetts, Amherst, for crucial support. And finally, turning editorial visions into printed pages, the director and staff of the University of Massachusetts Press have once again earned our warmest gratitude.

WOMEN IN THE RENAISSANCE

WILLIAM A. RINGLER JR.

The Nutbrown Maid *(a reconstructed text)*

INTRODUCTION

I

THE *Nutbrown Maid* has remained one of the most esteemed and popular of early Tudor poems ever since its first known appearance about 1503 in Richard Arnold's *Customs of London* (*STC* 782; often called "Arnold's Chronicle"). It was separately printed at an early date, probably in a quarto of twelve leaves (the text is too long for a broadside), and went through a number of editions. Though no copies of these quartos survive, their existence is attested by the fact that in 1520 the Oxford bookseller John Dorne sold a copy for a penny,[1] and that in 1558–59 John King was fined for printing the poem without license.[2] It was well enough known to be made the subject of a religious parody about 1537;[3] in 1575 it had a place in the library of popular "matters of storie" owned by the Coventry mason Captain Cox;[4] and in the mid-seventeenth century an abbreviated text was copied into the Percy Folio. It then dropped out of sight for a while; but in 1707 it was reprinted (from a transcript that had been made for Pepys from the 1503 edition) with an appreciative notice in the periodical called *The Muses Mercury*—an edition that inspired Matthew Prior's popular imitation, *Henry and Emma,* in 1709. Edward Capell printed it in his *Prolusions* in 1760, Bishop Percy included it in his *Reliques* in 1765, and from that time onward it has continued to be a popular selection in anthologies.

The poem is a version of the Griselda story, first given literary form by Boccaccio in the *Decameron* (x.x), redacted into Latin by Petrarch, and from Petrarch's Latin and a French translation paraphrased by Chaucer in his Clerk's Tale. It is an exemplum of the constancy of women's affection, of love that never varies however maligned. Boccaccio's version of the story moved Petrarch to tears, and the fourteenth-century author of the *Ménagier de Paris* found in it "too much cruelty, beyond reason." But the author of *The Nutbrown Maid* mitigates the pathos, for his Maid does not herself suffer; she is only presented with the prospect of suffering. It is the intention of the author to praise women by showing that they are superior in constancy to men, and by indicating that they may be

---

1. F. Madan, "The Daily Ledger of John Dorne," in Oxford Historical Society, *Collectanea*, First Series, ed. C. R. L. Fletcher (1885), p. 87.

2. Edward Arber, *A Transcript of the Registers of the Company of Stationers*, I (1875), 93.

3. Printed by W. Carew Hazlitt in *Remains of the Early Popular Poetry of England*, III (1866), 2–22.

4. *Robert Laneham's Letter*, ed. F. J. Furnivall, Ballad Society (London, 1871), p. 30.

3

even higher than men in the eyes of God, who "sumtyme provith such as he lovith." As Chaucer, following Petrarch, had said, every person "sholde be constant in adversitee," for God "preeveth folk al day." This is in accordance with the doctrine of St. Augustine's *De Patientia*, which quoted the Book of Wisdom iii.4–6: "And though they suffer pain before men, yet is their hope full of immortality . . . for god proveth them and findeth them meet for himself, he trieth them as the gold in the furnace." Nevertheless, Dr. Johnson's condemnation, in his life of Prior, of the moral confusion of that poet's imitation, applies equally to the original—the Maid's resolve "to follow an outlawed murderer . . . deserves no imitation," and the Man's expedients to try her constancy are "such as must end either in infamy to her, or in disappointment to himself"—and is not convincingly negated even by the larger religious perspective given by the end of the poem.

The Nutbrown Maid was first commended in *The Muses Mercury* in 1707 as a poem that will affect the "Minds of those that are to be touch'd by the Truth and Simplicity of Nature; for she cannot be better painted, if we will excuse the antique colouring"—a judgment that was substantially repeated by Percy in his *Reliques*. Child included it in the first two editions of his *Popular Ballads* (1864, 1878), but omitted it from his final edition. The poem is not a popular ballad and is not in the least an example of simple primitivism. It is a sophisticated work of art written by a poet who had a feeling for rhythm, a command of phrasing, and an ability to construct a story which were superior to those of most of his contemporaries.

The poem's great technical innovation is the application to narrative of devices from the newly developing secular drama. There had been dialogues before which told a story —such as *De Clerico et Puella*—but this poem is presented by actors who *impersonate* the characters. In the first four stanzas two actors come forward and in their own persons announce to the audience (see l. 16) that they will perform a piece to illustrate the virtues of women, and show that they have been unjustly maligned in the current attacks against them. The actors then assume the roles of Squire and Puella, and conduct a dialogue that develops and resolves a situation in the ensuing stanzas 5–29. In the last stanza the actors drop their dramatic roles, and, again in their own persons, comment in unison on the episode they have just performed. This technique is similar to that of Henry Medwall's *Fulgens and Lucrece*, c. 1487, which is almost the earliest example of purely secular drama in England. Medwall's play is primarily a debate on the qualities of true nobility. It begins with the actors, A and B, stepping out from among the audience and announcing the subject of the play; they then assume roles within the play as servants, and the action and debate proceed when the other principals enter. *The Nutbrown Maid*, then, has many of the characteristics of the earliest interludes, especially the element of *impersonation* by actors. A plot is unfolded which rises to a climax and has a surprising reversal at the end: all this is conveyed by dialogue; the only thing lacking to make it completely dramatic is physical movement of the characters during the performance. The poem may be considered as similar to the interlude, a form which its author obviously had in mind and on which he structured his piece. It does not, however, have a part in the historical development of the drama, for it is modelled on the already developed secular drama. Chambers, who classes the poem with carols and lyric, remarks that it might have been treated under the heading of drama; Warton had properly called it a "dramatic dialogue."[5]

5. E. K. Chambers, *English Literature at the Close of the Middle Ages* (1945), p. 121; Thomas Warton, *History of English Poetry*, III (1781), 140.

The poem is also notable for its competent handling of an intricate verse form and a sure sense of rhythm unusual for its time. The line is a septenary with double internal rhyme, and six lines are combined to form a stanza *aaaabB*, with a recurrent refrain. The form is found in Latin in the thirteenth century, and often in English from the fourteenth century onwards.[6] In contrast to much other verse at the end of the fifteenth and beginning of the sixteenth century, the rhythm has a sure flow. The basic pattern is iambic, but variety is introduced by substituting two unstressed syllables for a single unstressed syllable in any position. Only in four places (ll. 83, 99, 104, and 153) do headless part-lines occur, and these could be the result of textual corruption.[7]

II

Though the poem has been many times reprinted, there has been general uncertainty regarding its text, most editions of which have been eclectically emended. In 1760 Edward Capell, the first person to attempt a scholarly edition, reprinted the text of 1521 (the only one he knew of) with thirty-one acknowledged and fourteen unacknowledged conjectural emendations. In 1871 W. W. Skeat, in his *Specimens of English Literature 1394–1579*, produced a corrected version of the 1503 text, emended in thirty-six places by conjecture or with readings from the Balliol MS; and this eclectic procedure has been followed by the more recent editors F. Sidgwick and E. K. Chambers. No one heretofore has tried to determine the lines of descent and the relationships of the extant substantive texts, though ever since 1868, when F. J. Furnivall provided a *literatim* print of the Balliol and Percy Folio MSS in *Bishop Percy's Folio MS* (III, 174–86), most of the evidence has been publicly available. What has not been perceived heretofore is that Treveris' edition of Arnold's *Customs of London*, about 1521, was not a literal reprint of the first edition of about 1503, but was extensively corrected from another source, perhaps one of the lost quarto editions; and that even the late Percy Folio of about 1650, though it has suffered serious corruption, nevertheless retains readings which are of assistance in determining the earlier state of the text. It is time, therefore, to reassess the textual evidence and to attempt to reconstruct the wording of the original version of the poem.

As I have indicated, documentary evidence shows that a separately printed edition of *The Nutbrown Maid*, probably in quarto form, was produced as early as 1520 and reprinted about 1558, and that probably other editions were issued, possibly before and certainly after those dates; but no copy of any of these survives. There are extant, however, five early printed and MS sources to be taken into account in constructing a critical text: the earliest extant print in the first edition of "Arnold's Chronicle" about 1503 (which I will

6. Arthur K. Moore, *The Secular Lyric in Middle English* (Lexington, Ky., 1951), pp. 183–86.

7. I have resisted the temptation to create metrical regularity by emending lines 83 and 99 (against the testimony of all the substantive texts) to read "from deth many [a] one" and "Made of [fine] threde and twyne"; adopting the unique reading of *03* in line 104, "Ne may not faylle"; or preferring *21–03* "fynd me" in 153 against *B-P*. However, where omissions adversely affect the sense and also produce headless lines, I have adopted *21–03* readings at 48 and 66 against *B*, and the *03-P* reading at 143 against *B-21*.

refer to as *03*); the corrected reprint of this about 1521 (*21*); the transcript made shortly before or after 1521 in Balliol College Oxford MS. 354 (*B*); a religious parody, *The New Notborune Mayd vpon the Passion of Cryste*, printed about 1537 (*N*); and the corrupt and truncated transcript made about 1650 in the Percy Folio, British Museum MS. Additional 27879 (*P*). The first three texts are complete; *N* only occasionally echoes single words or phrases of its model; and the late version in *P* preserves only twenty of the original thirty stanzas. A number of unique errors in each of these texts show that none of them except *N* could descend exclusively from any other, so all four of the main texts are entirely or partly substantive.

The earliest text (*03*) is printed, incongruously, near the middle (sigs. N6–O2) of a folio anthology of commercial and legal items, several of which concern a Richard Arnold, a haberdasher of London who also conducted business in the Netherlands, and who was identified as the compiler by Bale.[8] The volume has no title, but has since been designated "Arnold's Chronicle," from its compiler and the historical annals that constitute its first item. The contents are not arranged in any logical or chronological order. The chronicle with which the collection begins extends to 1503; near the middle is a letter of exchange dated 1492; and near the end is a will dated 1473. So the compilation was probably put together in or shortly after 1503, which is accepted as the date of printing and also provides us with the latest date for the composition of *The Nutbrown Maid*. How much earlier the poem may have been composed there is no certain way of telling, though its language and style are consonant with a date of composition not long before that of the print. The British Museum Catalogue and the *STC* identify the printer as Adrian van Berghen of Antwerp. Since the text was set up by a foreign compositor, it abounds in obvious typographical and manifest verbal errors. The text of *The Nutbrown Maid*, which occupies only six pages, contains forty obvious typographical errors, and when collated with the other texts it is revealed to have fifty-one unique readings, at least a third of which are manifest errors. It is therefore an inaccurate and unreliable text. Whether Arnold copied it from a now lost MS or earlier print there is no way of knowing. Some of the verbal corruptions may have existed in his source, and others he may have introduced himself in the course of making his own MS copy; the compositor was certainly responsible for the typographical and probably for some of the verbal errors.

A second text (*21*) is the reprint of *03* published at Southwark without date by Peter Treveris.[9] In this edition an insert of five pages extends the chronicle to 1521, but otherwise the volume is a paginary reprint of the Antwerp folio. The text of *The Nutbrown Maid*, however, was extensively revised. All but two of *03*'s obvious typographical errors were corrected, and verbal variants were introduced in 66 of the 180 lines. The compositor of *21* had certain spelling preferences of his own ("nat" for "not," "betwayne" for "betwene," etc.), but in general he reproduced fairly closely the pattern of accidentals in *03* (29 "red," 34 "wheder," etc.). It therefore appears that *21* was set up from an annotated copy of *03* rather than directly from the source from which the corrections were taken.

8. John Bale, *Scriptorum Illustrium Brytanniae Catalogus* (Basle, 1559), Centuria IX, No. x.

9. Van Berghen's edition was reprinted at Antwerp by J. van Doesborch about 1515; but a single leaf of this edition in the British Museum, which does not contain the poem, is all that survives.

This is further indicated by the imperfect correction of some of the errors in *o3*, which shows that *o3* itself served as printer's copy. For example, *o3* in line 34 has "yed one" for "ye done," an error in spacing; but *21* prints "ye one," indicating that the compositor may have misinterpreted a line inked in before the "d" as a mark of deletion rather than as an indication of spacing; and where *o3* at l. 37 has "shomwhat" for "somewhat," *21* apparently prints "lomwhat" (though "l" and long "s" are difficult to distinguish).

It is clear that Treveris recognized the inaccuracy of the *o3* text of *The Nutbrown Maid* and sought out a better original by which to correct it. This was probably one of the now-lost quarto editions, for Treveris' corrections agree overwhelmingly with *B*, which also appears to be a transcript of a printed quarto. It is also clear that, instead of using the quarto as printer's copy, Treveris collated his copy of *o3* against the quarto, and entered the corrections between the lines and in the margins of his folio. Unfortunately he did not do a thorough job of collation, and allowed a number of *o3* errors to stand uncorrected (some of the more obvious are 29 "whan" for "what," 40 "make" for "take," 115 "yt" for "than," 136 "dede" for "rede," and 158 "of" for "in"). In addition, his annotations must have been difficult to decipher and his compositor worked carelessly, so that his text, though correcting *o3* in many places, contains sixteen new typographical errors and twenty-one new unique readings, all of which appear to be errors.[10]

Since *21* was set up from an annotated copy of *o3*, it cannot be depended upon as an independent authority where it agrees with *o3*, because in those passages it may merely repeat the testimony of *o3*. Therefore *21* is properly taken as substantive only where it differs from *o3*; but even in those passages its testimony is uncertain, because without corroborative evidence it is difficult to tell whether its variants are genuine corrections taken from an authoritative source, or merely new errors introduced by the *21* collator or compositor.

Fortunately this corroborative evidence is provided by a third text, *B*, which has every appearance of being a careful and accurate transcript of an authoritative original. This was transcribed in an anthology of poetry shortly before or after 1521 by the London merchant Richard Hill, probably directly from one of the lost printed quartos. Instead of long septenary lines extending across a folio page, it is copied in half lines, suggesting derivation from an original of smaller format. It is also the only text to preserve the speech headings of "Squire" and "Puella." Where *o3* has forty and *21* has seventeen obvious typographical errors, *B* contains no more than three obvious transcriptional errors (25 "it" for "is," 57 "deuyoyed" for "deuoyd," and 178 "be be" for "be"). Also, where *o3* contains fifty-one, and *21* contains twenty-one, unique verbal variants, all or most of which are errors, *B* contains unique readings in only twenty-four lines, no more than six of which are demonstrable errors.[11] Therefore *B* is the most accurate and dependable of all the early texts.

A fourth early witness, the religious parody *N* printed about 1537, is of no value in constructing a critical text. Though in each of its thirty stanzas it repeats the last phrase of the refrain and two or more rhyme words, within the lines it only occasionally echoes single

---

10. See in the apparatus lines 1, 9, 32, 34, 40, 59 (2), 61, 82, 86, 87 (2), 112, 116, 122, 158, 170, 174, 176, 177, and 179.

11. See in the apparatus lines 23, *25, 29, 40 (2), 45, *48, 49, 50, 52, *53, 57, *66, 68, 82, *91, *99, 116, 127, 130, 136, 147, 148, 176, 178 (2)—asterisks indicate errors.

words or phrases from its model. Most of its echoed words or phrases are invariant in the other texts, so only five passages provide possible evidence of textual relationships. In l. 1 *N* agrees in error with *P* against the other texts, "Ryght and no wrong," but this must be an accidental result of the independent substitution of similars. In two lines *N* agrees with *o3* against *B-21-P* (25 "Wherfore moche," 136 "wycked dede"), and in two other lines omitted by *P* it agrees with *o3* against *B-21* (41 "loo," 79 "Full well"). Since all four of these readings are probably errors in *o3*, the agreements indicate that *N* was modelled directly upon *o3* itself, and so is a derivative and not a substantive text. But even if it were substantive, *N*'s echoes of its model are so erratic and infrequent that its testimony would have to be ignored as textually insignificant.

The fifth text, in the Percy Folio (*P*), a century or more later in date than the others, was copied either from a late and corrupt lost quarto or from some other corrupt intermediary. It preserves only twenty of the original thirty stanzas and has verbal variants in almost every line. But though it is more of a paraphrase than a copy, it nevertheless preserves the main features of its ultimate original, and its testimony is overwhelmingly in favor of the readings of *B* against those of *o3* or *o3-21*. It agrees with *B-21* against *o3* in lines 6, 11, 18, 25, 36, 71, 98, 102, 113, 117, 123, 126, 136, and 163; and with *B* against *o3-21* in lines 7, 32, 87, 115 ("then"), 150, and 153. At 115 ("woman hood") *P* agrees in error with *o3* against *B-21*, at 139 it reads "vpbraid" with *o3* against *B-21* "owt brayde," and at 174 it reads "Thus" with *o3* against *B-21* "Than"; these are probably accidental resemblances resulting from the independent substitution of similars. But at 143 *P* preserves with *o3* the correct reading "me" which *B-21* omit, and at 176 it preserves with *o3* a partline which *21* omits and which *B* transcribes wrongly as the result of an eye-skip. *P* also corroborates the readings of *B* at 32, 87, 115, 143, and 150, and partially corroborates it at 147, 153, and 163. Therefore, despite its late date and corruption, *P* offers occasional evidence useful in the choice of readings.[12]

Of the four primary texts (*o3*, *21*, *B*, *P*), all except *B* abound in manifest errors. But when these manifest errors are eliminated, we find that the four texts fall into two groups identified by slight variations in phrasing in some fifty lines. The earliest group (represented by *o3*), I designate *X*; the later group (represented by *B*, the corrections in *21*, and *P*), I designate *Y*. I list below the salient readings of *B* and *o3* that distinguish *Y* and *X*.

12. In the earlier stages of my analysis I thought it might be possible to establish a precise stemmatic line of descent of the extant texts: *o3* and *N* from *X* (they agree together against the other texts at 25, 41, 79, 136); *P* from *Y* (*P* agrees with or approximates *o3* against *B-21* at 113, 115, 139, 142, 174, 176); *B* and *21* from *Y* via *Z* (they agree together against *P* and *o3* at 104, 113, 143, 174). But the evidential weight of these few scattered readings is slight indeed, especially when we take into account the phenomenon of independent substitution of similars. My final conclusion is the pattern of relationships described in the body of this essay: *o3* from *X* (or from an earlier print of the lost quarto *Y* via a scribally revised intermediary); *N* probably from *o3*; *B* and the corrections in *21* directly from *Y*; *P* from *Y* via corrupt intermediaries.

(*B* reading given first; *03* reading second)

6 from : and	87 and wete : or wete
7 wreten : writ	95 shortly gon : soon agone
11 whan . . . cam . . . to her :	98 Nether : nor drinke
from . . . whan . . . he cam	104 May not : Ne may not
23 tell me : telle	107 or : er
25 wherof gret : wherfore moche	110 your Knee : the knee
32 the . . . darke : My . . . derked	113 yff that . . . Do it as shortly as :
40 you owght : ye nought	And . . . doo it shortely as
41 to : loo	116 myn here : my here
45 bide : leue	117 I haue : haue I
50 of olde : and olde	123 like as : right as
52 for your : from your	127 it is : yet is
59 to Shewe : And sure	130 ye proved . . . ye loved :
65 wherby : By whiche	you proued . . . you loued
67 I say : I Thinke	136 by my cursed Rede : be wyked dede
68 to for sake : for your sake	139 owt brayde : vpbraid
75 socowrs : rescous	141-2 be as ye said / ye were . . . leve me :
76 ye . . . ffor fere wold draw :	as the sayde / Be so . . . leue
you . . . shul drawe for fere	145 you went : ye went
78 I will to / the grenwod go :	147 more fayre : fayrer
I too . the woode wyl goo	153 me fynd / softe : fynde . me softe
(*also* 102, 126, 150)	160 that ye shuld : you shuld
79 Right . . . but : Ful . . . ful	163 more gladder : more glad
80 it is : is it	170 Sith ye : sith you
81 with . . . or : amonge . . . and	171 myn herytage : my herytage
82 To helpe you with my :	174 Than : Thus
to greue them as I	178 God : Whiche

Most of the variants characterizing these two groups make almost equally good sense in context, and neither set can be clearly differentiated as an improvement over the other. Many of the variants are merely sense substitutions of one synonymous expression for another (as, for example, 45 bide *B* : leue *03*; 65 wherby : By whiche; 75 socowrs : rescous; 95 shortly gon : soone agone; 107 or : er; 123 like as : right as; 136 cursed : wyked; 139 owt brayde : vpbraid). Variations of this sort are too inconsequential to be the result of systematic authorial revision. Therefore one or the other set must be the work of a creative scribe who reproduced the general meaning rather than the specific wording of the text before him and frequently indulged in sense substitutions. If the scribe who made the substitutions wrote *X*, then *Y* best represents the lost author's original; if he wrote *Y*, then *X* would preserve the readings of the original.

It is, however, difficult to determine with certainty whether *X* or *Y*, the *03* or *B* variants, are authorial or the substitutions of a creative scribe. On impressionistic grounds fewer than a dozen *03* readings and a slightly larger number of *B* readings might appear preferable to an individual reader, but most of the other variants seem indifferent. Objective criteria are difficult to establish, though internal consistency of usage might be an indication of authorial readings. Uses of "my" and "mine," regularity of rhythm, and consistency of the refrain are examples. *B* always writes "mine" before a vowel; *o3* usually does, but in one place (71) has "my." *B* usually has "mine" before "h," but in one place (29) has "my"; *o3* is erratic and in two places (71, 101) has "mine," but in two other places (116, 171) has "my." The rhythm of the poem is in general remarkably regular for its time, and only in two places (83, 99) do headless part-lines occur in both *o3* and *B*; elsewhere *o3* has seven headless part-lines (16, 36, 49, 113, 136, 143, 178), all but the first, fourth, and sixth of which result from fairly obvious omissions; and *B* has only six headless part-lines (48, 66, 91, 104, 143, 153), all but the fourth and sixth of which result from fairly obvious omissions. In *B* the refrains of the Puella are invariant, except in 48 where "my" is obviously omitted; in *o3* the refrains of the Puella are also invariant, except in 36 where "my" is obviously omitted, and 60 where the substitution of "But" is a manifest error that destroys the sense. Except for the opening phrase, the refrains of the Squire are invariant in *B*; but in *o3* they vary in four stanzas (78, 102, 126, 150):

> wherfor I will to / the grenwod go / alon a banysshed man. (*B*)
> Wherfore I too / the woode wyl goo / alone a banysshed man. (*o3*)

Here *o3* substitutes "woode" for the otherwise invariant "grenwod." I cannot see that any purpose is served by maintaining the refrains of the Puella invariant, but varying the refrains of the Squire in four places as is done in *o3*. But since we have no other works of the unknown author to compare, we cannot be certain whether he himself was entirely consistent in his use of "my" and "mine," whether his sense of rhythm would lead him always to avoid a headless part-line, or whether he wished to keep all but the opening phrase of his Squire refrains verbally identical. However, the testimony of both *o3* and *B* indicates a considerable tendency on the parts of both their originals toward internal consistency, and since *B* is more consistent than *o3*, it may preserve the original author's reading more accurately than does *o3*.

There is the further fact that in several passages apparently acceptable variant synonyms in *o3* occur in combination with manifest errors. Thus in 68, though *o3*'s "for your sake" makes sense, the following "as ye haue said" indicates a misunderstanding of the structure of the sentence (see textual note); in 76 *o3*'s transposition of the phrase is acceptable, but its "shul" is an error for "shuld"; and in 136, though *o3*'s "wyked" is as appropriate in the context as *B*'s "cursed," its omission of the preceding "my" and its substitution of "dede" for "rede" are demonstrable errors (see textual note). We are therefore led to suspect that the *o3* synonyms that make sense may be scribal substitutions to the same extent that the manifest errors are. And finally there is the fact that in 1521 the printer Treveris rejected most of the *X* readings in *o3* and substituted *Y* readings for them.

However, none of these arguments is absolutely conclusive in proving authorial readings; and the final choice of the original to be constructed, *X* or *Y* (the original of *o3* or the original of *B*), must be made on pragmatic grounds. The only surviving witness to *X* is *o3*, a manifestly unreliable text which can be corrected only by conjectural emendation. It is impossible to reconstruct *X* with any certainty, because with only one text as a witness we cannot tell whether its variants from *Y* derive from the original *X* or are unauthoritative substitutions introduced by *o3* itself. On the other hand, the readings of *Y* are attested throughout by *B*, which contains remarkably few manifest errors, and are attested in part by the corrections in 21 and by *P*; the independent errors of *B* can be detected by the concurrence of 21-*P* and *o3*, and therefore the readings of *Y* can be reconstructed with a high probability of accuracy.

So the readings of *Y*, the lost quarto, the text that was most widely read in the sixteenth century, are the object of the present reconstruction. How accurately the critical text that follows reflects the wording of the author's earlier lost original remains to some extent problematic, though the balance of the evidence suggests that whatever deviations from the author's original may remain are minor.

III

From the above discussion, the principles upon which the critical text should be reconstructed are self-evident. *B* should be the copy text, because it contains fewer manifest errors than the others and because, since it is probably a direct transcript of the lost quarto, it is more likely to preserve the accidentals of its original than the others, which are demonstrably at further removes from their respective originals. The readings of *B*, where not manifestly in error, should be accorded primacy where variants occur in the other substantive texts. Second in order of authority are those passages of *21* that vary from *03*, because only the variant passages have an adequate likelihood of being substantive. Third in order of authority is *03*, and fourth *P*, because their general level of accuracy is demonstrably lower. The occasional testimony of *N* should be ignored because it is probably a derivative text.

Where variants occur, manifest errors should of course be discarded. Where variants in two or more texts make sense and are appropriate in their contexts, the agreement of *B* and any other text should be preferred against the agreement of the two remaining texts. Thus *B-21* should be preferred to *03-P*, *B-03* to *21-P*, and *B-P* to *03-21*. Where *P* omits a passage in question, *B* alone should be preferred against the agreement of *03-21*, because *21* was printed from a partially corrected copy of *03* and where it agrees it may only be repeating the testimony of *03*. When these principles are applied, it is found that *B* requires emendation in only thirteen passages. Three of these are obvious transcriptional errors in *B* (25, 57, 178), five others are manifest verbal errors in *B* (91, 99, 127, 148, 176), in four sense or rhythm indicate the superiority of *21-03* to *B* or *B-P* (48, 53, 66) or of *03-P* to *B-21* (143) and in one *21-03* supported by *P* overweigh an indifferent reading of *B* (147). Except for ten passages, all other readings in *B* are supported by the consensus of two or more authorities in accordance with the principles enumerated above.[13]

In the critical text that follows the copy text is *B* (Balliol College Oxford MS. 354, fols. 210v–213v), which is printed by generous permission of the Master and Fellows of Balliol College. The copy text is transcribed *literatim*, except that abbreviations are expanded and the thorn is transcribed "th." Punctuation, word division, and capitalization are editorial (there are only a few random capitals in the copy text, and the only punctuation in any of the originals is a virgule or period after the internal rhymes). The line numbering indicates complete septenaries, but each septenary is printed as two lines, which is the way the text was probably printed in the lost quarto and was transcribed in *B* and *P*, and which makes for greater ease in reading.

13. *B* alone is preferred against *21-03* in only nine passages (23, 29, 45, 49, 50, 52, 66, 68, and 178); *B-P* is preferred against *21-03* in only six passages (7, 32, 115, 145, 150, 171); and *B* alone is preferred against *21-03-P* on the basis of rhyme usage in one word (136 "rede"). All other passages in the critical text are supported by *B-21*, *B-03*, or a combination of three or all four of the substantive texts.

In the apparatus all substantive departures from the copy text and all verbal variants in *21* and *03* are listed. *P* is so late and corrupt that its complete verbal variants are listed only for the first stanza for illustrative purposes, and elsewhere only where variants occur in the other texts, because only in those cases may *P* readings be of textual significance. In order to eliminate insignificant detail from the apparatus, obvious typographical errors in *03* and *21* that would be automatically corrected by any reader or copyist are not listed but are separately enumerated below:

Forty Obvious Typographical Errors in *03*

1 cōplaiue, 4 fouour, 6 though, 7 bat, 9 witues, 14 too . . . they, 28 au, 29 her ttrewe, 34 yed one, 37 shomwhat, 46 neyer . . . lone, 48 lone bnt yon, 51 wantou, 57 lone . . . denoyd, 58 yonr, 63 mnst, 64 lyeue, 69 huute, 76 shul, 79 fiyght, 83 oue, 87 ou, 88 a bowe, 93 snre, 97 yEf, 98 before, 99 aud, 110 yout, 115 lougeth, 118 duth, 124 iu, 125 moman, 127 yEf, 128 lonid, 135 farest, 145 yEf, 158 iu . . . ener, 164 seeu, 170 destende, 173 cau.

Seventeen Obvious Typographical Errors in *21*

2 wayne, 6 tought, 16 your, 25 as, 35 where, 37 lomwhat, 47 all thought, 53 and ylle, 59 Towe, 77 Where, 94 were, 98 befor, 101 whan, 105 Sall, 130 Yed, 142 You, 174 and yerles.

The critical text I print is not perfectly consistent internally, because I have not posited a perfectly consistent author. I have tried to follow the lead of the four substantive authorities, even when their evidence results in slight textual inconsistencies. Perhaps I should have emended 83, 99, 104, and 153 to remove all headless lines, and 71 to make the use of "mine" before "h" absolutely consistent, and perhaps I should have printed "ye" as subject and "you" as object throughout. But poets at the turn of the century were seldom so precise.

THE NUTBROWN MAYDE   [210v

[1 First Player]
Be it right or wronge, thes men amonge
    on wymen do complayn,
affermyng this, how that it is
    a labowre spent in vayn
to love them well, for neuer a dele
    they love a man agayn.
For late a man do what he can
    ther favowre to attayn,
5 yet yf a newe to them pursue,
    ther ferste trew lover than
labowreth for nowght, for from her thowght
    he is a banysshed man.
[2 Second Player]
I say not nay, but that all day
    it is both wreten and said
that woman's feyth is, as who seyth,
    all vtturly decayde;
but neuerthelesse, right good witnes
    in this case myght be layde,
10 that they love trew and contenewe:
    recorde the Nutbrown Mayde,
which whan her love cam her to prove,
    to her to make his mone,

Title: The Nutbrown mayde *B*; A ballade of the notbrowne mayde *21 03*
   Table of Contents; The nutt browne mayd *P*.

1 Be it right or *B 21 03*; Right & noe *P*.   on *B 21 03*; as *P*.   wymen *B 03 P*;
   woman *21*.
2 how that *B 21 03*; what a thing *P*.   a *B 21 03*; of a *P*.
3 *omit P.*
4 late *B 21 03*; lett *P*.   attayn *B 21 03*; obtaine *P*.
5 yet *B 21 03*; & *P*.   ther *B 21 03*; the *P*.
6 labowreth *B 21 03*; he labours *P*.   for from *B 21*; and from *03*; fur from *P*.
   he *B 21 03*; for he *P*.
7 wreten *B P*; writ *21 03*.
8 womans *B 03*; womens *21 P*.
9 this *B 03 P*; his *21*.
11 whan . . . cam . . . to her *B 21*; from . . . whan . . . he cam *03*; whan . . . came . . . he
   come *P*.

wolde not departe, for in her hart
she loved but hym alone.
[3 First Player]
Than betwen vs let vs discvsse
what was all the maner
betwen them two; we will also
tell all the payn in fere
15   that she was in. Now I begyn,
so that ye me answere.
Wherfor all ye that present be,
I pray you geve an ere;
I am the knyght; I com by nyght
as secrete as I can,
saying, "Alas, thus stondith the caas,
I am a banysshed man."
[4] Puella
And I your will for to fulfill
in this will not refuce,
20   trustyng to shew, in wordes fewe,
that men haue an yll vse
to ther own shame wymen to blame,
and cavselesse them accuse.
Therfor to you I answere now,
all wymen to excuse:
"Myn own hart dere, with you what chere?
I pray you tell me anon,
ffor in my mynd of all mankynd
I love but you alon."
[5] Squyre
25   "It stondith so: a dede is doo
wherof gret harme shall grow.

12–17 *omit P.*
16 wherfor all *B 21*; Wherfore *03.*
18 caas *B*; case *21 P*; cause *03.*
19–24 *omit P.*
23 tell me *B*; tell *21 03.*
25 is *21 03 P*; it *B.*   wherof gret *B 21*; wherfore moche *03*; wherby great *P.*

---

13 *maner*: mode of action
14 *in fere*: together
18 *caas*: case; cf. l. 167

My destynye ys for to dye
  a shamfull deth I trow,
or elles to flee; the on mvste be.
  Non other way I know,
but to withdraw as an owtlawe   [211
  and take me to my bow.
Wherfor adewe myn own hart trew,
  non other rede I can;
30 ffor I mvste to the grenwode go,
  alon, a banysshed man."
        [6] Puella
"O lorde what is this worldes blis
  that changith as the mone?
The somer's day in lusty May
  is darke beffore the none.
I here you say ffarewell; nay, nay,
  we departe not so sone.
Why say ye so? Whether will ye go?
  Alas, what haue ye done?
35 All my welfare to sorow and care
  shuld chaunge, yf ye were gon;
ffor in my mynde of all mankynd
  I love but you alon."
        [7] Squyre
"I can beleve it shall you greve
  and sumwhat you dystreyne;
but afterward your paynes harde
  within a day or twayn
shall sone aslake, and ye shall take
  conforte to you agayn.

---

27 on *B 21 P*; ton *03.*
29 Myn own *B*; my owne *21 03 P.*
31 changith *B 03 P*; chaunged *21.*
32 the *B 21 P*; My *03.*   darke *B P*; derked *21 03.*   none *B 03 P*; mone *21.*
34 ye done *B*; ye one *21*; yed one *03*; you done *P.*
36 in my *B 21 P*; in *03.*
38–85 *omit P, except that 71–72 are substituted for 95–96.*

---

29 *myn own*: The testimony of *B* alone is here preferred to *21-03-P* "my owne," because elsewhere *B-21-03* always have "mine" before a vowel—cf. ll. 23, 149, 157

40   Why shuld you owght? For to take thowght
         your labowre were in vayn.
      And thus I doo, and pray you to,
         as hartely as I can;
      ffor I mvste to the grenwode go,
         alon, a banysshed man."
                 [8] Puella
      "Now sith that ye haue shewed to me
         the secrete of your mynde,
      I shall be playn to you agayn,
         lyke as ye shall me fynde.
45   Sith it is so that ye will go,
         I will not bide behynde;
      shall it neuer be said the Nvtbrown Mayd
         was to here love vnkynde.
      Make you redy, for so am I,
         allthowgh it were anon;
      ffor in my mynd of all mankynd
         I love but you alon."
                 [9] Squyre
      "Yet I you rede to take good hede
         what men will thynk and say;
50   of yong, of olde, hit shall be told
         that ye be gon away

---

40 you owght *B*; ye ought *21*; ye nought *03*.   take *B*; make *21 03*.
41 to *B 21*; loo *03*.
45 bide *B*; leue *21 03*.
46 it neuer *B 21*; neyer *03*.
48 my *21 03*; *omit B*.
49 to *B 21*; *omit 03*.   what *B*; whan *21 03*.
50 of olde *B*; and olde *21 03*.

---

40 *you owght*: you [do] aught; *21-03* read "ye" for "you," but the distinction between "ye" as subject and "you" as object is not consistently kept by either *B* or *03*—see variants in ll. 76, 130, 145, and 170

45 *bide*: *03* "leue" (meaning "remain") is probably a sense substitution uncorrected by *21*

48 *B*'s omission of "my" produces a headless line (see n. 7 above), and furthermore all other Puella refrains are invariant; thus the omission is a manifest *B* error

50 *of yong, of olde*: The *B* reading is accepted on the principle of *durior lectio* and because *B* is generally more authoritative than *21-03*. Line 55 echoes this line with the commonplace locution "of olde and yonge"

your wanten will ffor to fulfill
    in grenwode you to play,
and that ye myght for your delite
    no lengar make delay.
Rather than ye shuld thus for me
    be called an ylle woman,
yet wold I to the grenwod go,
    alon, a banysshed man."
            [10] Puella   [211v

55 "Thowgh it be songe of olde and yonge
    that I shuld be to blame,
thers be the charge that speke so large
    in hurtyng of my name;
ffor I will prove that feythfull love
    hit is deuoyd of shame,
in your distresse and hevynesse
    to parte with you the same,
to shewe all tho that do not so
    trew lovers ar they non;
60 ffor in my mynd of all mankynd
    I love but you alon."
            [11] Squyre
"I cownsaill you remembre how
    hit is no maydyn's lawe
nothyng to dowte; but to renne owt
    to wode with an owtlawe,
ffor ye mvste ther in your hond bere
    a bowe redy to drawe,

52 for *B*; from *21 03.*
53 an ylle *03*; a mysse *B*; and ylle *21.*
57 deuoyd *21*; deuyoyed *B*; denoyd *03.*
59 to shewe *B 21*; And sure *03.*   tho *B 03*; to *21.*   trew *B 03*; Towe *21.*
60 ffor *B 21*; But *03.*
61 no *B 03*; omit *21.*
63 Redy to *B 21*; to bere and *03.*

---

52 *for*: B preferred for the same reasons as in l. 50
53 *an ylle woman*: B's "a mysse woman" (a woman astray) is a possible form, but is not
recorded in the *OED*; also "ll" in print can be misread as long "ss," so B may have misread
58 *parte*: share
59 *tho*: those
62 *to dowte*: to fear

and as a theff thus mvst ye leve
    ever in drede and awe,
65 wherby to you gret harm myght grow;
    yet hade I lever than,
    that I had to the grenwod go,
    alon, a banysshed man."
            [12] Puella
    "I say not nay but as ye say,
    yt is no maydyn's lore;
    but love may make me to forsake,
    as I haue sayd beffore,
    to cum on fote, to hunte and shote,
    to get vs mete in store;
70 ffor so that I your company
    may haue I aske no more,
    ffrom which to parte it makyth my harte
    as colde as any ston;
    for in my mynde of all mankynd
    I love but you alone."
            [13] Squyre
    "For an owtlawe this is the lawe:
    that men hym take and bynde,
    withowt pite hangid to be
    and waver with the wynde.

---

65 wherby *B 21*; By whiche *03*.
66 I had *21 03*; I *B*.
67 say not *B 21*; Thinke not *03*.
68 to forsake *B*; for your sake *21 03*.   I *B 21*; ye *03*.
69 in store *B 21*; and store *03*.
71 my harte *B 21 P*; myn herte *03* (71 *appears as 95 in P*).
73–85 *omit P*.

---

64 *leve*: live; cf. l. 149
66 *had*: *B*'s omission of this word produces a headless line—see n. 7 above
67 *I say not nay*: cf. l. 7   *lore*: so spelled for rhyme; it echoes "lawe" in l. 61
68 *to forsake*: to withdraw (from the civilized world)—"as I have sayd before" refers to l. 45, "I wille not bide behind"; also the infinitive construction is in parallel with "to cum," "to hunte," and "to get." So *B* is preferable to the erroneous *03* and the only partly corrected *21* readings
69 *in store*: in reserve. "Store" in the phrase "mete and store" would refer to clothing and other household supplies, which would not all be got by shooting; so *03*'s "and" is an error
71 *my harte*: Elsewhere (ll. 101, 116, 171) *B* has "myn" before "h," but I have allowed the inconsistency to stand here because of the superior weight of *B-21* against *03*

75   Yf I had nede, as god forbede,
  what socowrs cowld ye fynde?
Forsoth I trow, ye and your bowe
  ffor fere wold draw behynde;
and no mervayle, ffor littill avayle
  were in your cownsell than.
Wherfor I will to the grenwod go,
  alon, a banysshed man."
    [14] Puella
"Right well know ye that wymen be
  but feble for to fight;
80   no womanhede it is indede
  to be bolde as a knyght;
yet in suche fere yf that yc were
  with ennemyes day or nyght,
I wold withstond with bow in honde
  to helpe you with my myght,   [212
and you to save as wymen have
  from deth many one;
for in my mynd of all mankynd
  I love but you alon."
    [15] Squyre
85   "Yet take good hede, for euer I drede
  that ye cowld not susteyn
the thorny wayes, the depe valeyes,
  the snowe, the froste, the rayn,
the colde, the hete; for drye and wete
  we mvste logge on the playn,

---

75 socowrs *B 21*; rescous *03*.
76 ye *B 21*; you *03*. ffor fere wold draw *B 21*; shul drawe for fere *03*.
78 will to the grenwod *B 21*; too the woode wyl *03*.
79 Right . . . but *B 21*; fVl . . . ful *03*.
80 womanhede *B 03*; women hede *21*. it is *B 21*; is it *03*.
81 with . . . or *B 21*; amonge . . . and *03*.
82 helpe you with my *B*; helpe with my *21*; greue them as I *03*.
86 the Rayn *B 03*; & rayne *21 P*.
87 and *B P*; nor *21*; or *03*. we *B 03 P*; Ye *21*.

---

 78 *03* also varies the refrain at ll. 102, 126, and 150; only at l. 150 does *21* fail to correct *03*; see p. 34 above
 83 The third part of the line is headless—see n. 7 above
 87 *logge*: lodge

and vs above non other roffe
    but a brake busshe or twayn;
which sone shuld greve you I beleve,
    and ye wold gladly than,
90   that I had to the grenwode goo,
    alon, a banysshed man."
        [16] Puella
"Sith I haue here ben partynere
    with you of ioye and blisse,
I mvste also parte of your woo
    endure as reason is.
Yet am I sure of on pleasure,
    and shortly it is this:
that wher ye be me semeth, parde,
    I cowld not fare amysse.
95   Without more speche, I you beseche
    that we were shortly gon;
for in my mynd of all mankynd
    I love but you alon."
        [17 Squyre]
"Iff ye go thyder ye mvst consider,
    whan ye haue luste to dyne,
ther shall no mete be for to gete;
    nether bere, ale, ne wyne;
ne shetes clen to lye betwen,
    made of threde and twyne;
100   non other hows but levis and bowes
    to cover your hede and myne.
Loo myn hart swete, this ill dyett
    shuld make you pale and wan;

---

91 of ioye *21 03*; of yoye *B*; in Ioy *P*.
95–96 *P substitutes* 71–72.   95 shortly gon *B 21*; soon a gone *03*.
98 Nether *B 21 P*; nor drinke *03*.
99 lye *21 03 P*; lay *B*.

---

   88 *brake bushe*: An unusual form for which I find no precedent. "Brake" (*bracken* or *fern*)
is not recorded as an adjective; therefore this is probably a combined form, "break-bush"
(bush used as a windbreak)
   99 The third part of the line is headless—see n. 7 above

wherfor I will to the grenwod go,
    alon, a banysshed man."
        [18 Puella]
"Amonge the wilde dere suche an archere,
    as men say that ye be,
may not fayll of good vytayll,
    wher is so gret plente;
105 and water clere of the rivere
    shall be full swete to me,
with which in hele I shall right well
    endure as ye shall see;
and or we go a bedde or two
    I can provide anon;
ffor in my mynde of all mankynd
    I love but you alone."
        [19] Squyre   [212v
"Loo, yet beffore ye mvst do more,
    yf ye will goo with me:
110 as cute your here vp by your ere,
    your kyrtyll by your knee,
with bow in honde for to withstonde
    your enymyes yf nede be.
And this same nyght beffore daylight
    to wodewarde will I flee;
yff that ye will all this fulfill,
    do it as shortly as ye can,
els will I to the grenwode go,
    alone, a banysshed man."

---

102 will to the grenwod *B 21*; to the wood wyl *03*; will I to the greenwood *P*.
104 may *B 21*; Ne may *03*; you shold *P*.
107 or we *B 21*; er we *03*; before I *P*.
110 vp by your . . . by your *B*; aboue your . . . aboue *the 21*; vp by your . . . by *the 03*;
    aboue your . . . aboue your *P*.
112 this *B 03 P*; the *21*.
113 yff that *B 21*; And *03*; *and if P*.   as shortly *B 21 P*; shortely *03*.

---

104 Another headless line—see n. 7 above
106 *hele*: health
107 *or*: before
110 *cute*: cut

[20] Puella

115 "I shall as now do more for you
 than longith to womanhede,
to shorte myn here, a bowe to bere
 to shote in tyme of nede.
O my swete moder, beffore all oder
 for you I haue moste drede;
but now adewe, I mvst ensue
 wher fortune doth me lede.
All this make ye; now lat vs flee,
 the day commeth fast vpon;
120 ffor in my mynd of all mankynde
 I love but you alon."

[21] Squyre

"Nay, nay, not so, ye shall not go,
 and I shall tell you whye:
your appetite is to be light
 of love I well espye;
for like as ye haue said to me,
 in likewyse hardely
ye wolde answer whosoeuer it were
 in way of companye.
125 It is said of olde 'Son whot, sone colde,'
 and so is a woman;
ffor I mvste to the grenwode goo,
 alone, a banysshed man."

[22] Puella

"Yf ye take hede, it is no nede
 such wordes to say by me;

---

115 than *B P*; That *21 03*. womanhede *B 21*; womanhod *03 P*.
116 myn here *B.*; my here *21 03 P.* a bowe to bere *B 03 P*; aboue to ere *21*.
117 I haue *B 21 P*; haue I *03*.
119 commeth *B 21*; cum *03*; *entirely different line P*.
122 of love I well *B 03*; Of my loue I well *21*; my loue I will *P*.
123 like *B 21*; right *03*; likwise *P*.
126 ffor I mvste to the grenwode *B 21*; wherfore I too the woode wyl *03*; therfore will
 to the greenwood *P*.
127 it is no *B 21*; yet is noo *03*; you doe not *P*. by me *21 P*; to me *B*; bee me *03*.

---

118 *ensue*: follow
119 *make*: cause [me] to do
123 *hardely*: boldly

125 *Son whot*: soon hot
127 *by*: concerning

ffor ofte ye prayd, and long assayed,
   or I you loved, parde.
And thowgh that I of avncetrye
   a baron's dowghter be,
130 yet haue ye proved how I ye loved,
   a squyre of lowe degre,
and ever shall whatso befall,
   to dye therfor anon;
ffor in my mynd of all mankynd
   I love but you alon."

      [23 Squyre]
"A baron's child to be begiled,
   it were a cursed dede;
to be felowe with an owtlawe,
   almyghty god forbede.
135 Yet better were the pore squyer
   alon to foreste yede,
than ye shuld say another day
   that, by my cursed rede,
ye were betrayde. Wherfor good mayd,
   the best rede that I can,   [213
ys that I to the grenwod go,
   alon, a banysshed man."

      [24 Puella]
"Whatever befall, I neuer shall
   of this thyng you owtbrayde;
140 but yf ye go and leve me so,
   than haue ye me betrayde.

---

130 ye . . . ye *B*; ye . . . you *21*; you . . . you *03*; you . . . *omit P.*
136 shuld *B 21 P*; shal *03.*   by my cursed Rede *B*; by my cursed dede *21*; be wyked
    dede *03*; by my accursed deede *P.*
139 what ever *B 21*; what so euer *03*; Let this *P.*   owt brayde *B 21*; vpbraid *03 P.*

---

  130 *proved*: learned by experience
  135 *yede*: went
  136 *rede*: advice; 21-03-P "dede" is the rhyme word of l. 133 above; nowhere else in the
poem is a word identical in form and meaning used as a rhyme
  137 *rede*: decision
  139 "owtbrayde" and "vpbraid" both mean "to cry out against"

Remembre you well how that ye dele,
 for yf ye be as ye said,
ye were vnkynd to leve me behynd,
 your love the Nutbrown Mayde.
Truste me truly that I shall dye
 son after ye be gon,
ffor in my mynd of all mankynd
 I love but you alon."

[25] Squyre

145 "If that you went ye shuld repent;
 for in the foreste nowe,
I haue purveyde me of a mayde
 whom I love more than you,
another fayrere than euer ye were,
 I dare it well avowe;
and of you both eche shold be wroth
 with other, as I trowe.
It were myn eas to leve in peas,
 so will I yf I can;

150 wherfor I will to the grenwod goo,
 alon, a banysshed man."

[26] Mayd

"Thowgh in the wode I vnderstode
 ye had a paramowre,
all this may nowght remeve my thowght
 but that I will be your;

141–42 for yf ye be as ye . . . ye were *B 21*; for yf ye as the . . . Be so *03*; you are not as
 you . . . you are *P*.
142 leve me *B 21*; leue *03 P*. your *B 03 P*; You *21*.
143 Trust me *03 P*; Truste *B 21*. I shall *B 21*; I *03*; I must *P*.
145 you . . . ye *B*; ye . . . ye *03 21*; you . . . you *P*.
147 Another fayrere *21 03*; An other more fayre *B*; *and* ffairer *P*.
148 shold *21 03 P*; will *B*.
150 will to the grenwod *B P*; to the wode wyl *21 03*.

---

143 "Trust me," *03-P*, provides a normal line; *B-21* "Trust" is headless—see n. 7 above
147 *fayrere*: *21-03* supported by *P*, against the single testimony of *B* "more fayre"
149 *leve*: live; cf. l. 64
150 See note to l. 78 above and p. 34

and she shall me fynd softe and kynd
    and curteys euery owre,
glad to fulfill all that she will
    comaund me to my powere.
155 For had ye, loo, an hundreth mo,
    yet wolde I be that on;
ffor in my mynd of all mankynd
    I love but you alon."
       [27] Squyre
"Myn own dere love, I se the prove
    that ye be kynde and trewe,
of mayde and wyf in all my lyff
    the best that ever I knew.
Be mery and glade, be no more sade,
    the case is chaunged newe;
160 for it were rewth that for your trewth
    that ye shuld have cawse to rewe.
Be not dysmayde; whatsoeuer I said
    to you whan I began,
I will not to the grenwode go,
    I am no banysshed man."
      [28 Mayd]
"Thes tydyinges be more gladder to me   [213v
    than to be made a quene,
yf I were sure they shuld endure;
    but it is often seen,
165 when men will brek promyse they spek
    the wordes on the splene.
Ye shape som wyle me to begile
    and stele from me I wene;
than were the caas wors than it was
    and I more woo begon,

---

153 me fynd B; fynd me 21 03; me ffind both P.
158 In all B 03 P; of all 21.
160 omit P.   that ye . . . cawse to B 21; you . . . causes 03.
163 more gladder B 21; more glad 03; are gladder P.
166 som B 21 P; sone 03.

---

153 me fynd: B is supported by P, but the second element of the line is headless; 21-03
"fynd me" provides a rhythmically normal line

ffor in my mynd of all mankynd
    I love but you alon."
        [29 Squyre]
"Ye shall not nede further to drede;
    I will not disparage
170   you, god defende, sith ye descende
    of so gret a lynage.
Now vnderstond to Westmorelond,
    which is myn herytage,
I will you bryng, and with a rynge
    by way of maryage,
I will you take and lady make,
    as shortly as I can.
Than haue ye wonne an erle's sonne,
    and not a banysshed man."
       [30 Both Players]
175   Here may ye see that women be
    in love meke, kynd, and stable.
Latt never man repreve them than,
    or calle them variable;
but rather pray god that we may
    to them be confortable.
God sumtyme provith such as he lovith,
    yf they be charytable;
for sith men wold that women shuld
    be meke to them echone,

---

170 *omit P.*   you god *B 21;* Your god *03.*   Sith ye *B 21;* sith you *03.*   a lynage *B 03;*   lynage *21.*
171 myn herytage *B 21;* my herytage *03;* my owne heritage *P.*
174 Than *B 21;* Thus *03 P.*   ye *B 03;* you *21 P.*   not a *B 03 P;* no *21.*
176 or calle them variable *03;* yf they be Charytable *B; omit 21;* nor call them varyable *P.*
177 we may to them *B 03;* we may To hym *21;* they to men may *P.*
178 God sumtyme *B;* Whiche somtyme *21 03; that* haue *P.*   provith such as he lovith *B;* proued such as he loued *21;* preuyth suche as loueth *03;* proued such as they loved *P.*   be *21 03 P;* be be *B.*
179 for sith *B 03;* Forsoth *21;* but *P.*
Subscription: omit 21 03; ffinis *P.*

---

176 *B's* error results from an eye-skip to l. 178
178 *God: B's* single testimony preferred above *21–03; P* is entirely different and of no evidential value here. The reference is to the Book of Wisdom iii.4–6— see p. 28 above
Subscription: Hill is the scribe, not the author

180   moche more owght they to god obey,
       and serue but hym alon.

Explicit quod Richard Hill
here endith the nutbrown mayd.

R. J. FEHRENBACH

A Letter sent by the Maydens of London *(1567)*

SOMETIME between late July and autumn, 1567, Henry Denham secured a license to print *"a boke intituled a mery metynge of maydes in London"*; shortly thereafter, Thomas Hacket received permission to print "a letter sente by the maydes of London to the vertuous matrons and mistres [ses] of ye same Cetie."[1] Hacket's pamphlet, printed by Henry Bynneman and dated November 13, 1567, was a reply to the one printed by Denham. The author of *A Letter,* which survives in only one copy, is impossible to identify, but the author of the now lost *The Mery Meeting of Maydens in London,* the title as it appears in *A Letter,* can be identified as the Elizabethan lawyer and moralistic versifier Edward Hake.[2] The exchange as reconstructed from *A Letter* provides another example of what Louis B. Wright in *Middle-Class Culture in Elizabethan England* (Chapel Hill, N.C., 1935) called the popular controversy over woman, but with certain fresh twists. First, *A Letter* provides some intimate glimpses of the life of ordinary maidservants in early Elizabethan London; second, the wit displayed throughout this curious piece has a special appeal, one that provoked John Payne Collier justifiably to describe the tract as a "remarkable" pamphlet.[3]

---

1. *A Transcript of the Register of the Company of the Stationers of London, 1554–1640 A.D.,* ed. Edward Arber (London, 1875; rprnt. 1950), I, 355 and 357.

2. As a reasonably young man entering the practice of law sometime between 1564 and 1567, Hake kept himself remarkably busy in 1566 and 1567, writing works of considerable variety. He is the likely author of a translation of Erasmus' colloquy, *Diversoria,* issued in 1566, and he certainly translated Thomas à Kempis' *Imitatio Christe,* brought out in 1567, the same year his *Newes out of Powles Churchyarde* first saw print. That first edition of *Newes* is now lost, but record of its entry in the *Stationers Register,* 1566–1567, attests to its earlier existence as mentioned by Hake in his second edition of that collection of "satyrs" printed in 1579. He may also be the author of the now lost *A Most Delectable Conference between the Wedded Life and the Single* (1566). During this busy time for Hake, *The Mery Meeting* was licensed for printing.

For more about Hake, see: the *DNB;* Charles Edmonds' introduction to his edition of Hake's *Newes out of Powles Churchyarde* (London, 1872); D. E. C. Yale's introductory comments to *EPIEIKEIA: A Dialogue on Equity in Three Parts* (New Haven, Conn., 1953), the only edition of Hake's manuscript treatise on equity; and Mark Eccles, "Edward Hake," *Brief Lives: Tudor and Stuart Authors, Studies in Philology,* 69 (1982), 58–59.

3. *A Bibliographical and Critical Account of the Rarest Books in the English Language* (New York, 1866), II, 267.

The only first-hand account of this work is by Collier (II, 267–72), and although he did recognize its "semi-humorous" character, his comments suffer from inaccuracies and misleading conjectures. F. L. Utley, finding the text inaccessible, relied on Collier and on Charles Edmonds, Hake's nineteenth-century editor, and thus made some inaccurate conjectures in his book on the early literary treatment of women.[4] These scholars and all subsequent evidence suggest that A Letter is a rejoinder to Hake's lost attack on what he perceived as the wantonness and sloth of London's female domestics.[5]

Authorship

George Turberville, translating Mancinus' moral verses into A plaine Path to perfect Vertue (1568), wrote in his prefatory remarks:

> I Neither write the newes of Poules,
>   of late set out to sale,
> Nor Meting of the London Maides:
>   for now that Fish is stale. (sig.*v.)

Turberville's first reference is to Hake's Newes out of Powles Churchyarde (1567 or 1568), and by coupling it with The Mery Meeting, he associates the latter with Hake, even if it is not certain that the use of "fish" is a play on Hake's name. If a pun, Turberville's note that the fish is stale may merely suggest that the pamphlet had run its popularity. The unfavorable reference might also suggest that Hake's pamphlet had been marred, perhaps by having been ignominiously punctured by A Letter.[6]

In none of his several subsequent works does Hake acknowledge seeing the rejoinder. But his unrestrained attack upon young women in a work published a few years after the exchange suggests a suspiciously disproportionate preoccupation with the activities of Elizabethan maidens, especially their reading and perhaps their writing habits. A Touchstone for this time present (1574) constitutes a moralistic tirade against various evils coupled with advice to parents and schoolmasters on how to train children, an harangue on slackness in rearing and teaching and on girls' depravity which Hake connects to their reading "amorous bookes, vaine stories and fonde trifeling fancies" (sig. C4). Hake singles out those "small number" of young women who have acquired some knowledge: "much better were it they should unlearne that againe which they have alreadie learned, then miserably to abuse it as they doe, or at the leaste wise (as we see them) to make equalle Pampheticall [sic] trifles with wholesome Doctrine and tryall of lyfe" (sig. C5). As the target of A Letter, Hake would have had particular cause to chide those who value "Pampheticall trifles" over what he pronounces "wholesome Doc-

---

4. The Crooked Rib: An Analytical Index to the Argument about Women in English and Scots Literature to the End of the Year 1568 (Columbus, Ohio, 1944), pp. 173–75.

5. Of incidental interest is the mention of "A merry meetinge" in a 1597 inventory of books owned by Richard Stonley, a teller of the Exchequer of Receipt dismissed for embezzling. See Leslie Hotson, "The Library of Elizabeth's Embezzling Teller," Studies in Bibliography, 2 (1949–1950), 58.

6. Another contemporary identification of The Mery Meeting with Hake's authorship is found in John Long's hortatory verses to the city of London in the 1579 edition of Newes out of Powles Churchyarde, where he says of Hake: "Of wanton Maydes he did also, / the slights a late detect" (sig. A5v).

trine." He remarks in *A Touchstone* that the few maidens who "have anye knowledge at all, doe so greatlye abuse it." But what Hake would have seen as an abuse of learning in *A Letter* would have produced laughter in the kitchens and pantries of London households and, more embarrassing to Hake the lawyer, probably in the chambers of the Inns of Court as well. One cannot resist wondering if Hake thought that a gaggle of city girls, armed with some measure of learning, had been able to compose a "Pampheticall' retort with such effect as to cause his *Mery Meeting* to fall quickly stale. To us, if not to Hake, the idea of domestic maidservants in the mid-sixteenth century collaborating on a mocking, humiliating riposte to the pontifications of a moralistic windbag has considerable appeal. The appearance of that collective authorship, however, is more likely than its reality.

Ironically, more is known about the author of the missing side of this exchange than about the writer of the work printed here. It is impossible to say whether the six maidens named on the title page of *A Letter* wrote the pamphlet, but much argues against their having done so. First, *A Letter* (sig. A7) makes clear that Hake had given six names to the participants of his dialogues as a way of representing London maidservants, although their characters as found in *A Letter* are doubtless quite different from Hake's representation of them. Second, however conventional the reply's *defensio* was and however literate the Elizabethan ordinary classes and women may have been by Continental standards, teen-age Tudor domestics probably would not have been able to write something as sprinkled with learning and as full of specialized knowledge as that found in *A Letter*.

If *A Letter* was not actually "*sent by the Maydens of London,*" the possibility remains that the author was a woman who was not only touched by the unfairness of Hake's attack on the city's domestic labor, but who was also angered by his assault upon a particular group within the class: women. One such a woman could have answered by directing her reply to matters of the rights and freedom of women as well as to their maltreatment by a society dominated by the likes of Edward Hake. Since no external evidence exists to identify the author, one must turn to internal evidence.

Of those characteristics that can be deduced about the author through the first-person-collective persona of *A Letter,* several provide indications of the writer's sex and class. First, the attitude of the author toward matrons and mistresses never seems anything but deferential and authentically respectful. Second, however sympathetic, the writer never patronizes the maidservants. Third, the author's acquaintance with the world of female servants is intimate, although uneven in its detail. And fourth, the author's knowledge of common, statutory, and customary law is both pointedly and casually demonstrated. However attractively the first three characteristics argue for a woman, particularly one of the lower classes, the last—the knowledge of law—argues for a man.

Legal knowledge is repeatedly demonstrated in *A Letter* by references to procedures and terms of law, by acquaintance with actual laws themselves, and by a habit of expression that reverberates with legal terms. To be sure, the author, in the guise of the six maidens, does say that "we wil borow a litle of the law, and laugh at" Hake (sig. A8), to explain the legal tone, style, and arguments. But the question of where a woman would have received such knowledge remains.

Barred from the profession of law, sixteenth-century women could be found at the

Inns of Court as prostitutes and domestics, but not as students.[7] That a scullion or a laundress employed at one of the Inns might have picked up such knowledge is, however appealing, very unlikely. Private training in the law, such as the tutoring in the humane studies given the educationally fortunate Margaret More Ropers by their fathers or others, does not seem to have existed for anyone, man or woman. In the end, whether any woman in the 1560s would have had the range of legal knowledge revealed in *A Letter* is, I think, the matter on which the sex of the author must turn, and not the slightest evidence exists to suggest that any woman was likely to have such knowledge. The author was thus likely a man, one who was able to create the persona of domestic maidservants by successfully adopting certain class attitudes and by effectively demonstrating an acquaintance with the domestic world, both easier to come by second hand than English law. But that the pamphleteer might have been Hake himself, as Collier suggests, is disproved by even a casual reading of the ridicule aimed at him in *A Letter*.

A Letter and the *querelle des femmes*

Whatever question exists about the author of the pamphlet, there is no question that at its center is the controversy over women, the medieval and Renaissance *querelle des femmes*. Its character and form were multi-faceted and resist brief summary. The subject was seriously treated by the great, like Erasmus and Agrippa, and by smaller fry like Stephen Gosynill, who was more interested in selling pamphlets than presenting a reasoned position, and seems to have written on both sides of the issue. Some were earnest and strident: John Knox, for instance. Others seemed bent on having as much fun as promoting an idea: the pseudonymous Oliver Oldwanton, for example. Some took the high road, Sir Thomas Elyot among them, and others took the low, Joseph Swetnam among those. There were dialogues, satires, sermonizings, arguments for and against marriage, pamphlets invoking scripture, tracts citing antiquity—and all these touched upon the matter of whether woman was good or bad, Mary or Eve.

The *querelle* had periods of especially high pitch. Sometimes these came as a result of a current event, such as the coincidental ascension of several women to positions of political power that caused John Knox in 1558 to blast his trumpet at the *Monstruous Regiment of Women*. Sometimes they followed a particularly provocative publication such as Gosynill's caustic *Scole house of Women* issued in the early 1540s from his anti-feminist position. The mid-sixteenth century was one such time of intense attacks and defenses..

The matters written about at this time were widely varied, limited only by the imagination of the participants, particularly the hot-eyed anti-feminists.[8] *A Letter*'s defenses are so unusual as to render it unique. For example, conventional subjects such as cosmetics and apparel, carnal appetites, vanity and pride are not at all the concern of *A Letter*. Nor does it weigh the virtues and vices of men and women, or treat the conflicts and jealousies of married and unmarried women or husbands or wives. It never

---

7. See Wilfred R. Prest, *The Inns of Court under Elizabeth I and the Early Stuarts, 1590–1640* (London, 1972).

8. Suzanne Hull writes in *Chaste, Silent, and Obedient: English Books for Women: 1475–1640* (San Marino, Cal., 1982), that "Favorite subjects for the Elizabethan and Jacobean satirist were women's apparel and cosmetics, jealousy, greed and extravagance, pride, lust and infidelity, gossiping or sharp tongues, and women's attempts to dominate men" (p. 111).

questions whether men or women should dominate. Rather, it focuses on basic freedoms of human beings who happen to be servants and women. Given what we know of Hake's attitude on the subject of women as presented in *A Touchstone* (1574) and *Newes* (1567, 1579), *A Letter* as a reply to Hake's attack on women in *The Mery Meeting* must have raised the level of the argument considerably. To be sure, the author of *A Letter* does strike more with tactics than substance, but the basis of *A Letter*'s defenses are ideas and arguments that not only speak to the mind rather than the spleen but are also generally lacking on both sides of the Elizabethan controversy. In addition, *A Letter* does not invoke revered figures, citing biblical or classical authority for its arguments. The one possible reference to Scripture is oblique, an alteration of the Pauline analogy of the body and the church that stresses the importance of those who serve: "For as there are divers and sundry membres in the body, the least whereof the body may not well want or spare . . . Even so are we to you (good Mistresses)" (sig. A4).[9]

The Letter

However refreshing the absence of stale ideas and hackneyed references to the ancients, it is the appeal to common sense rather than moralistic entreaty that sets *A Letter* apart from others in the *querelle*. The arguments are buttressed throughout by references to English Common, statutory, and customary law, but they always appeal to the rational rather than the legal mind.[10] Sometimes the author of *A Letter* simply enlists law as a rhetorical stalking horse for his argument by logic. For example, arguing by analogy, the author reasons that since established law prohibited a guardian from forcing his ward to marry one who is "maymed or disfigured" (sig. B1v), parents should likewise be prohibited from forcing daughters to marry men whom the young women would not personally choose. Love, after all, should be the "principall cause in mariage" (sig. B2). Giving such a free choice to their daughters may or may not have been a widespread practice among lower-class Elizabethan parents, but it certainly did not have the force of law that the author cunningly would give it by associating it with another practice that did.

Like Thomas More's *Utopia,* which often tends to look forward when it looks backward, *A Letter* seems enlightened when it is most traditional. When More argues, for example, what we might consider a modern sociological interpretation of the justice visited upon those who are forced by economic circumstances not of their making to turn to crime, he is actually arguing against the enclosures, against the disruption of a traditional bonding among classes. Similarly, one of *A Letter*'s more interesting and attractive arguments is that true freedom for both mistress and maidservant is found in the reciprocity between employer and worker (sigs. A5–A5v) with deep roots in custom. Old-fashioned customs coincide with modern freedoms; mutual

9. Cf. especially *I Corinthians* 12:12–31, but also *Romans* 12:4–5, *Ephesians* 4:4–16, and *Colossians* 3:14.

10. For example, the author argues that a widow should receive a portion of her husband's estate not just because it is the "laudable custom" of London, but because making provision for a widow, especially one with children, is unquestionably sensible. Accordingly, the circumvention by a husband of this custom through conveyance of that property to someone other than his wife upon his death, although legal, not only contradicts custom, but worse, it offends good sense.

care argues for individual liberty. The author's arguments do not depend on law, although he uses law when he can to defend the rights Hake would take from the maidservants with his narrow moralism. Neither do the arguments depend on the authority that many found in earlier writers. Apart from wit and style, the author's main weapons in *A Letter* are reason and good sense, qualities not in great supply in the literature of the controversy.

A Letter has a value apart from its unusual and forward-looking approach to the *querelle des femmes*. Incidental to his main purpose, the author provides glimpses of the ordinary life of the domestic world. Like so many of his contemporaries who offer social historians fragments of the homely, the author of *A Letter* unknowingly tantalizes us by stopping short of showing more, probably because such details as we would wish today seemed from the Elizabethan perspective so unworthy of note. Although a number of scenes presented in the pamphlet must have originated in the fictive dialogues of Hake's *The Mery Meeting,* we can still see something of the authentic life of maids and mistresses through *A Letter*, and it generally confirms what we know about their world from other, better known sources.

For example, the working conditions and schedules of the maidservants in *A Letter* reflect the sweeping government regulation of laborers and servants found in the Statute of Artificers of 1563 (5 Eliz. cap. 4)[11] and in various local proclamations. These include controlled terms of hire (sigs. B2v, B4, and B5v) and set wages and other remunerations (sig. A5v). Apart from providing these glimpses into regulated life of the maidservants, *A Letter* pictures as well the more personal world of Elizabethan young women as seen in their recreations, including their attendance at plays (sigs. B2v–B3), and as seen in their more private worlds, including "privie contracts" (sig. B1), probably marriages without benefit of parental approval, or perhaps even *per verba de praesenti,* marriages without benefit of clergy.[12]

Like the arguments the author presents, a good deal of the portrayed life of these Elizabethan maidservants and mistresses is, however, unusual, adding to or differing from what we know about the world of Tudor domestics. For instance, *A Letter* provides evidence that despite the regulation in the 1563 Statute, some servants apparently were summarily dismissed before the end of the term of their contract (sig. B4v). Also, several suggestions in *A Letter* hint at the existence of a flexibility in employment arrangements, including a brief trial period of work before a long-term contract was agreed to (sigs. B2v, B5–B5v). That temporary arrangement, although not unreasonable, has not previously been noted.

The most remarkable departure in *A Letter* from customary sixteenth-century manners, however, is the uncompromising attitude expressed by the female persona regarding the choice of husband. The maidens not only state that they have the right to choose, but they pronounce the practical and sensuous as equal motives in that choice (sigs. B1v–B2v). Possibly the author is presenting a portrait of young women that he

11. *Statutes of the Realm,* vol. IV, Pt. I, pp. 414–22, and abridged in *Tudor Economic Documents: Being Select Documents Illustrating the Economic and Social History of Tudor England,* ed. R. H. Tawney and Eileen Power (London, 1924), I, 338–50.

12. For a discussion of this and other binding marital contracts rather casually entered into during this period, see Lawrence Stone, *The Family, Sex and Marriage in England, 1500–1800* (New York, 1977), pp. 30ff.

knows will prick Hake's spleen. Yet perhaps the maidens' voice describes what actually occurred in marriage arrangements among the lower classes; little is recorded about their marital habits and motives.[13] It is hard to tell whether *A Letter* is ironic or straightforward in treating this matter. But a young woman agreeing to marry a man only if she loves him, if he can provide for her, and if he is attractive, seems very human, however unconventional, rebellious, and even wicked it might appear to Puritan anti-feminists of the mid-sixteenth century.

The uncertainty about this passage underscores the importance and sometimes the difficulty of determining the tone of the pamphlet, particularly as the multiple styles of the piece are rather sophisticated for the prose of a mid-Tudor pamphleteer. The author wields a clever pen, which he manipulates variously. Sometimes he is quite direct, as when he accuses Hake of presenting a "false surmise and suggestion" (sigs. A3–A3v) and an "unjust assertion without proofe" (sig. A3v), or even more baldly: "he wryteth that hee knoweth not," (sig. A5v). Generally the author is methodical, firmly leading the reader to his conclusion, sometimes it seems with sincerity—as when he argues for the same relief from work for servants that man gives his animals (sig. A5), and when he describes the unfortunate consequences of December-May marriages when young widows may be left saddled with children in a penurious condition (sig. B2). Often, however, the author's reasoning is ironical, as when he argues that Hake is chastening the "Lyon by the whelpe" in his attack on the maidens for attending "plaies and enterludes," in which criticism—the author would have us believe—Hake is actually charging the mistresses with doing nothing more than gadding about when they attend sermons, the purpose of both kinds of excursions supposedly being the same (sig. B3).

The attitudes he displays toward the main figures in his brief are consistent but his methods vary. To the matrons he is always respectful, ingratiating, ("If ye byd us go, we run, & are as loth in any thing to offēd you, as ye are to be grieved"[sig. A4v]), and frequently flattering ("we knew ye to be such as are not moved wyth every wynde, nor such as hang upon the blastes of every mans mouth"[sig. A3]). In his treatment of Hake, however, ridicule becomes his main instrument. The direct attack, always assured and confident, is nowhere more entertaining than when Hake's intelligence is questioned. Hake has "little wit" and "small skill & learning" (sig. A7), the "careful and serious studie" used to attain the latter having "dulled and cloyed" the former (sig. B4). Hake is but another Will Summers, a fool, who has written "ful fondly," and engages in nothing more than "babling (wherin he semeth to delight to heare him selfe to talke)" (sig. B5).

As always, however, ironic and indirect ridicule is more devastating. In several places *A Letter* mocks Hake's penchant for alliteration, seen even in the title of *The Mery Meeting of Maydens:* Hake has "cōbred his *capax* with our causes" (sig. A8), and "this mad mery man for his Mery meting of maydens madly mads in mery meter, merited only to be mockt" (sig. A8v). Feigning wonder as to why Hake would have written such a silly

---

13. See Stone, pp. 191–93, on the possibility that the young in the Elizabethan lower classes were likely to have been freer of their parents' direction in choosing a spouse than were their social betters. That freer choice, however, need not mean that they would choose out of "affective considerations." But one does not know; Stone admits that on marital arrangements for the poor "very little information is at present available for England" (p. 193).

piece as *The Mery Meeting,* the author conjectures that, being young, Hake was "desirous of glory by publishing of somewhat in Print what so ever it were"—anything for fame—or perhaps he "toke paines for the penny, thereto enforced by penury" (sig. A7)—anything for money. The author's rejoinder to Hake's charge that the girls gaze about church instead of paying attention to the service is merely to ask how Hake could have noticed them had he not been gazing about himself.

The ridicule is most devastating and effective when the author turns Hake's own legal profession on the lawyer and mockingly advises that he should have "medled in maters meter for his vocation. . . . The common law is his studie & profession, he might farre better have written of some Writte, as *Supersedeas,* or *Corpus cum causa,* or *De Idiota inquirenda,* or of some suche like argument, a great deale more meete for him" (sigs. A7v–A8). Whatever cunning relevance the first two writs concerned with matters of debt might have, the third, a common law writ that gives authority to inquire if a man is an idiot, is obvious as a matter "more meete" for Hake.

The arguments presented in *A Letter* appeal, as I have indicated, to good sense with an eye turned toward the law. Without claiming too much for it, I find the style of *A Letter* often reminiscent of the polemic by rhetoric and argument by wit engaged in by Thomas Nashe and his contemporaries some thirty years hence. Without question, the tract has its leaden moments, and the author's prose does not always seem up to his wit. Still, the irony, the straight-faced mockery, the legal patter turned against the pompous lawyer, the bursts of alliteration, the mischievousness hiding behind a disingenuous naiveté, and a spontaneity not unlike Nashe's "extemporal vein" together create a style that not only serves well the author's attempt to puncture self-righteous preachment but is remarkable for 1567 when English prose was not yet what one would call nimble.

The text printed here is reproduced from the unique copy in the Archepiscopal Library at Lambeth Palace, shelf listing 1576.5(4). The u/v and i/j are modernized, the superscribed forms *ye, yt, wt* are transcribed as *the, that,* and *with,* black-letter is reprinted in roman, and roman and italic types appear in italic. The punctuation of the copy-text, including the macron to indicate omitted nasals, has been retained save for two accidentals. Glosses have been kept at a minimum and are generally not provided when the sense is reasonably clear.

The copy-text, a small octavo, is in black-letter except for proper names and the title of Hake's pamphlet (in roman) and Latin phrases (in italics). It collates [A1, wanting]; A2, title-page; A2v, blank; A3–B6, text; B6v, Bynneman's printers' ornament (McKerrow, no. 149), and B7–B8v, blank. Fragments of a leaf with thread holes coinciding with all leaves through B8 exist in the valley preceding A2, providing evidence that the copy-text was issued with A1. With six other pamphlets, *A Letter* is bound fourth in a volume that bears the initials, R. B., for Richard Bancroft, Archbishop of Canterbury, 1604–1610. I am informed by E. G. W. Bill, Librarian at Lambeth Palace, that these initials do not prove the pamphlet was Bancroft's; it could have been owned by a predecessor. Yet Bancroft, strongly anti-Puritan and a participant in at least one flyting himself, revealed in the late 1580s that he valued wit and style when he suggested to Archbishop Whitgift that Martin Marprelate, satirical gadfly of the Anglican establishment, be answered in kind. Twenty years earlier in 1567, at 23 and just graduated B.A. from Christ's College, Cambridge, where he may have heard more Puritan expression than he would have wished, Bancroft perhaps found *A Letter,* part defense of the rights of women and domestics and part deflation of Puritan cant, a pamphlet attractive enough to give a penny for.

I am grateful to the American Philosophical Society, which supported my research with a grant during the summer of 1981, as did the Committee on Faculty Research at the College of William and Mary. The pamphlet is reprinted here with the kind permission of his Grace the Archbishop of Canterbury and the Trustees of the Lambeth Palace Library, to whom with the Librarian, Mr. Bill, and the staff of the Library at Lambeth, I express my sincere gratitude.

[A2]

A Letter sent
by the Maydens of
London, to the vertuous
Matrones & Mistresses
of the same, in the de-
fense of their law-
full Libertie.

Answering the
Mery Meeting by us
Rose, Jane, Rachell,
Sara, Philumias and
Dorothie.

Imprinted at London
by Henry Binneman,
for Thomas Hacket.

Anno. 1567.
To the right wise, sober,
and discrete Matrons, and Mistresses *of London, the Maidens of*
the same Citie send
greeting.

We were in a very evill case,[14] and ryght good cause had we to dread and to dispaire of oure well doings, (moste woorthie Matrones & Mistresses) wer it not that we knew ye to be such as are not moved wyth every wynde, nor such as hang upon the blastes of every mans mouth: for else what great mischiefe and trouble those fonde and malicious Dia-

---

14. unfortunate plight, with legal overtones; prejudicial circumstances.

logues of *The Mery meting of Maydens in London,* might have bred us siely[15] girles, what disquietnesse of minde and body also to you myghte therby have growne (if ye wer as light of credite, as the Author is of Judgement) your wisedomes well wote, and we are not to learne. For if at his false [A3v] surmise and suggestion, upon his bare word and letter, or upon his unjust assertion without proofe, ye shoulde have forthwith côdemned us of such things as he layeth unto our charges (& wherunto we pleade not giltie) and thereby also should have gone about immediatly to abridge us of our lawful libertie, such an inconvenience might have arisen and growne therby, that in a verie shorte time and space, ye shoulde have gotten very fewe or no servants at al, when such as are born in the countrey shoulde choose rather to tarie at home, and remaine there to take paines for a small stipend or wages with libertie: and such as are Citizens borne, shoulde repaire also to the coûtry, or to other Cities where they might be free, than to abide as slaves and bondewomen in London, *Libertas namque potior metallis.*[16] Then, the lesse inured and accustomed that every matron and mistresse were to toyle and drudge, the greater misse shoulde she have of hir mayde, the lesse [A4] paines that the mistresse were able to take, the more neede should she have of hir handmaid or servant. For as there are divers and sundry membres in the body, the least whereof the body may not well want or spare: and when any one of them is hurt or greved, the whole body suffreth smart therfore: Even so are we to you (good Mistresses) such as stande you in more steade, than some of the membres stande the body in, yea in as much steade we alone doe stande you in, as divers membres of the body altogether do stande the body in. For one might live although he lacked one of his eyes, one of his hands, one of his legs, and might also see, or handle any thing, and walke abrode. But ye (good Matrones and Mystresses) withoute your maides what coulde ye doe when now ye are paste paines taking youre selves, some by reson of age waxen unweldie, some by the grossenesse of your bodies, some by lack of bringing up in paines taking, and som for sundry and [A4v] divers other reasonable respects & causes, we are to you very eyes, hãds, feete & altogether. If ye byd us go, we run, & are as loth in any thing to offẽd you, as ye are to be grieved. And wherein from time to time we know that we may pleasure you, as

15. simple, helpless.

16. For indeed, freedom is preferable to money. See Morris P. Tilley, *A Dictionary of the Proverbs in England in the Sixteenth and Seventeenth Centuries* (Ann Arbor, Mich., 1950), L223: and F. P. Wilson, rev., *The Oxford Dictionary of English Proverbs,* 3rd edition (Oxford, 1970), p. 458.

redy we are to offer it, as ye are to demaũd it, as redy to obey you as ye to commaund us. The more & the greater that your businesse are (right worthie Matrones) and the lesse able that ye your selves are to accomplishe them, the more merite those your poore maidens, that take that toyle for you, whom it were to muche against reason, to intreate evill, when they have done their dueties to use as slaves or bondewomen, being free borne, and not rather to cherishe them, and make muche of them when they take intollerable paines for a trifle. How much against al reason were it, so straightly to deale with us, and so straitely to use us, that after all the toile we take in the whole weeke, we might not enjoye a piece of [A5] the holyday, to refresh our spirites, and to rest our wearied bones? Would ye not thinke him mad that would every day in the yeare journey his horsse? or that would course with his greyhound whilest his tayle will hang on? (as the Proverbe is)[17] or overflye his Hauke. If such good heede be taken in guiding of beasts, vermins[18] and foules, that they be not with too much labour spilt and marde: How much more heede oughte there to be taken, that christian people and reasonable creatures be not therwith oppressed: *Quod caret alternam requiem durabile non est.*[19] How much more circumspect[20] ought we [21] to be, that suche whose services we may not wel want, may be made off & cherished? partly for the preservation of their helth partly also that they being with honeste exercises and pastimes refreshed, may the better fal to their labor again, after that they have a little while rested? How much more ought they to be tendred, that cãby no meanes be separat? For as ye are [A5v] they that care & provide for our meat, drinke and wages, so we are they that labor and take paines for you: so that your care for us, and our labor for you is so requisite, that they can not be separated: so needeful that they may not be severed.

And where the Author doth so much invey against our overmuche libertie, in that he wryteth that hee knoweth not, and medleth of that that he hath no skill off. For, all the weeke dayes we are continually busied: and the Author findeth faulte but for the Holiday: the forenoone wherof we spend at Church, or about necessarie businesse at home: and

17. To hunt with hounds by sight, not by scent. I have not located any such proverb.
18. I.e., small animals generally.
19. The thing which lacks periodic rest does not endure.
20. respected.
21. Confusion in the voice exists in the next several sentences, with the reference to the maidens being made initially in the first person here, then switched to the third person in the next two sentences, to be followed by a return to the first person.

so muche time have we not in the after noone, that we can farre stray abrode, sith commõly they ring the first peale to Evẽsong before that we have washed up halfe our dishes. Then must we either to Church againe, or tary at home to dresse your suppers, for fewe commonly use to fast on Sundayes or Holy dayes, in London especially: No [A6] not the very Author of the Merie meeting of maidens himselfe, who would not be very mery, if he were therto cõstrained: as like a Divine as he taketh upon him to teache and preache of that that he hath nothing to do with, of thẽ that little set by it, and to them that do but laugh at it.

And where he alleageth that we doe mispend our time in the Church in gazing and looking about us, and that our comming thither is not to pray: surely he himself was not very well occupied in the Church, and prayed but litle (as it seemeth) when he stoode gazing & loking about him at us, to marke what we didde. And for oure thoughtes, sith they are so privie, that were he as cunning as the Divell, yet coulde he not knowe them, sithe God alone hathe that priveledge of all others, to know the thoughts of men, wemen, children, and of every living creature, so that he may as well lie, as say true herein, as it is more likely that he doth: therefore [A6v] ye may credite him as ye shal see cause: we dare take it upon our consciences that if ye beleve it not at all, it shal be nothing at al prejudicial to you, nor your lacke of beleefe therein shall any thing hinder your salvation. And thus this being well tried & examined, we have not past two houres at the most upon the Holy day for our talkes, meetings, drinkings, going to playes and sporting, &c.

Although his bragging and boasting title (of his *Mery meeting of Maidens*)[22] be farre worse than the worke it selfe, where in he hath as it were brought a milnepost to a pudding pricke:[23] wherein also at the first sight he doeth so threaten us, as though fewe or none of us were good, yea as though the best were too bad, how holily soever in the end of his worke he excuseth himself, wherin he breaketh our heads, and afterwards giveth us plaisters. Yet when he hath sayd what he can: he can shewe no good cause why our liberties should be re [A7] strained, as he so earnestly desired: and as on the one side the mã of likelihode is yong, and desirous of glory by publishing of somewhat in Print what so ever it were, or else

22. Nothing in the title of Hake's work as we know it fits this description. Perhaps the author is referring to a portion of a longer title that appeared in Hake's published piece in which he contended that his work revealed the outrageous faults of the maidens.

23. A large post has been discovered to be merely a small stick. See Tilley, M964, and Wilson, p. 821.

toke paines for the penny, thereto enforced by penury, so surely hath he chosen the most unfitte matter of al matters to entreat upon, if we regarded not more what became us maidens, than measured what hee hath merited & deserved. In which very choise of so many argumẽts, he hath no lesse declared his little wit, than he hath uttered his small skill & learning in the hãdling of it. For what one wise man will willingly meddle with a multitude, or contende with a whole company? He forgate certainly the Latine Proverbe, *Ne Hercules quidem contra duos,*[24] when he recited six of us by name, and under those sixe names above sixe thousand of us. O madde man that he was: Doth a Phisitian winne renoune by killing or by curing his pacients? Wotteth he not that the name of a pro-[A7v] moter[25] is odious? O most worthy Orator[26] what so ever he was, that for any cause could not be compelled to accuse any, but willingly for a trifle wold defend many. But surely either was this author not wel advised, or else remembred he not this Proverbe: *Ne sutor ultra crepidam,*[27] when he toke upon him, that that nothing at al appertained unto him. For sith Divinitie is not his profession, nor that he is admitted to the office of the ministery, nor to the order of Preaching, he might well have left that office of correcting and reforming of the maners of others to the preachers, & for his owne part farre better might he have folowed that Counsell of holy *S. Augustine,* who saith: *Medice primum teipsum cura.*[28] After his serious study he wold have found out some honester recreation, and medled in maters meter for his vocation, wherein also his skill and knowledge had bene greater: and in that the common law is his studie & profession, he might farre better have [A8] written of some Writte, as *Supersedeas,*[29] or *Corpus cum causa,*[30] or *De Idiota*

24. Not even Hercules could struggle against two. See also Tilley, H436, and Wilson, p. 370.

25. *promater* in the text, a form that does not appear in the *OED*. The second syllable which serves as the catchword on sig. A7, however, is spelled *mo.* Although originally an officer of the crown appointed to prosecute criminal offenders, a *promoter* came to be known as a professional accuser or informer.

26. The modern equivalent would be *plaintiff;* in Roman law, an orator is an advocate, one who defends or pleads for another.

27. Let the shoemaker not go beyond his last, a proverb attributed to Apelles, the 4th-century B. C. painter. Legend has it that his art was critically commented upon by a shoemaker whose opinion about shoes Apelles had sought regarding a slipper in one of his paintings. In sum, "Let everyone mind his own business."

28. Physician first heal thyself. Biblical (*Luke* 4:23), although without *primum,* and not known to have any particular association with Augustine. See Tilley, P267, and Wilson, p. 622.

29. A writ staying a proceeding.

30. Apparently more properly described as a writ of *Habeas corpus cum causa,* which transferred a case from one court to another.

inquirenda,[31] or of some suche like argument, a great deale more meete for him, and agreeable for his gravitie, being incident and appertinet to his science,[32] more correspodent also to his facultie, and might well have letten us poore maidens alone, and not have cobred his *capax*[33] with our causes, nor have intermedled[34] in our libertie. He might have spent his time farre better, than in a common consequent upon so fond an argument. Wherin, if according to his promise he proceede and make you laugh, we will borow a litle of the law, and laugh at him for company,[35] we wil lay apart, and part of [36] our bashfulnesse, and deale merily with a mery man in meeter, *ut impleatur Proverbium, Qui moccat moccabitur.*[37] But even as he was at the first procured by povertie[38] to make any thing merily for money, so nowe by chance Nidiot[39] it may fal forth, that moved with melacholy[40] he wil proceede [A8v] frantikely (which we are as loth shold chaunce, as he should be to procure it.) We must the of necessitie addresse our selves to Replie in defense of our liberty, and eke of our honesty, least our silece yeld us gilty. It is also right expedient[41] that so it should be, *ut si quam male dicendo voluptatem caeperit, eam male audiendo ammittat.*[42]

He thought perhaps to have discredited us marvelously when he hath nowe most of al hurt himself, & hindred us very lytle or nothing. For whereas the chefest point of a Gentleman is to defende and save harmlesse[43] to his uttermost, the poore and silly women when they are wronged and oppressed: and many have thereby onely woon them selves an immortall fame, so hath this mad mery man for his Mery meting of

31. A writ, the purpose of which was to inquire whether a person be an idiot.

32. occupation.

33. head.

34. A legal term suggesting interfering without right. The whole preceding sentence is replete with legal language.

35. good fellowship.

36. *lay . . . part of:* put aside.

37. As provided by the proverb, he who mocks shall be mocked. See Tilley, M1031, and Wilson, p. 537.

38. *procured by povertie:* acted for money, but with the salacious overtones carried by the term "procuring."

39. idiot.

40. violent anger.

41. proper, fit.

42. The Latin makes no sense, but the idea is probably "he who is pleased by saying what he should not, will be displeased by hearing what he would not," a variation on a common proverbial phrase that has origins in Terence and Erasmus. See Tilley, S115 and Wilson, p. 762.

43. protect.

maydens madly mads[44] in mery meter, merited only to be mockt and laughed to skorne for his labor, and well declared how base his byrthe and bringing up are, and how farre unlike a Gentleman he is to seeke to hurt them [B1] whom he ought to helpe: to make so great boast to bring to small roast, to barke so loude and to byte nothing.[45] For what be the causes wherefore he wold have us restrained of our liberties? "Forsoth bycause of privie contracts, he wold not have us resort to Playes:[46] he findeth fault with our great expences in banqueting, and accuseth us with pilfering and pycking of meate and candels from you for mother B,[47] by whome (as he saith) we are boldned and encoraged to be stoute and stubborne to you, being alwayes placed by them in service, if at any time we be destitute."

This is the whole summe (good Matrons and mistresses) of all his three Dialogues, saving that he accuseth Rachel to occupie for hir selfe,[48] which sith she is better able to denie than he to justifie, there nedeth no further ado in that mater. But for the rest, as the privie contractes especially, surely it is a thing that we do not very well allow,[49] nor yet

44. The present tense of *mads,* a verb meaning "rages," is not in keeping with the rest of the sentence. Such inconsistency of tenses, however, is not uncommonly found in pamphlets that affect the oral delivery. See Susan Clark, *The Elizabethan Pamphleteer: Popular Moralistic Pamphlets, 1580–1640* (East Brunswick, N.J., 1983), pp. 249–50. Still, the compositer may have mistaken the secretary terminal *e* for an *s* in the manuscript, printing *mads* instead of an authorial *made.*

45. These two proverbs convey essentially the same meaning: great expectations aroused, but little delivered. See Tilley, B488, and Wilson, p. 333 on the first, and Tilley, B85 and B86, and Wilson, pp. 30–31, on the second.

46. *Forsoth . . . Playes.* The connection between "privy contracts" and attendance at plays is not made in the defense that follows; see sig. B2v. The author probably did not intend to connect the two here either; he not uncommonly ties two independent clauses with a comma. In any case, the accusations he defends against are four, not three.

47. A figure criticized at length by Hake in *Newes out of Powles Churchyarde* (1567, 1579), where he excoriates this old woman, a kind of Elizabethan female Fagin, who, he says, entices "siely girles," and "simple maydes" (*Newes,* sig. F8v). Hake's attack on Mother B. in *Newes* allows us to understand something about the references to this woman in *A Letter.* To Hake she is a special danger to "The countrey maides that come from far, / as straungers to the towns: / Whome still the Trottes doe tittle so, / that straight all shame layde down" (*Newes,* sig. F8v). All too frequently, according to *Newes,* these maidens travelling to the city to work as servants are enticed by Mother B. to steal from their masters and mistresses and then to leave their employment only to be placed elsewhere—by implication with Mother B.'s connivance—to continue their "whoredome, theft, and filching" (sig. G1). Whatever the letter "B" stood for (perhaps Broker, probably Bawd), Mother B. is a curious figure: to Hake a sinister force; to the author of *A Letter* an example of pitiable poverty. Whichever she was, one assumes that the old woman and the argument about her meant more to the writers' contemporaries than they do to us, however intriguing we find the character four centuries later.

48. *to occupie . . . selfe:* suggestive of prostitution.

49. Here and in the following sentence meaning *praise* rather than *permit.*

alto-[B1v] gether discommende. Allow it we may not, Condemne it we
can not. For as our parentes advise is alwayes to be asked in the choyce of
our husbands, so is it not alwaies to be followed, namely when we can not
frame our selves to love the partie that our parentes have provided for us.
Is it not a ruled case in the law,[50] that the Warde for sundry lawful causes
may lawfully refuse to marie, when mariage is by his Garden[51] tendred to
him? As if his Garden wil marie him to one that is bond, to one that is
maymed or disfigured, & such like: how much more may we refuse such
olde doting fooles as somtimes ar procured by our parētes to be suters to
us, & have a thousand worse impedimentes, and nothyng but their goods
and money to mary them, no not so much as any one good propertie or
qualitie. Lette us say nothing of their extreme covetousnesse, (*Cum enim
omnia vitia in sene senescunt, Avaritia solummodo invenescit,*)[52] and divers other
their crooked and crabbed condicions. [B2] What great gaine shall a
yong mayden have by matching with any of them, when cōmonly they
leave at their death behinde them many yong children, and litle or
nothing to kepe them with? For as they may give all to their wives, if
they list, so notwithstanding the most honest laufull and laudable cus-
tome of this most famous Citie to the contrary, they may in their lyfe
time by unconscionable conveyance convey all from them,[53] if they lyst,
as seldom litle they leave them, in respect of that they deserve, unlesse it
be upon condition not to mary againe, whilest they live. Thus have their
poore wives a very evill recompense for their painfull services and
diligence, and are put to a very hard choise, eyther to ende theyr lives
with beggery, or being yong and bound from mariage and driven (the
more is the pytie) to live (as some chanceth) incontinently. And sith love
should be the principall cause in mariage, why shold we be blamed, for
chosing wher we most love and fansie? *Concordia res par-*[B2v] *vae crescunt,*

50. Arrived at by judicial action, not by statute. The specific reference is to the law of
disparagement, which had for centuries provided that guardians could not marry their wards to
any who would, for a variety of reasons, from defects of body or mind to lower station of birth,
discredit the ward. For full discussion of this legal tradition, see Joel Hurstfield, *The Queen's
Wards: Wardship and Marriage Under Elizabeth I* (Cambridge, Mass., 1958), pp. 138ff.

51. guardian.

52. Although all vices decline with age, avarice alone increases. See Tilley, S479 and M568,
and Wilson, p. 737.

53. In England, local custom or a practice with a long tradition often took legal precedence in
a locale over more widely applied statutory law. According to London custom, a wife was
guaranteed at least one third of her husband's real and personal property upon his death. He
could, however, arrange through legal means, while he still lived, to convey that property to
others to circumvent this local London customary law of inheritance.

discordia maxima dilabuntur, With concord and good agreement small things encrease and wax great, with discord the greatest things of all decay and come to naught.[54] Blame us not if we wold avoid so great inconveniences in the choyse of them whom we must serve all our lyfe tyme, when no wise wench willingly wold be hyred of any for a yeare, without a profe of time of liking.

The author of the Dialogue seemeth to be unmaried, else surely shold he finde by experience, that all things[55] are almost to few to make good agreement to last and continue in maried couples. As we are not so wynching wood[56] to choose boyes or lads that lacke experience and the trade to live, so loth we to be coupled in mariage with such as are lothsom to looke upon, *Medium tenuere beati.*[57]

Now in that he findeth fault for our going to plaies and enterludes, your wisdomes know well, that in a godly play or enterlude (if it be well made and under-[B3] standed) may be much learning had: for so lively are in them set forth the vices and vertues before our eyes, in gestures and speach, that we can bothe take learning and pleasure in them. But as for you (right worthy and vertuous Matrons) many resort to sermons, also not so much for your pleasure (as we take it) as ye do for your good instruction and edifying. But herein the author playeth the crafty marchant, by casting that in our teeth, for which he rather mysliketh[58] you that are our mistresses, as who wold say he chastened the Lyon by the whelpe.[59]

Our great costes and charges in good chere and banketting objected by him against us, sith he hath named no great deynties, nor yet any great shot or reckning,[60] he hath but sayd a thing that he hath not proved, and so have we the lesse to say therein: and so much the rather sith he him selfe against his will, or more than he remembreth, hath sayd metely well for us in that behalf. For when *Rose* would have sent for wyne, *Jane* [B3v] wold not suffer hir, and so had they but bare beere alone that we heard of. Now at that feast or rather a bare beere banket, there were but they

54. The first part of the Latin passage, which is translated in the text, is the motto of the Merchant Tailors. See Tilley, U11 and Wilson, P. 854.

55. material goods.

56. insane.

57. Happy people keep to the middle course.

58. disapproves of.

59. *chastened . . . whelp:* a proverbial phrase by which the author charges Hake with criticizing the matrons' actions indirectly by attacking the similar actions of their maidservants. See Tilley D443 and Wilson, p. 37.

60. *shot . . . reckning:* both are terms for a bill presented at a tavern.

two alone, the day was halfe spent and more, for it was well in the after noone. And they are no such quaffers but that a quart would serve them well when they had well dronken before at their dynner. Also a quart of the best beere may be boughte for a peny, so that they two that daye spent eche of them a halfepeny. *Summa totalis* of all that was spent that daie betwene them two at the costely banket, was a peny.

Thus have you a quicke reckening and a slow payment, a marvellous expence and a mischevous charge.

For our pilfring and picking from you (our Mistresses) for mother B. &c. If that matter were proved, it could not be well with us, although that in other things he listed to dally, yet here he jested but homely,[61] in charging us with that felony: but his witnesses herein are as far [B4] to seeke as were his wittes, being dulled and cloyed (as he wrote) with carefull and serious studie: ye your selves are farre better hable to answere for us, and to excuse us, than he is hable to accuse us. For why? Ye knowe that we admit no poore women (whome in dispight he nameth B.)[62] to help us without your leave and licence, and not without good cause do ye licence them sometimes to helpe us: for such do ye hire at your pleasures for a trifle and for a small time, when ye nede not to be at charges with them all the yere, your provisions also being dayly made in the shambles[63] and markets, we cannot lightly[64] be false in robbing of your poudering tubbes;[65] and ye are not so slender[66] huswives, but ye would easily espie it, and quickely misse it: & a candles ende is not so costly, that giving it to a poore woman to light hir home in a dark night for[67] breaking hir face or shinnes, would undoe you, or greatly hinder you. But he is loth that poverty should have any relief at your handes: what thinke ye [B4v] would he have you to give at your dores in almes to beggers that do nothing for it, when he is thus offended that poore women should have their hire[68] for their paynes, a few scraps of broken

---

61. *although . . . homely:* this final charge the author appears to find more serious, suggesting that Hake was with his other accusations not really touching on matters of major concern to the matrons. With the charge that the servant girls steal from their mistresses, and are in the pay and influence of a quasi-underworld figure, Hake is causing real trouble or is showing a poor sense of humor.

62. probably Bawd, perhaps Broker. See note 69.

63. meat market.

64. easily.

65. tubs in which meat was powdered, or salted, that is, pickled.

66. lax.

67. to keep from.

68. wages.

breade meete for their toyle and travaile? For their broking[69] and helping of servantes to services is but a tale of a tubbe,[70] such poore peoples credit is not halfe so great, that they can shew any so great a pleasure,[71] yet surely were it not amisse, if any such brokers were, then servants sodenly without warning put out of service, should not by any necessitie be constrayned to lyve unhonestly. As what would not one do pinched with penury? hunger breketh stone walles (as the proverb is)[72] and why should we be afrayd in honest wise[73] to complayne to our Maisters and Mistresses when we finde any thing a misse, & desire their good leave to depart, when they wil not redresse it? What a long tale told he of *Dorothy,* when she would serve no longer? how she was brought before the Aldermans Depu- [B5] tie,[74] what gained hir master thereby? Although at the first the officer spake some what stoutly, yet spake he at last full resonably, and *Dorothy* might depart laufully, there was no cause to the contrary. For why? she was by the yere hired, hir time was expired, she ought[75] no longer service, she was overcharged with worke, she had complained and found no amendment, she sought for more easement,[76] she liked not that intertainment.[77] *Sed ut caedas canem, facile reperitur baculus.*[78] The man would fayne have picked a quarrel, but he fared like wil Sommer:[79] for some by likelihode had angred him, and bicause he could not with his staffe reach them, he stroake them that stode next unto him: but our trust is that your wisdoms wil way but lightly that that he hath writen ful fondly: and for al his babling (wherin he semeth to delight to heare him selfe to talke) we hope that you wil be as good Mistresses unto us as heretofore ye have been. Accept our services as ye finde us. First trie us, then [B5v] trust us: Faire words and

---

69. This and the reference to *brokers* later in the same sentence carry pejorative associations ranging from the dealings of a dishonest go-between, suggestive of a bawd, to those of a dishonest legal agent.

70. a tall-tale, a lie. See Tilley, T45, and Wilson, p. 803.

71. *such poore . . . pleasure:* poor people do not have the kind of influence required to place servants in employment.

72. See Tilley, H811, and Wilson, p. 392.

73. *in . . . wise:* candidly.

74. The law provided that disputes between London servants and masters over terms of service were to be adjudicated by city officials.

75. owed.

76. redress of grievances.

77. employment or treatment.

78. If one wants to beat a dog, he will easily find a stick. See Tilley, T138, and Wilson, p. 769.

79. Will Summers was the jester of Henry VIII, and jesters were known to use their staffs or bladders to strike in slapstick style those nearest them.

g̃etle entreating of us shal do more a gret deale with us, than a thousand of threattes & stripes,[80] we would not wish you to kepe that servãt that serveth you not in a maner as much for your love as for your money. *Oderint dum metuant,*[81] was the saying of a moste cruel tyrant, of all men to be rejected, of no man to be allowed nor accepted: whẽ al is done, frendeship is the surest garde. Let us have, we besech you, our honest accustomed libertie, sith ye know no just cause to the contrary, intreate us as we shall deserve, we will deserve to be well entreated. So much are we busied this terme[82] by reason of the greate resort[83] that cõmeth to your housen (good Mistresses) of your kinsfolkes frendes and guestes, that for this time we are constrayned to make an end. Wherfore we wil commit you all to the holy Tuytion[84] of the most blessed Trinitie, whom we most humbly besech to send unto you our Mistresses long life, great encrease of worship, & all felicity: & unto us your pore h̃ad maides [B6] and servantes good health, hartes ease, and the grace to do our duties to you. Scribled in haste this xiii. of November. 1567.

Your handmaydens and ser-
vants *Rose, Jane, Rachell, Sara,
Philumias & Dorothy.*
FINIS.

Imprinted at London
by Henry Bynneman for
Thomas Hacket.
Anno. 1567.

---

80. beatings, lashes.

81. "Let them hate provided they fear me," is said to have been spoken by the Emperor Tiberius.

82. The calendar was divided according to the quarterly sessions of the court, the specific term referred to here being the Michaelmas Term.

83. throng.

84. protection.

TINA KRONTIRIS

Breaking Barriers of Genre and Gender: Margaret Tyler's Translation of The Mirrour of Knighthood

IN 1578, approximately midway between the publication of Isabella Whitney's *The Copy of a Letter . . . to her unconstant Lover* (1566–1567) and Jane Anger's *Protection for Women* (1589), Margaret Tyler published her translation of the Spanish romance, *The Mirrour of Princely deedes and Knighthood*.[1] As in the case of other women writers of this period, very little is known about Tyler, but from the Dedication and the Preface to her translation it appears that she had been a servant in the household of the parents of Lord Howard.[2] From the same documents we also gather that she was probably advanced in years when she engaged in translating and that she had been an early reader of romances.[3] Unfortunately, no other information is available. It seems amazing that an ex-servant could know so thoroughly a foreign vernacular language that was rarely studied even by educated men of her time. Although diplomatic and commercial ties with Spain had existed ever since the days of Catherine of Aragon, it was not until the defeat of the Armada in 1588 that Spanish as a language gained some currency. Prior

---

1. The work was licensed by the Stationer's company on 4 August 1578, but it probably did not come out until 1580. For evidence of dating see J. Perott, "The Mirrour of Knighthood," *The Romanic Review* 4 (1913), pp. 397–402. For its relationship to other chivalric romances, see H. Thomas, *Spanish and Portuguese Romances of Chivalry* (Cambridge, Eng., 1920).

2. In her recent edition, *First Feminists: British Women Writers 1578–1799* (Bloomington, Ind., 1985), Moira Ferguson includes a short biographical note on Tyler. In it she says: "it appears that she was a member of and possibly a servant in the household of the aristocratic and Roman Catholic Howard family . . . the father of the dedicatee would be Thomas, Third Duke of Norfolk, who was executed in 1572." She also says there is "a slim possibility" that Margaret Tyler's real name was Margaret Tyrrell. The Tyrrells were a prominent Roman Catholic family living at the time of the Howards (p. 51).

3. In the preface she refers to writers of "as aged years," and to the reader's interpretation of "my name and years," while in the dedication she tells us that she took up the translation partly to reacquaint herself with her old reading.

to that time even Spanish dictionaries seem to have been rare.[4] Further-more, until the days of the Armada, the circulation of Spanish literature in the original had been restricted to people who were on diplomatic mission or who were friends of diplomats traveling to the peninsula.

Tyler's publication of her translation of *The Mirrour of Knighthood* marks a significant point in the history of romantic fiction. Her book set a vogue which lasted almost to the end of the seventeenth century. Before Tyler published her translation, the chivalric romance had not been widely read in England. A few titles from the French and English material, such as *Morte d'Arthure, Bevis of Hampton,* and *Guy of Warwick,* had been regularly reprinted, but the entire group of Spanish and Portuguese romances, which had already enjoyed great popularity on the continent and which were to flood the English market in the last twenty years of the sixteenth century, had not yet made their full appearance in England.[5] Thomas Paynell's publication in 1568 of *The Treasurie of Amadis of France* contained only extracts from Books 1–12 of the *Amadis* series. Tyler was the first to translate a complete chivalric romance from the peninsular group and the only one to do so directly from the Spanish rather than through the French. Following the publication of Tyler's translation, chivalresque romances became a vogue and were rapidly translated into English.[6] *The Mirrour* was one of the most popular and influential, although it was not necessarily recognized as superior in merit to others in the same group. It went through several editions, and authors like Spenser, Shakespeare, and Bunyan are said to have bor-rowed plot material from it.[7]

Tyler's *Mirrour* is not only a contribution to the history of romantic

4. See John Underhill, *Spanish Literature in the England of the Tudors* (London, 1899), esp. pp. 328–38 and 228–59.

5. R. S. Crane, *The Vogue of Medieval Chivalric Romance During the English Renaissance* (Menasha, Wis., 1919), p. 16.

6. Tyler's *Mirrour* was so successful commercially that the printer, Thomas East, soon commissioned the translation of *The Second Part of The Mirrour of Knighthood* (1583), with a different translator, possibly because Tyler was too old for such another laborious task. Her successor was one R. P. (Robert Perry). The translation was then continued by one L. A., and the entire series was completed in eight volumes by 1601. The Spanish originals of *The Mirrour* were written by four different authors: First Part, 3 books: Diego Ortuñez de Calahorra, 1562; Second Part, 2 books: Pedro de la Sierra, 1581; Third and Fourth Parts, 2 books each: Marcos Martinez, 1589.

7. See Dorothy Atkinson, "Busirane's Castle and Artidon's Cave," *Modern Language Quarterly* 1 (1940), 185–92; J. Perott, "The Probable Source of Shakespeare's *Tempest*," *Publications of the Clark University Library* 1 (1905), 209–16; and Harold Golder, "Bunyan's Valley of the Shadow," *Modern Philology* 27 (1929), 55–72. See also Crane, pp. 24–29.

fiction. It also occupies a significant position as the literary product of a Renaissance woman. Like Isabella Whitney before her, Tyler is an early example of women producing secular literature; Tyler was the first Englishwoman to publish a prose romance. She was also the first woman to confront, in a Preface prefixed to her translation, male divisions of genre and gender. Her Preface has attracted some critical attention,[8] but the book she translated has been almost totally ignored. My purpose in this study is to examine both the Preface and *The Mirrour* in relation to the translator's sex and culture. Why does Tyler need to defend her task and her choice in the first place? The bold terms she employs in her defence would seem to imply that *The Mirrour* is an oppositional book. If it is, how does it oppose conventional notions of gender?

II

As a number of recent writers have suggested, Renaissance women's literary activity was greatly circumscribed. Male definitions of feminine propriety limited what women could take up in writing. Underlying such definitions were various assumptions about woman's "nature" and proper place. Woman was thought to be man's intellectual inferior, born to be a mother and housewife at home, not the equal of man competing with him in the public world. Furthermore, she was thought to be sexually insatiable and potentially another unruly Eve, who had to be kept under surveillance. The wider her contact with the outside world, it was feared, the greater the threat to her chastity, a quality emphatically required of her. Conservative theoreticians thought it would be dangerous to allow women to be educated, for it would make them scorn the simple duties they were supposedly born to perform. In *A mirrhor mete for all mothers, Matrones and Maidens* (1579) Thomas Salter, translator of Giovanni Bruto, conveniently proposed the "Distaffe, and Spindle, Nedle and Thimble" as replacements for the pen.[9] More liberal humanists, such as Vives, More, Hyrde, Elyot, and Mulcaster, argued that books, the right sort of books, could teach women wisdom and the precepts of virtuous living.[10] Yet learning was one thing and publishing another, for to publish meant to engage in public self-display. Hence a woman who

8. See E. D. Mackerness, "Margaret Tyler: An Elizabethan Feminist," *Notes and Queries* 190, 6 (1946), 112–13; Betty Travitsky, ed., *Paradise of Women: Writings by Englishwomen of the Renaissance* (Westport, Conn., 1981), pp. 144–46; and Moira Ferguson, pp. 51–57.

9. Ruth Kelso, *Doctrine for the Lady of the Renaissance* (Urbana, Ill., 1956), pp. 59–60.

10. Kelso, pp. 62–63.

appeared in print was suspected of seeking male attention, or of trying to compete with men. Nevertheless, women would be allowed to write and publish if they stayed within the safe areas of religion and domesticity. The first was woman's prerogative; the second was her granted dominion. Neither of the two jeopardized her chastity. Secular literature was considered a threat to a woman's sexual purity and therefore unacceptable. Martial affairs, and epic literature particularly, were thought to be especially inappropriate for a female writer, for only men could deal with such weighty matters; besides, women had no experience in fighting battles. In any case, authorship of imaginative literature was a distinctly male activity. Only a man could father a text. Creative energy in a woman was thought to be anomalous, hermaphroditic, unfeminine.[11]

Tyler's preface, "M. T. to the Reader," is a defense of her translation of *The Mirrour of Knighthood* against these restrictions. Tyler defends her right to translate a book about chivalry, "a matter more manlike then becommeth my sexe." Lack of experience in a subject, she asserts, does not preclude writing about it: "But as for the manlinesse of the matter, thou knowest that it is not necessary for every trumpettour or drumstare in the warre to be a good fighter. . . . I trust every man holds not the plow, which would the ground were tilled: & it is no sinne to talk of Robinhood though you never shot in his bow" (A3–A3v).[12] Even if it were granted that it is "bolde" for females to actively "intermeddle in armes, so as the auncient Amazons did, and in this story Claridiana doth," she argues, there should be no objection to women writing about battles which, although fought by men, also concern women: "yet to report of armes is not so odious but that it may be borne withal, not onely in you men which your selves are fighters, but in us women, to whom the benefit in equal part apperteineth of your victories" (A3v).

Tyler takes even greater pains to defend her choice of non–religious

11. For Renaissance women's literary activity and public role see Travitsky (1981); Margaret Hannay, ed., *Silent But for the Word: Tudor Women as Patrons, Translators, and Writers of Religious Works* (Cambridge, Mass., 1986); and Mary Beth Rose, ed., *Women in the Middle Ages and the Renaissance* (Syracuse, N.Y., 1986), esp. pp. 1–27. For Renaissance notions of women see Ruth Kelso (1956); Suzanne Hull, *Chaste, Silent, and Obedient: English Books for Women, 1475–1640* (San Marino, Cal., 1982); and Linda Woodbridge, *Women and the English Renaissance: Literature and the Nature of Womankind, 1540–1620* (Sussex, Eng., 1984). Sandra Gilbert and Susan Gubar treat the relationship between author and father in *The Madwoman in the Attic: the Woman Writer and the Nineteenth-Century Literary Imagination* (New Haven, Conn., 1979).

12. Textual citations here and throughout refer to the 1578 British Museum copy of *The Mirrour of Princely deedes and Knighthood*, STC 18859. Signatures are used for the prefatory material and page numbers for the text of *The Mirrour*, but pagination is irregular.

subject. With arguments which again reveal both her society's restrictions on women's intellectual activity and her own critical discernment, she tells the reader why she chose to translate a secular piece of literature, "a story prophane," as she calls it, and why she "preferred this story before matter of more importance." Although in places she assumes a defensive stance, as when she downplays the translator's role (A3v), open confrontation is Tyler's principal strategy. She asserts her right to literature by exposing the biases and contradictions in patriarchal theories and practices. Initially citing but quickly dismissing the commonplace excuse that the work was "put upon me by others," and that worse books than *The Mirrour* are daily published by men, she declares:

> But my defence is by example of the best, amongst which many have dedicated their labours, some stories, some of warre, some phisick, some lawe, some as concerning government, some divine matters, unto diverse ladies & gentlewomen. And if men may & do bestow such of their travailes upon gentlewomen, then may we women read such of their works as they dedicate unto us, and if we may read them, why not farther wade in them to the serch of a truth. (A4)

Tyler challenges the ideologies which grant men exclusive right to knowledge and restrict women to specific areas of learning: "But to retourn whatsomever the truth is, whether that women may not at al discourse in learning, for men lay in their claim to be sole possessioners of knowledge, or whether they may in some manner that is by limitation or appointment in some kinde of learning, my perswasion hath bene thus, that it is all one for a woman to pen a story, as for a man to addresse his story to a woman" (A4–A4v). I mentioned above that religion and domesticity were the only acceptable areas for women of literary ambition. Translation was also a permitted area, as it called for a relatively passive role and indirectly reinforced the idea of author as patriarch. But the permission to translate did not also carry with it a license to cross the boundaries of designated subject areas. Tyler's need to defend her choice of a secular work is evidence of that.

III

Yet the defense was also necessary because Tyler was dealing with a genre which Renaissance men had generally condemned as immoral. Sidney, one-third of whose *Arcadia* is traceable to *Amadis de Gaul,* found a didactic purpose in romances, but he was one in a very small minority. Moralists and theoreticians on education almost unanimously castigated romantic literature and forbade the reading of such literature for both sexes, but especially for women. Thus in the *Instruction of a Christian Woman* (published in a translation by Richard Hyrde in 1529) Vives prohibits among other amorous material "those ungracious books, such as be in my country in Spain, the *Amadis,* Florisand, Tristan and Celestina the bawd, mother of naughtiness; in France, Launcelot du lac, Paris and Vienne, Ponthus and Sidonia. . . . In England, Parthenope, Geranides, Hippomadon, William and Melyour, Libius and Arthur, Guy, Bevis, and many other."[13] Thomas Salter concurs with Vives and severely criticizes fathers who allow their daughters "to come and learn by heart bookes, ballades, songes, sonnettes and dities of daliance, excityng their memories thereby."[14]

The moralists evidently feared that romances and other types of amorous literature would corrupt the minds of readers, especially of young women, turning them into unruly lovers. The connection between reading romance and the production of sexual desire is suggested by the language of the moralists themselves: "[S]till desire doth from knowledge grow," says Saltonstall in his condemnation of amorous reading (*Picturae Loquentes. . . . With a Poeme of a Maid,* 1631), echoing the fears of his earlier colleagues. Sexual knowledge is directly linked to desire and by implication to the overturning of the established roles between the sexes. The fears of the moralists mounted as more and more women actually read the type of literature branded as immoral. Indeed, studies of Renaissance women's reading show that in the last quarter of the sixteenth century, when the market of recreational books (mostly romances of all types) exploded in England, a large number of women read prose fiction, for by the turn of the century a female reading audience had emerged as distinct from the male.[15] L. B. Wright informs us that romances were a favorite form of reading among women and that although they later came to be the literary fare of the lower ranks, "they were not abandoned by any group and remained popular with

13. Quoted by L. B. Wright in "The Reading of Renaissance Englishwomen," *Studies in Philology* 28 (1931), p. 147n.

14. Wright, p. 141.

15. Hull, esp. pp. 75 and 78–82; Wright, pp. 152–56. In the chivalric romances which followed Tyler's translation, the appeal to female readers is obvious. *The Ninth Part of The Mirrour of Knighthood* (1601), e.g., is advertised as dealing with "the high chevalrie of the gallant Ladies." Similar appeals were made by other authors and publishers.

women of all classes."[16]

The chivalric romance was a continuation of a literary tradition that had given prominence to women and had been the medium of expression for the revolutionary ideas of courtly love, a form of love that aristocratic women of the Middle Ages had actively helped to develop. The new ideas spread all over Europe through romances and love lyrics. As Joan Kelly-Gadol suggests, the notion of courtly love, which was based on the idea of homage or service to a lady (and which corresponded to the feudal relationship of lord and vassal), had several liberating implications for aristocratic women. It allowed for the expression of sexual love and introduced the notions of equality and mutuality. A woman had to honor her lover as a friend, not as a master, while the signs or pledges of love had to be mutual. In courtly love literature, adultery became a precondition for the existence of passionate love, for within the constraints of marriage as practiced in medieval society, love was deemed impossible. Marriage was a system of political and property alliances while courtly love was a relationship free of any bargains. The only form of chastity that courtly love literature required, and that actually served to justify sexual love, was fidelity between the two lovers.[17]

Some critics, like Gillian Beer, think these ideas subverted the order of feudal society.[18] Joan Kelly-Gadol believes that they actually supported it by reinforcing existing institutionalized practices such as that of policital marriage.[19] What is not debatable, however, is that in the sixteenth century notions of courtly love posed a threat to the order of the home, which explains why in this period the romance was suppressed in favor of classical (patriarchal) literature. In the Renaissance, marriage was elevated and love was bonded to it to make up the romantic concept of marriage.[20] At the same time, certain criteria for female conduct—chastity, obedience, and sexual modesty above all—were foregrounded

16. Wright, p. 154. Possibly upper class women passed their taste to lower classes. Maids were frequently employed as readers by their mistresses (cf. the *Diary* of Lady Anne Clifford). Crane, cited above, gives a comprehensive account of the taste for chivalric romances and the role of the printers in it.

17. This is a summary of Kelly-Gadol's section on love and the medieval lady, pp. 141–48 of her influential essay, "Did Women Have a Renaissance?" in *Becoming Visible: Women in European History*, ed. Renate Bridenthal and Claudia Koonz (Boston, Mass., 1977).

18. Gillian Beer, *The Romance,* Critical Idiom series (New York, 1970), p. 23.

19. Kelly-Gadol, p. 145.

20. According to Ian Watt, there are signs of reconciliation between courtly love and the institution of marriage at least as early as Chaucer's "Franklin' Tale." See *Rise of the Novel* (London, 1974), pp. 136–37.

and emphasized. The church, too, modified its views on desire and sexuality, citing marriage and procreation as justification for the hitherto sinful act of sexual intercourse.

The chivalric romance of the sixteenth century accommodated these new ideas of love, marriage, and female conduct. Accordingly, it presented marriage as the desired end in a heterosexual love relationship and eliminated adultery as a positive context for passionate love. Adultery became at best an indiscretion to which the hero was usually led by some supernatural power. In addition, the chivalric romance adopted the attribute of modesty as a requirement for acceptable female conduct.

However, despite these important concessions that the chivalric romance made to survive among an audience that was no longer exclusively courtly and which no longer recognized a privileged code of behavior for aristocratic women, it did not completely assimilate the values of the new social order. For one thing, the associations with courtly love were not completely cut off. Perhaps Spenser ousted courtly love concepts from the romance,[21] but other writers—the French[22] and Spanish writers, for example, did not. They continued to favor several concepts associated with courtly love, at least two of which are present in the type of chivalric romance to which *The Mirrour* belongs: the idea of male homage to a lady and the idea of passionate love as a physically inspired feeling that tyrannizes both lovers. Although these concepts intermingle with Renaissance restrictions on women, some of their liberating implications still obtain. Unlike the sonnet which presents an icy picture of woman and detaches her from the actions and inner turmoil of her lover, the romance portrays her as a human being who can reciprocate her lover's feelings and pledges of love. Furthermore, the romance ignores Renaissance restrictions, inherited from classical literature, on the affective behavior of men. It allows them the sort of emotional overreaction that Ovid and his followers had attributed to women only. In this respect the romance counters traditional stereotypes and helps bridge the gap that such stereotypes create between the two sexes.

Several other features rendered the chivalric romance an oppositional

21. This is C. S. Lewis' point in his discussion of *The Faerie Queene* in *The Allegory of Love* (Oxford, 1958), pp. 297–350. Lewis argues that the third and part of the fourth books of *The Faerie Queene* are about the victory of married love in its struggle with courtly love.

22. Ian Watt notes in passing (p. 137) that the French tradition in fiction differed from the English in its use of courtly love.

genre in the sixteenth century. First, by its portrayal of daring heroines the romance often encouraged women to ignore social restrictions. Especially within a group of romances to which *The Mirrour* belongs, the heroine characteristically opposes conventional authority. Often, for example, she decides to deceive or disobey her father/guardian in order to love a man of her own choice and usually of unknown origin. "The decision she faces in accepting the unknown knight pits her individual will against the social order. Her judgment of observed worth is more reliable than her father's judgment on the basis of social convention."[23]

Secondly, by its construction of an ideal world, the romance could suggest a comparison with the real one. In the ideal world of the romances the heart was placed higher than the mind, personal virtues such as courage were put above heredity, and class barriers were often removed. Love affairs almost always ended happily, and evil was punished. Where the real world fostered violence against women, the chivalric one protected them without lowering their status. The chivalric hero always undertakes to rescue women from rape, disinheritance, or force of will. Such a contrast could make the female reader critical of her position in the real world.

Thirdly, romances tended to provide experiences unattainable for women in actual life. Amazons and warrior women are found primarily in romantic fiction. The presence of lady knights–errant meant among other things that female readers had the opportunity to identify with members of their sex who at least on the printed page were engaging in traditionally male activities—travel, adventure, and outdoor sports. Sir Thomas Overbury suggests this idea in one of his *Characters* (1614); his chambermaid "reads Greene's works over and over, but is so carried away with the *Mirror of Knighthood,* she is many times resolv'd to runne out of her selfe, and become a lady errant."[24] Similarly, the elaborate descriptions of amorous scenes found in romances could vicariously satisfy the affective needs of the female reader which her society did not.[25] Although as I mentioned earlier the female heroines of sixteenth-century romances are not nearly as free in matters of sexual conduct as their twelfth–century counterparts, they are not subject to the strict

23. Barbara Louise Magaw, "The Female Characters in Prose Chivalric Romance in England 1475–1603," Ph.D. Dissertation, University of Maryland (1973), p. 62.

24. Quoted by Wright, p. 148.

25. Janice Radway, in her book *Reading the Romance: Women, Patriarchy and Popular Literature* (Chapel Hill, N.C., 1985), makes this point about readers of Harlequin romances today.

rules on subordination and distance between husband and wife expounded in sixteenth-century conduct books. Furthermore, the notion of a Bower of Bliss, so frequently included in the romance formula, could encourage the type of behavior moralists sought to suppress. It could, of course, reinforce stereotyped notions of woman as seductress, but at the same time, since the author has no control over how the reader will construct meaning, it could equally serve as a source of vicarious sexual pleasure for women and control over the sexual behavior of men. (This would seem to hold true especially in texts like *The Mirrour,* where the author seldom interjects moral lessons.) Arguably, such compensatory function of reading romance may have diverted energies that might otherwise have been spent in social protest, but it probably also stimulated the mind to imagine other possibilities in an age when women were constantly indoctrinated with theories about their own inferiority.

Finally, the *act* of reading the romance could be potentially subversive in the sixteenth century as it might be even today. For women like Lady Anne Clifford, reading a romance was apparently no different than reading books on Turkish history. The entries in her *Diary,* which include *The Faerie Queene, The Arcadia,* and Ovid's *Metamorphoses, The Government of the Turks,* and Chaucer,[26] do not communicate any sense of impropriety in reading these types of books. But this was apparently not the case with women of lower social position and less liberal educational background. There are several contemporary references to women secretly reading amorous material. Referring to *Venus and Adonis,* John Davies says that "the coyest Dames / In private read it for their Closet-games."[27] And one N. W. informs us that "Ladies entertaine Bandel or Ariosto in their Closets."[28] Janice Radway, speaking about women readers of modern popular literature, suggests that the act of reading a romance constitutes a gesture of independence.[29] Given the prohibitions on love literature in the early modern period, it would also seem to constitute an act of disobedience. Thus the very act of reading, as surely as the narrative itself, could undermine dominant ideologies.

IV

Before I discuss *The Mirrour,* let me briefly summarize the plot. In the

26. See Lady Anne Clifford, *Diary* (London, 1924), pp. 47, 52, 66, 76, and 104.
27. Quoted by Wright, p. 150.
28. Wright, p. 148.
29. Radway, pp. 211–12.

monastery of the river lives the beautiful princess Briana, at a distance from her parents' court. Her father, the Emperor of Hungary, has waged war of expansion on Greece. But he is militarily not strong enough, so he makes an alliance with the British king. The terms of the alliance are: 20,000 troops and the personal help of the British king's son, Edward, in exchange for the hand of the Princess Briana. So Briana, daughter of the king of Hungary, is to marry Edward, son of the king of Great Britain. The two have never met. But the plans become thwarted. The Emperor of Greece, against whom Edward is to fight, falls in love with Briana's reported beauty. So on the way to the monastery of the river he kills Edward and presents himself to Briana as Prince Edward, with documents and all. Briana and Trebatio (alias Edward) are married by the archbishop in the monastery. Briana has been advised by her father not to consummate her marriage before her husband goes to war, but she disobeys his advice. She becomes pregnant, and Trebatio disappears not to go to war but to search for the enchanted chariot which in his dreams has carried off Briana. She gives birth to two sons who become the narrative's new heroes. One of the sons is named Rosicleer, the other Donzel del Febo (or Knight of the Sun). From a very young age, each of the two disappears separately from the mother's abode in the monastery of the river. They search for adventure and their father. They travel far and wide in Asia, Africa, and Europe, performing deeds of chivalry. They rescue women and reinstate the dispossessed. Rosicleer falls in love with Olivia, daughter of the king of Great Britain, and she with him. The affair is secret and Olivia is worried, for Rosicleer's birth is of doubtful origin. Her father intends to marry her off to an heir of a neighboring state. Meanwhile, after twenty years, Trebatio returns to the monastery of the river. He offers explanations for his absence and he is glad to find his wife waiting for him. Deciding not to introduce himself to her father, he elopes with her to Greece.

Like other sixteenth-century chivalric romances, *The Mirrour* combines courtly and chivalric elements with Renaissance ideas about love, marriage, and sexual conduct. As the setting and structure of the plot clearly derive from the chivalric tradition, so do the ideals the book upholds. The heroes are carried to distant parts of the world through a series of adventures which purport to prove their courage and honor. Possessed of superhuman strength, they fight endless battles against giants or others who exploit the disadvantaged. At least one of the two major love relationships in the book is conducted according to the concept of male service inherited from courtly love. At the same time, the relationships between men and women clearly show that love is allied to marriage and so is sex. Olivia is distressed to find out that the man she loves may not be eligible as a husband, and Briana can experience sexual intercourse only when she is married. Even then she has to appear modest and relatively passive; we are told that she consents "somewhat against her will," because Trebatio is after all "hir lawfull husband" (Ch. 7, p. 12). Sexual passion and expression of sexual desire is an attribute of the man.

The Mirrour opposes some conventional ideas and practices while endorsing others. The text works not as a radical critique of sixteenth-century culture, but as a series of appropriations. While sometimes criticism of oppressive structures is placed in the mouth of specific female characters, usually particular areas of culture are contested by endorsement of other conventional areas or by appeal to higher ideals. The text also opposes dominant ideologies and practices by following, at least in part, the chivalric code of justice. Below I discuss *The Mirrour*'s oppositional attitude in relation to three areas: marriage and class, the double standard, and women and violence.

In the sixteenth century marriage theory and practice was based on the need of the aristocratic class to maintain its power through inheritance. Although in earlier Utopian social theory members from different castes might be allowed to marry, nowhere else was such a practice encouraged. The conflict that resulted from the individual's desire to marry for love and the tragic consequences of disinheritance recurs in Renaissance literature, especially in drama. The socio–political changes that took place in the transition from a feudal to an early modern state necessitated regulation of membership in a hereditary nobility—hence also the increase in the concern over legitimacy of birth. Marriages were based on alliances made between families with titles to property. Despite humanistic ideas about love and marriage, property and political alliance remained the most important criteria in the marriages of the upper classes.[30] Through the threat of disinheritance, the parents controlled their children's choices. Often marriages would be arranged when the children were still very young. And legal practice supported the parents' power, for parental consent was required by law for most marriages. Theory supported cultural practice in this respect, and the material motive of the aristocracy was coupled with the Renaissance concern to

30. Lawrence Stone, *The Family, Sex and Marriage* (London, 1977), p. 193.

establish the patriarchal family. Middle–class marriage manuals advised people to marry within their own social rank and often interpreted a woman's desire to choose a husband from the lower class as an attempt on her part to gain control over the man. (William Googe speaks of the arrogance of some women in marrying men of lower rank.)[31] *The Mirrour* seems to undermine several of these ideas and practices. It shows the utter incompatibility between love and material marriage and strongly challenges barriers of caste. Interestingly, the text views this matter mainly from a female perspective and shows the binds that women are placed in when they are treated as commodities.

Two parts of the narrative, the story of Briana and Trebatio and that of Olivia and Rosicleer, show the conflicts of class and gender and finally affirm the primacy of love. Trebatio is not a chivalric hero, but he seems to uphold some chivalric ideals. He stands against imperialism and for love without bargains. Attracted to the reported beauty of Briana, he kills his materialist adversary Edward vowing that "although thou wast mine enemie and come in favour of the kinge Tiberio to take from me my land and high estate, yet woulde I not have bene so cruel an enimie unto thee, but that entire love of the princesse Briana drave me more therto, then mine owne enmitie" (Ch. 9, p. 15). Edward is the one who has accepted woman (Briana) as a commodity. He has come to buy her with his 20,000 men and his military skill in her father's expansionist enterprises. Trebatio too displays a certain degree of aggression in claiming Briana. He too treats her as his prerogative, and in this respect he is more a Renaissance male than a chivalric hero. But he at least does not participate in the system that puts a price on women and uses them as pawns in military alliances.

Briana is presented in conventionally acceptable terms. In *Amadis* and other romances of the same type, the leading female character disobeys or deceives her father in her decision to follow her lover.[32] In *The Mirrour* Briana is made to appear much less deceitful and rebellious, at least on the surface. Trebatio's disguise as Edward frees her from the responsibility of disobeying her father's will.[33] In fact her initial recognition of filial duty and obedience would have been applauded by any sixteenth-century theorist on female conduct: "I will accomplish that which the duetie of obedience unto the king my father forceth me unto, for that I must

31. Kelso, p. 94.
32. Magaw, p. 58.
33. Magaw concurs, p. 89.

subject my wil unto his commaundement, yet I so consider of this your offer and request, as that from this time I will dare to compare with you in like happinesse" (Ch. 6, p. 10v). But her last statement in this passage would not have been applauded, for it implies a little too much forwardness and hope for equality. Equally troubling would be her decision at the beginning of the book to consummate her "marriage" and at the end to elope with Trebatio to Greece. Here the portrayal of an ostensibly dutiful and virtuous daughter supports the woman's sexual responsiveness and her final act of disobedience.

The union between Trebatio and Briana is not a case of expediency, and the story itself reads like an example of how to thwart an arranged marriage. We are shown that the Trebatio–Briana marriage succeeds because the material motives attendant on the original match between Briana and Edward have been removed. The narrative is constructed so that the reader will approve the change in circumstances. It is important to note here that Edward's replacement is rendered necessary not by the plot but by his materialistic motives, which preclude him as a candidate for the role of chivalric hero.

Furthermore, the Briana–Trebatio relationship may be seen as oppositional also on account of its conventional elements. Briana's specific situation accentuates her characteristics as a *feme covert*. Her geographical isolation may be part of the romance convention, but her seclusion also inadvertently serves as a symbol for the condition of sixteenth–century women and their exclusion from the public sphere, the world of action. She is a woman who is acted upon by men and who has very little control over what happens to her. Even the man who loves her leaves her pregnant and disappears for twenty years. She has to live a life of patience and pain, trying to hide her children in order to prevent social disgrace. This is a sympathetic representation which has the potential to elicit identification from the female reader and make her aware of oppression. At the end, like a faithful Penelope, Briana gets her man back, but the narrative does not in any way imply that this fact justifies the pain she undergoes. (And even if it did, the potential for identification could not be erased.) It shows, rather, that Trebatio owes some explanations for his actions. This is unlike the type of representation one finds in books like *Penelope's Web* (1587) where obedience, chastity, and silence are not only expected but taken for granted.[34]

34. See Hull, p. 81, about the Penelope and Griselda theme in recreational literature addressed to women.

The Olivia–Rosicleer affair in the book likewise undermines sixteenth-century theory and practice with regard to marriage and caste. Here Don Silverio, a less crude version of Edward, is the representative of the status quo who serves as antagonist to the chivalric hero, Rosicleer. Like Edward, Don Silverio appears ready to claim the benefits that the traditional system of marriage offers to men of his title and social position. More confident about his material assets than his love for Olivia, he comes to ask for her in marriage, "presuming upon his byrth and livelihood that she should be graunted unto him" (Ch. 32, p. 83). Olivia's father, King Oliverio, supports this system of marriage as political property alliance. He attempted such an alliance when he sent his son Edward to Hungary, and now he tries it with the marriage of his daughter. He explains to her why Don Silverio is a good match: he is "a comly knight of personage, valiant in armes, of a couragious spirite above, all vertuous, and in his dealinges circumspect, courteous of speach and of highe estate. . . . Ther are besides to commend this match the entercourse of trafficke betweene our subjectes, and the friendshippe between his parents and mee" (Ch. 55, p. 177v). This type of marriage is a self-reproducing system within the propertied class. *The Mirrour* shows the restrictions that the system imposes on women especially and, through Olivia, criticizes the values of the class that upholds it. Olivia is first set up as a supporter of aristocratic practices and values, but is soon turned into a critical opponent of these. Caught between her love for Rosicleer and what she believes to be the barrier of class between them, she makes the most eloquent case in favor of abolishing noble birth as a criterion for marriage within the aristocratic class. Her speech, a long discursive passage within the narrative, is one of the most important statements in a book translated by a woman and largely read by members of her sex. As the text of *The Mirrour* is not readily available, the passage is worth quoting at length:

What a wicked world is this, wherein men of force must neglect other mens vertues, and magnifie their owne nobilitie wythout deserte: were it not more reason to rayse this man to the toppe of honour that in him his posteritie may glory, then for lacke of auncestors famous for like qualities, to suppresse his vertue and keepe under the magnanimitie of his courage? When began my fathers and grandfathers to be nobles, but when with the winges of vertue they soared above the vulgar sort, and if by their means onely I am advaunced to be a Princesse, what thancke is there to mee of my highnesse? and thou Rosicleer if by those rare and sovereygne vertues . . . thou dost mount in credit . . . art not thou worthy of greater renowne then we others whych clymbing by vertue in lyke sorte, never yet came to the possibylytie of like worthinesse?

Is not this a forgery of the world and a playne [m]ingling wyth nobility, when we must make more account of one which perhaps by disorder of life defaceth the honour of his race, then of one which reacheth by the ignobilitie of his stock, wherein consisteth nobilitye in the opinion of men, or in vertue in deede? and doo men inherit vertue as the chylde entereth uppon the fathers lande beeinge lawfull heyre? No, heere wee receyve naught but what our selves sowe, and hee that reapeth not maye be a loute for all his Lordshippe, as in tyme appeareth, whiche judgeth freely and wythout affection. And for mee, if the eyes of my understandinge were not dymmed, I shoulde soone confesse lesse merite in me to deserve Rosicleer then wanteth in him to bee worthy of me. . . . But sith of force I must yeelde to the time and rather dye then acknowledge the contrary, *sith my Fortune is such that I must live by the immagination of other men,* and sith my estate may not be yoked with hys basenesse, have at it, I will for ever shutte him from my presence for the savegard of myne honour. (Ch. 39, pp. 114–114v) [emphasis added]

This passage and indeed most of Chapter 39 is very similar in spirit to Tyler's Preface. Both deal with restrictions on women, one focusing on gender, the other on class. Both show the binds that culture and class create for women. Olivia vacillates in her decision to accept the love of Rosicleer, a man of supposed low birth; but her vacillation is not between Rosicleer and Don Silverio. The narrative as a whole encourages both the heroine and the reader to abandon patriarchal standards of judging human worth.

The Mirrour's opposition to dominant ideology is also evident in its criticism of the double standard. The strongest and most articulate objection is raised with regard to adultery. One of the feats of the Knight of the Sun, brother of Rosicleer, is the defense of the Duchess Elisandra, who has been accused of adultery and dispossessed of her property. The Knight of the Sun and his father Trebatio are on their way to the monastery of the river when they hear the cries of distressed gentlewomen. The latter are representatives of Elisandra, Duchess of Pannonia. Married for eight years, Elisandra has no children. Her husband, fearing that in the absence of children her inheritance would revert to her kin, accuses her of adultery to get rid of her. To present his case convincingly, he makes one of his friends (Arydon) his accomplice. The whole scheme is described as follows:

For a plot of ground adjacent to his segniories, his accusation lyeth thus that with himselfe [Arydon] she committed adultery. . . . The Duke presently complaineth to the king, and both partyes are sent for in all hast. Arydon being first asked confesseth it, and is acquitted by his confession. *As (by the way) our lawe in this case acquiteth the man once confessing it though otherwise never so great an offender, and onely stretcheth to the woman in respect of hir faythe given at marriage.* (Ch. 40, p. 166v) [emphasis added]

The only hope of this woman, we are told, is to find a knight who will defend her innocence in a battle with the mighty Arydon. The Knight of the Sun undertakes the task, and in the ensuing battle, which takes place in the presence of the king and other judges, kills Arydon, who at the last minute confesses his part in the Duke's plot against his wife. The Duke is ordered to be executed, and the story ends by abolishing the double standard in the law governing adultery: "For albeit many of his nobles entreated for their pardon, yet the king so abhorred the villany that nought availed: and at this time was the lawe first enacted in Hungary that *the law of punnishment for whoredome should stretche aswell to the man as to the woman,* and that *equall penaltie* should be assigned to lyke offendours, whereas before the men escaped the women onely were in danger"(Ch. 54, p. 175) [emphasis added]. The bias in the law described in the above two passages is not much different from that which existed in most countries of sixteenth–century Europe, including England. Such passages show, among other things, that where matters of sexuality were concerned the law assumed the innocence of the man and the guilt of the woman. They evince once more the close link between the interests of patriarchy and the legal rights of women.

In the sixteenth century the double standard in sexual conduct was widespread. Fidelity within marriage was in theory required of both men and women, but only women were morally condemned for their lack of chastity. Western literary tradition reinforced the double standard by giving the hero, married or not, complete freedom in his sexual behavior. As a form which derived from the epic, the chivalric romance kept several of its conventions, including the sexual enchantment of the hero. But the chivalric code required fidelity from both lovers. *The Mirrour* registers the disparity between the two traditions, a disparity made especially apparent by the author's attempts to provide excuses for Trebatio's behavior. When Trebatio, a married man, becomes enchanted in the Castle of Lindaraza (the equivalent of Acrasia's Bower of Bliss in the *Faerie Queene*), apologies are offered to the reader: "And you must pardon the Emperour if by this he was wholy possessed with hir [Lindaraza's] love, and forgot his late wife the Princesse Briana"(Ch. 9, p. 16v). His enchantment, we are told further, was due to "the secreate of the place." He was "deprived of his understanding," in a state of semi–consciousness or "sweet sleep" (Ch. 9, p. 16v). When he finally returns to Briana in the monastery of the river, she is made to ask: "My Lorde and onely lyfe what cruell Fortune hath detayned you from this lande, and bannished you so long from my presence"(Ch. 51, p. 169). To which Trebatio replies:

> Madame . . . you may call that Fortune cruell, for it hath offered you a great wronge by forceing you to endure a farre greater penaunce then Penelope dyd by Ulysses absence: but one thinge you maye assure your selfe of that the fault was not in mee thoughe I am not to bee excused, for if I had had lyfe and lybertie and judgement, all the world should not have stayed me from you.
>
> Since my freedome if I have not had as loyall a regarde of your constancye and my duetie, then blame all mankinde for my sake of unstedfastnesse and wronge, and for this tyme let these things slippe wyth lesse griefe to entertayne our present joye. (Ch. 51, pp. 169–169v)

However naive-sounding, such passages clearly imply that apologies are needed, that Trebatio's lack of constancy cannot be presented as an assumed right. They also have the effect of legitimating opposition to the double standard.

As I mentioned earlier, *The Mirrour* does not advocate the type of sexual equality that was found in the courtly love romances of the twelfth century. Sexual modesty is an attribute of the female character mainly, although it is occasionally found in the male one also. (Rosicleer, for example, is abashed when he faces Olivia in public after he has fallen in love with her, Ch. 34, p. 96v.) But the fact remains that *The Mirrour* foregrounds and criticizes at least the crude forms of the double standard just discussed.

The Mirrour also foregrounds the issue of violence against women. It reiterates the chivalric rule that violence against a woman is a crime. And insofar as violence against a woman includes also violence against her will, the defense of women runs counter to sixteenth–century theory and cultural practice. It is of course one of the conventions in chivalric romances for the hero to seek adventures and to try to right the wronged. But in *The Mirrour* the victims which the heroes succor are almost always women. In the course of the book there are no fewer than eight incidents in which women come running for help because they are threatened by rape, forced marriage, or disinheritance. Two of the incidents are particularly interesting.

The first concerns one Arguirosa, heiress to the kingdom of Thessaly. Her father married a woman of questionable character. When he died, his widow married her lover Rolando, who seizes the throne by force, excluding Arguirosa, the rightful heiress. Rolando and his kinsmen are so strong that Arguirosa is powerless. "But that which is worst of all was, that to undoe hir rightefull claime, hee mindeth to marrye hir with a

kinsman of his and to give [her] onely some lyttle towne to dwell in"
(Ch. 47, p. 157v). Arguirosa has come to the tournaments at the British
king's court hoping to find a knight who will undertake her quarrel.

The second incident also involves an heiress but the offense is even
more personal. Princess Radamira is the heiress to Cyprus. Raiartes, a
great giant, hears of her beauty and comes to her island to demand her for
his wife. Her father refuses and Raiartes kills him in a duel. Through
sheer strength, Raiartes takes over her property, carries her against her
will to his country, and forces her to accept him as husband. Radamira,
"abhoring nothing so much as the company of Raiartes," finally makes a
deal with him: if she finds a knight who will defeat Raiartes in battle, she
will be set at liberty. Thus Radamira rides through the courts of Europe
to find a knight who will undertake her cause.

The first of these incidents involves mainly loss of title and property,
while the second concerns loss of personal freedom as well. Both
incidents take place in a patriarchal society where power clearly belongs
to men. Such incidents involving loss of inheritance and forced marriage
were commonplace in the sixteenth century and earlier. The difference
was that in actual life there was no court to which women could appeal
in order to defend their cause. Moreover, Renaissance legal and social
practice formally brought under the man's control the very rights which
are defended by the chivalric heroes here. A woman could be forced
through the threat of disinheritance to accept a husband she disliked and
her right to property could be manipulated by the male heirs. (The case
of Lady Anne, Countess of Clifford, is one obvious example.) *The
Mirrour* reaffirms the restitution of women's legal rights. Even in
chivalry, however, such feats are exceptional, the heroes are as formida-
ble as the wrong-doers. Rosicleer and his brother are no ordinary
mortals. But the fact that *The Mirrour* undertakes the defense of such
issues on any level constitutes an act of opposition to dominant ideology
and practice. And it is important to notice that the text prioritizes the
issues on which women must be defended: whims are not treated
seriously.[35]

35. That *The Mirrour* prioritizes the issues and draws the attention away from defense as a mere
game is evident from an incident in Chapter 52 in which a woman demands a defense of her
beauty. The Knight of the Sun laughs at her cause, although he finally does what she asks, and the
chapter ends with a lesson on misplaced preoccupation with beauty. This differs from the
emphasis in many other chivalric romances and in Queen Elizabeth's own court. On February 26,
1588, Cumberland and Essex made challenge that "they will runne all corners to maintain that
the Queen is most worthiest and more fairest Amadis de Gaule." (Recorded by Miller in *The
Professional Writer in Elizabethan England* [Cambridge, Mass., 1959], pp. 80–81.)

While *The Mirrour* challenges dominant sixteenth-century ideology and social practice, there are absences from the text which are equally important. For one thing, the text uses no language that denotes subordination. It is true that sexual modesty is mainly a female characteristic, but there is nothing which explicitly states the idea of woman's subordination to man. In this respect *The Mirrour* observes the chivalric code. Similarly, there are almost no stereotyped views of women. In the few instances where they do occur, they are disproved by the narrative itself. Olivia, for example, reproaches herself in terms traditionally used against her sex ("O inconstant and frayle womankinde . . . lyght in beliefe, light in judgement," Ch. 41, p. 130). But the narrative shows that she does not deserve such self-reproach since she has good reasons to worry about her lover's social rank. Moreover, Olivia criticizes herself and is not censured by others.

There is also an overall absence in *The Mirrour* of the type of adjectives that describe women as dainty and coy. None of the female characters is endowed with these traditionally feminine attributes. The portrait of the Amazon Claridiana in Chapter 45 may be revealing in this respect. Claridiana, daughter of the Queen of the Amazons, first appears chasing a wild boar. Three knights happen to see her and they are awestruck by her grace and beauty, but "the Lady more bolde then the men" wakes them up as it were with a blow on her horn. After introductions and courtesies are exchanged, Claridiana's entourage (consisting of thirty gentlewomen and thirty or more male knights) arrives, but not before she has had a chance to devise a trick she will play on her knights to amuse herself and the strangers. The jest is finally revealed, and she invites the three new knights to her parents' court where she is shortly to be knighted. The combination of beauty and masculine skill in hunting that Claridiana displays are probably commonplace attributes in representations of warrior women, and so too might be the description of her untypical upbringing and heritage. (She was trained in hunting, we are told, since early youth and her mother "achieved such enterprises that in hir time there was no knight more famous.") But noticeably absent are those signs of femininity that Simon Shepherd notices in Spenser's *Faerie Queene*—Britomart's smock and hair revelation, and the "dainty parts" in the encounter with Radimund.[36] Unless it were Claridiana's "softe paces" (Ch. 45, p. 141v), nothing else in the description implies traditional notions of femininity. In fact the roles seem somewhat reversed. It

36. See *Amazons and Warrior Women* (Sussex, Eng., 1981), esp. pp. 5–17.

is the men who are unhelmeted and it is male beauty that is being revealed. The women are among the admirers: "wherat smiling they all unbuckeled their helmets Bargandel and Liriamandro beeing then of the age of 20 yeares, seeming so beautifull that as well the gentlewomen as the knights were amazed at them" (Ch. 45, pp. 151v–153). Claridiana behaves with greater ease than the men. When they pay her a compliment, she returns one freely and displays, in addition to her skill in hunting, a natural playfulness, a sense of humor, and a freedom in movement and expression.[37]

In the preceding analysis I have tried to show how *The Mirrour* may have constituted a critique of prevailing ideologies and cultural practices in the Renaissance. The oppositional elements I have pointed out hardly seem to warrant the strong defense Tyler advances in her preface. But viewed as ideas in a book translated by a woman in the 1570s in England, they acquire a larger significance. For any woman to publish a piece of secular literature then was an achievement; to publish a romance which critiqued the current social norm was an even greater achievement. In 1621 Mary Wroth published her own original romance, *The Countesse of Montgomeries Urania,* with a considerable degree of confidence, which she maintained even during the public quarrel that unfortunately led to the suppression of her book. Undoubtedly, part of this confidence can be attributed to her title as the niece of the accomplished Philip and Mary Sidney. But in addition, by the time she came to write, a number of other women writers and translators had paved the way. Margaret Tyler can certainly be counted as one of these women.[38]

37. Interestingly, these qualities became associated with sexual immorality, for eventually the name Claridiana in England came to be used as a synonym for mistress (Thomas, pp. 272–73).

39. This study is part of a larger research project funded by the Greek State Scholarship Foundation.

ELLEN M. CALDWELL

John Lyly's Gallathea: A New Rhetoric of Love for the Virgin Queen

> I greve, and dare not shewe my discontent;
> I love, and yet am forst to seem to hate;
> I do, yet dare not say I ever meant;
> I seem stark mute, but inwardly do prate;
> I am and not, I freese, and yet am burn'd;
> Since from myself, my other self I turn'd.

THE love-sick speaker in this lyric, a woman, languishes from a common Petrarchan malady of holding oxymoronic feelings. Able neither to show nor to speak her love, she stands bound in contradictions which threaten her sanity, surely, but more to the point, her identity. "I am and not . . . / Since from myself, my other self I turn'd." Who is this "other self"? The speaker's beloved, who is spurned? Love himself, the god of such painful pleasure? Or is it a part of the woman's own nature which must be denied in order, apparently, that reason rule? Before answering these questions, we might ask another: who, indeed, is the lyricist? Rather surprisingly, we find it to be Queen Elizabeth herself, writing farewell verses in 1582 to her suitor, the Duke of Anjou.[1]

Though hardly evidence of strong royal sentiment, Elizabeth's lyric nevertheless articulates the strain which passionate feeling seems to put upon the female psyche. And it is this curiously disruptive symptom of

---

1. Of the poem's three extant versions, I use the text of the poem in John Nichols' *Progresses of Queen Elizabeth* (London, 1823), II, 346, taken from the Bodleian Ashmole 781, p. 142 (written c.1620–30). The text shows very few variants from Bodleian Tanner 76, p. 162 (written c.1600). The third MS is British Museum Stowe 962, fo. 231 (written in the seventeenth century). Both Ashmole and Stowe say that Elizabeth wrote the poem on the occasion of Monsieur's departure, at the end of marriage negotiations in 1582. Tanner 76 suggests that the poem was written to the Earl of Essex. In his edition of *The Poems of Queen Elizabeth I* (Providence, 1964), Leicester Bradner supplies this information (p. 73). Bradner, however, doubts that the Queen would write such a poem and suggests either that it was written for political effect or that it was authored and circulated by someone else (p. xiii). I, however, accept the record of all three MSS that the poem was written by Elizabeth, though perhaps more as a sign of polity or wit than of feeling.

Subsequent references to Nichols will be cited parenthetically by volume and page number within the text.

love which John Lyly examines in *Gallathea*. Traditionally a master of finely crafted prose, Lyly offers here a satirical look at the rhetorical extremes of both passion and restraint in the language of his characters. He notes, thus, the unreason and psychic self-questioning of the woman in love as well as the vitriolic petulance of her who disdains love. While obviously arguing in his play for some mean between these two extremes, Lyly realized that before Elizabeth, his principal spectator of the 1588 court performance, such a message needed to be tactfully presented.

And he *is* tactful. Lyly makes a most persuasive argument for marriage, not as fulfillment of natural, divine, or political dictates, but as a method of uniting the parts of a woman's divided nature, of her competing urges for separateness and union, or for chastity and love. Gallathea and Phyllida, the two women who fall in love with each other, cannot, because of their disguises and their conflicting emotions, be themselves until the end of the play. That desire to be free of either a life-threatening female identity or of a confining male disguise seems to motivate the women far more than the satisfaction of mere sexual passion, something which only the nymphs are forced, comically, to endure in the play. Even more than a "marriage of true minds," then, Lyly calls in *Gallathea* for a marriage or reconciliation of conflicting responses within the mind of a woman, perhaps the Queen herself, torn between the trials of love and the frustration of chastity.

To make the argument for marriage, by now one which a variety of able poet-courtiers had attempted unsuccessfully, Lyly reinterpreted his Ovidian sources, heightened the ambiguity of the strategies employed in the entertainments provided for Elizabeth's amusement, and abandoned the conventional platitudes espoused in Renaissance treatises on the sacrament. The definition of marriage in the play also overturned the arguments Lyly had made earlier, advocating an active, political career over marriage in *Alexander and Campaspe* and the reasoned control of emotions over the blandishments of love in *Sapho and Phao*. *Gallathea,* on the other hand, offers a personal, not public, reason for marriage. It seeks to locate a new rhetoric between the extremes of Petrarchanism and common lust to woo Elizabeth to the idea of marriage. Finally, Lyly not only rewrites the terms of marital contract, but substitutes, at least symbolically, the man and woman who are normally joined in marriage for two complementary features of a woman's own nature.

Lyly's plot is a thinly disguised allegory of a woman's reluctance to face the sexual demands of marriage. Two doting fathers wish to save their virgin daughters from being sacrificed to Neptune, who demands every five years the most beautiful maiden of the countryside as his price for not flooding the Humber River. Both daughters are dressed as boys and hide in the forest, where they see and fall in love with each other. Unable to reveal their love without forsaking the safety of their disguise, both Gallathea and Phyllida dote as discreetly as possible, lament their plight, and worry (rightly, they learn) that the object of their affections may not be a man but another disguised maiden. The main plot is reinforced by a subplot, for the forest is also the hunting ground of Diana's virgin nymphs, who have fallen under spiteful Cupid's powers and become infatuated with the two disguised youths. Diana alternately cajoles and threatens her nymphs to withstand the machinations of the mischievous love-god, who has disguised himself as a nymph. The chaos is ultimately resolved through a compromise between Venus and Diana, nominally overseen by Neptune. Gallathea and Phyllida will be changed into a conventional male-female pair of lovers in order that they might be wed.

While Lyly follows the plotline of his Ovidian source, he nevertheless chooses a radically different method to persuade his audience of love's value. In Ovid's Iphis and Ianthe story, the metamorphosis of mortal woman to man satisfies both conventional and emotional dictates. The necessary sexual transformation in Lyly's story, however, is downplayed. Constancy, not metamorphosis or transformation, is celebrated, and the love of Gallathea and Phyllida seems to remain at the same pitch, no matter under what physical guise they are allowed to express it.[2]

In both Arthur Golding's and George Sandys' translations of the Iphis and Ianthe story (*Metamorphosis,* IX),[3] there are significant details which Lyly chooses to exploit in the argument of his play. Both translations do justice, as does Lyly, to Ovid's clear depiction of heterosexual and homosexual love; while Ianthe loves Iphis whom she assumes to be male, Iphis knowingly falls in love with another woman, but not without insistent reservations. Here is Golding's version: "And hereupon the hartes of both, the dart of Love did streeke / And wounded both of them alieke. But unlike was theyr hope / . . . . Iphys loves whereof she thinkes

---

2. My emphasis on constancy in love differs from Leah Scragg's emphasis on metamorphosis in the play. However, we concur in seeing antithetical properties in the play (p. 32) and in identifying Gallathea / Phyllida as an "epicoene figure" (p. 34). See *The Metamorphosis of Gallathea* (Washington, D.C., 1982).

3. I use the following editions: for Golding, *The 15 Books Entytuled Metamorphoses* (1567); for Sandys, *Ovid's Metamorphosis Englished, Mythologiz'd, and Represented in Figures,* 3rd ed. (1632). Page numbers will be cited parenthetically in the text.

she may not bee / Partaker, and the selfe same thing augmenteth still her flame. / Herself a Mayden with a Mayd (ryght straunge) in love became" (pp. 121–22). And both the unnaturalness of this love and the impossibility of its being satisfied are bluntly proclaimed in Iphis' soliloquy: "A Cow is never fond / Uppon a Cow, nor Mare on Mare. The Ram delyghts the Eawe / . . . . But never man can shewe, / That female yit was tane in love with female kynd. / . . . Beholde the blissful tyme / The day of Mariage is at hand. Ianthe shalbee myne, / And yit I shall not her enjoy. Amid the water we shall thirst" (p. 122r-v). However, unlike this outpouring of concern, none of the soliloquies in Lyly's play, even where Gallathea and Phyllida suspect each other's true female natures, raises the issue of unnatural desire. Frustration, certainly, arises from its unspoken presence, but Lyly takes pains never to present the love of the two women as anything but genuine, superior to the other infatuations in the play's subplot, and completely independent of the often frivolously aimed arrows of Cupid.

Although written well after Lyly's play, Sandys' commentary nevertheless is a useful compilation of the age's associations with the Iphis-Ianthe story. What most fascinates Sandys—the transformation—is what Lyly deliberately downplays. Sandys finds three lessons in the myth: the power of the gods, the necessity of trusting to Providence rather than presuming through unlawful or unnatural means to order one's own life, and the evidence that women become ennobled by being changed into men (pp. 449–50). While merely listing the first two, Sandys offers several examples of the third, drawn from sources such as Pliny and Montaigne. He particularly emphasizes the fact that men are never transformed into women: "that as it is preposterous in Nature, which ever aimes at perfection, when men degenerate into effeminacy; so contrarily commendable, when women aspire to manly wisdome and fortitude" (p. 450). The message is, of course, wholly inappropriate for Lyly's intended audience, and *Gallathea* seems quick to disclaim this moral. The transformation which Lyly celebrates is not the sexual one, which allows the marriage, but the psychological one, which reconciles oppositions as much within the individual as between the physically incompatible couple. Both Golding (p. 121) and Sandys (p. 449) note that the name Iphis is suitable for either sex; in that androgynous symbol, Lyly may also have seen the basis for a psychological union of the Queen's two natures—one desiring to marry, the other desiring to remain chaste— and for her wish to play simultaneously the roles of spouse and sovereign, which her age saw as canceling each other out. Lyly's purpose, however, was not so much to reconcile these two roles as to depict the matrimonial role as one compatible with the Queen's independent temperament. From the literary efforts of his contemporaries, Lyly saw how difficult it was to pose any but a judiciously ambiguous argument for marriage.

II

As late as 1575 Elizabeth was being regularly accosted with pleas to listen to nature, to good sense, to woman's true calling, and to her duty as a sovereign, to marry. In the 1575 entertainment at Kenilworth Castle, George Gascoigne offered the story of Zabeta, one of Diana's best-loved nymphs, who had been lost in the woods for the past seventeen years, the period of Elizabeth's reign. When found Zabeta proves to be an excellent and wise sovereign, but still a virgin. To persuade her to matrimony, Iris offers the conventional reasons:

> Wherefore, good Queene,
> > forget Dianae's tysing tale.
> Let never needlesse dread presume
> > to bring your blisse to bale.
> How necessarie were
> > for worthy Quenes to wed,
> That know you wel, whose life alwaies
> > in learning hath beene led.
> Then give consent, O Queene,
> > to Juno's just desire,
> Who for your wealth would have you wed,
> > and, for your farther hire,
> Some Empress wil you make,
> > she bad me tell you thus.
> Forgive me, Queene; the words are hers.
> > I come not to discuss:
> I am but messenger.   (Nichols, I, 510)

Gascoigne had Iris anticipate his sovereign's annoyance, an indication, perhaps, of the frequent vexation with which Elizabeth met similar messages.[4]

4. In "The Tudor mask and Elizabethan court drama," Marie Axton notes Gascoigne's pointed advocacy of Robert Dudley's suit. In arguing for marriage, Iris invokes Juno's power, seeking to override the claims of Diana. But the favoring of Juno over Diana was not popular with Elizabeth. Axton claims that with rare exception "the iconography of chastity is nowhere in evidence in the court masks early in Elizabeth's reign. The cult of Cynthia or Diana was not imposed; it was a hard-won personal triumph, not firmly established until the 1580s" (p. 34). The entertainments prepared by Dudley, however, are remarkable in the bluntness of their message. Other courtiers and poets were not so rash. See *English Drama: Forms and Development,* ed. Marie Axton and Raymond Williams (Cambridge, 1977), pp. 24–47.

Some of the entertainments during the Queen's summer progresses made pleas for marriage while also ambiguously praising Elizabeth's virginity.[5] Henry Goldingham's maske presented as part of the 1578 Norwich entertainment opened with this apology: "Gods there be also which cannot come, being tyed by the tyme of the yeare, as Ceres in Harvest, Bacchus in Wines, Pomona in Orchards. Only Himineus denyeth his good-will, eyther in presence, or in person: notwithstanding, Diana has so countre-checked him therefore, as he shall ever hereafter be at your commaundement" (Nichols, II, 160). The notion of Diana chastising the god of marriage for refusing to attend Elizabeth's entertainment seems farfetched. Would she not approve his absence? Moreover, would Elizabeth resent or relish the absence of these illustrious gods, almost all of whom are associated with human as well as agricultural fertility? By mentioning this divine boycott, Goldingham reminds the Queen that her continued celibacy has denied her realm vitality and stability. Options, however, are left open to her. Of the deities in attendance who offer the sovereign gifts, two are significant. After Apollo, Pallas Athena, and Neptune have presented uncontroversial tributes, Diana offers her gift of bow and arrows tipped with silver, with these verses:

> Who ever found on earth a constant friend
> That may compare with this my Virgin Queene?
> Whoever found a body and a mynde
> So free from staine, so perfect to be seene,
>
> . . . .
>
> Thou, thou arte shee, take thou the onely prayse
> For chastest Dame in these our happy dayes.
> Accept my Bowe, since best thou dost deserve,
> Though well I knowe thy minde can thee preserve. (Nichols, II, 163)

In what seems to be competition with Diana's gift, Cupid presents one of his own: a golden shaft. Almost as an aside, Cupid establishes his character as playful and untrustworthy god of love: "A ha, I see my mother's out of sight. / Then let the boy now play the wag awhile, / I

---

5. Several entertainments in the period of *Gallathea*'s composition and performance presented marriage debates. In an Appendix to "Landscape with Figures: The Three Realms of Queen Elizabeth's Country-House Revels," (*Renaissance Drama,* n.s. 8 [1977], 112–15), Bruce R. Smith lists extant texts for four entertainments between 1575–91, each following debate format. Rather than resolving the argument of love or chastity, debate format in the Renaissance provoked ambiguity, since the object of a debate was to test ideas, not to determine the truth. See Joel Altman, *The Tudor Play of the Mind* (Berkeley, 1978) on the nature of debate (pp. 21–30) and its specific purpose in *Gallathea* (pp. 196–216).

seeme but weake but weake is not my mighte, / . . . . Who so do think, I speak this but in jest, / Let me but shoote, and I shall quench his rest" (Nichols, II, 163). After this rather disrespectful comment, Cupid makes his presentation with at least a tinge of irony: "Shoote but this shafte at King or Caesar: he / And he is thine, and if thou wilt allowe, / It is a gift, that many here would crave, / Yet none but thou, this golden shaft may have" (Nichols, II, 164). Although there is no record of Elizabeth's response, we may assume that she accepted the contradictory gifts, with ironic intent of her own.

Ambiguity continued to characterize the chaste life in subsequent entertainments. In a show devised by Thomas Churchyard for the Queen's progresses to Suffolk in August, 1578, Chastity bluntly offers Elizabeth part of the spoils she and her maids have taken from Cupid: "Thou shalt (good Queene) by my consent and voyce / Have halfe the spoyle; take eyther bowe or cloke [of Cupid's]. / The bowe (I thinke) more fitte for such a one / In fleshly forme, that beares a heart of stone / That none can wound, nor pearce by any meane" (Nichols, II, 192). Although the plot clearly glorifies "chast life" at the expense of "leawd life," neither the bluntness nor the violence of Dame Chastity can go unremarked. In the pageant she and her maids, Modesty, Temperance, Good Exercise, and Shamefastness, put on quite a display of unvirtuous behavior in turning Cupid out of his coach, trampling his finery, and stealing his possessions. The action ends with the maids singing in praise of the chaste life. Such sentiments earned for the author "gracious words of the Queene openly, and often pronounced by hir Highnesse" (Nichols, II, 190). In the midst of a tribute to chastity, however, Churchyard allowed ambiguity to remain. Although Elizabeth herself is praised as being immune to the arrows of Cupid, she is given Cupid's bow in order that she might win a suitor of her own selection: "Wherefore take heere the bowe, and learne to shoot / At whome thou wilt; thy heart it is so cleane, / Blind Cupid's boltes therein can take no roote" (Nichols, II, 192). While appearing to be a paean to virginity, the Suffolk entertainment actually offered to reverse the traditional sexual roles by making Elizabeth the pursuer, with divine powers at her disposal to effect a match. As in the entertainment at Norwich, the allegorical image of chastity, whether it is Diana or Dame Chastity, places in Elizabeth's possession the means of abandoning celibacy for marriage.

The desire to retain the iconography of the Virgin Queene while also encouraging a politically advantageous marriage no doubt created this confusing mix in the mythic tributes accorded Elizabeth.[6] Yet even in Protestant England, the Roman Catholic image of the Virgin Mother Mary provided the model for a hybrid identity. From this mixture of divine and human qualities in the character of the sovereign, it was an easy step to see the amalgamation of her other opposites, notably sexual, in the image of the sovereign. If Christ's identification with the Phoenix could represent a self-generating unisexuality,[7] then the Virgin Queen could acquire the nature of semi-divine androgyne in assuming the historically masculine role of ruler while also retaining her traditional gender role. Conventional arguments for marriage to which Lyly and his fellow poets and courtiers might have appealed offered only slight evidence of the sort of liberated marriage which might have attracted Elizabeth.

III

There is no need in this discussion to emulate the tediousness of Renaissance treatises on marriage with a detailed survey of them. Besides being a frequent subject for sermons, marriage enjoyed popularity as a topic during both the tumultuous marriage and divorce proceedings of Henry VIII as well as later in the thirty-year-long flirtation with suitors which Elizabeth maintained. An early example of the marriage tract was William Harrington's *The commendation of matrymony* (1528), a grim treatise detailing the lawfulness and "substantial" nature of marriage and the rules to be kept by those who married. In *A right fruitful epistle in laud and prayse of matrymony*, translated by Richard Taverners in 1530, Erasmus justified the sanctity of marriage, argued for its necessity, and offered exemplary illustrations of tragic marriages. The epistle was relieved by personal anecdotes upon married life, a technique which John Heywood used as well in his *Dialogue of Proverbs* (1546).[8] Another manual written in a style similar to Heywood's was Henrich Bullinger's *The Christen state of matrimonye* (1541). The translation by Miles Coverdale, which enjoyed four editions in five years, featured realistic discussions of marriage's

6. See Camille A. Paglia's discussion of androgynous iconography associated with Queen Elizabeth in "The Apollonian Androgyne and the *Fairie Queene*," *English Literary Renaissance* 9 (1979), 47–48. The article offers close readings of Britomart's behavior in Book III.

7. This point is made by William Slights in an excellent study of Shakespearean androgny and its classical backgrounds. See "'Man and Maid' in *Twelfth Night*," *JEGP* 80 (1981), 327–47. The comment is on p. 330.

8. For a discussion of these and other treatises on marriage, see Rudolph E. Habenicht's Introduction to the edition, *John Heywood's A Dialogue of Proverbs* (Berkeley, 1963), pp. 35–39.

pitfalls, written in colorful and proverbial language. Less engaging were the caveat treatises, such as that written by Andrew Kingsmill concerning his widowed sister's remarriage. Kingsmill's *A Godly advise touchyng mariage* (1580) recalled, as Peele's play would later, the judgment of Paris. After Kingsmill described four suitors to his sister, he advised her to consider the fourth suitor of "plain byt pure metal" (sig. K1). It was a sober and passionless examination of love.

The treatises were generally cautionary, zealous in determining rules of conduct, and often mired in the language and mentality of contractual law. There were, however, exceptional treatises which urged something quite different. *A right Godlye treatise of matrimonye* by Hermann of Wied, translated in 1548 by Richard Ryce, offered this definition of marriage: "the conjunction and coupling of two parsons, that is to saie one man and one woman into one mete and lawfull flesh and bodye, accordinge to the ordynaunce and institution of God indissoluble, without separacion fast knyt and bounde, of equall auctoritye and power, on both parties" (sig. B6). Honored perhaps more in the breach than in the observance, this definition of conjugal equality was at least familiar to the Renaissance from classical sources. David Clapham's translation of Agrippa's *The commendation of matrimony* (1534) provided a similar definition:

For what felowship mought happen amonge men, more holy and pleasaunt? what more surer? what lesse carefull, what more chaste? then the life of manne and wife? When either of theim is the same that the other is, in one agreeable minde two bodies, in two bodies one minde and one consent. Only man and wife, one envieth not the other, they alone love eche other, out of measure, in as much as either of theim hole hangeth of the other, one fleshe, one minde, one concorde, one hevinesse greeveth them both, one mirth equally rejoyceth both. (sigs. A7–A8v)

Mutuality is exhaustingly emphasized in the treatise. But the image in which the age found greatest potential was not mutuality, but the mingling in marital love of two separate natures. An emblem was ready in the image of the androgyne, and it is this image with which Lyly experiments in *Gallathea*.

Etienne Pasquier's *Monophylo: a philosophical discourse, and division of love* (1572), translated by Geoffrey Fenton, recalls the discussion in Plato's *Symposium* where the androgyne is depicted as "a man composed of the Masculine and Femenine sexe, and he standing in his state of perfection, swelled in such mortall pryde agaynst the Gods, that by that meanes he was afterwards divided into two" (Bk I, 34). By dividing the androgyne, the gods destined humans to search for that other component which would make them whole. Attached to the androgyne myth in the Renaissance was the Ovidian story of Hermaphroditus and Salmacis (*Metamorphosis,* IV). Here the gods sympathetically assist the love-struck Salmacis by binding her flesh eternally to that of her beloved Hermaphroditus.

The androgyne and the hermaphrodite enjoy a curious relationship, the latter being an attempt to recover the perfection which the former represents. With tact, Lyly could apply both images to the character of Elizabeth. Since according to *Monophylo,* the androgyne is associated with the prelapsarian Adam (p. 34), it is an image of unusual completion and perfection which would flatter the Queen. Yet the image could also express, as Gabriele Jackson argues, "an all-consuming fantasy of self-sufficiency."[9] As Spenser depicts his androgynous Britomart in *The Fairie Queene,* the state of androgyny appears to be a stage between egocentric immaturity and heterosexual maturity.[10] Perhaps the comic shrillness of Diana and Cupid's mockery of the nymphs' abstemiousness in *Gallathea* reflect these negative associations.[11] Resting then at the edge of Lyly's compliment to Elizabeth is a rebuke of his monarch's refusal to provide a stable future for England through marriage.

Just as with the androgyne, the image of the hermaphrodite provoked opposite responses in the Renaissance. On the one hand, it symbolized the perfect union within marriage; on the other, it was a grotesque image of comic depravity. While Barthelemy Aneau's *Picta Poesis* (1564) used the

9. Jackson's comment refers to Ben Jonson's use of androgyny and appears in "Structural Interplay in Ben Jonson's Drama," in *Two Renaissance Mythmakers,* ed. Alvin Kernan (Baltimore, 1977), pp. 113–45. She is quoted in Slights's analysis of hermaphroditism on p. 338. While Slights emphasizes the androgyne's significance as both grotesque image and pure idea of mental harmony, A. R. Cirillo's study, "The Fair Hermaphrodite: Love-Union in the Poetry of Donne and Spenser," (*Studies in English Literature* 9 [1969], 81–95) traces the hermaphrodite topos of the union of two souls through mutual love. It is important to see the image's ambiguity. Slights's discussion is particularly useful in pointing out the comic potential of Plato's androgyne fable in *The Symposium.* Another study tracing the image's ambiguity is that of Donald Cheney, "Spenser's Hermaphrodite and the 1590 *Fairie Queene,*" *PMLA* 87 (1972), 192–200.

10. Paglia comments, "Within the poem [Britomart] is the adolescent Apollonian androgyne, but this is merely the pre-adult stage of her development. . . . [Britomart] begins as her descendent Artemis and ends as the primeval great goddess" (p. 59). Despite Britomart's move toward heterosexuality, however, Paglia notes that the founders of the British line, Britomart and Artegall, are both hermaphrodite. The higher characters of the poem must "internally subsume the extremes of masculinity and femininity, chastened and moralized" (p. 58).

11. On this point Anne Begor Lancashire concurs. See her Introduction to *Gallathea and Midas* (Lincoln, Neb., 1969), p. xxi. Quotations from *Gallathea* are taken from Lancashire's edition and will be identified parenthetically within the text.

emblem of the hermaphrodite to idealize marriage,[12] the anonymous author of *La Metamorphose d'Ovide figuree* (1583) emphasized the image's monstrosity in its brutal retelling of the Hermaphrodite-Salmacis story.[13] It is the Platonic interpretation of the image, however, where the grotesque physical union is veiled by the spiritual allegory of a marriage of spirits, that Lyly emphasized in *Gallathea*. Pasquier's *Monophylo* affirmed that "the unitie of the two halfes [of the Androgyne] is not ment by a conjunction of the bodyes, but by the communion of the mindes" (p. 34). In accommodating the myths of androgyny and hermaphroditism to the argument for marriage posed to Elizabeth in *Gallathea,* Lyly incorporated both the Queen's cult of the chaste sovereign and the Platonic notion of united souls. In plot as well, *Gallathea* departed from the format conventional for love stories. Joseph W. Houppert has noted Lyly's variation on the love triangle, from *Alexander and Campaspe,* where two men pursue one woman; to *Sapho and Phao,* where two women pursue one man; to *Gallathea,* where not only Gallathea and Phyllida, but the nymphs who pursue them, are all women.[14]

Why in *Gallathea* does Lyly depict true love only between those of the same sex? Because, he seems to claim, it is the purest form of love, a welcome alternative to the sacrifice which awaits fair virgins in this play. In the last scene, when confronted with the disappointing discovery that Gallathea and Phyllida are women and that Nature and necessity, according to Diana, require them to "leave these fond, fond affections" (5.3.125–26), neither woman will renege upon her devotion. Says Gallathea, "I will never love any but Phyllida. Her love is engraven in my heart with her eyes." "Nor I," says Phyllida, "any but Gallathea, whose faith is imprinted in my thoughts by her words" (127–30). And Venus, overriding the objections of both Diana and Neptune, allows this love and faith to survive, convinced that the women's devotion is "unspotted, begun with truth, continued with constancy, and not to be altered till death" (136–38).

Perhaps there is additional significance in depicting a female couple who refuse to surrender a love which is conventionally termed unnatural. The hermaphrodite image may as well represent the union of two separate natures within the one woman as it does the separate natures of

---

12. The woodcut is reproduced by Slights, p. 336.

13. The version appears on sig. D4, and is summarized by Slights, p. 335.

14. *John Lyly* (Boston, 1975) Twayne Series no. 177, p. 85.

male lover and female beloved.[15] When Lyly's argument for marriage is advanced by two women who wish to be joined, it acquires the force of a psychological plea for the union of oppositions within the nature of the female protagonist, whether she be Gallathea or Queen Elizabeth. Just as the play magically resolves the gender difficulty, it also seems to promise as easy a reconciliation of the internal struggle between desires for autonomy and for shared intimacy. The play makes a point of presenting Gallathea and Phyllida as nearly alike as possible—in social situation, psychological make-up, and in emotional commitment to each other. Lyly could offer no more androgynous an image of marriage than that of two so similar human beings, threatened with immediate separation when their true natures are discovered, who are rescued from this fate by the metaphorical rejoining of the androgyne's divided self.[16]

Venus's mastery of the last scene of *Gallathea* brings not only harmony to the troubled natures of the two women, but order to the world of gods as well as of mortals. In mutually conciliatory gestures, Neptune offers to abolish the barbaric rite of Virgin sacrifice and Diana agrees to return Cupid to his mother Venus. The goddesses also agree to disagree about the relative merits of love or chastity. Meanwhile, mortals need no longer fear the Humber River's flooding, nor nymphs the threat of Cupid's arrows. Both brutal rape and comic Petrarchan infatuation, then, are dismissed in favor of the steadfast love of two women. Lyly, moreover, lays the emphasis on the couple's spiritual, rather than physi-

---

15. According to Slights, twins are the alternate representation of the androgyne in classical art (p. 327). Although sexual taboos prevent the physical union of twins, their shared origin makes them psychological intimates. While the point bears directly upon his argument for *Twelfth Night,* it also helps to explain the relationship of Gallathea and Phyllida. While not twins, as women Gallathea and Phyllida appear to represent the desire for psychic rather than mere physical union in a relationship of true love.

16. Juliet Dusinberre also notes the unusual nature of the relationship of Gallathea and Phyllida; however, she describes it as an affectionate friendship, as opposed to the "fantastic, grotesque, lyrical, asexual . . . pastime for gods and nymphs" which is the image of love in the play. "Lyly's love-struck girls inhabit the same uncomplicated emotional climate as the boys in the Elizabethan friendship plays," claims Dusinberre (p. 257), and the comparison accurately points out the innocent virtue of this love untainted by stale convention. See her discussion of *Gallathea* in *Shakespeare and the Nature of Women* (London, 1975), pp. 351–65. While offering an important discussion, Dusinberre occasionally overlooks Lyly's subtleties in favor of Shakespeare's. Dusinberre claims that Shakespeare's use of disguise "gives a woman a double image of herself," which allows her to "integrate her experience as a man with her feelings as a woman." Disguise as Lyly uses it is merely "mechanical plot device . . . innocent of any symbolism of harmony between the masculine and the feminine" (p. 265). My interpretation, however, seeks to prove that Lyly's purposes are much closer to those of Shakespeare.

cal, compatibility. To allow natural urges to be satisfied, Venus will change one woman to a man, but both Gallathea and Phyllida are content to wait until the moment of their marriage to see which will be which.[17]

IV

As he did in *Alexander and Campaspe* and *Sapho and Phao,* Lyly again focuses in *Gallathea* upon the psychologically disruptive effects of love.[18] Whereas Alexander must renounce love for greater political responsibilities and both Sapho and Phao must reject a love which violates social hierarchy, Gallathea and Phyllida find the means for reconciling the emotional with the rational part of human nature. But before Lyly offers his new definition of love, he debunks the florid rhetoric of infatuation, noting the self-destructiveness which it breeds among the nymphs of Diana. In a bitter argument with herself, Teleusa, one of Diana's company recently pricked by Cupid's arrow, offers a soliloquy upon her self-division: "Fond girl that I am, to think of love; nay, vain profession that I follow, to disdain love" (3.1.25–27). This scene, where two other nymphs also confess their infatuation with the two disguised mortal women (who have taken the names of their fathers, Tityrus and Melebeus), ends in a curious lament:

17. Altman suggests that the audience can easily surmise which of the two maidens will be transformed (p. 209), and Houppert argues that the solution must be withheld to sustain dramatic tension (p. 85). I agree, instead, with Lancashire (pp. xxv–xxvi) that the play's ending calls attention to the arbitrary nature and relative unimportance of the physical transformation in a play which celebrates Platonic union.

18. In terms of theme and focus, *Alexander and Campaspe* and *Sapho and Phao* (both written 1583/4) seem far from the world of *Gallathea.* Devotion to military conquest and to his counsellor Hephestion helps Alexander banish the thought of personal happiness possible in marriage. In delivering Campaspe to another suitor, Alexander scorns his previous emotional weakness: "Thou shalt see that Alexander maketh but a toye of love, and leadeth affection in fetters; using fancy as a foole to make him sport, or a minstrell to make him mery. . . . It were a shame Alexander should desire to commaund the world, if he could not commaund himselfe" (5.4.132–34, 150–51). Alexander turns to conquest while Phao, denied any further intimacy with Queen Sapho by reason of his lowly status, resigns himself to the role of dutiful servant. Although Sapho at first endures a tortuous infatuation of her own, she finds herself falling out of love at play's end: "I feele relenting thoughtes, and reasons not yeelding to appetite . . . I cannot love, Venus hath hardened my heart" (5.2.36–37, 44). In both plays Lyly stops the examination of his lovers' psyches before their dilemmas may be resolved. Instead, love is merely banished or else held remorselessly in check. Not so in *Gallathea.* Yet the early plays are also crucial forerunners of important themes in *Gallathea.* Peter Saccio comments that Sapho's startling action of luring Cupid away from his mother Venus unites love and chastity in the play, a "marriage" which finds more perfect expression in *Gallathea* (p. 166). See *The Court Comedies of John Lyly* (Princeton, 1969).

For dating of the plays I follow Saccio, p. 225. Quotations of the plays are taken from *The Complete Works of John Lyly,* ed. R. Warwick Bond (Oxford, 1902), II.

Eurota.	Talk no more, Telusa; your words wound.
	Ah, would I were no woman!
Ramia.	Would Tityrus [Gallathea] were no boy!
Telusa.	Would Telusa were nobody! (113–16)

To escape their pain, the nymphs offer to sacrifice their sexuality or that of the object of their pain, Tityrus–Gallathea. Telusa, in despair, offers her very life. What has prompted such outbursts? Judging from Cupid's detailing of the emotion to one of Diana's nymphs, it is love, burdened by the cliched excesses of Petrarchan hyperbole:

A heat full of coldness, a sweet full of bitterness, a pain full of pleasantness, which maketh thoughts have eyes and hearts ears, bred by desire, nursed by delight, weaned by jealousy, kill'd by dissembling buried by ingratitude, and this is love. Fair lady, will you any? (1.2.16–20)[19]

The nymph scorns Cupid's ironic rehearsal, of course, and to assuage his wounded pride, Cupid forces Diana's votaries to plunge irrevocably into foolish Petrarchan pining for their lovers.

The extremes to which the nymphs are brought are comically overstated, but not before they reinforce a more serious dilemma raging within the psyches of the disguised mortal women. With every scene, Gallathea and Phyllida chafe all the more under the male disguise which protects their chastity but which frustrates the desires they are barely able to articulate. Lyly devotes a soliloquy to revealing Phyllida's self-division:

Go into the woods . . . and transgress in love a little of thy modesty. I will—I dare not; thou must—I cannot. Then pine in thine own peevishness. I will not—I will. Ah, Phyllida, do something, nay, anything, rather than live thus. Well, what I will do, myself knows not, but what I ought I know too well, and so I go resolute, either to bewray my love or suffer shame. (2.5.5–12)

In Euphuistic prose, such rigidly balanced antitheses are not unusual. But the dissonant rhythm of the assertions and denials, the insistent tone, and the dramatic spontaneity of the soliloquy (an internal debate, really) mark the prose as anything but orderly and balanced. Where balance exists in the last sentence, contraries cancel each other out. The anaphoric and parallel clauses ("what I will . . . what I ought") really offer no solution. Phyllida admits that she ought to declare her love–though whether she will have the courage to do so openly, she cannot determine.

19. Jonas Barish cites this speech as an example of Lyly's use of antithesis. See "The Prose Style of John Lyly," *ELH* 23 (1956), 14–35.

The paratactic speech in fact avoids logic by avoiding any subordination of ideas. While lines 7–8 asyndetically splice together contradictory assertions, "I will—I dare not," lines 10–12 polysyndetically string the contradictions together. The conjunctions "but," "and so," and "either ... or" suggest a mind still so at odds with itself that it can exert neither ordering principles of logic upon thought, nor of grammar upon expression.[20]

When Phyllida and Gallathea next meet, this desire both to unmask and to maintain the cover of safety involve the women in tedious puns and obvious hints of their true sexual identity:

Gallathea.	I would not wish to be a woman, unless it were because thou art a man.
Phyllida.	No, I do not wish to be a woman, for then I should not love thee, for I have sworn never to love a woman. (3.2.7–10).

Lyly still offers no hope of an easy resolution. Either Gallathea and Phyllida must return to their roles as maidens and to the threat of being sacrificed to Neptune, or they must remain trapped in their male roles, victims of frustrated passions. The discrepancy between what they appear to be and what they are leads each to question not only her own identity but that of her beloved. "Come let us into the grove," invites Phyllida, "and make much one of another, that cannot tell what to think one of another" (3.2.55–56). Indeed this maiden knows not what to make of herself, as she remarks, "Poor Phyllida, what shouldst thou think of thyself, that lovest one that I fear me is as thyself is?" (4.4.37–38). The dilemma of Gallathea and Phyllida illustrates graphically the lament of Queen Elizabeth which began this essay: "I am and not ... since from myself my other self I turn'd." Friendship provides at least some outlet for this frustrated affection. But its verbal expression is riddled with puns and equivocations, rhetorical tokens of the speakers' divided natures.

The alternative to maintaining a male disguise and thwarting passions, though, is a grim one: sacrifice to Neptune. Hebe, the maiden chosen for

---

20. Here is an example of what Barish might call "the excessive logicality of Lyly's style" (p. 27). The passion for logical structure precipitates Lyly's reliance upon syntactic relationship alone to provide a tenuous logical relationship between words or ideas (p. 29). In "Metamorphosis by Love in Elizabethan Romance, Romantic Comedy, and Shakespeare's Early Comedies," *Review of English Studies* 35 (1984), 14–44, R. S. White suggests that the rhetorical balance evident in Gallathea's soliloquy (2.4.4–9) emphasizes "the enforced restraint which holds violent emotions at bay" (p. 25). It is also possible, I suggest, to see strained logicality and rhetorical restraint as irony directed against the speaker or, in this case, the subject matter.

sacrifice when Gallathea and Phyllida cannot be found, offers a plaintive outcry against these gods and men who rule her destiny: "Art thou the sacrifice to appease Neptune and satisfy the custom, the bloody custom, ordained for the safety of thy country? Ay, Hebe, poor Hebe, men will have it so, whose forces command our weak natures" (5.1.10–14). Hebe has likened the Neptune sacrifice to a virgin's sexual initiation—through rape, not through love or marriage. The connection is apparent in her horrible invitation to the river god:

Come, Agar, thou unsatiable monster of maidens' blood and devourer of beauties' bowels, glut thyself till thou surfeit, and let my life end thine. Tear these tender joints with thy greedy jaws, these yellow locks with thy black feet, this fair face with thy foul teeth. Why abatest thou thy unwonted swiftness? I am fair, I am a virgin, I am ready. (5.2.50–56)[21]

But Hebe, not as fair as Gallathea and Phyllida, is unacceptable as a sacrifice to appease Agar. And when she is rejected, Hebe laments her reprieve, stung that she cannot offer this ecstasy of sexual martyrdom.

Extravagant use here of balanced phrases and alliteration warns us that Lyly is treating this excessive language with irony. If not in her hyperbole, then surely in Hebe's response to rejection by Agar, we suspect a rhetoric inflated by pride. In grim mockery of the prothalamion's invitation, Hebe announces herself the ready victuals of Agar's banquet, though such unappealing self-descriptions as "beauties' bowels" and "tender joints" fail to win our sympathy. In antithetically balancing the anatomical parts of Hebe and Agar, "Yellow locks . . . black feet," and "fair face . . . foul teeth," Lyly effectively injects verbal, if not physical, violence, into the play, but the unconscious double entendres rob Hebe's words of the sympathetic response they might otherwise be accorded.

Hebe's strident supplication for a sexual and literal death, with its grim apostrophe and relentless tricolon ("I am fair, I am a virgin, . . ."), matches the rhetorical excesses of her mentor, Diana. And just as Hebe is stung by Agar's rejection, Diana chafes under the joke played by Cupid. Furious, she berates the nymphs:

Now, ladies, doth not that make your cheeks blush that makes mine ears glow, or can you remember that without sobs that Diana cannot think on without sighs? What

---

21. Here is an example of the simplest type of antithesis identified by Barish: a thing defined by its opposite, or the mention of one thing evoking the mention of its opposite (pp. 17–18). I emphasize the importance of antithesis in the language of the play because of its connection with the paradoxical union of opposites thematically presented in the action.

greater dishonor could happen to Diana, or, to her nymphs, shame? . . . Shall it be said, and shall Venus say it, nay, shall it be seen, and shall wantons see it, that Diana, the goddess of chastity . . . shall have her virgins to become unchaste in desires, immoderate in affection, untemperate in love, in foolish love, in base love? (3.4.17–35)

Lyly reveals his lack of sympathy for Diana's concern by having her use ironically the characteristics of a Petrarchan lover—blushes, sobs, sighs—to describe her embarrassment over the nymphs' behavior. Diana seems more concerned with the potential damage to her reputation than to the chaste honor of her nymphs.[22] The anaphoric gradatio, "shall it be said . . . shall it be seen . . ." builds her periodic sentence ironically to that which Diana most adamantly disapproves. Love, emphasized by epistrophe, "intemperate in love, in foolish love, in base love," is placed rhetorically in just the climactic position which Diana wishes to deny it.

Perhaps because we can recognize the rhetorical pyrotechnics of both Hebe and Diana, we are willing to find in the actions and language of Gallathea and Phyllida more poignant and psychologically revealing matter. It seems clear, now, exactly what Gallathea and Phylliaa have tried to avoid: not merely a patriotic duty to save their country from a jealous river god, but a marital duty—the initiation to passion which neither the young women nor their fathers seem ready to accept. The flight to the woods, which provokes both guilt on the part of the daughters and rage on the part of Neptune, is an escape from the brutish concupiscence which, for Ovid and Lyly, characterizes Neptune. The alternative, discovered by Gallathea and Phyllida, is not one predicated in such destructive sexual terms or in the Petrarchan clichés of the nymphs' infatuations; rather, it is an agape of friendship, which matures to an amor blessed by Venus.

Language offers an index of the self-division and confusion suffered by those caught in love, both in the comically portrayed infatuation of the nymphs and in the genuine emotional attachment of the mortals. The declarations of devotion by Gallathea and Phyllida allow each finally to supplant the confusion and rebellion brought on initially by the threat of virgin sacrifice to appease the Humber river god. While confusion and deception are dispelled, however, ambiguity remains, specifically in the message which Lyly hoped his Virgin Queen might draw from the play. Here is the message found by Michael Shapiro: if gods learn to respect each other's claims in the play, "then mortals must surely abandon absolute devotion to a single idea, learn to fuse or balance opposing

22. Lancashire also notes the tirade's excess (p. xxi).

impulses, and achieve union through the give-and-take of ordinary human relations."[23] In short, "yield to love"(Epilogue, 5) seems to be the message. Indeed, the play has mocked rhetorical and philosophical extremes in favor of some sort of reconciliation. But Lyly does not allow such an easy resolution.

We expect in the play's Epilogue to get a straightforward statement of Venus' power to conquer all through love. Instead we find there a statement which Lyly intended his audience to see as simplistic. First, throughout the play, Lyly has made a careful distinction between the rakish and mean-spirited Cupid and his mother, the conciliator, Venus. But in the Epilogue, Gallathea urges the ladies of the audience to yield to Venus, to love, to Cupid—with no distinction. Second, in the play, Lyly never makes Gallathea and Phyllida subject to the infatuation produced by Cupid's arrows. Their love is nurtured by genuine amor, over which Venus presides. Yet in the Epilogue, Gallathea seems not ony to equate the powers of Cupid and Venus, but to suggest that the ladies of the audience are as much potential victims of Cupid as were the nymphs earlier in the play.

In fact, there is nothing straightforward about the Epilogue. Lyly takes fullest advantage of theatrical irony in having a boy actor deliver the lines of a woman who has been impersonating a man, who may indeed be changed momentarily into a man by Venus. From such a self-conscious example of sophisticated humor, how can we expect anything but tongue-in-cheek irony from Gallathea in these words: "Confess [Cupid] a conqueror, whom ye ought to regard, sith it is unpossible to resist, for this is infallible, that love conquereth all things but itself, and ladies all heart but their own"(Epilogue, 9–12). Elizabeth, Lyly knows, will never confess Cupid a conqueror, and Lyly has as much as engineered this response through his playful challenge to Her Majesty in the Prologue: "Your highness hath so perfect a judgment that what-soever we offer we are enforced to blush" (Prologue, 9–11).[24]

What Elizabeth heard in the Epilogue was a conventional message,

23. See *Children of the Revels* (New York, 1977), p. 182. Lancashire finds the ending much more capricious (pp. xxv–vi). White reaches the same conclusion about the ending as I do, that "the external transformation is less fundamental than the initial emotional change caused by love" (p. 26).

24. My reading of Cupid's role differs from Robert Meyer's argument that "all of the paradoxes and thematic tensions in the play are absorbed into and resolved through the metamorphoses of Cupid's character" (p. 208). See "'Pleasure Reconciled to Virtue': The Mystery of Love in *Gallathea*," *Studies in English Literature* 21 (1981), 193–208.

but what she saw was entirely different: in the person of Gallathea, she saw an emblem of the androgyne, both male and female: independent, complete, and speaking in the ringing tones of authority. Alone on stage, Gallathea pointedly claims, "'tis I only that conclude all," and it is she who finally resolves within herself the contradictions of constancy and fickleness, courage and cowardice, modesty and lightness—not Venus, as the Epilogue claims (2–4). We are left with the image of woman as union of opposites and as controller of her destiny, who shrewdly mouths praise of a love which conquereth all, when she permits it to do so.

The message, in 1588, to an aging queen still clinging to her professed chastity, is that marriage need not mean a submission to Cupid or Neptune, to madness or lust. It may be a bond forged not by Cupid but by deeper realities of the heart, where friendship and agape, rather than concupiscence, reside.[25] Think of it, says Lyly, as a marriage of minds, not bodies; as a marriage of women, not of man and woman; and as a way to satisfy both the duties of one's kingdom and the conflicting urges of the heart. Finally, think of it as a marriage of the self which need never turn away from her other self again.

25. Emphasizing the power of the gods over the love of mortals to resolve tensions in the play, Peter Berek offers a different reading in "Artifice and Realism in Lyly, Nashe, and *Love Labor's Lost,*" *Studies in English Literature* 23 (1983), 207–21. Berek claims that "Lyly resolves the complications of his plot by actions which affirm the principles of hierarchy" (p. 209). But his argument fails to consider that Venus, not Neptune, determines the action's outcome. Neptune even surrenders his claim to virgin sacrifice in order to compensate Diana. Harmony, not hierarchy, seems the point. I favor Saccio's argument, which finds the union of Gallathea and Phyllida representing "the simultaneous divinity of Venus and Diana, the harmonious coexistence of the eternal powers of love and chastity" (p. 147). This union seems all the more powerfully expressed in the image of androgyny presented both by the single character of Gallathea and in the union of Gallathea and Phyllida.

GABRIELE BERNHARD JACKSON

*Topical Ideology: Witches,
Amazons, and Shakespeare's Joan of Arc*[1]

> Glory is like a circle in the water,
> Which never ceaseth to enlarge itself
> Till by broad spreading it disperse to nought.
> With Henry's death the English circle ends;
> Dispersed are the glories it included.
>   *1 Henry VI,* 1.2.133–37[2]

THIS wonderfully evocative description of the everything that is nothing, an exact emblem of the rise and disintegration, in Shakespeare's first tetralogy, of one new center of power after another, is assigned to Joan of Arc, the character whom most acritics agree in calling a coarse caricature, an exemplar of authorial chauvinism both national and sexual, or at best a foil to set off the chivalric English heroes of *1 Henry VI.* Her portrait, says Geoffrey Bullough in his compilation of Shakespeare's sources, "goes far beyond anything found in Hall or Holinshed or in the Burgundian chronicler Monstrelet."[3] Bullough ruefully lauds Shakespeare's mastery in discrediting the entire French cause through Joan; many subsequent critics have shared Bullough's admiration, although not his compunction, over the skill with which Shakespeare delineated an "epitome of disorder and rebellion" to pit against the "epitome of order and loyalty," the English hero Talbot: "She is absolutely corrupt from beginning to end," rejoices the author of

---

1. This essay was first presented at the 1986 World Shakespeare Conference in Berlin and, in another form, at the Northeast Modern Language Association on 3 April 1987. It shares a common concern about Joan's ideological ambiguity with an independent study by Leah Marcus in her *Puzzling Shakespeare* (Berkeley, 1988), but we arrive at different conclusions. Professor Marcus emphasizes Queen Elizabeth's complex projected image and its reception by her subjects, while the present essay examines late Elizabethan literary embodiments of the strong woman; Professor Marcus' discussion of topical references in *1 Henry VI* is much more extensive than mine and will surely be the definitive treatment of that matter.

2. Citations are from *The First Part of King Henry VI,* ed. Andrew S. Cairncross, *The Arden Shakespeare* (London, 1962).

3. Geoffrey Bullough, *Narrative and Dramatic Sources of Shakespeare* (New York, 1960), III, 41.

one book on Shakespeare's history plays.[4] When the play was presented in 1591 or 1592, English troops were once again in France, once again supporting a claim to the French crown, a claim by another Henry— their religious ally Henry of Navarre. "A play recalling the gallant deeds of the English in France at an earlier period . . . would be topical," Bullough rightly says.[5]

The portrait of Joan, by this calculus of relation between drama and social context, takes its place among "English attempts to blacken the reputation of Joan of Arc"[6]—an easy task in the Elizabethan period, when women "who refuse[d] the place of silent subjection" could, like Shakespeare's Joan in Act 5, be carted to execution as witches.[7] By this reckoning, the character of Joan of Arc becomes a regrettable sign of the times.

Neither the content nor the form of Joan's words about glory easily supports such a reading. Joan's image of the circle in the water is not only the most poetically resonant statement in the play, it is also specifically borne out by the action. The eloquence of her recognition that all human achievement is writ in water, one of the play's thematic pressure points, sorts ill with a lampooned character "coarse and crude in language and sensibility."[8] Yet *1 Henry VI* does contrast English chivalry, especially in the figure of heroic Talbot, with the pragmatism of the French, especially Joan, and Act 5 does dispel both Joan's power and her pretensions

4. Robert B. Pierce, *Shakespeare's History Plays: The Family and the State* (Columbus, Oh., 1971), pp. 46–47. In the same spirit, Don M. Ricks identifies the tone she sets as "treachery, depravity, and insolence" in *Shakespeare's Emergent Form: A Study of the Structures of the Henry VI Plays* (Logan, Utah, 1968), p. 45. So common is the critical view of Joan as a moral write-off that she is sometimes assigned reprehensible behavior that does not even occur in the text, as when Catherine Belsey remarks that she "puts heart into the enemy by her rhetoric," in *The Subject of Tragedy: Identity and Difference in Renaissance Drama* (New York, 1985), p. 183. At the very least she is presumed to be the butt of continuous irony (e.g., by David Bevington in "The Domineering Female in *1 Henry VI*," *Shakespeare Studies* 2 [1966], 51–58 and John Wilders in *The Lost Garden: A View of Shakespeare's English and Roman History Plays* [Totowa, N.J., 1978], p. 36). A signal exception is H. M. Richmond in *Shakespeare's Political Plays* (New York, 1967), who allows her "heroic power" and even some "magnetism"; he also goes quite against the current of critical commentary by alluding to "her subtlety and finesse" (p. 23), but he agrees on "the harshness of the portrait" (p. 22).

5. Bullough, pp. 24–25.

6. Lisa Jardine, *Still Harping on Daughters: Women and Drama in the Age of Shakespeare* (Sussex, 1983), p. 124.

7. Belsey, p. 184.

8. Marilyn French, *Shakespeare's Division of Experience* (New York, 1981), p. 47.

to divine aid in a series of progressively less dignified scenes.[9]

First she vainly offers diabolical spirits her blood and sexual favors in exchange for continued French success; subsequently captured, she rejects her old father to claim exalted birth; finally, faced with the prospect of death by burning, she claims to be pregnant, shifting her allegation of paternity from one French leader to another in response to her captors' insistence that each of these is a man whose child should not be allowed to live.

Perhaps it is a reflection as much on accepted critical standards of aesthetic unity as on the gullibility of individual critics that several have read this last scene as Joan's admission of sexual activity with the whole French camp. Ridiculous as such a reading is, it does at least integrate Act 5 with what precedes, undercutting Joan's claims to virginity just as her conjuring undercuts her claims to divinity. Such an interpretation of Act 5 makes it synchronic with previous acts in meaning; only the revelation of that meaning is postponed. Similarly, Joan's claims to divine mission, which she never mentions again after her introductory speeches in Act 1, become in such an interpretation synchronic with the action which follows them. In the long central section of the drama, according to such a unified interpretation, Joan's prior assertion of godliness struggles against Talbot's repeated assertions of diabolism until Act 5 vindicates Talbot. The unstated premise of this kind of reading is that temporally multiple suggestions of meaning collapse finally into an integrated pattern that transcends the temporal process of dramatic presentation. In this final pattern, all suggested assignments of value are reconciled and each plot line or character allotted its proper plus or minus sign *sub specie unitatis.* The individual incident or dramatic effect has no more final autonomy than a number in a column for addition has in the sum below the line. These assumptions are very clear in Riggs' influential 1971 summation of Joan's character: "Beneath these postures, Joan is generically an imposter. . . . Hence the scenes in which she is exposed and burnt as a witch, like the stripping of Duessa in *The Faerie Queene,* serve a formal expository purpose that supersedes any need for a controlled, sequacious

---

9. See David Riggs, who admirably elucidates the play's structure in *Shakespeare's Heroical Histories:* Henry VI *and Its Literary Tradition* (Cambridge, Mass., 1971), pp. 100ff. On the play's ideology we disagree.

plot."[10]

Now of course the typical Shakespearean play does have a very powerful sense of ending, partly brought about by a "formal expository" resolution of difficult issues. I want to emphasize, however, that it is equally typical of Shakespeare to present unexplained and suggestive discontinuities. One might remember the complete reversal of Theseus' attitude to the lovers in *Midsummer Night's Dream:* having backed up Hermia's coercive father in Act 1 by citing the unalterable law of Athens, Theseus reappears in Act 4 (after a two-act absence) to overrule the same father and the same law with no explanation whatever. A more subtle version of this kind of turnabout occurs when Othello, calmly superior in Act 1 to the accusation that he has used sorcery in his relationship with Desdemona, informs her in Act 3 that the handkerchief which was his first gift to her is a magical talisman. In these instances, the critic's expectation of unity forces interpretive strategy back on unspoken motivations and implicit character development, raising such questions as whether Othello deliberately lied to the senate in Act 1, or when exactly he gave Desdemona the handkerchief. I want to propose that these are unsuitable strategies and questions for a phenomenon that has little to do with unity of character and much to do with the way in which a character is perceived by the audience at a particular moment of dramatic time. I would argue that in Act 1 Othello had not given Desdemona a magic handkerchief as his first gift, but in Act 3 he had. It is a matter of the character's consonance with the key into which the movement of the play has modulated.

This is not the place to make a detailed case for such an interpretive approach or to try to identify for these examples the reasons—external to a concept of character as coherent selfhood—that direct a change in Shakespeare's presentation. Applying such an approach to the problem of Joan's significance, however, permits us to recognize and give individual value to the phases of her portrayal, which, not untypically for

---

10. Riggs, p. 107. Riggs' view has been more recently affirmed by Norman Rabkin, *Shakespeare and the Problem of Meaning* (Chicago, 1981), pp. 88–89 and n. 39. Riggs and David Sundelson also make explicit, in slightly different ways, a criterion of integration to explain the last act: "her final degeneration in Act V is but a spectacular demonstration of the unsaintliness which has been implicit in her words and behavior all along. There is nothing contradictory, therefore, about the two views of Joan as Pucelle and as 'Puzzel' [whore]" (Ricks, p. 46); "Shakespeare himself seems unable to tolerate any uncertainty about the source of Joan's potency. He resolves the matter with a scene in which she conjures . . . , thus confirming Talbot's explanation" (David Sundelson, *Shakespeare's Restorations of the Father* [New Brunswick, N.J., 1983], p. 20).

Shakespeare, is partially continuous and partially disjunct. The changing presentation allows Joan to perform in one play inconsistent ideological functions that go much beyond discrediting the French cause or setting off by contrast the glories of English chivalry in its dying moments.[11] As Bullough long ago suggested, the play's ideology is topical, but in what way and to what end cannot be answered as simply as he or some of the play's subsequent critics have believed.[12] To characterize its main military hero, Talbot, the play alludes specifically to the contemporaneous French expedition led by Essex, as John Munro first suggested, but it incorporates far more ideologically ambiguous detail than has been recognized. Similarly, for its presentation of Talbot's national and sexual opposites, the three Frenchwomen who are the play's only female characters, it draws heavily on the current controversy about the nature of women and on the interrelated types of the Amazon, the warrior woman, the cross-dressing woman, and the witch, all figures that—for a variety of reasons—were at the end of the sixteenth century objects of fascination both in England and on the continent.

It is now generally accepted that the play dates from 1591/92, when English troops under Essex had been sent to France for the particular purpose of besieging Rouen; the play unhistorically dramatizes that city's recapture from the French. Actually, Rouen had never been retaken, nor was it after this hopeful piece of stagecraft. But the parallel does not remain general and wishful. The play explicitly links Talbot to the current effort through a neatly turned compliment to Queen Elizabeth which has, oddly, been deflected by critics to Essex alone. Bearing away the fallen Talbot and his son, the English messenger declares: "from their ashes shall be rear'd / A phoenix that shall make all France afeard" (4.7.92–93). The phoenix was one of Elizabeth's emblems; Shakespeare uses it again in *Henry VIII*. She had not up to this time fulfilled the

---

11. See, e.g., Rabkin, pp. 86–87.

12. Detailed proposals of the play's topicality have been made by T. W. Baldwin, *On the Literary Genetics of Shakespeare's Plays 1592–1594* (Urbana, Ill., 1959), pp. 324–40. Less extended suggestions of parallels have come from J. Dover Wilson in the introduction to his edition of *The First Part of King Henry VI* (Cambridge, 1952), pp. xviii–xix; Emrys Jones, *The Origins of Shakespeare* (Oxford, 1977), pp. 119–26; John Munro in *TLS* October 11, 1947; Hereward T. Price, *Construction in Shakespeare*, University of Michigan Contributions in Modern Philology No. 17 (Ann Arbor, Mich., 1951), pp. 25–26; and Ernest William Talbert, *Elizabethan Drama and Shakespeare's Early Plays: An Essay in Historical Criticism* (Chapel Hill, N.C., 1963). Leah Marcus offers a most thorough treatment of many of the play's topical allusions that takes full account of their complexity in "Elizabeth," a section of her *Puzzling Shakespeare*. See note 1 above.

messenger's prediction: early military success against French forces in Scotland had been completely cancelled by a disastrous occupation of Le Havre in 1563. The vaunting compliment can only refer to the most recent French expedition. Its leader—the dashing young popular favorite, Essex—would be an eminently suitable candidate for the role of Talbot redivivus.[13] In 1591 the becalmed campaign was serving as backdrop for his exploits, one of them mimicked by another of the play's departures from its sources. Encamped before Rouen, "Essex sent a challenge to the Governor of the town daring him to fight either a duel or a tournament," which was, not surprisingly, declined.[14] In *1 Henry VI,* Talbot similarly challenges Joan and her supporters as they stand victorious on the walls of Rouen (2.2.56ff.).[15] He is contemptuously rebuffed by Joan in one of those moments when English chivalry confronts French pragmatism: "Belike your lordship takes us then for fools, / To try if that our own be ours or no" (3.2.62–63). A critic guided by the play's obvious national sympathies could plausibly feel that Joan's reply, however momentarily amusing, lacks magnanimity.

A closer look at the topical link between Talbot and Essex, however, suggests a more complicated ideological situation. Both the expedition and its leadership were controversial. Henry IV had broken his promise of reinforcements for a first set of troops, sent in 1589, and Elizabeth sent the second army with misgivings, putting the hot-headed Essex in command with a reluctance well justified by the results. "Where he is or what he doth or what he is to do," she wrote angrily to her other officers, "we are ignorant."[16] Halfway through the expedition she ordered her uncontrollable deputy home, although he talked her into sending him back. A likely rescripting of this sequence of events appears in Act 3, where Talbot interrupts his conquests to go and visit his sovereign "with

13. John Munro first interpreted the lines about the phoenix as a reference to Essex. J. Dover Wilson follows suit in his introduction to the play, where he also suggests that "Talbot was intended to stand as in some sort the forerunner of Essex" (p. xix). T. W. Baldwin, in his study of the play's "literary genetics," is dubious about Munro's identification but agrees that the allusion is to "the English armies in France 1589 and following" (p. 334). E. W. Talbert similarly cites Munro and also accepts the play's connection with the Essex expedition (pp. 163–64 and p. 163 n. 6).

14. J. E. Neale, *Queen Elizabeth I* (Garden City, N.Y., 1957), p. 337.

15. Dover Wilson sees the parallel between Talbot's and Essex's challenges, but interprets it simply as a reminiscence of Essex's gallantry (p. xix). He considers the play "an outlet for the growing sense of exasperation, anger, and even despair which was felt in London at the impending failure of an invasion of France" (p. xvi).

16. Neale, p. 335.

submissive loyalty of heart" (3.4.10) and receives acclaim, reward, and a commission to return to battle (3.4.16–27, 4.1.68–73). In the second of these scenes, Talbot strips a coward of his undeserved Order of the Garter and makes a long speech about the value of "the sacred name of knight" (4.1.33ff.)—another touchy subject after Essex's temporary recall, for he had just knighted twenty-four of his do-nothing soldiers. Lord Treasurer Burghley kept this news from Her Majesty as long as he could; Elizabeth was notoriously stingy with new titles—holding, in fact, rather the attitude expressed by Shakespeare's Talbot. She had wanted to deny Essex the privilege of dubbing knights, and remarked caustically on hearing of the twenty-four newcomers to fame unsupplemented by fortune, "his lordship had done well to have built his almshouses before he had made his knights."[17]

Are these portions of Talbot's behavior and speech, then, aligned with the latest news from France in order to celebrate Essex?[18] Or do they obliquely defend him by rewriting his indiscretions in more acceptable terms, sympathetically dramatizing the "real" meaning of his grand gestures? Or do Talbot's loyal actions, on the contrary, undercut the play's apparent endorsement of Essex by showing how a truly great champion acts? The answers are not at all clear.[19] What is evident is that the play situates itself in an area of controversy easily identifiable by its audience, an area of growing ideological conflict in which a "war party" contested, if it did not openly confront, the Queen's favored policy of negotiation, delay, and minimal expenditure. Far from playing down the controversial aspects of Essex's command, the drama singles them out for reenactment, but presents them in such a manner that either side could claim the play for its own. In light of the play's tendency to go both

17. Neale, p. 336. Elizabeth called the campaign "rather a jest than a victory" and ordered Essex home for good in January 1592 (Neale, p. 337).

18. That a steady stream of ephemera carried bulletins from France to English readers is evident from the entries in the Stationers' Register. The diversity of possible attitudes to the expedition is perhaps suggested by the contrasting titles of two such pieces: an obviously enthusiastic "ballad of the noble departinge of the right honorable the Erle of ESSEX lieutenant generall of her maiesties forces in Ffraunce and all his gallant companie" (23 July 1591) and a possibly more ominous-sounding "letter sent from a gentleman of accoumpte concerninge the true estate of the Englishe forces now in Ffraunce under the conduct of the right honorable the Erle of ESSEX" (6 September 1591).

19. The well-known compliment to Essex in *Henry V*, 5, Cho. 30–34, is also ambiguous in light of the sentence that follows it (ll. 34–35). That this passage refers to Essex has been generally accepted, but the identification has been challenged by W. D. Smith. See G. Blakemore Evans, "Chronology and Sources," *The Riverside Shakespeare,* ed. G. Blakemore Evans (Boston, 1974), p. 53.

ways, Joan's sardonic reply to Talbot's challenge acquires an integrity of its own, sounding surprisingly like the voice of Her caustic Majesty Queen Elizabeth. Is the play, then, lauding chivalry or correcting it? Is it pro-war or not? This irritable reaching after fact and reason that Keats found so uncharacteristic of Shakespeare is not soothed by the parallels between Talbot and Essex or by the tone of Joan's voice. The coexistence of ideologically opposed elements is typical of the play's dramatic nature and foreshadows the mature Shakespeare.

Critical examination of the play's three women has not proceeded on this assumption. The perceived dominance of patrilineal and patriarchal ideology in Shakespeare's era and in the play's action has been the basis of most interpretations, whether feminist or masculinist.[20] The three women have been seen as a trio of temptresses,[21] of threats to male and particularly English hegemony and to the chivalric ideal,[22] as incarnations of what Marilyn French calls the "outlaw feminine principle."[23] This kind of negative reading, like the purely positive reading of the play's military expedition, has support in the action. All three women are in different ways unconventionally strong and all three threaten the English with losses. Coppélia Kahn's claim that Shakespeare is here exposing, but not sharing in, male anxieties about women is surely counsel of desperation.[24] Fortunately, it is not the only alternative to pathological or paternalistic Shakespeare. Like the positive militaristic reading, with which it is closely connected, the negative misogynist one neglects both the play's topicality and the historical moment's ideological complexity.

The nature of women had long been under discussion in western Europe in a semi-playful controversy that became especially active in sixteenth–century England. Contributors to this controversy buttressed or undercut female claims to virtue by citing *exempla,* worthy or unworthy women chosen from history, the Bible, and legend. As Linda Woodbridge's recent account of this literary sub-genre in England points out, "The formal controversy did not always appear full-blown, in

20. E.g. Marilyn French (n. 8 above), following L. C. Knights and Northrop Frye, calls the play a search for legitimacy (p. 43). She believes that legitimacy is presented as a strictly masculine principle—"Shakespeare's women can never attain legitimacy"—although, somewhat confusingly, she also claims that it can contain "the inlaw feminine principle" (p. 49).

21. Bevington (n. 4 above), pp. 51–58.

22. Riggs (n. 9 above).

23. French (n. 8 above), p. 51.

24. Coppélia Kahn, *Man's Estate: Masculine Identity in Shakespeare* (Berkeley, Cal., 1981), p. 55 and p. 55 n. 11.

carefully developed treatises; it was sometimes sketched in cameo, with the names of a few exemplary women stamped on it like a generic signature."[25] The 1560s had seen a spate of plays about individual *exempla* in the controversy. By the time *1 Henry VI* appeared, the controversy had already been naturalized into narrative fiction by George Pettie's *A petite pallace of . . . pleasure* (1576) and Lyly's best-selling *Euphues* (1578). In these fictional contexts, the old techniques "could be used to characterize, to comment on the action, even to advance the plot."[26] *1 Henry VI* incorporates just such a cameo controversy. The play's three women are surrounded by allusions to legendary females which problematize their evaluation. The Countess of Auvergne compares herself to Tomyris, a bloody warrior queen, and is connected by verbal echo with the Queen of Sheba—two entirely opposite figures.[27] Margaret of Anjou is cast in her lover's description of his situation as Helen of Troy (5.5.103ff.), a woman claimed by both attackers and defenders in the controversy. Joan appears amidst a tangle of contradictory allusions: she is among other identifications a Sibyl, an Amazon, Deborah, Helen the mother of Constantine, and Astraea's daughter to the French, but Hecate and Circe to the English. Of the women alluded to in *1 Henry VI*, eleven appear as *exempla* in the formal controversy. The genre itself was tolerant of, not to say dependent upon, divergent evaluations of the same phenomenon: a number of its *exempla*, like Helen of Troy, appeared regularly on both sides, and some writers handily produced treatises both pro and con. It would come as no surprise to readers of the controversy that one man's Sibyl is another man's Hecate.

1 Henry VI should be classed with what Woodbridge calls the "second

25. Linda Woodbridge, *Women and the English Renaissance: Literature and the Nature of Womankind 1540–1620* (Urbana, Ill., 1984), p. 61. Shakespeare's interest in this controversy is evident not only in his frequent allusions to its *exempla* (Woodbridge cites references, pp. 126–28, and there are many more) but in his use of at least ten of them as characters in his works, four as protagonists. His is an impressive roster even in a period when plays about the controversy's *exempla* were a growth industry (Woodbridge, pp. 126ff.). The four protagonists are Venus, Lucrece, Cressida, and Cleopatra; the other characters, Volumnia in *Coriolanus*, Portia in *Julius Caesar* and Portia in *The Merchant of Venice* (carefully identified, as Woodbridge notes on p. 127, with "Cato's daughter, Brutus' Portia"), Octavia, Helen of Troy, and Hippolyta (Thisbe should also be mentioned). The maligned and repudiated Mariana in *Measure for Measure*, too, may be a relative of Mariamne, Herod's defamed second wife, another favorite of the controversialists.

26. Woodbridge, pp. 61–62, 66.

27. Cairncross, 2.3.7–10n., and Bevington.

FIGURE I. Two Amazons. From Sir John Mandeville, *The Voiage and Travaile of syr J. Maundevile,* 1568 (STC 17250), sig. G8v.

FIGURE II. Boadicea. From Raphael Holinshed, *The Firste Volume of the Chronicles of England*, 1578 (STC 13568A), "The Historie of England," p. 61. Reprinted by courtesy of Special Collections, the Van Pelt Library, University of Pennsylvania.

FIGURE III. Woada and her daughters. From Raphael Holinshed, *The Firste Volume of the Chronicles of England,* 1578 (STC 13568A), "The Historie of Scotland," p. 45. Reprinted by courtesy of Special Collections, the Van Pelt Library, University of Pennsylvania.

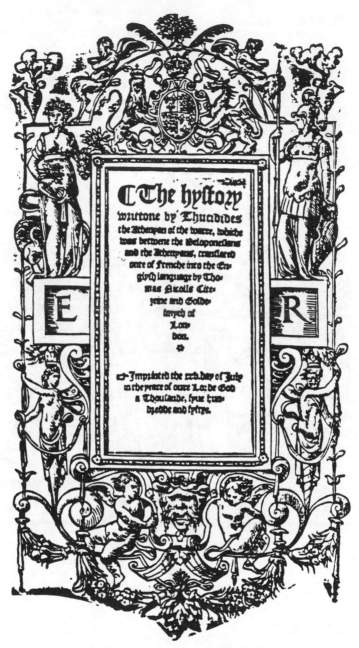

FIGURE IV. Flora (left) and "armed Pallas" as joint patrons of Thucydides' history. Their foothold on the queen's initials suggests that they may be intended for aspects of her. From R. B. McKerrow and F. S. Ferguson, *Title-page Borders used in England & Scotland 1485–1640* (London, 1932 [for 1931]), plate 74. Reprinted by courtesy of Special Collections, the Van Pelt Library, University of Pennsylvania, and the publisher.

flurry of plays centering on prominent *exempla* of the formal controversy," which "appeared in the late 1580s and 1590s."[28] Its deployment of
these stock figures is as germane to its ideology as its structural alignment
of the female characters, but whereas the play's structure points in the
direction of synthesis, of the synchronic or temporally transcendent
reading, the *exempla* point towards differentiation, the temporally disjunctive reading.

Joan is evaluated by the French choice of *exempla* at the beginning and
by the English choice at the end. At all times before Act 5, however,
because of the armor she is described as wearing and the military
leadership she exercises, she is an example of what the Elizabethans
called a virago, a woman strong beyond the conventional expectations
for her sex and thus said to be of a masculine spirit.[29] The increasing
fascination of such women is evident in the proliferation of Amazons,
female warriors, and cross-dressing ladies in the English fiction and
drama of the late sixteenth century.

The Amazon and the warrior woman were already established as two
of the most valued positive *exempla* of the controversy over women. Joan
is identified with both immediately on her entry into the play's action:
"thou art an Amazon," exclaims the Dauphin, "And fightest with the
sword of Deborah"(1.2.104–05). The power of this combination reaches
beyond the arena of the formal debate. Spenser had just used it in *The
Faerie Queene,* published 1590, in praise of "the brave atchievements" of
women (3.4.1.3): those "warlike feates . . . Of bold Penthesilee," the

28. Woodbridge, p. 126. Woodbridge's account of the controversy is invaluable. I cannot
agree with her, however, that the plays written in and after the later 1580s were probably not
influenced by it; her own evidence (and there is more she does not cite) seems to point
overwhelmingly the other way. She observes that "the drama had many other potential sources,"
which is true but does not account for the upsurge in plays devoted specifically to *exempla* from the
controversy, and she points out that dramatists often treated these *exempla* differently from
controversialists—but this objection assumes that to influence is to produce a copy.

29. The term was almost entirely positive and denoted either physical or spiritual prowess. For
the virago's "manly soul," see Simon Shepherd, *Amazons and Warrior Women: Varieties of Feminism
in Seventeenth-Century Drama* (Sussex, 1981), pp. 34–35. Various contemporary allusions to the
Queen invoked the pun *virgo/virago,* and her "masculine" spirit was frequently remarked upon
with admiration. See Winfried Schleiner, "*Divina virago:* Queen Elizabeth as an Amazon," *Studies
in Philology* 75, 2 (1978), 163–80. I am grateful to Louis Montrose for calling this extremely useful
article to my attention.

Amazon who aided the Trojans, or the blow with which "stout Debora strake / Proud Sisera" (3.4.2.4–5, 7–8).[30] For him these two fighters define Britomart, his female knight in armor, who in turn defines Queen Elizabeth, "whose lignage from this lady I derive along" (3.4.3.9). Both Amazons and women warriors already had some degree of British resonance because the Trojans who received Penthesilea's help were the supposed ancestors of the British, while a proud chapter in legendary English history recounted Queen Boadicea's defense of her country against Roman invasion. The evocation of heroines related to England is continued by Joan's association with Saint Helen, the mother of Constantine; though not a warrior, this finder of the remains of the true cross was by popular tradition British.[31] The Dauphin's welcome to Joan is thus calculated to arouse the most unsuitably positive and even possessive associations in an Elizabethan audience.

Elizabethan literature of course contained many other Amazons besides Penthesilea; the race had a long and honorable history, derived from such respected authorities as Plutarch, Ovid, and Apollonius of Rhodes.[32] In the sixteenth century Amazons became a topic of current relevance when exploration of the Americas and Africa began bringing reports of Amazonian tribes sighted or credibly heard of.[33] Within a brief period after *1 Henry VI,* both Ralegh (1596) and Hakluyt (1599) would specify the Amazons' exact location. Perhaps because of their increased timeliness, Amazons were also about to become a vogue on stage; they would appear in at least fourteen dramatic productions from 1592 to

30. All citations from *The Faerie Queene* will be identified by book, canto, stanza, and line numbers in my text; these refer to Edmund Spenser, *The Faerie Queene,* ed. R. E. Neil Dodge (Cambridge, Mass., 1936).

31. I am indebted to F. J. Levy for calling my attention to this fact.

32. Ironically—or as a calculated symbolic counterstatement to the Maid?—Henry VI's Paris coronation pageant included "la sage Hippolyte" and her sister Menalippe, as well as Penthesilea and Lampeto, as female worthies. See Robert Withington, *English Pageantry: An Historical Outline,* Vol. I (Cambridge, Mass., 1918), pp. 138–39 n. 4. Celeste Turner Wright calls attention to Henry's coronation pageant in "The Amazons in Elizabethan Literature," *Studies in Philology* 37 (July 1940), 437 n. 41 (n.b.: because of a numbering error in this volume, Wright's article begins on the *second* occurrence of p. 437).

33. See Abby Wettan Kleinbaum, "The Confrontation," in *The War Against the Amazons* (New York, 1983). I appreciate being directed to this book by Daniel Traister, Curator of Rare Books at the University of Pennsylvania.

1640.[34]

Elizabethan stage Amazons are all either neutral or positive, an evaluative convention generally in line with their ever more frequent mention in Elizabethan non-dramatic literature. On the other hand, *The Faerie Queene* contains an evil Amazon alongside its positive allusions. For the Amazon figure was inherently double: although "models of female magnanimity and courage" who appeared regularly in lists of the nine female worthies and were venerated both individually and as a race, Amazons were also acknowledged to be at times cruel tormentors of men.[35] From the very beginning, then, Joan's ideological function is complicated to the point of self-contradiction: she seems both French and English, both a type of Penthesilea who helps her countrymen in battle and an unspecified Amazon who may embody threats to men—in fact, a representative of the full complexity of late Elizabethan perception of the strong woman.

34. Schleiner (see n. 29 above) also identifies as "Amazons" the female characters in a mock tournament of 1579, presented for the Queen and the Duke of Alençon's representative (p. 179), although her quotation from her source refers only to "ladies" (pp. 163–64 n. 3). *Tamburlaine* mentions Amazon armies, but they do not appear. Greene's *Alphonsus*, an obvious offspring of *Tamburlaine*, may have preceded 1 *Henry VI* in presenting visible Amazons as well as a warrior maiden, but this play has never been satisfactorily dated. Rabkin believes it was "probably written 1587," but does not given his reasons (introduction to Robert Greene, "Friar Bacon and Friar Bungay," *Drama of the English Renaissance. I: The Tudor Period,* ed. Russell A. Fraser and Norman Rabkin [New York, 1976] p. 357). The play's general derivative quality suggests, however, that Iphigina is more likely to be a daughter of Joan than the reverse. The other productions I know of containing Amazons are "A Masque of the Amazons . . . played March 3, 1592" (Henslowe's diary, quoted in William Painter, *The Palace of Pleasure,* ed. Joseph Jacobs, 3 vols. [London, 1890], I, lxxxi); "field pastimes with martiall and heroicall exploits" staged for Prince Henry's christening in 1594 (John Nichols, *Progresses, Public Processions, &c. of Queen Elizabeth,* 3 vols. [London, 1823], III, 355); *Midsummer Night's Dream,* 1595; Marston's *Antonio and Mellida,* 1602; *Timon of Athens,* ?1605–1609; Jonson's *Masque of Queens,* 1609; Beaumont and Fletcher's *Two Noble Kinsmen,* ?1613, *The Sea Voyage,* 1622, and *Double Marriage,* 1647; the anonymous *Swetnam, the Woman-Hater,* 1620; Heywood's *Iron Age,* 1632; Shirley's dramatization of the *Arcadia,* 1640; and Davenant's *Salmacida Spolia,* 1640. There is a discussion of Fletcher's *Sea Voyage* and some Amazon dramas 1635–1685 in chapter 11 of Jean Elisabeth Gagen, *The New Woman: Her Emergence in English Drama, 1600–1730* (New York, 1954).

For many of these titles and the beginnings of all my information about Amazons, I have relied on the encyclopedic Wright (n. 32 above). Her non-chronological organization assumes, however, that the degree of interest in Amazons and writers' attitudes towards them remained stable throughout the period from which she takes her examples (some undated). Her evidence suggests otherwise.

35. Wright, pp. 442–43, 449–54. Wright's data are difficult to get around in chronologically, but it looks as though doubts about the Amazons—including skepticism about their existence—may have increased in England after 1600, although the Amazonian vogue lasted right up to the Civil War.

These contradictions continue for as long as Joan appears in the role of woman warrior. Although she triumphs over the English and so must be negative, she carries with her a long positive tradition reaching back to Plato's assertions that women could and should be trained for martial exercise and to the figure of the armed goddess Minerva. These classical

---

Although there are Elizabethan accounts of the Amazons' ruthless origins and habits, I do not agree with Shepherd (n. 29 above) that the period's overriding feeling was "Elizabethan distress about Amazons" (p. 14), in support of which view he instances Radigund and the egregious misogynist Knox. Shepherd wants to extrapolate Spenser's opposition between Radigund and Britomart into a pervasive Elizabethan distinction between Amazons and warrior women: "Against the warrior ideal there is the Amazon" (p. 13). This schema will not hold up in the face of a mass of evidence for Elizabethan Amazon-enthusiasm. Shepherd's own evidence for the Elizbethan period is slender and largely extrapolated from Stuart texts. Although he does say that the negative meaning of Amazon "coexists with the virtuous usage" (p. 14), this concession, in itself inadequate, is forgotten in his subsequent loosely supported account.

Nor can I agree with Louis Adrian Montrose's implication in his otherwise insightful and imaginative "'Shaping Fantasies': Figurations of Gender and Power in Elizabethan Culture," *Representations* 1, 2 (Spring 1983), 61–94, that English Renaissance texts about Amazons generally express "a mixture of fascination and horror" (p. 66). The passages he quotes detail the Amazons' origins and/or customs; others of this type are often flat in tone and delivered without comment, like Mandeville's (1499, rpt. 1568), while some mention no horrors at all. Even the Amazon-shy Spenser compliments the supposed South American tribe: "Joy on those warlike women, which so long / Can from all men so rich a kingdome hold!" (*F.Q.* 4.11.22.1–2). Although Montrose calls attention to the association sometimes made between Amazons and the destruction of male children, and in some travel books between Amazons and cannibalism, in an equal number of accounts they produce male children for neighboring tribes and are thought of as desirable breeding stock. By far the greatest number of Amazon allusions, moreover, refer to specific Amazons and appear in a positive context. Penthesilea, the hands-down favorite, is always treated with admiration and respect, as is Hippolyta.

My observations are based on the following Tudor texts: Agrippa, tr. Clapham, *The Nobilitie of Woman Kynde,* 1542 (STC 203), p. 360v; Anghiera (Peter Martyr), tr. Eden, *Decades of the Newe World,* 1555, ed. Arber, *The First Three English Books on America,* 1885, pp. 69, 177, 189; Richard Barckley, *The Felicitie of Man,* 1598 (STC 1381), III, 266–68; Boccaccio, *De Claris Mulieribus,* 1534–47, ed. Wright, EETS (London, 1943), pp. 39–42, 66–67, 103–05 and *Tragedies,* tr. Lydgate, 1554 (STC 3178), I, 12; Quintus Curtius, tr. Brende, *History of ... Alexander,* 1553 (STC 6142), pp. Pii–Piii; Anthony Gibson, tr., *A Womans Woorth,* 1599 (STC 11831), pp. 5, 37v; Richard Madox, *An Elizabethan in 1582: The Diary of Richard Madox ...,* ed. Elizabeth Story Donno, Hakluyt Society second series No. 47 (London, 1977), p. 183; Sir John Mandeville, *The Voyage and Travel ... ,* 1568 (STC 17250), pp. Gviii verso; Ortuñez de Calahorra, tr. T[yler], *The Mirrour of ... Knighthood,* 1578 (STC 18859), 26.91v, 55.219; Hieronimus Osorius, tr. Blandie, *The Five Books of Civill and Christian Nobilitie,* 1576 (STC 18886), II, 25v; Ovid, tr. Turberville, *Heroycall Epistles,* 1567 (STC 18940.5), p. 23; William Painter, *The Palace of Pleasure,* 1575, ed. Joseph Jacobs, 3 vols. (London, 1890), II, 159–61; Sir Walter Ralegh, *The Discoverie of ... Guiana,* 1596 (STC 20636), pp. 23–24 and *History of the World,* 1614 (STC 20637), I.4.195–96; William Shakespeare, *King John,* 1594–96, ed. Herschel Baker, in Evans; Sir Philip Sidney, *The Countess of Pembrokes Arcadia,* 1590, ed. Robertson (Oxford, 1973), pp. 21, 36; Edmund Spenser, *The Faerie Queene,* I–III, 1590, IV–VI, 1596 (see n. 30); Andre Thevet, *The New Found World,* tr. 1568 (STC 23950), pp. 101–74 (*recte* 103); William Warner,

references as well as invocations of the Old Testament Deborah and Judith figured repeatedly in the formal defenses of women. Female military heroism under special circumstances carried the prestigious sanction of Elyot, More, and Hoby, and Joan's actions conform to the pattern they approved as well as to the current literary conventions defining a praiseworthy female warrior. She fights in defense of her country, "particularly under siege," and converts the Duke of Burgundy to her cause with a simile that likens France to a dying child (3.3.47–49)—defense of her children being a recognized motivation of the virtuous woman fighter.[36] Like Spenser's Britomart and countless others, she deflates male boasts and engages in a validating duel with a would-be lover.

As Spenser's connection of Britomart with Queen Elizabeth suggests, the tradition of the woman warrior acquired particular contemporaneous relevance from her existence. The maiden warrior-goddess Minerva provided an irresistible parallel with the virginal defender of Protestantism, who even before the year of the Armada was called "for power in armes, / And vertues of the minde Minervaes mate" by Peele in *The Arraignment of Paris* (1584).[37] Deborah, a magistrate as well as her country's savior in war, was also adopted immediately into the growing iconology of Elizabeth: the coronation pageant contained a Deborah, and the name was frequently used thereafter for the queen.[38] Not unexpectedly, Spenser identifies the Trojan-oriented Penthesilea as an analogue of his Belphoebe, the avowed representation of Queen Elizabeth.[39]

In light of these accumulated associations, a Minerva-like French leader who is a Deborah and Amazon, and is also called "Astraca's

Albion's England, 1586 (STC 15759), pp. 25–26; and two accounts of Spanish voyages known in England, those of Francesco Orellana and Gonzalo Pizarro, *Expeditions into the Valley of the Amazons,* tr. and ed. Clements R. Markham, Hakluyt Society (New York, n.d.), pp. 13, 26, 34, 36). I have also found useful Kleinbaum's chapters "The Net of Fantasy" and "The Confrontation."

36. Woodbridge, p. 21.

37. Cited by both Wright and Shepherd.

38. Wright, p. 455.

39. He makes this identification in 1590, just a year and a half after the Armada crisis (see discussion below, in text). Penthesilea was frequently used as a comparison for Elizabeth, especially around this time (see Schleiner [n. 29 above], pp. 170–73). The Amazon analogy was still current in 1633, when Phineas Fletcher likened his "warlike Maid, / *Parthenia,*" a recognizable variant of Elizabeth, to Hippolyta in *The Purple Island* 10.27–40 (STC 11082), pp. 141–44.

daughter" (1.6.4) at a time when Astraea, goddess of justice, was another *alter ego* of Elizabeth, must be reckoned one of the more peculiar phenomena of the Elizabethan stage.[40] But it is likely that Joan was more than peculiar: she was probably sensational. For the odd fact is that despite all the outpouring of Elizabethan literature both cultivated and popular on the subject of Amazons and warrior women, there seems to be only one rather obscure woodcut of real—as opposed to allegorical— armed women to be found in the English printed books, pamphlets, broadsides, and pictorial narrative strips of the entire era, nor had any such personage (as far as I have yet discovered) ever appeared on the stage.[41] Two Amazons that illustrate Mandeville's *Travels* are clad with impeccable feminine respectability (Fig. 1, following p. 96). The coronation Deborah (1559), despite the pageant verses' reference to "the dint of sworde," was equipped with Parliament robes, not with a deadly weapon as in Spenser's fantasy.[42] Holinshed's Boadicea (1577) had a wide skirt and long hair (Fig. 2, following p. 96). What is more, there seem to be no pictures of women in men's clothing of any kind. It looks as though there was an unspoken taboo on such representations, a taboo just beginning to be breached occasionally in the 1570s, when Holinshed included in his *History of Scotland* an illustration of Woada's daughters (Fig. 3, following p. 96). In this same decade come the first mentions of real Elizabethan women wearing articles of real male apparel, though not armor or weapons, a fashion that was soon to grow into a fad. It is not until the 1580s that a very few cross-dressing ladies appear on stage, and not until after *1 Henry VI* that Amazons, women warriors, and girls in male disguise become a triple dramatic vogue. In 1591/92, dressing Joan in armor was a stunning *coup de théâtre*.

40. In "Elizabeth," Leah Marcus also connects Joan with the queen and comments on the contradiction between Joan's "idealized symbolic identities" and her status as an enemy (p. 51).

41. For information on woodcuts I am most grateful to Ruth Luborsky, who is currently completing a catalogue of all woodcut-illustrated printed English documents in the period, keyed to the STC. For pictorial narratives, I have consulted David Kunzle, *The Early Comic Strip: Narrative Strips and Picture Stories in the European Broadsheet from 1450–1895* (Berkeley, Cal., 1983). I have examined the engraved representations in Arthur M. Hind, *Engraving in England in the Sixteenth and Seventeenth Centuries,* 3 vols. (Vol. III ed. Margery Corbett and Michael Norton) (Cambridge, 1952–64); in Ronald B. McKerrow, *Printers' and Publishers' Devices 1485–1640 in England and Scotland* (London, 1913); in Ronald B. McKerrow and F. S. Ferguson, *Title-page Borders Used in England & Scotland 1485–1640* (London, 1932 [for 1931] [sic]); and in Margery Corbett and Ronald Lightbown, *The Comely Frontispiece: the emblematic title-page in England, 1550–1660* (London, 1979).

42. Nichols (n. 34 above), II, 53–54.

It had, however, been anticipated. Outside the world of the stage lived a connoisseur of theatrical effect as daring as Shakespeare. In 1588, on the eve of the expected Spanish invasion, Queen Elizabeth visited her soldiers in the camp at Tilbury "habited like an Amazonian Queene, Buskind and plumed, having a golden Truncheon, Gantlet, and Gorget," according to Heywood's later description.[43] Leonel Sharp, afterwards James I's chaplain and in 1588 "waiting upon the Earl of *Leicester* at *Tilbury* Camp," reported as eyewitness that "the Queen rode through all the Squadrons of her armie, as Armed *Pallas*"[44]—a figure whose iconographic conventions of plumed helmet, spear, and shield (Fig. 4, following p. 96) coincided with descriptions of Amazon queens.[45] This was the occasion of her famous speech: "I know I have the bodie, but of a weak and feeble woman, but I have the heart and Stomach of a King, . . . and think foul scorn that . . . any Prince of Europe should dare to invade the borders of my Realm. . . . I my self will take up arms, I my self will be your General."[46] This grand gesture of virago-ship, which combined visual uniqueness with enactment of time-honored conventions identify-

43. Quoted from Thomas Heywood's *Exemplary Lives*, 1640, by Shepherd (n. 29 above), p. 22.

44. Leonel Sharp, Letter to George Villiers, Duke of Buckingham, n.d. [1623–25], *Cabala, Mysteries of State, in Letters of the great Ministers of K. James and K. Charles* (1654), p. 259.

45. Stow in his *Annals* (1615) calls the Queen at Tilbury "Bellona-like" (quoted by Miller Christy, "Queen Elizabeth's Visit to Tilbury in 1588," *EHR* 34 [1919], 58), and an anonymous poem of 1600 appeals to her as "Thou that . . . bearest harnesse, speare, and shielde" (Schleiner [n. 29 above], p. 174). Schleiner, who does not know the Sharp letter, calls Heywood's 1640 description "probably only theatrical imagination" (p. 176). There seems little doubt, however, that Elizabeth did wear armor, and that Heywood was only recreating the spectacle staged by a superior dramatist when in 1633 he brought his two-part stage biography of the Queen to its climax with a final Tilbury scene: "Enter . . . Queen ELIZABETH, completely armed." See Thomas Heywood, *The Second Part of If You Know Not Me, You Know No Bodie* (1633), in *Thomas Heywood's Dramatic Works*, ed. J. Payne Collier (London, 1853), II, 156; for the date see editorial note [xxiii]. (The 1606 version of the play does not contain this stage direction, but may of course have used the same costume.)

I do not know where Paul Johnson gets his circumstantial description of a white velvet dress, etc. in *Elizabeth I: A Study in Power and Intellect* (London, 1974), p. 320, which Montrose (n. 35 above) follows, p. 77. The description is not in any of the sources Johnson cites in his footnote.

46. Sharp, p. 260. J. E. Neale, "Sayings of Queen Elizabeth," *History* n.s. 10 (October 1925), pp. 212–33, considers this speech substantially authentic (pp. 226–27). Sharp, who recounted it soon after 1623, must have received a copy of it in 1588, for at Tilbury he had been "commanded to re-deliver" the oration to "all the Armie together, to keep a Publique Fast" (Sharp, p. 259) after Elizabeth's departure.

For evidence that Elizabeth's rhetorical self-presentations often implied androgyny, see Leah S. Marcus, "Shakespeare's Comic Heroines, Elizabeth I, and the Political Uses of Androgyny," *Women in the Middle Ages and the Renaissance,* ed. Mary Beth Rose (Syracuse, N.Y., 1986).

ing the woman warrior, is surely the shadowy double behind the sudden appearance in the French camp of Joan, the puzzlingly Astraea-connected Amazonian, to lead her army against the invaders of her country.[47]

This probability does not make life any easier for the critic of *1 Henry VI*. One could simplify the situation by seeing Joan as a sarcastic version of such a figure, an anti-Elizabeth, a parodic non-virgin whose soldiership (finally) fails. Perhaps that was the point, or one of the points. But such close mirroring is hard to control. It is difficult to keep doubles separate. An obviously parodic presentation of a figure so suggestive might slide over into parody (dare one breathe it?) of the queen herself.[48] At the same time, the strong honorific associations of the Amazon-Deborah-Elizabeth combination exert their own pull in the opposite direction from parody. If Joan, parodied, functions as inferior foil for English chivalry, Joan honored also functions as its superior. It seems likely, then, that Joan in armor is as fair and foul as the traditional double-potentialed Amazon, and that what she says or does is as likely to undercut "the glorious deeds of the English in France" as to set off their splendor. She is a powerful warrior and a powerful enemy, but also an inverted image of both. Lest this interpretation seem an implausibly modern critical recourse to ambiguity, we should take notice of one elaborate European visual representation in the Elizabethan period of women in armor, Bruegel's *Dulle Griet* or Mad Meg. As described by Natalie Davis in her account of the sociological phenomenon she calls "women on top," the painting sends a similar double message. It "makes a huge, armed, unseeing woman, Mad Meg, the emblem of fiery destruction . . . and disorder. Bruegel's painting cuts in more than one way, however. . . . Nearby other armed women are beating grotesque animals from Hell."[49] This visual oxymoron sorts well with the double-valenced Amazon figure which is the period's prototype of the powerful and active woman.

Amazon, goddess, or queen, the numinous representative of a strength that in its very transcendence of social convention becomes salvific is

47. In "Elizabeth," Leah Marcus notes numerous similarities between Joan and the queen, including the proposed celebration of a saint's day commemorating each woman (p. 68) and the identity in name between two of Joan's supposed lovers and two of Elizabeth's suitors (p. 69).

48. Leah Marcus, in "Elizabeth," does interpret Joan as a figure of parody that "brings into the open a set of suppressed cultural anxieties" about Elizabeth (p. 51).

49. Natalie Zemon Davis, "Women on Top," *Society and Culture in Early Modern France* (Stanford, Cal., 1975), p. 129.

from another perspective a potential subverter of established order and belief, an overturner of values. Nowhere is this clearer than in the disparity between Elizabethan or Jacobean fictions of cross-dressing women and accounts of real ones from the same period. Both attest to the fascination of the time with gender subversion, as does the cross-dressing phenomenon itself. Fiction could delight in Mary Ambree (1584), who avenged her lover's death in battle by putting on armor to lead the English troops, or in Long Meg of Westminster, said to have lived in Henry VIII's reign: she came from the country to work in a London tavern, dressed in men's clothes, fought and defeated obstreporous males, and went with the soldiers to Boulogne, where she achieved victory over the champion of the French and was honored by the king.[50] Long Meg's story was told in two ballads, a play, and several reprintings of her pamphlet life, all between 1590 and about 1650. And no wonder; for when Long Meg had overcome the (Spanish) aggressor Sir James and humiliated him in the tavern by revealing her womanhood, she "sat in state like her Majesty."[51] Once again the warrior woman is assimilated to that modern numinous exemplar, Queen Elizabeth. But during the same

50. "The Life of Long Meg of Westminster," *The Old Book Collector's Miscellany*, ed. Charles Hindley, Vol. II (London, 1872). See also Shepherd (n. 29 above), pp. 70–71. The outlines of Long Meg's story exhibit striking similarities with the outlines of Joan's; according to Hall, Joan too came from the country and "was a greate space a chamberleyn in a commen hostrey" (Bullough, p. 56) before going off to lead the army against the English champion and being honored by the Dauphin.

51. Hindley, p. xii, quoted by Shepherd, p. 73. The ballad of Mary Ambree is given in Thomas Percy, *Reliques*, Vol. III (1823), pp. 46–51 (series 2, Bk. 2, no. 19). She was a well-known figure, mentioned by Fletcher and Ben Jonson (Percy, p. 46). Long Meg was even more familiar; she is referred to by Lyly, Nashe, Harvey, Deloney, Taylor, Dekker, Jonson, Beaumont and Fletcher, Middleton, and William Gamage's collection of epigrams (see Hindley and Shepherd).

All modern critics who discuss Long Meg give a wrong date of 1582 for the first pamphlet account of her life. This edition's title page and colophon are forged from an unrelated book published 1582; the rest of the text is ca. 1650. See William A. Jackson, ed. *Records of the Court of the Stationers' Company 1602–1640* (London, 1957), pp. 112–13 and n. 6 (this information is incorporated in the STC's revised Vol. II, ed. Katharine Pantzer). The earliest mention I know of Meg's story is the 18 August 1590 entry in the *Stationers' Register* for her life, followed on 27 August the same year by an entry for a ballad about her. On 14 March 1594/95, another ballad is entered. The first extant life would thus become one printed in 1620 (STC 17782.5), followed by further editions in 1635 and 1636 (STC 17783, 17783.3). After these would come the "1582" (*recte* ca. 1650). Hindley, who reprints the 1635 edition, includes in his introduction another reprint, which he believes to be an abridged version (n.d.) of the supposed 1582 text. It does seem to be Elizabethan, for it contains the casual reference to "Her Majesty"; later, this phrase was economically altered by the printer to "she sat in her Majesty" (1635; I have not seen the 1620 edition). Thus the life in Hindley's introduction may be the version registered 1590; if so, it is our earliest text.

period, women who really do participate in the growing fashion for wearing men's clothes, including ultimately weapons, are complained against with mounting sarcasm and hysteria. It is one thing to embody, in the encapsulated realm of fiction or of royalty, transcendence of social constraint—quite another to undermine on the street the customs around which society is organized.[52]

If Joan's initial presentation plays with the numinous aura and royal superiority of the virago, her portrayal in the play's middle section brings to the fore a special form of the virago's potential for subversion.[53] Uncommitted to convention, Joan is also uncommitted to the ethical stereotypes that structure the consciousness of other characters. This is her most threatening and most appealing function. It can be clearly seen in her comment after her eloquent speech has persuaded Burgundy to return to the French: "Done like a Frenchman! [*Aside.*]—turn and turn again" (3.3.85). Although this is a topical throwaway for the audience, its effect is very like that of early asides by Richard III, or of Falstaff playing first Henry IV and then Hal. It is characteristic of her persistent demystification of cherished idealisms, an ideological iconoclasm that does not spare her own achievements once she has finished with her original claim to divine aid.

Joan's speech constantly invites skepticism at the very moments when values are in need of affirmation, as when Rouen is captured, when Burgundy is about to desert, when Talbot falls. We should recall her sardonic response to Talbot's chivalric challenge—modeled, it is worth remembering, on Essex's conception of chivalry. Her conversion of Burgundy uses a different mode but achieves a similar shift of perspective, suddenly presenting an audience that enjoys "the gallant deeds of the English in France" with a point of view that sees "the cities and the towns defac'd / By wasting ruin of the cruel foe" (3.3.45–46) and forces

---

52. Lawrence Stone believes that female cross-dressing was a reflection of the Jacobean court's homosexuality and that "The playwrights noticed what was happening and gave it further circulation"; see *The Crisis of the Aristocracy 1558–1641* (Oxford, 1966), pp. 666–67. Given the early beginnings of both real and fictional cross-dressing, however, behavior at the Jacobean court comes much too late to be an explanation.

53. There is contemporaneous evidence for the possibility of regarding Joan as a heroine. Gabriel Harvey in his commonplace book set her between Alexander and her shepherd-analogue David (Shepherd, p. 35). By the 1620s, she was publicly entered among warlike and valorous women in Thomas Heywood's *Gynaikeion* (Jardine [n. 6 above], p. 137 n. 66) and admitted to membership in the long-running formal controversy in Christopher Newstead's *An Apology for Women,* a positive *exemplum* after all (Woodbridge [n. 25 above], p. 80).

them to look at the enemy "As looks the mother on her lowly babe /
When death doth close his tender dying eyes" (3.3.47–48). This clash of
perspectives becomes extreme, and reaches beyond momentary effect,
when the issue is the meaning of death itself. After the messenger who is
searching for Talbot has recited the hero's titles of honor, performing
unawares the eulogistic function of a traditional funeral oration, Joan
observes: "Here is a silly-stately style indeed! / . . . / Him that thou
magnifiest with all these titles, / Stinking and fly-blown lies here at our
feet" (4.7.72–76). Like the cross-dressing woman she is, Joan perceives as
futile convention what representatives of the status quo perceive as a
visible sign of inner nature, be it formulaic titles or formulaic clothing. If
her view is allowed, honor's a mere scutcheon, as her fellow subversive
Falstaff later agrees. Like Falstaff, Joan must be neutralized on behalf of
stable values, but like his, her point of view is too compelling to be
forgotten even when her circle in the water disperses in the humiliations
of the fifth act. Although Talbot is the play's ostensible hero and
nobility's decay its subject, it is Joan who expresses most forcefully both
the vanity of all ideologies and an unorthodox *consolatio*. Like the cross-
dressing festival ladies of misrule,[54] Joan offers relief from idealistic codes
of behavior—and thus from the need to mourn their demise.

The need to neutralize the virago, however, even the admired virago,
is as pervasive in the period's writing as the evident fascination with
her—indeed, it is probably a tribute to the force that fascination exerted.
This hypothesis helps in understanding some oddities in the presentation
of the period's literary Amazons and warrior women.

Two sets of stage Amazons have no lines at all, nor any action relevant
to the plot. Three more are actually men in disguise.[55] But by far the most
popular strategy for neutralizing the manly woman was to feminize her.
Hippolyta in both Shakespeare and Beaumont and Fletcher is a bride,
while in an Elizabethan translation from the French, she is said to have
become so eager to serve Theseus that she licked his wounded shoulder
with her tongue.[56] Less crude and more congenial was the ancient story

---

54. Davis (n. 50 above), pp. 138–39.

55. The Amazon army in Greene's *Alphonsus* stands by silently while its non-Amazon leader
fights; the Amazons in the masque of Shakespeare's *Timon* sing and dance. Since these are early
manifestations of the Amazon vogue in drama, their extraneousness probably reflects their initial
use as spectacle rather than integrated content. Marston's *Antonio and Mellida*, the anonymous
Swetnam the Woman-Hater, and Shirley's dramatization of the *Arcadia*, which fall into the later part
of the period, contain men disguised as Amazons.

56. Anthony Gibson, tr., *A Womans Woorth* (1599), cited by Wright (n. 32 above), p. 437.

that when Penthesilea had been slain by Achilles, her helmet fell off and revealed her beauty, causing Achilles to fall in love with her—sadly, luckily, too late. Amplified by the addition of a flood of golden hair loosed from the fallen helmet, the incident enriched Spanish and Italian romance and made its way to Elizabethan England, where at least six Amazonians, including Britomart, met with a version of this accident—all of them deliciously powerless to hide from admiring male gaze their quintessential femininity.[57] Holinshed's Boadicea with her long tresses and Mandeville's two gowned Amazons present the same feminized picture. Britomart, who sleeps "Al in her snow-white smocke, which locks unbownd" (3.1.63.7), having overcome her opposite number, the wicked Amazon, immediately changes all the rules of Amazon-land and "The liberty of women did repeale, / Which they had long usurpt; . . . them restoring / To mens subjection" (5.7.42.5–7). Even robust Long Meg, who looses her hair voluntarily to embarrass her vanquished opponent, returns from her French conquests to recant; having married a soldier who "had heard of her manhood" and "was determined to try her" in a combat with staves, she silently accepts "three or four blows" and then, "in submission, fell down on her knees, desiring him to pardon her, 'For,' said she, ' . . . it behoves me to be obedient to you; and it shall never be said, . . . Long Meg is her husband's master; and, therefore, use me as you please.'"[58] The strength of her subversive attraction can be measured by the violence with which she is reintegrated into conservative ideology. She is too powerful to be wedded in another key.

We may anticipate, then, what those in Shakespeare's audience familiar with the conventions defining the woman warrior must also have anticipated: that the more free play Joan's attractive force is permitted, the more completely she will have to be feminized at the end of the play. Her scenes in Act 5 should be read in light of this expectation, in full acceptance of their radical difference from her earlier behavior. Her conjuring, once established, assigns her to an overwhelmingly female class of malefactors: informed estimates place the proportion of women

---

57. Ortuñez's Claridiana (tr. 1585), Spenser's Britomart and Radigund (although the latter's loss of helmet releases no golden hair), Ariosto's Bradamante (tr. 1591), Tasso's Clorinda (tr. 1600), and Phineas Fletcher's Hippolyta (*The Purple Island,* 1633). See Wright, p. 441, and Shepherd, pp. 9–10. Mary Ambree (1584) removes her helmet to astonish the besieging forces; Shepherd says she "was forced to reveal her true gender to avoid being killed" (p. 222 n. 2), but the tone of the ballad is triumphant. Nevertheless, Ambree does share in the woman warrior's climactic feminization.

58. Hindley (n. 51 above), p. xx; quoted in a slightly different form by Shepherd, pp. 71–72.

executed as witches at about 93%.[59] Her rejection of her father reduces to female vanity the serious social claim implicit in her male clothing, for, as a number of recent writers point out, cross–dressing attacks the concept of natural hierarchy on which, for the Elizabethans, social class is built.[60] Her terrified snatching at subterfuges in the face of death would count as peculiarly female behavior; and when, finally, she claims to be pregnant, naming everyone and anyone as a lover, her feminization becomes irreversible. She has lost her helmet forever. Her captors' harsh reactions to her pleas are the equivalent of Long Meg's beating: Warwick's sadistically merciful directions, "And hark ye, sirs; because she is a maid, / Spare for no faggots, let there be enow" (5.4.55–56) are followed by York's unequivocal "Strumpet, . . . / Use no entreaty, for it is in vain" (84–85).

The witch is Joan's last topical role. Executions for witchcraft in England reached peaks in the 1580s and 1590s, high points on a long curve that Belsey considers "coterminous with the crisis in the definition of women and the meaning of the family"; she notes that in the last two decades of the sixteenth century "the divorce debate was also reaching a climax."[61] These events coincide with the beginnings of the vogue for Amazons and women warriors on stage and with the early phases of the fad for cross–dressing. But of all that twenty-year span, 1591 was the year of the witch in England. It brought to London the pamphlet *Newes from Scotland,* a full account of the spectacular treason–cum–sorcery trials King James had supervised there in the winter of 1590–1591, in which large numbers of his subjects were accused of having made a mass pact with the devil in order to raise storms against the ship bringing the King and his bride from Denmark.[62] The pamphlet had political overtones, as did

59. Belsey (n. 4 above), p. 185. Christina Larner gives the proportion of females among those put on trial for witchcraft in England at close to 95–100% in *Witchcraft and Religion: the Politics of Popular Belief,* ed. Alan Macfarlane (New York, 1984), p. 85. Belsey's figure is taken from earlier work by Larner.

60. Cf. Mary Beth Rose's comment that cross–dressing women are "obscuring . . . the badge of their social status as well, and thereby endangering critically the predictable orderliness of social relations" ("Women in Men's Clothing: Apparel and Social Stability in *The Roaring Girl,*" *English Literary Renaissance* 14 [1984], 374).

61. Belsey, p. 185. Overall, Belsey is concerned with an extended period of "crisis" lasting from 1542 to 1736, when the last statute against witchcraft was repealed.

62. This tract, with its new emphasis on the spectacular pact with the Devil, which had not previously been a factor in Scottish witch trials and was never very important in English ones (Larner, pp. 4, 8, 80–81, 88), seems to have evoked a little spate of conjuring dramas in the early 1590s, including *Dr. Faustus* and possibly *Friar Bacon and Friar Bungay* (written between 1589 and 1592).

the trials. King James, described to the English by the tract as "the greatest enemie the Devil hath on earth," was after all an aspirant to their throne. The trials provided him an opportunity to dissociate himself from the memory of his mother's crimes as well as gain a sort of posthumous revenge on his father's probable murderer by urging savage reprisals against a female suspect known to have been Bothwell's friend.[63]

It is not at all clear, however, that James' "forwardness," as the English ambassador called it in a letter to Burghley,[64] elicited the kind of acclaim that could help us read Joan's treatment by York and Warwick as pro-Jamesian political doctrine. There are indications that his self-interested zeal may have worked the other way. The woman he particularly wanted disemboweled was acquitted. Moreover, it appears that popular opinion in Scotland did not support the political aspects of the prosecution.[65] Perhaps still more serious, "the picture of himself as the principal target for witches" might easily look foolish, to say no worse, in a more sophisticated country that had never been as harsh or consistent in its punishment of witches as the continent, where James had first acquired his demonological ideas. As Larner says, "there was a possibility that his new-found interest in witchcraft . . . could . . . damage his image, especially in England."[66] Although England executed witches, it did not burn or torture them, and one wonders what an English audience made of James' vindictiveness or of Warwick's call for plenty of faggots and extra barrels of pitch for Joan's stake (5.4.56–57).[67] Furthermore, it was absolutely standard practice in both England and Scotland to put off a witch's execution if she was pregnant, as was the woman whose grisly punishment James unsuccessfully urged. Although Joan is only pretending, her captors are at best playing cat and mouse with her as they condemn her supposed child to death anew each time she assigns it a different father. Joan is the butt of the brutal joke here, but it is unlikely that York and Warwick come off unscathed by the negative associations of their total violation of English custom: "we will have no bastards live.

63. Larner, pp. 69, 9–10, 12.
64. Larner, p. 12.
65. Larner, pp. 12–13.
66. Larner, pp. 14, 4, 10–11, 15.
67. Warwick does say "That so her torture may be shortened" (5.4.58), but it seems at best a mixed recommendation. As for the usual English treatment of witchcraft, although it sounds sufficiently grim to us, it was "fairly far down the scale" of intensity compared with that of other countries, sufficiently different to be often called "unique" by recent investigators, although Larner is not willing to go that far (pp. 70–71).

... It dies and if it had a thousand lives.... Strumpet, thy words condemn thy brat and thee" (5.4.70, 75, 84).

It is altogether difficult to be sure how an Elizabethan audience might have reacted to Joan's punishment. Opinion on witches in 1591 was by no means monolithic. Skepticism about witch-trials was gathering force; on the continent Montaigne had commented as recently as 1588, "After all, it is putting a very high price on one's conjectures to have a man roasted alive because of them,"[68] and at home Reginald Scot had even earlier published his 600-page attack (1584) on "those same monsterous lies, which have abused all Christendome" and been the undoing of "these poore women."[69] Scot's book was clearly labeled as subversive when it was (appropriately) burnt by the hangman. Later, James attacked Scot by name in his own tract *Daemonologie*. This makes it all the more interesting that the portrayal of Joan divides into a subversively Scot-like main section and a Jamesian demonological coda. In the long middle section of the play already discussed, her triumphs are based simply on boldness, common sense, and resourcefulness. Comically, this supposed witch is the most down-to-earth pragmatist in the play: "had your watch been good / This sudden mischief never could have fallen" (2.1.58–59). In consequence, Talbot's repeated insistence that she is a witch sounds not dissimilar from the deluded allegations recounted by Reginald Scot. Joan herself, unlike Talbot and the French leaders, never falls back on metaphysical notions about her opponent. Whereas her companions suggest that Talbot is "a fiend of hell" or a favorite of the heavens (2.1.46–47), Joan simply expresses realistic respect for his prowess and invents several plans to evade it. Her successes are well served by Scot's commentary: "it is more strange, that we will imagine that to be possible to be doone by a witch, which to nature and sense is impossible; ... [for in other legal cases] the judge dooth not attend or regard what the accused man saith; or yet would doo: but what is prooved to have beene committed, and naturallie falleth in mans power and will to doo."[70] Yet in Act 5, Joan appears as a witch engaged in a diabolical compact, a demonological feature never very important in English witch trials but topically responsive to James' recent proceedings.

The presentation of Joan as witch is almost as diverse in its implications as her Amazonian image, of which it is a kind of transformation.

68. Michel de Montaigne, "Ignorance and Witchcraft," *Witchcraft in Europe 1100–1700: A Documentary History,* ed. Alan C. Kors and Edward Peters (Philadelphia, 1972), p. 337.

69. Reginald Scot, "Credulity and Witchcraft," Kors, pp. 327, 326.

70. Scot, in Kors, pp. 318–19.

The common folk belief in witches with beards, like the tradition of the Amazon's armor, renders visible the concept of a woman who "exceeds her sex" (1.2.90).[71] Hall calls her "This wytch or manly woman,"[72] as if the two were so close that he could hardly decide between them. A comment by Belsey illuminates this aspect of Joan's witchhood: "The demonization of women who subvert the meaning of femininity is contradictory in its implications. It places them beyond meaning, beyond the limits of what is intelligible. At the same time it endows them with a (supernatural) power which it is precisely the project of patriarchy to deny. On the stage such figures are seen as simultaneously dazzling and dangerous."[73] Joan's dazzle is of course neutralized by her fifth-act humiliations, but her danger persists in her final curse on England. Quickly, she is taken off to be neutralized more thoroughly at the stake. Her helplessness vis-à-vis her male captors may serve to remind us that despite folk belief, there were no Elizabethan pictures of witches with beards or any other kind of power-laden sexual ambiguity.[74] Joan's fate enacts that annihilation fantasized for the cross-dressing woman by the anonymous author of a Jacobean pamphlet: "Let . . . the powerful Statute of apparell [the sumptuary law] but lift up his Battle-Axe, so as every one may bee knowne by the true badge of their bloud, . . . and then these *Chymera's* of deformitie will bee sent backe to hell, and there burne to Cynders in the flames of their owne malice."[75] Yet in a final twist of meaning, as we have seen, the terms of Joan's reintegration into conservative ideology recognizably damage her captors' own ideological sanction.

In my reading of *1 Henry VI,* the disjunctive presentation of Joan that shows her first as numinous, then as practically and subversively powerful, and finally as feminized and demonized is determined by Shakespeare's progressive exploitation of the varied ideological potential

71. This phrase and its variants (sometimes in Latin) were regularly applied to Queen Elizabeth. James' eulogistic inscription on her monument identifies her, typically, as "*super sexum*" (see Schleiner [n. 29 above], pp. 172–73).

On witches' beards, Belsey (p. 186) cites Keith Thomas' *Religion and the Decline of Magic,* p. 678. Thomas Alfred Spalding, *Elizabethan Demonology* (London, 1880), p. 99, instances *The Honest Man's Fortune, The Honest Whore,* and *The Merry Wives of Windsor*—besides, of course, *Macbeth,* to which both Belsey and Spalding refer.

72. Bullough, p. 61.

73. Belsey, p. 185.

74. For information on pictures of witches, I am again indebted to Ruth Luborsky. Many illustrations are also reproduced in Kors, including some of witches with animal heads and limbs, but none with transsexual characteristics.

75. *Hic Mulier,* C1v, cited by Rose (n. 61 above), p. 375.

inherent in the topically relevant figure of the virago. Each of her phases reflects differently upon the chivalric, patriarchal males in the play, especially Talbot, who also have topical referents outside the drama. At no stage is the allocation of value clearcut.

Neither is the definition of dominant ideology clearcut in the play's social context. To bring detailed topical considerations into an assessment of the ideology of *1 Henry VI* is to come upon some truisms worth restating: that there is probably more than one opinion on any crucial issue at any time in any society, and that it is often hard to sort out the relationship between views and power. If the queen considers a French expedition disadvantageous but her subordinate succeeds in continuing it, is the dominant ideology war or peace? If pamphleteers complain that women are becoming moral monsters by cross-dressing, but a fad for Amazons arises and women cross-dress more than ever, what is the ideological situation? This kind of uncertainty complicates the concept of subversion, which I have invoked from time to time in my analysis.

Given the multiple uncertainties within the play's milieu and the uncertainties the play itself generates, it becomes strikingly evident that *1 Henry VI,* like so much of Shakespeare's later work, locates itself in areas of ideological discomfort. It uses culturally powerful images ambiguously, providing material for different members of a diverse audience to receive the drama in very different ways. Although one must agree with the critical judgment that in this play "the individual consciousness never engages in an *agon* with its milieu, and never asks the great questions,"[76] the presence of Joan does provide a form of *agon,* if a less profound one than in the great tragedies. Even the ending with its strategies of neutralization cannot disqualify the questions raised.

Finally, once the ways in which disturbing ideological positions are neutralized by the play have been made clear, it seems well to point out that the theater is an illusionistic medium and that to neutralize on stage is not necessarily to neutralize in reality. In fact, it is possible that maintaining the illusion that an ideological tendency can be reliably neutralized may help to enable toleration of threatening ideas.[77]

76. Ronald S. Berman, "Shakespeare's Conscious Histories," *Dalhousie Review* 41, 4 (Winter 1961–62), 486.

77. The research for this essay has relied greatly on the knowledgeable and generous help of Georgiana Ziegler, curator of the Furness Collection at the University of Pennsylvania, to whom I owe much gratitude.

SUZANNE GOSSETT

"Man-maid, begone!": Women in Masques

THE distance between an actor and the person he represents varies throughout theatrical history. At some times the relation is close: the actor is typecast or methodically lives the part. At other times the relation is remote. Brecht urged his actors not to identify with their roles; Greek actors wore masks. On the Elizabethan and Jacobean stage potentially different relations existed simultaneously. The theaters of the time employed all male casts, with boys taking the roles of women. Therefore Kemp may have been a "real" clown, or Burbage a convincing Hamlet, but the boys could only be women according to an understood convention. The audience was expected to ignore defects in their presentation—Cleopatra does not want to be played by a squeaking boy—and to supply the necessary imaginative effort to dissociate the part from the player. Occasionally, as in Shakespeare's comedies, the dramatist would make a series of jokes based on the sex disguise, jokes which assumed that on one level the audience knew all along that Rosalind, for example, was "really" a boy. Usually, however, the plays did not encourage conscious comparison between the actor, man or boy, and his part.[1] The boy-player-queen and the man-player-king existed in the same fictive realm; their personal identity and their physical sex were irrelevant.

In Jacobean and Caroline masques, however, the conventions governing audience response were more complex. The performance of a masque regularly required two different kinds of audience consciousness, one for the professional singers, speakers, or antimasquers whose personal identities were to be ignored, and one for the masquers, recognition of whose identity was central to the meaning of the masque. The audience was asked to perform a kind of mental gymnastics, finding "the

---

1. Lisa Jardine notes that "the taking of female parts by boy players actually occasioned a good deal of contemporary comment, and created considerable moral uneasiness," and argues that the appeal of the allusions to the boy players' actual sex was homoerotic. She suggests there was more awareness of the performers in comedy "where role-playing and disguise is part of the genre" than in tragedy, where "the willing suspension of disbelief does customarily extend . . . to the taking of the female parts by boy players." *Still Harping on Daughters: Women and Drama in the Age of Shakespeare* (Sussex, Eng., 1983), pp. 9–36. For further discussion of these issues, see Phyllis Rackin, "The Boy Heroine on the English Renaissance Stage," *PMLA* 102 (1987), 29–41, which appeared after this article was completed.

relationship between the reality and the symbol, the impersonators and the impersonation . . . of crucial importance" for the masquers, while keeping in mind that should the professional actor remove his disguise the revelation would be "trivial."[2] The presence of women masquers, including Queens Anne and Henrietta Maria, called for particular awareness of this distinction, since it meant that there might be both women and men taking the roles of women within the same performance. Any misplaced audience interest in the person behind the role could injure the total effect: one must recognize that the queen is playing Bel–Anna, and one must ignore any ridiculous overtones created by the boy playing the moon goddess. The normal stage solution, of treating the whole as a consistent illusion, was not possible.

During the Elizabethan and Jacobean period the audience received fairly consistent signals aiding them in interpreting the presence of women. Real women participated only as silent dancing masquers, thus forming primarily a physical contrast to the disguised men, especially the antimasquers who, like the female masquers, usually danced. Such a contrast was present even in the masques with male masquers, since every masque ended with mixed dancing in the revels and hence drew in real women. During the Caroline period, however, two significant innovations exacerbated the inherent difficulties. First of all, by 1632 women's voices had been heard on the masque stage. Once women were actively involved throughout the performance, comparisons would more naturally arise between the female singers or masquers and the men speaking or singing the roles of personified female abstractions or goddesses. In addition, as Charles' reign continued, courtiers were scattered throughout the performances, instead of appearing only as masquers. Eventually they took speaking or dancing parts previously reserved for professional performers. The dual consciousness implicitly demanded by the earlier masques broke down. It became reasonable, or even necessary, for an audience to consider the identity, including the sex, of all participants in a masque.

The treatment of women in masques can best be traced in the queens' masques of the Jacobean and Caroline period. This is the period when the masque, in the hands of Ben Jonson and a few other poets, and with the significant collaboration of Inigo Jones, developed into a complex literary and spectacular form. Its effects depended partly upon audience acceptance of its governing conventions. Yet from the comments on the

2. Stephen Orgel, ed. *Ben Jonson: The Complete Masques* (New Haven and London, 1969), p. 5; Stephen Orgel, *The Jonsonian Masque* (Cambridge, Mass., 1965), p. 118.

decorum of Anne's and Henrietta Maria's early masques, from the ambivalent literary treatment of both queens, from the incidental commentary on women, and from the renewed experimentation in the late Caroline masques, it appears that neither poets nor audience could always make the necessary dissociations between actor and part, or adjust to having real women on the stage. The most notorious objection to women acting, Prynne's *Histriomastix* (1633), was just one of a number of possible responses to the innovation; the masques themselves constitute a more interesting commentary on the new developments.

Anne's earliest dramatic offenses arose from the decorum, or indecorum, of her costuming. Dudley Carleton's comments are instructive. In Anne's first masque, Samuel Daniel's *Vision of the Twelve Goddesses* (1604), she played Pallas in a costume which differed from those of the other ladies: "Only Pallas . . . had a trick by herself, for her clothes were not so much below the knee that we might see a woman had both feet and legs which I never knew before."[3] Carleton no doubt understood that "allegory, symbol and myth are the substance of masques,"[4] but he chose to react instead to the physical presence of a female in the masque. He ignored the appropriateness of the costume to Pallas in observing its inappropriateness to Anne.

Carleton was even more horrified by the queen's appearance a year later in Jonson's first masque, *The Masque of Blackness*. At Anne's own suggestion the women were disguised as blackamoors:

Apparell was rich, but too light and Curtizan-like for such great ones. Instead of Vizzards, their Faces, and Arms up to the Elbows, were painted black, which was Disguise sufficient, for they were hard to be known; but it became them nothing so well as their red and white, and you cannot imagine a more ugly Sight, then a Troop of lean-cheek'd Moors. . . . [The Spanish Ambassador danced with] the queen, and forgot not to kiss her Hand, though there was Danger it would have left a Mark on his Lips.[5]

Carleton could pretend to stupidity when he wished: for instance, he refused to see more than a "great Engine" in the scenery of *The Masque of Blackness* (I, 89). Nevertheless no parallel objections exist to the parts or costuming of the princes in James' reign, or later of King Charles himself.

Reaction to these two masques was educational for Anne, who apparently learned that her costume could not even temporarily demean

3. Samuel Daniel, *The Vision of the Twelve Goddesses,* ed. Joan Rees, in *A Book of Masques in Honour of Alardyce Nicoll,* ed. T. J. B. Spencer (Cambridge, 1967), p. 41.

4. Stephen Orgel and Roy Strong, *Inigo Jones: The Theatre of the Stuart Court* (London and Berkeley, 1973), I, 11. All further citations from this work will be given in the text by volume and page. The text of the masques of Ben Jonson is that established by Orgel for the Yale *Ben Jonson.*

5. Orgel, ed. *Ben Jonson: The Complete Masques,* p. 4.

her royal dignity. Thereafter she took parts which effectively eliminated any discrepancy between her historical and dramatic roles: Bel–Anna, Tethys, the Queen of the Orient. *Blackness* was also educational for Jonson. If the queen could not appear briefly as a figure requiring improvement or transcendence, then transformation would have to involve two groups of characters, masquers and antimasquers. The reaction to *The Masque of Blackness* partly explains the necessity for the two–part form: it also suggests why Jonson's first real venture into that form is *The Masque of Queens*.[6]

Even as it initiates the clear division between masque and antimasque, *The Masque of Queens* also neatly reveals Jonson's own divided feelings about women. Again Jonson gives Anne partial directorial credit, this time for shaping the masque into its two–part form: "her majesty . . . commanded me to think on some dance or show that might precede hers and have the place of a foil or false masque" (I, 132). From this point on women in masques must be either true or false, queens or hags. The new method called for men or boy actors to play female roles in the anti-masques, embodying the distorted vision of women, and for aristocratic women to play the masquers. The message conveyed to the audience is that "real women" are, or should be, like the masquers. Jonson's allegory was thus supported by the sex discrepancy between the boys and the female masquers. If the audience were to glance behind the fiction to the players' reality in both parts rather than just in the masque proper, the meaning of the masque would only be reinforced.

Jonson's attitude toward women, an ambivalence verging on antip-athy, is evident in the structure and commentary of his masques from *Blackness* on.[7] Surface compliment in the early queens' masques only slightly conceals fear and dislike of women. In *Blackness* the audience sees that the black daughters of Niger are ugly, petulant, and frivolous, "as women always are." Despite the sun's fervent love, which "shows / That in their black the perfect'st beauty grows" the women are "as women are / Most jealous of their beauties," and unreasonable: they have "a settled thought / As women's are" (I, 91). The confirmation of

6. In *The Gypsies Metamorphosed* Jonson returned to the type of transformation he had attempted in *Beautie* and *Blackness*. The Duke of Buckingham and other noblemen were dyed brown with an ointment, and they reappeared changed at the end. This masque was King James' favorite and was performed three times. However, it was not produced at court, and Jonson never again tried this kind of transformation using women.

7. Anne Barton addresses the question of Jonson's changing treatment of women and notes that Mistress Fitzdottrel, in *The Devil is an Ass* (1616), is the "first woman in a Jonson comedy who can fairly be described as a heroine." *Ben Jonson, Dramatist* (Cambridge, 1984), p. 224.

their desires by Aetheopia, the moon goddess, is not reassuring, since the moon itself is traditionally identified with women, instability, and lunacy. The recurrent phrase, "as women are," suggests that women are an unchanging, possibly unteachable, essence.

Jonson is compelled by his allegory to transform the black daughters for *The Masque of Beautie,* but even there the structure denigrates their new perfection. Repeatedly criticism of the women precedes excuse. For instance, they are accused of "coarse and most unfit neglect," for not coming at their appointed time two years earlier (I, 93). This, Boreas explains, was not their fault but caused by envious, and female, Night. The women are potentially dangerous: "say the dames should, with their eyes, / Upon the hearts here mean surprise, / Were not the men like harmed?" Yet here, "no such deceit is mixed" (I, 96). Finally Jonson audaciously raises the accusation:

> Had those that dwell in error foul,
> And hold that women have no soul,
> But seen these move, they would have then
> Said women were the souls of men. (I, 96)

The last line refutes the error, but even to suggest in a queen's masque that women have no souls is astonishing. And the reply, while it passes in the song and the rhyme, does not assert that women have souls. The compliment is addressed to the men, who aspire neoplatonically. The women are without separate identities.

Even in *The Masque of Queens,* where male actors emphasize the symbolic distance between the antimasque witches and the masque queens, Jonson did not present the queens as the active agents he knew they were. His new formula idealized the masquers but also made them passive. A comparison of Jonson's notes about the queens to what the spectators saw is instructive. Inigo Jones' designs and Jonson's poetry give little hint that many of these women were historically or tradition-ally powerful, dangerous, even masculine. The only suggestions are Heroic Virtue's references to Penthesilea as "the brave Amazon," whom Jones shows with a sword (I, 140); to "Victorious Thomyrsis," whom he shows with a scepter (I, 143); and to "the wise and warlike Goth, Amalasunta," for whom no design survives unless it is the very feminine figure of the unidentified queen (I, 153). But in the commentary which Jonson wrote at Prince Henry's request and published in the quarto he tells the reader that Camilla led "*a squadron of horse . . . a virgin warrior*"; that of Artemisia, Xerxes wrote, "*men have shown themselves to me women, yet women have shown themselves men*"; that Hypsicratea was assistant to her husband *"in all labours and hazards of the war, in a masculine habit,"* and therefore cut her hair; that Bonduca *"managed the whole war, and*[her] *mind was a man's rather than a woman's"*; and that the Bohemian queen Valasca *"to redeem herself and her sex from the tyranny of men which they lived in under Primislaus, on a night and an hour appointed led on the women to the slaughter of their barbarous husbands and lords . . .* [and] *lived many years after with the liberty and fortitude of Amazons"* (I, 136–37).

Jonson is at pains to suppress these attributes on the stage for two reasons. First, the presence of the male actors representing the hags required a contrasting emphasis on the more delicate femininity of the "real" female masquers—in this masque, to be too masculine could mean to be male. Second, *The Masque of Queens* is an allegory which strips the actual queen of political significance, depicting her, quite accurately, in the dependent position of a consort–queen. The witches are chased away by "Fame's loud sound and Virtue's sight," that is, by the appearance of the House of Fame in which sit the Queens, and by the descent of Perseus, *"expressing heroic and masculine virtue."* Perseus is the active agent. He is the father of fame, whose house is built of "Men-making poets, and those well made men / Whose strife it was to have the happiest pen / Renown them to an after-life," that is, the heroes Achilles, Aeneas, and Caesar. Perseus represents King James, whose fame rested in part on his poetry; Bel–Anna is only a reflection of his masculine virtue. "Far from self-love, as humbling all her worth / To him that gave it," from him she passively receives "the lustre of her merit" (I, 135). It is true that masques conventionally turn their compliments to the king, but, by contast, in the nearly contemporary *Oberon, The Fairy Prince,* the prince is directly praised, "the height of all our race" (I, 207), who will be the heir "to Arthur's crowns and chair" (I, 209). In the *Masque of Queens* Bel–Anna has no individual merit except as a projection of James. Thus Jonson has succeeded in reducing the significance both of the power-wielding queens like Bonduca and of the ceremonial queen Anne, even while praising them.

This pattern is repeated in *Love Freed From Ignorance and Folly,* where the antimasque is she-fools (played by men) and the masquers are daughters of the morn who are freed from the Sphinx when Love, not they, solves the Sphinx's riddle by looking in the king's face. In *The Lord's Masque,* Campion follows Jonson's lead. This was not a queen's masque but was offered by eight lords and eight ladies at the Princess Elizabeth's marriage. Presented by Mania, who is ugly like the Sphinx in *Love Freed,* the antimasquers are twelve frantics, six men and six women. These were, of course, all played by male dancers. Campion specifies five of the six male frantics: "the lover, the self-lover, the melancholic man . . . the schoolman . . . the over-watched usurer" (I, 243). The undifferentiated women make up the rest of the *"medley of madness,"* presumably resembling the she-fools in *Love Freed* and gathering impact in performance from the sex disguise. The allegory of the main masque accentuates ideal female passivity in contrast both to the men and to the antimasquers. The male masquers are stars who become "men fit for wars"; the female masquers are statues, made by Prometheus and twice transformed until they become "women fit for love" (I, 245).

The remaining years of James' reign saw no more queen's masques or masques for women. As a result, Jonson avoided the complications of having male and female "women" in the same fiction. He wrote either masques with no female parts at all (for instance *Love Restored, The Irish Masque, News from the New World, Pleasure Reconciled to Virtue*) or masques with comic antimasques whose female characters might have been imported from the London stage. Among these are the deaf tire woman in *Christmas his Masque,* the Welshwomen in *For the Honor of Wales,* the wenches in *Gypsies Metamorphosed,* the Lady Alewife and two women in *The Masque of Augurs,* the "laced mutton" and poulterer's wife in *Neptune's Triumph,* and Eleanor Rumming, Mary Ambree, and Long Meg in *The Fortunate Isles.* These women occasionally have a line or two; frequently they only dance. The emphasis is on their comic or ridiculous qualities, which male dancers would have accentuated.

That Jonson nonetheless found the issue of sex disguise both persistent and annoying we can infer from the debate between Rabbi Zeal-of-the-Land Busy and the puppet Dionysius at the end of *Bartholomew Fair.* By 1614 Jonson had completed all of his masques for Queen Anne. He had recently written *Epicoene,* which can be interpreted as a self-referential theatrical statement that it is possible for a boy to pass convincingly as a woman. In *Bartholomew Fair* the puppet's response to the Puritan's *"old stale argument against the Players"* that *"*the Male among you, putteth on the apparell of the *Female,* and the *Female* of the *Male"* is to take up his garment and show that *"we haue neyther* Male *nor* Female *amongst vs."*[8] While a perfect gesture of contempt and a proper *reductio ad absurdum* of Busy's complaints, the response is false when applied to the masque stage. In his comedy Jonson can argue for the primacy of the dramatic illusion and the irrelevance of the players. In masques, however, the "players"

---

8. *Ben Jonson,* ed. C. H. Herford and Percy and Evelyn Simpson (Oxford, 1925–1952), VI, 135–36.

contain the central meaning of the performance. Furthermore, the frequent attention to the proper behavior of women traceable in the queen's masques requires the audience to recognize and separate the male and female performers, not to confound them. Although the problem became dormant for the remainder of the Jacobean period, it revived as soon as Charles came to the throne. From then on questions of women as performers and of "woman" as idea persisted on the masque stage until the masquing itself stopped because the Puritans' "old stale arguments" prevailed.

Jacobean methods for the inclusion of women in masques proved inadequate to the new queen, Henrietta Maria. Only fifteen when she arrived in England, she was a fun-loving adolescent with the habits of the Catholic French court. Her problems were similar to Anne's but more intense: her ideas of decorum caused scandal, her notions of appropriate masquing roles for men and women courtiers broke down the traditional divisions of awareness which separated masque from antimasque, and the fad for Platonic love which she encouraged made the symbolism of the later masques extreme and occasionally incoherent. The greatly increased importance of the queen at court meant that women had to be taken seriously; this very importance was one cause of the notorious political controversy which her acting eventually provoked. It is no wonder that the final masque in which both she and the king danced has been taken as a symbol of the entire Caroline court.[9]

Henrietta Maria began her English dramatic career by presenting a pastoral which she had seen at the French court seven years earlier. She and her ladies took all the parts. Although the performance was "conducted as privately as possible," it gave offense on two counts of decorum: the Venetian report says "*the English objected to the first part . . . being declaimed by the queen,*" and Chamberlain wrote to Carleton that the queen "herself acted a part, and some of the rest were disguised like men with beards" (I, 384–85). Henrietta, who was used to actresses, apparently assumed that if the English accepted men dressed as women on the public stage, they would not object to women dressed as men in a private presentation.

She appeared equally oblivious of violating class distinctions in the court performances of the next year. Although the masque of November, 1626 is lost, we know that it was danced by the queen and ten ladies, and that the antimasque, based on Rabelais, featured the tall

9. C. V. Wedgwood, "The Last Masque," in *Truth and Opinion* (London, 1969), pp. 139–56.

porter (a court notable) as Gargantua, being instructed by the Duke of Buckingham as a fencing master, the Earl of Holland as a school master, and George Goring as a dancing master. Predictably there were private protests: "His grace [i.e., Buckingham] took a shape . . . which many thought too histrionical to become him . . . never before then did any privy counsellor appear in a masque."[10]

For Henrietta Maria performing was a game; at this point in her life she did not worry much about allegorical significance. She was more concerned with amusing herself, and possibly with maintaining an appropriate distance between the queen and professional actors, than she was with the symbolic coherence of the performances. She and Buckingham, defying expectations of decorum by casting great lords in the antimasque, either did not notice or did not care that such casting violated the two levels of consciousness which had previously organized the masque. If the Duke is to be recognized in the antimasque—and what is the fun if he isn't—then the audience is alerted to consider the identity of all the players. No clear literary separation tells the spectators when to accept the illusion and when to look behind it for a meaningful relation of actor and part. As a result the audience becomes actively, rather than subconsciously, aware of the sex disguises. (The antimasque in 1626 included "double women," matrons, nurses, and Gargamella, Gargantua's mother.) Soon this innovation became common; courtiers began playing a variety of parts, including comic or even repugnant ones such as furies. Once again, masque writers were compelled to adapt their styles to royal whim.

Jonson was first called upon to write for the new king and queen in 1631. There had been only one masque, now lost, since the offending performance of 1626.[11] By 1631 the marriage of Henrietta Maria and Charles was firmly cemented: Buckingham was dead and the queen was

---

10. Anonymous letter to the Rev. Joseph Mead (I, 389). The writer either had not heard of or ignored *The Gypsies Metamorphosed*. He also did not know that "at Salisbury, August 5, 1620, Buckingham spoke the lines of an Irish footman in an entertainment in which the Marquis Hamilton was a pirate and Sir William Fielding a Puritan." Under James, however, such performances did not take place at court. Harbage traces the cavalier taste for private theatricals to Buckingham, noting "the tendency of the courtiers to appear in [interludes and masques] so conspicuously was the ostentation of a privileged clique, and was neither highly approved nor widely imitated" Alfred Harbage, *Cavalier Drama* (New York, 1936), p. 192.

11. Apparently there was a queen's masque performed, perhaps at Denmark House, in January, 1627; a king's masque for Shrovetide, 1628, seems to have been cancelled: see Gerald Eades Bentley, *The Jacobean and Caroline Stage* (Oxford, 1941–1968), VII, 63, 66–67. In their Calendar of Masques Orgel and Strong indicate uncertainty about both of these masques (I, 86).

her husband's closest friend. Jonson's masques show his attempt to adjust to the very different relations between this king and queen and the preceding pair. For the first time he allows a masque for male masquers to move towards a central female focus. In *Love's Triumph Through Callipolis* Charles, representing heroic love, presents his triumph to "the queen of what is wonder in the place! / Pure object of heroic love alone!" (I, 406). Although the queen, representing beauty, does nothing, she is allegorically more significant than Anne had been in her own masques. Henrietta's presence is essential to complete the "mysterial" union of Beauty and Love, rose and lily, Mary and Charles with which the masque ends. Otherwise Jonson uses the divisions of his earlier masques: the audience is required only to recognize the king and his companion lovers and can ignore the personal identity of the depraved lovers of the antimasque and the gods and goddesses of the remainder, most or all of which was sung.[12] So far no conflict arises between the implied new attitude toward women and the casting.

Chloridia proved more intractable. All of Jonson's masques for Queen Anne had emphasized the passivity of the queen and her ladies, and he had difficulty breaking with that pattern. In *Chloridia* the queen plays the nymph Chloris, who, once transformed into Flora, will enrich the earth with flowers. Yet Chloris is essentially decorative. Juno, goddess of marriage, is the real power. She can stop the havoc caused by Cupid, or love, in rebellion: "*Here, by the providence of Juno, the tempest on an instant ceaseth*" (II, 421). The flowers are "Preserved by the Hours / At Juno's soft command"; she employs Iris "to guard the Spring" (II, 421–22). Meanwhile "Chloris sits, a shining star / To crown and grace our jolly song" (II, 421). Jonson's motives were both practical and allegorical. Juno must speak, and therefore could not be played by the queen. (Although Henrietta recited in private pastorals, masquers were invariably silent). Additionally, attributing female power to the goddess of marriage was one way to emphasize that Henrietta Maria acquired her significance from her marriage to the king. *Chloridia* ends with a compliment to Henrietta Maria which with each succeeding line more closely

---

12. All of the sections are identified as sung except one poem of Amphitrite. Willa McClung Evans points out that "among the characters of the masque-world were four, sometimes five, allegorical personages, such as those forming the Constellation in *Love's Triumph*, making their entry for the final scene, seated on clouds, in chariots, or on spheres suspended in mid-air. Professional musicians played these parts." *Henry Lawes, Musician and Friend of Poets* (New York, 1941), p. 60. It is difficult to determine whether the singing made the sex change more or less obvious.

confines her within her sexual identity as the king's wife:

> Chloris the queen of flowers
> The sweetness of all showers,
> The ornament of bowers,
> The top of paramours! (II, 422)

In *Chloridia* the bi-polar opposition between male and female, anti-masque and masque of Jonson's earlier queen's masques is complicated by the large number of female parts played by men. Some of these characters, such as Jealousy, Disdain, Fear, Dissimulation, and Tempest, come from Hell; masculine awkwardness in these parts would be appropriate. Others, however, like Spring, Juno, Iris, the Naiades, Fame, and Fame's four supports, Poesy, Architecture, Sculpture, and History, are from the world of the masque. Dressed as women, they would gain from femininity.[13] The Naiades, who are identified as "*the nymphs, fountains and servants of the season*" (II, 420), dance. Nothing in the text inhibits the audience from contrasting the dance of the queen and her ladies, who are also called "nymphs" (II, 421), with the dance of these Naiades as well as with the absurd dances of the antimasquers. Yet the allegory would not be enhanced by a failure of the Naiades to be as feminine as the queen and her ladies. Audience response to the presence of the "real" and acted women is not sufficiently delimited by the masque itself, and the full implications of having so many female figures are not worked through.

For the conclusion of his masque Jonson recalled an earlier masque for a different queen. *The Masque of Queens* reached a climax in the appearance of Fama Bona from the *machina versatilis,* and *Chloridia* ends with the flight of Fame. But where Fame in *The Masque of Queens* was the daughter of Heroic and Masculine Virtue and central to the allegory, this section of *Chloridia* is merely recapitulation: "Who hath not heard of Chloris and her bower, / Fair Iris' act, employed by Juno's power" (II, 422). It is this part of the masque whose performance Jonson criticized in his "expostulation" with Jones. His lines spread contempt on Jones' machinery and on the female figures who, instead of the man-making poets of the *Masque of Queens,* accompanied Fame in *Chloridia:*

---

13. The sexes can be determined from the text, from Jones' designs, especially those reprinted in Orgel and Strong, II, 437–38, and from Jonson's "Expostulacon wth Inigo Jones," quoted below. Jones changed Fear from a male figure in his model, Vico's *Pavor,* into a female figure (II, 438).

Th' ascent of Lady Fame which none could spy
Not they that sided her, Dame Poetry,
Dame History, Dame Architecture too,
And Goody Sculpture, brought wth much adoe
To hold her vp.[14]

Though Orgel defends the mythological coherence of *Chloridia* (I, 56–57), for Jonson himself the masque was not a success. The multiple anti-masques based on the *ballet de cour* were foreign to his style, he broke with Jones over the title page attribution, and he complained that masques had become shows whose soul was "Painting & Carpentry." The court had changed, the old formulas did not work. The next year the commission went to Aurelian Townshend.

Like Jonson, Townshend was to write a pair of masques, the first for the king at Twelfth Night, the second for the queen a month later. In the first, *Albion's Triumph,* he is groping for the form and closely imitates Jonson's *Love's Triumph* of the previous year. The triumph itself, the group of gods on the cloud (Jonson's "Constellation"), and the final compliment to Mary-Charles are all copied. The masque falls into sections with different kinds of performers for each part: singers for the gods, male or female; actors for Publius and Platonicus; dancers for the seven antimasques; and the king and his companions for the masquers. One change Townshend did make elevated the symbolic significance of the queen. Where in *Love's Triumph* the queen is passive, only "reflecting" the "lines of love" (I, 406–07), in *Albion's Triumph* she is Alba, goddess of the island. Albanactus is originally mortal. When he is "subdued to love and chastity by Cupid and Diana . . . they show him the Queen. The King yields, and presents himself a suppliant to the goddess Alba. She embraces him, and makes him co-partner of her deity" (II, 454).

Townshend also reflected the queen's interest in neo-platonism in the interlude between the patrician and the plebian, Platonicus and Publius. Platonicus, who has seen Albanactus Caesar "with the eyes of understanding," represents the ideal courtier. Although there are some jokes at his expense (as there are jokes about the Platonic Persian youths in Davenant's *Temple of Love* three years later), it is Platonicus' way of thinking—the queen's way of thinking—which shapes the entire masque. In fact, Orgel calls *Albion's Triumph* "a Platonic fable about the creation of a sacred monarch" (I, 61).

14. *Ben Jonson,* VIII, 403.

Five weeks later, in *Tempe Restored,* the English court saw one of the most experimental masques of the period. It is not clear to whom we can attribute the innovations: "*All the verses were written by Master Aurelian Townshend. The subject and allegory of the masque, with the descriptions and apparatus of the scenes, were invented by Inigo Jones*" (I, 61–62).[15] In the poetry of this masque the tensions generated by the new court attitudes towards casting and towards women finally rose to the literary surface.

Tempe Restored is about transformation, the central subject and action of most Jacobean and Caroline masques. Rarely had the complexities of the issue been so fully explored. The masque begins with the Fugitive Favorite, a young gentleman who was changed by Circe into a beast and now, restored to his former shape, is escaping from her. Circe is unable to recapture him because "it is consent that makes a perfect slave" and he has decided to "fly to virtue" (II, 480). The king of course represents this virtue, but the re-transformation has already occurred and is sustained by the favorite's will. For consolation, Circe is amused by the antimasquers, who are divided into "*Indians and barbarians, who are naturally bestial, and others which are voluntaries, and but half transformed into beasts*" (II, 481). Once again emphasis falls upon the function of the will in transformation; those half-transformed should be more grotesque than those naturally bestial. The attitude conveyed in this entire section is opposed to transformation.

Jones and Townshend underlined their point by the casting, which formed the natural climax to Henrietta Maria's theatrical experiments since her arrival in England. The young gentleman was played by twenty-year-old Thomas Killigrew, at this time a court page, and Circe was played by the first woman singer on the English stage, Madame Coniack. In other words, the court watched an action in which the major performers were not transformed by sex or class: in a sense they played themselves, as the masquers always had. All court gentlemen had to exercise their wills to overcome the temptations of female Circes. Even the actors who took the parts of the transformed and partially transformed antimasquers were in a sense representing the actor's art.

The next part of the masque continues the extraordinary emphasis on non-transformation. The antimasquers, according to the text, simply pass off the stage; presumably they are vanquished by the appearance of Harmony and the fourteen "influences" of the stars that are to come. Harmony was another woman singer, Mistress Shepherd, and the influ-

15. Paul Reyher points out that much of the masque is borrowed—Reyher says plagiarized—from Beaujoyeulx's *Ballet Comique de la Reine;* Reyher objects both to the copying and to the changes that Townshend and Jones introduced. *Les Masques Anglais* (Paris, 1909), pp. 201–02.

ences, who danced, were fourteen noble children, seven boys and seven girls. These were the literal as well as metaphorical "products" of the stars, Henrietta Maria's ladies. In the main masque, which follows, the queen, Divine Beauty, is surrounded by these ladies costumed as stars. Their descent is accompanied by the music of the spheres, sung by the court musicians. The allegory, in which Divine Beauty is attracted by Heroic Virtue, is transparent and conventional, merely reversing the allegory of *Love's Triumph*. Orgel examines Jones' use of lighting and machinery and concludes "the work makes its moral point far more significantly through Jones' engineering than through the action of Circe and her erstwhile lover" (I, 61). Indeed, the entire production might seem naïve and unself-conscious were it not for the final section. But this last conversation, between Cupid, Jupiter, Circe, and Pallas, instead signifies that the authors were aware of their innovations, and used them to further the meaning of their masque.

The appearance of a final group of singers after the main masque had become standard by 1632. Here Jupiter, Pallas, and Cupid consider what should be done with Circe.[16] She has injured Cupid's subjects and usurped Jupiter's "soil"; these two want to torment her. Yet, as the allegory states, "Circe here signifies desire in general, the which hath power on all living creatures, and being mixed of the divine and the sensible, hath divers effects, leading some to virtue and others to vice" (II, 482). Transformation, in other words, can raise men up the Platonic ladder as well as reduce them to beasts. Circe, not entirely evil, cannot be condemned outright. She herself reminds her companions that "the gods more freedom did allow / When Jove turned Io to a cow." Her example, chosen to equate her own actions with Jupiter's, ignores his condemnation of "the hecatombs she brings" which "scent of earth"; in the new world created by Divine Beauty and Heroic Virtue only the "pure incense" arising from virtue is acceptable. Irate at Circe's analogy, Pallas dismisses Jupiter's past errors: "Are mortal creatures grown so proud / To tax the sky for every cloud?" To her Circe indignantly replies, "Man-maid, begone!" (II, 482).

At this point in the masque—and in masque history—the casting and the masque subject intersect. Circe, who is a female singer, turns on the male singer dressed as a woman and condemns him/her for the very transformation which has been forbidden to Circe. Masque tradition gave uncertain directives about who should play Pallas. When Anne of

16. This discussion has no parallel in the *Ballet Comique*, where Circe is instead first overcome by Jove's thunder and then escorted to the king by a silent Pallas.

Denmark took the role in Daniel's *Vision of the Twelve Goddesses,* her martial appearance exposed her to Carleton's contempt. In *The Golden Age Restored* the part was played by a professional actor from the King's Men. The goddess was a perfect locus for conflict between the attitudes frequently articulated in masques, attitudes extolling beautiful passivity in women, and the classical praise for the goddess' wisdom and martial prowess. In *Tempe Restored* Pallas is the only significant character who embodies a sex–transformation, and there is a kind of logic in Circe's attitude that she does not belong in the newly established "age of gold" if transformation is banished from it.

The masque is consistent in assuming that throughout the performance the audience might look behind the roles to see who the performers are. Influences, stars, and gentleman are all significantly related to their parts: even Nicholas Lanier, Master of the King's Music, performs as the "highest sphere." Pallas' threat ("I could turn thee to a stone") shows that she does not understand the character of this newly stable world. Circe knows better: she yields all she has to "this matchless pair," Charles and Henrietta Maria. Although Jones' allegory requires that Circe "voluntarily deliver her golden rod to Minerva," in Townshend's verses this does not happen. Pallas, like Circe, is corrected (Jupiter says, "Dear daughter, cease!"), and Cupid and Jupiter debate who has brought Circe to resign. Male and masculine Pallas is transcended in the final reconciliation.[17]

Townshend's point was apparently lost on Henrietta Maria. The very next year the queen and her ladies again performed at court, this time in Walter Montague's pastoral *The Shepherd's Paradise.* The queen herself played the Princess of Navarre, but some of her ladies played in "men's apparell," as Prynne phrased it in *Histriomastix.* The outraged response accentuated the basic conflict between those who thought the person behind the performer was paramount and those who thought the players insignificant. For Prynne, women actors were always women (and notorious whores), and men actors playing women were compromising their masculinity. *Tempe Restored* had toyed with realistic casting, but under attack the masque retreated to its original position, that the whole was a perfect fiction except for the relation between the masquers and

17. The phrase "man-maid" for Pallas appears to be conventional. In *The Forrest,* 10, Jonson writes: "PALLAS, nor thee I call on, mankinde maid, / That, at thy birth, mad'st the poore Smith affraid, / Who, with his axe, thy fathers mid–wife plaid." (*Ben Jonson,* VIII, 107) Jonson's poem first appeared in an appendix to Robert Chester's *Love's Martyr* in 1601. But in *Tempe Restored* the presence of the first female singers and the theme of transformation give the phrase a force particular to the context.

their roles. As far as we know, the experimental use of female singers
was not repeated. Townshend's non-transformation was not suited to the
court because the question it raised was indirectly related to such larger
issues as the dispute between Puritans and Anglicans over the significance of ceremony and symbols; these issues could not be resolved within
the confines of the stage.

The masques following *Tempe Restored* mix two possible methods of
dealing with female roles or real women on the masque stage: an intense
platonizing which implies that the sex of all performers is ultimately
irrelevant, and the older technique which allows some of the comedy of
the antimasques to come from the partially recognized sex disguise when
men play women's roles. One last attempt to bring the masque up to date
without modifying casting methods was *The Temple of Love.* Here Davenant took the dichotomous vision of women which had been constant in
masques since *The Masque of Queens* and reworked it to fit the new
Platonic mold. The queen and her ladies are the influences who will
reestablish the temple of chaste love; they "raise strange doctrines and
new sects of love, / Which must not woo or court the person, but / The
mind" (II, 601). The magicians who oppose them attempt to hinder
destiny by presenting antimasques of the elemental spirits. The female
figures among these, such as "amorous women" or "witches," had all
been seen on the masque stage before and could all be recognizably men
to add to their comic disorder. Indamora and her ladies have "all / That
wise enamoured poets beauty call," but they use their beauty to lead
"unto the virtues of the mind." The masque's implied ladder from the
(male) unchaste women of the antimasque to the (female) chaste queen at
the top simply ignores questions of the sex of the speaking or singing
figures, Divine Poesy, "*a beautiful woman,*" "*Sunesis a man of a noble aspect,*"
"*Thelema a young woman,*" and the group of ancient Greek poets including
"*Sappho (a poetess)*" (II, 600–04). Davenant assumes that the audience has
not been misled by masques like *Tempe Restored* into trying to identify
anyone but the masquers.

An incidental difficulty of the Platonic sexless vision which Charles
and Henrietta Maria came to prefer in their masques was that the royal
couple nevertheless had to be praised for prolifically producing heirs to
the English throne. *The Temple of Love* ends with a wish for the king and
queen: "May youthful blessings still increase, / And in their offspring
never cease" (II, 604), just as if the anti-Platonic magician had not said
that Platonic lovers practice generation "not / Of bodies, but of souls"
(II, 601). *Luminalia,* which gives the queen a disembodied role as "queen

of brightness," still admits:

> Though men the blessed estate of angels praise
> 'Cause not perplexed with what we sexes call,
> Yet you by such a human difference raise
> Your virtue more because 'tis conjugal. (II, 709)

In *Luminalia* and *Salmacida Spolia,* the last two masques in which the queen took part, growing incoherence prevented definitive answers to questions about woman's place in masques and about the relation between actor and character. Because the queen and her ladies were intensely platonized, little could be done to vary their roles: having been a queen of brightness in *Luminalia,* Henrietta became the "chief heroine" full of brightness in *Salmacida Spolia.* The use of courtiers throughout the masques increased: in *Luminalia* "most of the antimasques were presented by gentlemen of quality" (II, 707). Talent, rather than appropriateness, determined roles. No systematic comparison of performers to roles in these masques was possible, since the courtiers were haphazardly mixed with professionals. For example, in *Luminalia* one antimasque was described as follows:

A cavalier in a dream being enamoured of a beautiful gentlewoman seeks by his page to win her to his love, which she seems to entertain, but he coming near to court her, suddenly is turned into a fury, which much affrights them. Represented by the Earl of Antrim and Master Bartholomew de Mountain, his page. (II, 708)

The beautiful lady turned fury must have been a professional actor or dancer. Similarly, the female fury whose *"breasts hung bagging down to her waist"* who opens *Salmacida Spolia* was an actor; he/she was joined by three additional furies played by Mr. Charles Murray, Mr. Seymour, and Mr. Tartareau (II, 731).[18] Only the queen, masqued as a heroine sent from heaven by Pallas, was to be identified with her role. But the ultimate sign of growing indifference to coherence is that the masque as performed had no indication of who sent the queen. Only a reader could follow the logic of the allegory.

The gradual disappearance of the neat formula which had differentiated masquers and antimasquers put the greatest strain on the women's parts. The complications, even absurdities, arising from having male and female "women" in one performance could be ignored so long as the audience received consistent signals for interpretation. Once these signals disappear, an entire range of possibilities emerges: professional male

18. Some of the antimasquers in *Luminalia* and *Salmacida Spolia* are identified by Reyher, who notes that the first included more "hommes de qualité" and the second "des pages et des valets de la cour" (pp. 89–90).

actors or singers may play women with no significance attached to the sex disguises, or according to the Jonsonian mode, the male performers may be used to reveal the falseness of the women they represent; courtiers may play women (William Murray, later the first Earl of Dysart, was the mistress of an old-fashioned Englishman, Mr. Ashton the wife of a country gentleman, Mr. Rimes the wife of a Dutchman, in *Salmacida Spolia*), in which case recognition of the actor seems called for but we don't know whether the actor's sex was trivial or part of the meaning; and finally the women may be represented by women singers, whose sex under the circumstances was itself very conspicuous. With its symbolic adjuration, "Man-maid, begone!" *Tempe Restored* is the climax of Caroline attempts to find a systematic method for including women. It was not only Puritan abhorrence of sex disguises but the internal logic of the masque itself which demanded changes. The line must have echoed in the ears of Killigrew and Davenant when they undertook to recreate English theatrical life in the Restoration.

The difficulty which masque writers had in presenting women in their masques, their uncertainty about the relationship between divine beauty and the wife of the jealous Dutchman, did not result exclusively from the internal theatrical situation. The writers lived in a world profoundly ambivalent about women. Although the political forms of patriarchy were still in place, family relationships were changing, rapidly for the middle class, more slowly for the aristocracy.[19] For fifty years before the accession of James, England had been ruled by queens, and the polite lies about Queen Anne's importance to her husband were true in the case of Henrietta Maria and Charles I. Prynne's book reveals not only an abhorrence of sex disguises and of the stage, but a deep distrust of women themselves. He too would banish the man-maid, but offers no substitute; female actresses are as "abominable" and intolerable as male actors in female clothes. The masque, which is a codified expression of the values of society, could not continue to exist in a world prepared to take its disagreement over those values into civil war. Thus the tensions which had grown within the masques themselves merged with the general social malaise of the 1630s. By the time solutions were found, the masque in its Jacobean and Caroline form had ceased to exist.

---

19. Lawrence Stone dates the beginning of the shift from the open lineage family to the closed domesticated nuclear family to the period 1630–1640. *The Family, Sex and Marriage in England 1500–1800,* Abridged Edition (New York, 1979).

SARA JAYNE STEEN

Fashioning an Acceptable Self: Arbella Stuart

MANY studies of Renaissance women in the last decade have focused on theories of ideal womanhood, theories that converge in a model of, as one recent book title has it, chastity, silence, and obedience.[1] The research reveals Renaissance stereotypes of a good woman to have been remarkably consistent and sanctioned by the patriarchy. English law, religion, and—notwithstanding independent female characters like Moll Cutpurse—literature supported the image of the ideal woman as humble, submissive, quiet, nurturing, sexually chaste, pious, and obedient to appropriate male authority. Even Renaissance humanists like Thomas More and Juan Luis Vives who supported education for women and encouraged their active participation in religious life did not challenge the basic notion of female subordination: man should be woman's father, teacher, husband, and spiritual guide. Conduct books proclaimed the appropriateness of this hierarchy, and popular literature on the whole reinforced it, praising the Penelopes and Constances and condemning as shrews or harlots those women whose language or actions flouted conventional sex roles. Queen Elizabeth, always conscious of the value of propaganda, was symbolically the Virgin Queen, owing sovereignty to no earthly husband.

This model of female submission dovetails neatly with King James' theories of absolutism. James saw himself as a ruler in "the stile of *Gods*,"[2] a king by divine right against whose decisions no disagreement or rebellion could be tolerated or justified. In fact, in his treatises on kingship, James explicitly draws on the patriarchal tradition to make his

---

1. Suzanne W. Hull, *Chaste, Silent, & Obedient: English Books for Women, 1475–1640* (San Marino, Cal., 1982). On these theories, see also Katherine Usher Henderson and Barbara F. McManus, *Half Humankind: Contexts and Texts of the Controversy About Women in England, 1540–1640* (Urbana and Chicago, Ill., 1985); Linda Woodbridge, *Women and the English Renaissance: Literature and the Nature of Womankind, 1540–1620* (Urbana and Chicago, Ill., 1984); and the introductory materials in Betty Travitsky, ed., *The Paradise of Women: Writings by Englishwomen of the Renaissance* (Westport and London, 1981).

2. *Basilikon Doron*, as cited in Jonathan Goldberg, *James I and the Politics of Literature: Jonson, Shakespeare, Donne, and Their Contemporaries* (Baltimore, Md., 1983), p. xi.

point about obedience. He argues that the state is a marriage in which he is the husband and head to whom his subjects are to submit in all, as a wife and children dutifully submit to a husband and father. James' expectations of his subjects, then, were willing deference and obedience; what was owed to God the Father should be given to James, His earthly representative.[3] Presumably the great misogynist expected even greater deference from female subjects; he disdained the sex as a whole and, preferring male favorites, rarely enjoyed the company of women.

The gap between ideology and practice, however, was sometimes large, and the relationship confusing.[4] Were the models of submissive woman and subject consciously imitated? Were they unconsciously imitated? To what degree did the ideas of subordination become internalized, part of a self-image? Could the models be subverted? Could they be ignored? Certainly James was both disobeyed and manipulated, and if women always had fulfilled the ideal or even attempted to, there would have been little need for conduct books or cautionary negative stereotypes. While it is difficult to know how theory interacted with practice, the letters of Arbella Stuart (1575–1615) provide an opportunity to examine that interaction in the writing of a woman of rank and education.[5]

Arbella Stuart, like most of us, was a person of contradictions, but one thing she was not was the model of humble woman or subject. Raised to be a queen, she was once dismissed from Elizabeth's court, some said for haughtiness. Her childhood was spent in the company of servants who addressed her as "your Highness," and she sometimes complained bitterly against what she felt was the injustice of her dependent position at James' court. A highly educated woman who knew six languages and loved to read, she surely had a good sense of her culture's ideal woman, but the women of rank around her in her youth—Mary Queen of Scots,

3. Jonathan Goldberg, "Fatherly Authority: The Politics of Stuart Family Images," in *Rewriting the Renaissance: The Discourses of Sexual Difference in Early Modern Europe,* ed. Margaret W. Ferguson, Maureen Quilligan, and Nancy J. Vickers (Chicago, Ill., 1986), esp. pp. 3–5. On the effect of James' theories on contemporary writers, see Graham Parry, *The Golden Age Restored: The Culture of the Stuart Court, 1603–42* (1981 ; rpt. New York, 1985) and Jonathan Goldberg, *James I and the Politics of Literature.*

4. See, e.g., Stephen Greenblatt's work including and since *Renaissance Self-Fashioning: From More to Shakespeare* (Chicago, Ill., 1980), as well as the recent work of critics like Jonathan Dollimore, Jonathan Goldberg, and Alan Sinfield.

5. This article is part of a larger study of Stuart, including an edition of her letters, that has been supported in part by the NEH, the Folger Shakespeare Library, and Montana State University.

Queen Elizabeth, and Bess of Hardwick—were active and aggressive, and Stuart's actions in marrying against James' command and attempting to escape to France made her, from the King's perspective, subversive.[6] But although her practice might differ from prevailing theories, those visions of ideal woman and subject nonetheless inform the values contained in Stuart's letters to James and other members of his court. Whether or not she internalized those concepts of subordination, even in part, in her letters Stuart rhetorically shaped a persona, a submissive self, that would be acceptable at James' court—and thereby help her achieve her ends.

Literary analysis is appropriately applied to Stuart's letters. Critics in recent years have recognized that the letter, like the autobiography, is more than a source of historical information: the letter is a literary genre, and was considered one in the Renaissance.[7] Stuart, moreover, was a highly conscious writer who took her court letters through draft after draft. Because of her rank and political importance as niece to Mary Stuart, cousin to King James and significant claimant to the throne of England, many of her letters and drafts were filed and eventually became state papers or part of private collections. As a result, her sometimes multiple drafts are extant, and it is possible to see the process by which she resolved contradictions in her thinking and rhetorically defined the Arbella she formally presented. These letters at the same time serve to extend Stephen Greenblatt's work by demonstrating that what he has said in *Renaissance Self-Fashioning* about male power to fashion a self applies as well to females.[8] To read the revisions in Stuart's court letters is to watch an intelligent and well-educated Renaissance woman craft a self in prose.

Stuart's extant letters can be divided into three forms of writing:

6. The most recent biography is David N. Durant's *Arbella Stuart: A Rival to the Queen* (London, 1978).

7. Claudio Guillén, "Notes Toward the Study of the Renaissance Letter," *Renaissance Genres: Essays on Theory, History, and Interpretation,* ed. Barbara Kiefer Lewalski, Harvard English Studies, 14 (Cambridge, Mass., 1986), pp. 70–101. Virginia Woolf pointed out the letter's importance as a literary activity for Renaissance women when she wrote of Dorothy Osborne: "Had she been born in 1827, Dorothy Osborne would have written novels. . . . But she was born in 1627, and at that date though writing books was ridiculous for a woman there was nothing unseemly in writing a letter" ("Dorothy Osborne's *Letters,*" *The Second Common Reader* [New York, 1932], p. 60).

8. Barbara K. Lewalski provides a parallel study of a woman who in a different manner self-fashioned in "Lucy, Countess of Bedford: Images of a Jacobean Courtier and Patroness," *Politics of Discourse: The Literature and History of Seventeenth-Century England,* ed. Kevin Sharpe and Steven N. Zwicker (Berkeley, Cal., 1987), pp. 52–77.

loosely structured letters from Hardwick Hall, informal letters from James' court, and formal Jacobean court letters. Although I will focus most closely on the third group of letters, the other two modes of writing provide useful comparisons. The first form is the stream of consciousness that can be therapeutic, cathartic, and lead to self-discovery. Sometimes letters that begin conventionally and with a clear sense of audience shift into writing that is an outpouring of fears, evasions, justifications, recriminations, and anger. Stuart's usual highly controlled syntax becomes more relaxed and her structure of ideas more associational, closer to what composition theorists now call freewriting. Even her handwriting may change from a formal presentation hand to a scrawl more consistent with speed and frustration. There is no way short of photographic reproduction to capture the different emotional content suggested when Stuart's ornate, upright, elegant presentation script shifts to the plain, slanted, heavier hand used in drafts and informal writing, or even when a careful informal hand becomes hasty and blotted.

Nearly all of the writings in the first category, and they are few but lengthy, are from early 1603, when Elizabeth still ruled and Stuart was under enormous psychological pressure. In late 1602, at the age of twenty-seven, the young woman that Elizabeth had hinted would succeed her was unwelcome at court and living in Derbyshire as a virtual state prisoner in the home of her maternal grandmother, the redoubtable Bess of Hardwick. Bess was in her late seventies, and as she had aged, she had found it more and more difficult to understand or control the granddaughter she had educated for the throne. As a result, Bess had become increasingly restrictive, monitoring conversations and dismissing servants who seemed too close to Stuart, a practice that led to further confrontations between the two women and redoubled Stuart's sense of confinement. She determined to escape through marriage and during the Christmas holiday secretly sent a messenger to the Earl of Hertford suggesting that if he was still interested in an engagement between her and his grandson—she had been told of such a proposal—he should send the young man to her in disguise. The alarmed Earl turned message and messenger over to Robert Cecil, Elizabeth's chief counselor, and within a few days, Sir Henry Brounker arrived at Hardwick Hall to investigate. Brounker found an offended and outraged Bess and a distraught and desperate Stuart, both well aware of the potentially severe consequences of Elizabeth's wrath.

Some of Stuart's letters over the next few months are startling to anyone familiar with Renaissance epistolary form: Stuart begins in the usual, formal style, but then anger and defensiveness overcome discretion until even the pretense of politeness is gone. For example, in a letter to Brounker from March of 1603, her "most earnest and reasonable suites that I might attend on hir Ma.^ty· or be from my Grandmother at least" having been thwarted, she angrily expostulates against the unjust counselors who have poisoned Elizabeth against her:

are the Stanhopes and Cecilles able to hinder or diminish the good reputation of a Stuart hir Ma.^ty· being iudge? haue I stained hir Maties· bloud w^t unworthy or doubtfull marriage? haue I claimed my land these .ii. yeares though I had hir Maties· promise I should haue it and hath my Lo. of Hartford regarded hir Maties· expresse com̄aundment and threatned and felt indignation so much? haue I forborne so long to send to the K. of Scots to expostulat his unkindnesse and declare my minde to him in many matters and haue no more thanckes for my labour?

She continues in this vein for pages, in language that is rhetorically impressive but politically inflammatory. Writing hurriedly and with virtually no revision, Stuart argues that her enemies at court have gathered

euery unlikely possible conceite w^t a deale of trash of theyr owne inuention and lining it w^t secret whisprings, and shaping it as best pleaseth theyr fancy who haue made you present hir Ma.^ty· w^t a mishapen discouloured peece of stuffe fitting none nor fitt for hir Ma.^ty· to looke upon which if either I might be suffered or not hindered I will not say helped but why should I not be helpt I pray you in such a peece of worke? should haue binne presented to hir Ma.^ty· in a forme well beseeming hir Ma.^ty· whearas now it is so tossed up and downe that it hath almost lost the glosse, and euen by the best slubbred up in such hast that many wrong stitches of unkindnesse must be picked out which nedd not haue binne so bestowed and many wrong placed conceits ript out whearof som̄ may be cast away but most being right placed will do very well, the more you thinck to make the more you marre when all is donne I must take it hand, and shape my owne cote according to my cloth, but it shall not be after ye fashion of this world god willing but fitt for me, and euery way becom̄ing of that vertu in me whither it be a natiue property of that bloud it cam̄ of, or an infectiue vertu of the E. of Essex who could go neither frend nor foe knew whither till he arriued amongst his unwitting enimies. . . .⁹

The run-on syntax and fluid, associational style reveal Stuart's distraught state of mind, and the content reflects a lack of regard for appropriate-

---

9. Cecil Papers, vol. 135, ff. 130v–34. Quotations from the Cecil Papers are made with the kind permission of the Most Hon. The Marquess of Salisbury, Hatfield House, Hatfield, Hertfordshire.

ness of tone or subject, especially in a letter addressed to Elizabeth's representative. Stuart's lack of caution is rarely more clear than when she suggests a parallel between her case and that of the Earl of Essex, who had been executed for treason in 1601 and was a particularly painful topic with Elizabeth. Her good friend Essex is gone, Stuart laments, also victimized by enemies, and she has never more needed a friend than now, when she is so miserable that she has spent the day verbally portraying her grief and unhappiness. One can hope the day's furious writing at least relieved some tension and frustration.

In these letters Stuart not only lashes out at her enemies, but also bemoans her fate, tries to exonerate herself, and even develops a fictional lover to force waning court attention back to her situation, using personas by turns evasive, arrogant, submissive, and flamboyant. Had such pieces remained at Hardwick, they might well have provided the catharsis of freewriting and done no more; had Stuart remodeled them, as she did her later letters, she might have made a reasonable case; had she been aware of the severity of Elizabeth's illness, she might have been more politic. However, the writings went to court and damaged her in the eyes of those who could have helped her. Even as Stuart wrote, she acknowledged her "scribling melancholy" to be a "kinde of madnesse,"[10] but if her writing was a conscious strategy to indicate the degree of her distress, it did not work as she would have hoped. In April Stuart indeed was removed from her grandmother's custody, and such writing ceased, but Brounker was annoyed and angered, and the response from Robert Cecil, to whom her letters were passed, was that the lady must have had "some strange vapours to her braine."[11] The experience may have suggested to Stuart the virtues of restraint in writing to the court.

The second form of writing among her extant papers is the informal letter, usually written to her uncle and aunt, Gilbert and Mary of Shrewsbury, after James had succeeded to the throne and been convinced to bring his cousin to court. Stuart wanted to maintain contact with the relatives to whom she felt most close and from whom she was most willing to take counsel; their side of the correspondence, unfortunately, has not survived. In Stuart's letters, written between 1603 and 1610, the Arbella persona she creates is often at ease, teasing, allusive, affectionate,

10. Cecil Papers, vol. 135, f. 135.
11. Cecil Papers, vol. 135, f. 163v.

and, especially in the early examples, an observant recorder of life at the Jacobean court.[12] From these letters come intimate glimpses of court activities—the plays at Christmas, the hunting, the lavish gifts presented by the Spanish ambassador at sumptuous dinners, the court ladies raiding the dead Queen Elizabeth's wardrobe for costumes for a masque—and revelations that are the more interesting because they come from the perspective of a well-educated woman of rank. Stuart was not always pleased with what she saw, and said so directly:

But out of this confusion of Imbassages will you know how we spend our time on the Queenes side[?] Whilest I was at Winchester theare weare certein childeplayes remembred by the fayre ladies. Viz. I pray my Lo. giue me a Course in your park. Rise pig and go. One peny follow me. &c. and when I cam̄ to Court they weare as highly in request as euer cracking of nuts was. so I was by the m.ʳˢ· of the Reuelles not onely compelled to play at I knew not what for till that day I neuer heard of a play called Fier. but euen perswaded by the princely example I saw to play the childe againe. This excercise is most vsed from .10. of the clocke at night till .2. or .3. in the morning but that day I made one it beganne at twilight and ended at suppertime.

And she mocks herself as well: she goes on, "Thear was an enterlude but not so ridiculous (as ridiculous as it was) as my l[etter] which heare I conclude wᵗ many prayers to the Almighty for your happinesse."[13] Stuart was equally direct about political issues at court, ranging from when to issue thanks for patents received—"I thinck your thanckes will com̄ very vnseasonably so neare Newyearestide. especially those wᵗ which you send any gratuity"[14]—to her relief at having been exonerated of guilt in the Main Plot to remove James and put her on the throne: "I am a witnesse not onely of the rare guifte of speach which God hath giuen him[Robert Cecil], but of his excellent iudgement in chusing most plausible and honourable Theames as The defending a wronged Lady."[15]

The informal letters contain not only court news and politics, about which Mary early cautioned Stuart to be more circumspect,[16] but casual

12. Letters written to Gilbert after Stuart's fall from grace in 1610 concern the disposition of servants she can no longer care for; in these letters, her persona is serious and concerned, but the tone of the letters is still informal.

13. 8 December 1603, to Gilbert, Talbot Papers II, f. 209v. Quotations from the Talbot Papers are made with the kind permission of the Marquess of Bath, Longleat House, Warminster, Wiltshire.

14. 8 December 1603, to Gilbert, Talbot Papers II, f. 208v. As a tactical ploy, she suggests he attribute the delay in his thanks to her or Mr. Hercy, who had not acquainted him sooner with the good news about his patents.

15. 18 December 1603, to Gilbert, Talbot Papers II, f. 210.

16. Stuart refers to the caution in her response to Mary, September 1603, Talbot Papers II, f. 192.

discussions of health and gifts and messengers and financial woes, from Stuart's toothaches, colds, and swollen eyes to her appreciation for gifts of red venison from the north. Her affection is clear and open: she writes to Mary, "your loue and iudgement together makes me hope you know I can like nor loue nothing better, then the loue and kindnesse of so honorable frends as you and my vncle,"[17] and she urges Mary to "comend me to my uncle Charles and my Aunt, and my .2. prety cousins I thinck I shall many times wish my selfe set by my cousin Charles at meales."[18] She even tries to reconcile her uncle Gilbert and her grandmother, whose former severity Stuart is willing to overlook, and her mock-threatening tone gives a good sense of the warm relationship she had with her uncle:

I found so good hope of my Grandmothers good inclination to a good and reasonable reconcilation betwixt hir selfe and hir deuided family, that I could not forbeare to impart to your Lo. w[t] all speede. Thearfore I beseech you putt on such a Christian and honorable minde, as best becometh you to beare to a Lady so neere to you and yours, as my Grandmother is. And thinck you cannot deuise to do me a greater honour, and contentme[n]t then to let me be the onely mediatour moderator and peacemaker betwixt you and hir. You know I haue cause onely to be partiall on your side so many kindenesses and fauours haue I receaued from you and so many unkindenesses and disgraces haue I receaued from the other party; yet will I not be restrained from chiding you (as great a Lord as you are), if I finde you either not willing to harken to this good motion, or to p[ro]cede in it as I shall thinck reasonable.[19]

Her persona here is both respectful and affectionate as she banters with her uncle; her syntax is controlled, and her ideas are stated forthrightly. And Stuart's informal letters, like the lengthy pieces written from Hardwick, appear rarely to have been significantly revised, although, happily, copies often were kept.

That first self, openly angry and frustrated, and that second self, observant, teasing, and lively, only rarely appear in the third mode of writing, formal letters to those associated with James and his court. These letters were written both during the years of relative calm from 1603 through 1609, when Stuart was acknowledged a ranking member of the royal family, and during the years of crisis, from her betrothal in 1610 until her death in the Tower of London in 1615. Stuart's fall from grace in 1610 was sudden and complete: having obtained James' permission to

17. 8 December 1603, to Mary, Talbot Papers II, f. 206.
18. Undated, likely March, 1608, to Mary, Talbot Papers II, f. 255.
19. 3 February 1604, Talbot Papers II, f. 222.

marry as long as she did not choose a foreign prince, Stuart immediately became engaged to William Seymour, an Oxford scholar who had a claim to the throne in his own right and, ironically, was a grandson of that Earl of Hertford who in 1603 had been so quick to turn Stuart's message over to the crown. James forbade the marriage; and although Seymour argued that they had never intended to wed without the King's consent, he and Stuart were married secretly in her apartments at Greenwich. When the ceremony was acknowledged, both were imprisoned, Stuart in Lambeth in the custody of a trusted counselor and Seymour in the rooms over Traitor's Gate in the Tower. They escaped, hoping to join each other in France, but Seymour was late, and because Stuart refused to land at Calais until she knew her husband was safe, she was recaptured and committed to the Tower. (Seymour lived in exile in France during Stuart's subsequent years of imprisonment and eventual death.) One would expect to find a marked difference in style between the court letters Stuart wrote during the peaceful years and the court letters she wrote during more tumultuous times, but the letters from the two periods are far more alike than different.

Before and after 1610, Stuart's court letters are written with a high degree of structure and formality, a formality to which her "freewriting" and informal letters form an illuminating contrast. In the court letters, Stuart rarely allows a glimpse of the open anger and stream of consciousness that occur in the writings from Hardwick Hall. And what in a newsy letter to her aunt or uncle would be the direct "Let me interrupt you with a request" becomes in a court letter the formal "I acknowledge my selfe greatly bounde to your Lo.P· and haue sent this bearer my seruant to attend your pleasure, whose important affaires I am constrained to interrupt w^t this necessary importunity."[20] What in an informal letter would be "I thank you for your help" becomes in a court letter "I aknowledge my selfe greatly bounden to your Lo: of whose patience I presume in reading these needlesse lines, rather then I would by omitting your due thanckes a short time, leaue your Lo: in the least suspence of my thanckfulnesse to you, whose good opinion and fauour I highly esteeme."[21] Stuart's rhetoric in the court letters was praised by her contemporaries, and her appeals were considered models to be read aloud in the presence chamber and commended for style. These were the letters over which she slaved in draft after draft throughout her years at

20. 26 June 1603, to Robert Cecil, Cecil Papers, vol. 100, f. 134.
21. 30 June 1603, to Robert Cecil, Cecil Papers, vol. 134, f. 39.

James' court, because her ability to use words was one way to achieve her ends through the "good offices" of those who had more power than she did.

The persona she created was humble and lowly, in accordance with the modes of the day; in fact, "humble" may be the adjective she most often applies to herself in these letters. She sends "humble thanks," and "humbly" wishes happiness and honor, and signs herself a "humble" servant or handmaid. Even for an age of flattery, however, Stuart's court letters sometimes are so deferential that we cringe at what is to us heavy-handed obsequiousness. Not all Jacobean writers carried the role of humility to such extremes as this thank you to Andrew Sinclair for serving as messenger:

> S^r. you hauing not onely performed the kindnesse I required of you in deliuering my letters to theyr Ma.$^{ts.}$ but returned me so great and vnexpected a fauour as his Ma.$^{ts.}$ letters, haue doubly bounde me to you, and I yeild you thearfore many great thanckes, beseeching you to continue in preseruing theyr Ma.$^{ts.}$ fauour to me, for which good office I most desire to become obliged to you so worthy and reverent a person.[22]

Nor were all letter-writers at court in so dependent a position: a single woman, the second lady in the land by rank and expected to conduct herself in accordance with that rank, but without income beyond a "diett" from the king's table and a small pension. Not long after Stuart arrived at court, she wrote her aunt Mary about the cost of traditional New Year's gifts and her inability even to provide presents for any but the king and queen: "This time will manifest my pouerty more then all the rest of the yeare. . . . [M]y quarters allowance will not defray this one charge I beleeue."[23] Stuart's fragile political and economic situation magnified the need for support from others and therefore for flattery and self-deprecation. In later years, soliciting others to intercede with the King about her freedom must have seemed a familiar task, given the number of times she had been forced in earlier years to seek mediators for her suits for better maintenance or payment of her pension.

Much as I would like to have found a protofeminist in the woman who escaped from imprisonment in men's clothing like one of Shakespeare's heroines, Stuart was not one. She believed that women as a sex are more virtuous than men; she wrote her uncle Gilbert "ours shall still be the purer and more innocent kinde. Theare went 10000 Virgins to heauen in

---

22. 1606, draft, Harley MSS., vol. 7003, f. 45.
23. 8 December 1603, Talbot Papers II, ff. 206v–207.

one day, looke but in the Almanack and you shall finde that glorious day."[24] But she had little understanding of the limitations placed on Queen Anne and other women at court and little sense of affinity with them. Perhaps she would have been happier had she been able to share confidences with other court women; instead, she was frustrated with what she saw as the frivolous and thoughtless activities of the "fair ladies" at court, like playing children's games until three in the morning or raiding the late Queen's wardrobe. Her informal letters make her general attitudes clear. "Our great and gratious Ladies," she writes her aunt Mary with some scorn, "leaue no gesture nor fault of the late Queene unremembred as they say who are partakers of theyr talke as I thanck God I am not."[25] Even though Stuart danced in some of the numerous court masques other women seem to have enjoyed, she preferred her books to "Court sportes"[26] and laments to her uncle Gilbert that women at court participate in the general dissipation: "I dayly see som euen of the fairest amongst us misled and willingly and wittingly ensnared by the Prince of darknesse."[27]

Rhetorically, however, she does on occasion call attention to herself as woman. Sometimes Stuart incorporates the vision of the ideal, submissive female into the formal court letters, crafting, for example, a picture of herself at her needlework—women's work[28]—making "trifles" for others to honor her by accepting, a picture that links Stuart to her aunt Mary Stuart, who also passed time with needlework and was even farther from fulfilling the submissive ideal. When Stuart asks Andrew Sinclair in 1606 to pass along a small gift of needlework to the Queen of Denmark, she emphasizes the degree to which she places herself below him: "Thus am I bold to trouble you euen w[t] these womanish toyes whose serious minde must haue som relaxation and this may be one to vouchsafe to discend to these petty offices for one that will euer wish your happinesse increase and continuance of honour."[29] She thanks

24. 8 December 1603, Talbot Papers II, ff. 208v.

25. 23 August 1603, Talbot Papers II, f. 190.

26. 8 December 1603, to Mary, Talbot Papers II, f. 206.

27. 8 December 1603, Talbot Papers II, f. 208.

28. Needlework was one of the few occupations considered appropriate for a woman at court and indeed for Renaissance women in general. Bruto urged fathers to see that daughters plied the respectable needle, not the dangerous pen (Ruth Kelso, *Doctrine for the Lady of the Renaissance* [Urbana, Ill., 1956], pp. 59–60). See also Merry E. Wiesner, "Spinsters and Seamstresses: Women in Cloth and Clothing Production," in *Rewriting the Renaissance*, pp. 191–205.

29. 1606, draft, Harley MSS., vol. 7003, f. 45.

Denmark's queen for accepting that gift which she has given "with blushing at the unworthinesse thearof . . . onely out of the confidence of the Sympathy of your gratious disposition, w^t that I found in the most puissant and noble King your husband,"[30] a man whose drunken excesses she surely deplored. Stuart perpetuates the ideal of womanly submission even as she uses submissiveness to achieve her ends—in this case to improve her position at James' court by a close relationship with his brother-in-law and sister-in-law.

Writing from confinement after her marriage, Stuart is especially conscious of the images of womanhood. She may refer to herself as another's "handmaide" or as a "poore aff[l]icted gentlewoman" or an "unfortunat woman" as she appeals to James or an unnamed intercessor or the Chief Justices of England.[31] In an entreaty to the Queen she argues that she can address herself to no one more confidently than to another woman, in this case "your Royall person (the mirrour of our sexe)."[32] She creates a verbal picture of herself to be conveyed to the Queen, along with a gift of gloves, again evoking a vision of herself at her needlework and linking the hands that sewed with the hands that would wear the work, hands that Stuart gladly would kiss in homage: "I pray you likewise present hir Ma.^{ty}· this peece of my worke which I humbly beseech hir Ma.^{ty}· to accept in remembrance of the poore prisoner hir Ma.^{ts}· most humble seruant that wrought them in hope those Royall handes will voutchsafe to weare them which till I haue the honour to kisse I shall liue in a great deale of sorrow."[33] She even once attempts to persuade James that her marriage was appropriate womanly chastity and submission to God's law; since her conscience told her that after a betrothal "I was then the wife of him, that nowe I am," to have done otherwise would have made her a "harlott." Surely, she says, a king of such "Princelie wisedome and judgem^t" would not want to see any woman so reduced in virtue, but especially not "one who hath the hono^r (howe otherwise vnfortunate soeuer) to haue anye dropp of yor Ma.^{ts} blood in them."[34]

In fact, however, Stuart's submissiveness is a conscious creation, to the

---

30. 1606, draft, Harley MSS., vol. 7003, f. 49.

31. Undated, draft, Harley MSS., vol. 7003, f. 85; undated, draft, Cotton Vespasian F. III., f. 75; undated, draft, to the Chief Justices of England, Harley MSS., vol. 7003, f. 152.

32. October 1610, State Papers Domestic, James, vol. 57, doc. 224.

33. Undated, draft, Harley MSS., vol. 7003, f. 66.

34. Undated, in her secretary's hand, Harley MSS., vol. 7003, f. 87.

extent that what she does can only be called fictionalizing, a strategy often adopted by the powerless. The drafts make clear that she frequently revised in order to add the proper flattery and convey a sense of hierarchy, especially in the last years when her ability to shape language might mean freedom. Stuart's multiple drafts, incidentally, refute the occasionally voiced argument that Renaissance women only wrote spontaneously and are therefore less worthy of study than writers who crafted their words. In a letter to her cousin Drummond, written after her fall from favor because of her relationship with Seymour, she asks that her cousin "present this letter to hir Ma.ty.," then, rethinking, inserts "in all humilitie." She wants her cousin to thank the queen "for the gratious comiseration and respect" already shown, then crosses out "and respect," as though respect, something that hints of equality, is too much to suggest. Her hope to be restored to "hir Ma.ts. fauour" is modified to "hir Ma.ts. seruice," and James' "gratious disposition" becomes "his *iust and* gratious disposition" [italics mine], as she wants to emphasize the honesty of her cause.[35] Punishment that was "onely an effect of his Ma.ts. displeasure," suggesting her guiltlessness and James' capriciousness, becomes "a signe of his Ma.ts. displeasure";[36] his "compassi[on]" becomes "that gratious disposition which moueth your Royall minde to compassion."[37] Repeatedly, Stuart's revisions illustrate a genuine sensitivity to the nuances of language, and to the creation of an appropriately deferential tone.

The longer passages that she decided to omit are sometimes even more revelatory of the shift between her initial thinking and the guarded, submissive self she finally fashioned. In a letter to Queen Anne, likely written at Christmas in 1611 after her disgrace, Stuart first wrote that the season increased her hopes of pardon "because his Ma.ty. I am sure forgiueth greater offences as freely as he desire[th] to be forgiuen by him whose Sacrament he is to receiue." Her revised version is more demure and does not suggest that the king has committed offences for which he should ask pardon: she says only that she is presenting a petition "at this time when his Ma.ty forgiueth greater offences."[38] In a letter to James, perhaps from 1610, Stuart initially wrote directly: "I haue giuen your Ma.ty. no true cause of displeasure when it shall please your Ma.ty.

35. Undated, draft, Harley MSS., vol. 7003, f. 61.
36. Undated, draft, Harley MSS., vol. 7003, f. 90.
37. 1611[?], draft, Harley MSS., vol. 7003, f. 82v.
38. Drafts, Harley MSS., vol. 7003, ff. 82v, 78.

throughly to consider of it," indicating his censure to be both unwar-
ranted and ill-considered. She then inserted "*your iust* displeasure"[italics
mine], as though to flatter him, but the change only furthered the idea of
his injustice, and she scratched out the passage entirely. The sense of it
reappears later in the letter, more humbly phrased, as "But I assure my
selfe if it please your Ma.^ty· in your owne wisdome to consider throughly
of my cause theare will no solide reason appeare to debarre me of iustice
and your princely fauour which I will endeuour to deserue whilest I
breath."[39]

The revisions in another letter to the King, written in 1611 and asking
for additional weeks to recover from her illness before being sent to the
north, well illustrate Stuart's understanding of how to manipulate James.
In an early draft she argued with some resentment that she had not been
feigning illness, as her enemies had suggested, but had tried to make her
weakness known to James "by my Lo. Fenton, and to the Lords of your
Ma.^ts· most ho. priuy counsell by writing. and many other waies. . . . But
my misfortune being such as not onely . . . any protestation of my owne
but the reiterated testimonies of such graue persons as aduertised the like
. . . seemed of lesse weight then the traducements of some whisperers."[40]
In the final version she eliminates all criticism of James' judgment and
advisors, saying only that she has "first endeauored by all good meanes to
make my extreame weakenesse knowne to your Ma:^tie" and goes on to
praise James. She thanks him for the respite she has already had—
"certenlie I had sodaynlie perished if your Ma:^tie had not speedelie had
compassion of me in graunting me this time of stay for my recouerie"—
and asks for more time: "if itt maie please your Ma:^tie of your gratious
goodnes to add 3. weekes more, M^r. Doctor Moundford hopes I maie
recouer so much strength as may enhable me to trauell. And I shall euer
be willinge whilst I breathe to yeild you^r Maiestie moste humble and
dutifull obedience as to my Soueraigne for whose felicitie for euer in all
things I cease not to praie."[41] According to Dr. Moundford, Stuart's
submission won her time; he says, "This letter was penned by her in the
best terms (as she can do right well) & accompanied with matter best
befitting his Highness & her. It was often read without offence, nay I
may truly say even commended by himself [James] with the applause of

39. Draft, Harley MSS., vol. 7003, f. 82.
40. Harley MSS., vol. 7003, f. 79.
41. Harley MSS., vol. 7003, f. 80.

prince & Councill."[42] During the weeks that followed, Stuart and Seymour prepared to escape to France.

One of the drafts of this successful letter is of particular interest because it was handwritten by someone else, perhaps because of Stuart's illness and likely at her dictation, and has angry marginal notes in a voice that sounds much like the Arbella of Hardwick Hall. Clearly it was never intended to turn up in a collection entitled Original Letters of State. For example, Stuart had been told that the King desired her obedience only as a point of honor. Beside her promise of obedience is a note indicating her disbelief: "this [promise] wth out the Jorney is inoughe if the K: desire but his hor salved." Next to her statement that she will after three weeks undergo the journey north without resistance is a bitter "as thoughe I had made resistans &c. and so the Jorney more perilous & painefull by my selfe wherevppon I must confess I bely my selfe extreemely in this." To "the dutie I owe you as my Soueryne," she comments, "I take it to bee more then I owe by my allegiance to be separated from my husband dvringe his pleasure." To "that grace & goo[d]nes from you wch one in my case may hope for," she says, "What man of grace this is I cannot guess nor in what case I am." Beside her profession that James has "my obedyant hart," she adds, "as thoughe none but this would serve."[43]

Occasionally, the anger and spirit of the freewriting and informal letters slip through in what appear to be final drafts of court letters, as when in 1607 she had to send Thomas Cuttinge, her favorite musician, to Denmark to serve the Danish king and tells the king that the loss is a sacrifice, especially since for kings "the difficulty is not to obtain a crowd of those who most excel in any art, but to limit their number";[44] or when, not long after her wedding, she excuses her actions to James by pointing out his inconsistency and neglect:

I humblie beseech your Ma: tie to consider howe impossible itt was for me to ymagine itt could be offensiue vnto yor Ma: tie havinge fewe Dayes before geven me yor Royall consent to bestowe my selfe on anie Subiect of your Ma: ts (wch likewise yor Ma: tie had done longe since). Besides neuer havinge ben either prohibited any or spoken to for anie in this land by your Ma. tie these 7 yeares that I haue liued in yor Ma: ts house I could not conceiue that yor Ma: tie regarded my Mariage att all.[45]

---

42. Sloane MSS., vol. 4161, f. 61v.

43. Harley MSS., vol. 7003, f. 83v.

44. Harley MSS., vol. 7003, f. 37; as trans. from the Latin in E. T. Bradley, *Life of the Lady Arabella Stuart* (London, 1889), 2:220.

45. Draft in secretary's hand, Harley MSS., vol. 7003, f. 57; draft in Stuart's hand, f. 82.

Despite the "I humblie beseech," her tone is hardly submissive here; instead, her indignation is only lightly veiled.

More often when the situation is important, however, Stuart increases the rhetoric of deference. Writing likely within a short time of her marriage, Stuart creates a picture of herself "humbly on my knees"; her plea is that if she has displeased James, he will "lett itt be covered wth the Shadowe of yor gratious benignitie, & pardoned in that heroicall mynd of yo.^rs wch is never closed to those who carrie A most Loyall hart to yor Soveraintie, [and] A most sincere & Dutifull affeccon to yor p[er]son."[46] As the years of imprisonment stretched out and she became increasingly fearful that she would never rejoin her husband or even be freed, the degree of submission in her rhetoric well indicates the degree of her desperation. She writes, for example, to beg a lord's intercession with those close to the king: "my weaknesse not permitting me to write particulerly I haue made choice of your Lo. humbly beseeching you to moue as many as haue any compassion of my affliction to ioyne in humble mediation to his Ma.^ty. to forgiue me the most penitent and sorrowfull creature that breathes."[47] Despite her unhappiness and her illness, Stuart was still consciously revising to create the deferential tone: the "humbly beseeching you" was an addition.

What has traditionally been thought the last petition drafted to James before Stuart's death in 1615 is written on a torn sheet of paper that appears stained with tears. For the only time in the extant letters, she clearly indicates regret for her marriage, whether she means it or not, and she does so in rhetoric that should have been humble enough to satisfy the most absolutist king, rhetoric that to a modern ear sounds an ironic note: "In all humility the most wretched and vnfortunate creature that euer liued prostrates it selfe at the feet of the most mercifull King that euer was desiring nothing but mercy and fauour, not being more afflicted for any thing then for the losse of that which hath binne this long time the onely comfort it had in the world, and which if it weare to do againe I would not aduenture the losse of for any other worldly comfort, mercy it is I desire, and that for Gods sake."[48] It is not certain that James received the petition; in any case, no mercy was forthcoming.

Those who received Stuart's court letters were aware that she was not reared to fulfill the traditional models of woman or subject, but to rule.

46. Harley MSS., vol. 7003, f. 85.
47. Harley MSS., vol. 7003, f. 149.
48. Harley MSS., vol. 7003, f. 146.

Certainly those who knew her at all well must have seen a contradiction between the rhetoric of her court letters and her speech and actions, which in her early years at James' court were sometimes imperious— Thomas Cooke wrote to her aunt Mary with some alarm in 1604 that she had "wrastled extraordenaryly" with the king's advisors for access to the king,[49] and Ian McInnes describes her as having had scores to settle at court and using her tongue sharply to do so.[50] Surely there were times when her humble persona provoked amusement from those who could well imagine the thoughts behind the words. And sometimes the contradiction between her words and her actions may have meant that her rhetoric was received with annoyance or resentment by those who realized they were being manipulated. The one time James accepted Stuart's statements of submission and granted her an extension before her journey to exile in the north, she used the time to recuperate and plan an escape to France. No matter how unjust were many of James' choices in relation to Stuart, it is understandable that he would not easily accept his cousin's words of humility or penitence at face value.

That Stuart felt little affinity for the submissive role and that her other forms of writing contain such strikingly different personas make it all the more significant that the models of deferential woman and obedient subject so strongly inform her court letters. Apparently she believed that her society's expectations of a woman and her King's expectations of a subject were entrenched enough that any other self would receive less approval and have less success in achieving her goals, perhaps even threaten her precarious position at James' court. To that extent the theories mattered in practice; they affected what she wrote. And the creation of the humble persona must have evoked for Stuart the contradiction between the court dominance for which she was educated and the subservience dictated by James' accession and supported by her society. While Stuart may never have fully reconciled what Mary Beth Rose describes in women's autobiographies as "the felt conflict between self-effacement and self-assertion, between private and public life, and between individual personality and social role,"[51] it is heartening to see that cultural expectations did not altogether color what Stuart thought

49. Lambeth Palace Library, MSS. 3203, f. 182.

50. *Arabella: The Life and Times of Lady Arabella Seymour, 1575–1615* (London, 1968), pp. 133–34.

51. "Gender, Genre, and History: Seventeenth-Century English Women and the Art of Autobiography," in *Women in the Middle Ages and the Renaissance: Literary and Historical Perspectives,* ed. Mary Beth Rose (Syracuse, N.Y., 1986), p. 247.

of herself. In her informal letters she often sounds lively and confident; and in the unrevised drafts and marginal notes of the court letters we hear a voice that certainly did not speak as humble woman or subject. Stuart chafed at the role.

What may be most important in terms of our understanding of Renaissance women is that Stuart's revisions argue her submissive persona to have been carefully fashioned. That she employed the persona does not mean she accepted her subordination as right and just; it does mean that she was aware of the social and literary conventions as conventions and saw that they could be manipulated to her advantage. Even though she had little interest in women in general, and even though she ultimately failed to achieve her goals, Stuart's creation of a deferential self was an attempt to exploit the patriarchal models and use the language of flattery and obedience as an indirect means of achieving control when overt power was unavailable.

Stuart may have taken pride in her ability to craft an acceptable self so well and promote her ends, especially in her early years at court, when, despite her rank and attendants, she was only a poor relation. After her marriage and escape, no rhetoric would have been good enough to ease James' compulsive fears of the threat she and any child of hers could pose to him and his heirs. From my perspective as a modern feminist, Stuart perpetuated the roles by adopting them, and it is sad that she felt she had to do so. At the same time it is fascinating to watch a verbally talented woman give rhetorical shape to a self she thought would be more acceptable to a misogynistic king and his court than her unreformed one ever could be.

CAROLYN RUTH SWIFT

Feminine Identity in Lady Mary Wroth's Romance Urania

IN 1621 Lady Mary Wroth published *The Countesse of Mountgomeries Urania* (STC 26051), a beautiful folio divided into four lengthy books, approximately 600 pages of prose and poetry that concludes with the sonnet sequence *Pamphilia to Amphilanthus*. An unpublished 145-page manuscript, evidently in Wroth's own hand[1] and now at the Newberry Library, continues the story into a second generation but remains incomplete. Generally ignored today, Lady Wroth was recognized by many of her contemporaries. But while patronage may explain the attention of Jonson, Wither, and Chapman, still many of her 120 songs and sonnets, as well as much of *Urania*, can justify both her own contemporaries' praise and the study of modern scholars.[2]

Herford and Simpson in their edition of Jonson describe briefly Lady Wroth's *Urania* as "gracefully" continuing "the Arcadian-Sidneyan tradition of her uncle" (I, 54–55). But Wroth seems to have begun her book with a deeper interest in the nature of women than is apparent in Sidney's *Arcadia*. While her title, *The Countesse of Mountgomeries Urania*, is deliberately reminiscent of *The Countesse of Pembrokes Arcadia*, Sidney's subject is the "alienation of men" from "the idyllic world to which they have

1. Margaret Witten-Hannah, "Lady Mary Wroth's *Urania:* the work and the Tradition," Diss. University of Auckland (1978), p. 110.

2. See also Josephine A. Roberts and Paul Salzman cited below, G. F. Waller, ed. *Pamphilia to Amphilanthus, Elizabethan and Renaissance Studies,* 64 (Salzburg, Austria, 1977); May Nelson Paulissen, *The Love Sonnets of Lady Mary Wroth: A Critical Introduction, Salzburg Studies in English Literature,* 104 (Salzburg, Austria, 1982); Josephine A. Roberts, ed. *The Poems of Lady Mary Wroth* (Baton Rouge, La., 1983). Contemporary praise of Wroth is in Joshua Sylvester, *Elegaic-Epistle Consolatorie* (1614), sig. Y1; George Chapman, *Homer Prince of Poets* (1610), sig. Ff2; George Wither, *Abuses Stript and Whipt* (1613), sig. X4; Ben Jonson, *The Alchemist* (1612), and *Underwood,* 23, Herford and Simpson, II, 393. Roberts quotes seventeenth-century praise of *Urania* by William Davenport in his annotations, Introduction to *Poems* p. 29.

retreated."[3] Wroth's subject is the alienation of women from men.

Sidney's prose romance begins when Urania leaves Arcadia (*NA*, 20).[4] She appears so seldom, however, that she soon becomes a symbol of lost simplicity and virtue.[5] In what seems a deliberate reversal, Wroth's *Urania* begins with Urania's search for her parents, a symbol of the female quest for identity that shapes much of the long narrative. While Urania is only one of many women seeking to find themselves, she is also the most important commentator on the book's many courtly adventures. Queen Pamphilia's constant love for the unfaithful King Amphilanthus is the central story, from which myriad friends and relatives depart and return to narrate mirroring adventures. Wroth's double emphasis on the spiritual quests of women and the heroic adventures of knights offers us insights into the ambivalence with which a seventeenth-century woman viewed a society that subordinated even the most talented of her sex.[6]

Within her Jacobean awareness that the world is dangerous and that human life implies betrayal,[7] Wroth reveals the loss of identity that women experience in a society that victimizes them; both the narrator and characters sometimes devalue women as Wroth and her work were devalued in her own life. Two months after publication, for example, Wroth had to withdraw *Urania* from sale when Edward Lord Denny complained bitterly that she had satirized his family. In reply, Wroth vigorously defended her "harmless book." She transformed Denny's

3. A. C. Hamilton, "Sidney's *Arcadia* as Prose Fiction: Its Relation to Its Sources," *English Literary Renaissance*, 2 (1972), pp. 36–37. Another book which may have influenced Wroth's choice of title was Guillaume de Salluste Du Bartas' "L'Urania," *La Muse Chrestiene* (Bordeaux, 1574), translated into English by James I (1585) and by Joshua Sylvester (1605), who admired Wroth. Du Bartas' Urania urges him to write new religious verse with courage. Perhaps Wroth saw herself as equally exploring new insights.

4. There are two texts of *Arcadia:* the *Old Arcadia* which circulated in MS but was not published until the twentieth century and the *New* (or revised) *Arcadia* (*NA*), published in 1590 and 1593. References are to the ed. by Albert Feuillerat (Cambridge, 1912).

5. Myron Turner compares Sidney's Urania to "the heavenly Venus of Renaissance Platonism" in "The Disguised Face of Nature; Image and Metaphor in the Revised *Arcadia*," *English Literary Renaissance*, 2 (1972), 116. Roberts says of *Pamphilia to Amphilanthus* that it concentrates on Pamphilia's "ambivalence between self-assertion and dependence, skeptical detachment and trust." "The Biographical Problem of Pamphilia to Amphilanthus," *Tulsa Studies in Women's Literature*, 1 (1982), 51.

6. Hilda L. Smith, *Reason's Disciples; Seventeenth-Century Feminists* (Urbana, Ill., 1982), p. 6, discusses feminists in the latter half of the century. Wroth's *Urania* suggests that women's consciousness of female subordination existed earlier.

7. The intricate examples of perfidy in Jacobean drama are too numerous to require specific documentation.

of mortalls all, butt I would nott bee
for sone was lightes inthroned to see,

Soe loue of all things hath most styles
and noe thing more then loue is stylde,
then Cupid take thy honor right,
thou'rt neither God, nor Earthly spright:/

The winde a sifting, and often a troublous companion whispering, and offring into euery corner, and euery so doe mischiefe, as if in spite, or soone as I had writen thus, I confess foolish lines, and read them, laying them by, the trecherous Boreas wth a curld blaste blew the paper from mee, raising itt a pritty height, soe as I beleued itt would nott rest till itt were at distance from mee, Fame quick of foote folowed itt, chasing as the lightning as it to express my folleys or more then mine owne eyes, wch I had ill thus euer kept secret, though by many besought to shew some, I still answering thus, imagined more in mee then was, for I could neuer make lines owragie, but now they flew to som tune, for after I had run a pretty way, I saw the paper lighte, I then ran faster, and thinking to stoope to take itt vp, I saw the brauest knighte that euer had ouer beheld, lifting him self a little vp in that poore thing in his hand to read them, hauing don besseiged what can this bee, this is the flannel dedicated to loue, and can his greatnes bee thus reuiled, and condemned in his owne Souerainities, O Gods see what reason is this, then looking of the paper parceauing mee, but if you bee that iealser circle bee, you will quickly make a rebellion, and Crowne yodein Venus place, then heauily rising, surprised, and I amased all soe vnexpected, and admireable a sighte, hee then came towards mee, I amased stood still, senceles, of certainty I had fled, when hee in a seemly and yett fearfull maner, least offence mighte proceed from itt, spake these to mee, Most to bee admired, and yett feared if this bee yours, and your opinion against him soe strict, giue mee leaue to aske some question of you wherby to bee assured to whom I speake, that my respectiue dueties may now bee mistaken: Fairest of ladyes (O pardon mee farr more excelling, and in comparison deemest Beauties) my owne guiltines of such wants makes mee blush to death, rather then bee able to proceed in soe high a straine wth rather, and surely wrought from the high straine of his witt, then from any defect in mee poore mee a rag of the rich piece of beauty indeed, cutt of as the fag end of perfections truely in beauties Court, as shreds bee of whole peeces, Sweet Madame sayd Exampliana disprise vs nott the happines to haue all the story, since you speake in this temple him self who is as worthy as or temples may bee, and of whose wordes, and true judgment in all things I am extreamly well assured nor is braue Andromarko any thing att all mistaken in that his comending of your perfections, since had hee sayd lesse, hee had infinitely lessened his owne judgment, and him an vnworthy beholder of such vertues, if nott by him (who can as well as any sett them forth) hee had sluggishly, or poorely spoke of such surprising, and truly conquering perfections, wch wth soe much ease do itt sett though tortures to others make such safe victories, therfor proceed sweetest surely, for you that knowe the powers rule allmost matchles, shallbee infinitely pleased to heare relations of his loue way to shew surprising...

satiric poetic attack that she was an "hermaphrodite, in show, in deed a monster," into an attack on his drunken dyspepsia, his "hateful words" and "Dirty doubt." Wroth vigorously rejected the stigma of female writer as "female anomaly" that Margaret Cavendish would accept only fifty years later.[8] Even so, in an age when women rarely published, her book was doomed, and Wroth published nothing else, ending what Josephine A. Roberts has called a "pioneering venture in publication."[9]

But despite Wroth's apology in her letter to the Duke of Buckingham that she never intended her book to be published,[10] her prolific poetry and prose as well as her forceful response to Denny indicates her pride in authorship. She also emblazoned her own name on an elegantly engraved title page, although she lived in an age when women authors were usually "Anonymous." Perhaps she tried to validate her own writing by including also the names of her uncle and aunt, Sir Philip Sidney and Lady Mary Herbert, the Countess of Pembroke. Certainly Wroth's insistence on Denny's folly reveals her pain at her book's suppression. Ironically, her book's fate proved the truth of her theme—that society limited women unreasonably and harmed them in the process.

Although critics caution each other to treat literary characters as wholly imaginary creations, the characters in *Urania* clearly reveal a talented woman author's creative reaction to the restrictions of her age. Scholars have revealed a close connection between the plot and characters of *Urania* and Wroth's own life. Roberts associates the male lover in Wroth's poetry (Amphilanthus) with Wroth's lover, the Earl of Pembroke; it follows that in *Urania* Pamphilia may represent Wroth herself.[11] Roberts and Paul Salzman also have noted that Lord Denny was probably correct in charging that Wroth had drawn upon his family history

8. See Dolores Poloma, "Margaret Cavendish: Defining the Female Self," *Women's Studies,* 7 (1980), 55–66. Roberts in her Introduction to *The Poems,* p. 34, points out that Cavendish quoted Denny's attack on women writers in her *Sociable Letters* (Menston, Eng., 1969), sig. b.

9. "An Unpublished Literary Quarrel Concerning the Suppression of Mary Wroth's 'Urania' (1621)," *Notes and Queries,* (Dec. 1977), 533–34, and the Appendix to *The Poems.*

10. Historical Manuscripts Commission, *Appendix to the II Report,* p. 60, 15 Dec. 1621, photographed and quoted by Roberts in *The Poems,* p. 77, and Appendix, p. 236. Roberts points out that Wroth also wrote an unpublished play, *Love's Victorie,* now at the Huntington Library (MS HM 600.) Witten-Hannah, pp. iv, 67, argues that *Urania* was pirated, but I believe she contradicts her own argument by citing Wroth's gift of the book to Lord Buckingham.

11. Roberts, *Notes and Queries,* (Dec, 1977), 533–34, *TSWL,* 1, 48–49, 51; Paul Salzman, "Contemporary References in Mary Wroth's *Urania,*" *Review of English Studies,* 29 (1978), 178–81. See also Roberts' Introduction to *The Poems,* pp. 30–35. Witten-Hannah calls *Urania* "documentary," pp. iv, 46.

when she condemned a father "strange" enough to threaten to kill his only daughter because he identified with his irrationally jealous son-in-law (pp. 438–39). Denny's recorded self-recognition confirms my claim that Wroth's diligent portrayal of unfaithful knights and unhappy ladies reflects the world she knew. The point is further supported by a letter from George Manners, Earl of Rutland, asking Wroth to decipher her code: "You once showed me a manuscript in your study at Barnard's Castle. Meeting here with your *Urania,* I send the enclosed and beg you to interpret the names as I have begun them."[12] Like Denny, Rutland evidently recognized his friends in Wroth's chivalric romance. In addition, Wroth's characters even embody their author's awareness of real societal injustice to women.

But reality was often intertwined with chivalric romance in the sixteenth and early seventeenth centuries. As Queen Elizabeth surrounded her life with romantic fictions,[13] so letters reveal that courtiers gilded life with chivalry. Wroth's father, for example, wrote to his wife about their "young knight," his son. A 1613 ledger in the Rutland MSS. also reminds us that men in fact wore accoutrements of fully armed knights still seen in their paintings: "Item paid to knight that drew the armes with helmet, crest, and mantlines in 4 escocheons, upon 2 banners for 2 trumpetes."[14] As popular romances today embellish heterosexual family life in middle-America,[15] so the seventeenth-century chivalric romance gave courtly readers in Renaissance England a model and validation.

Because *Urania,* like all fiction, can be understood on some levels through its own stated standards, its action, and its character, this essay does not unravel topical allegories that caused contemporary scandals. Section I compares Wroth's view of women's abilities in *Urania* with the view in traditional romances. Sections II and III examine Wroth's tales of women's "ruine" (p. 395) in romance and marriage. Section IV concludes that Wroth viewed society as destructive of woman's sense of self. To show how Wroth's views differ from the views of Renaissance

12. *MSS. of the Earl of Rutland,* I.520. R. T. Olney of the Royal Commission of Manuscripts, wrote me that "There is no report here of the survival of the enclosure." Rutland refers to "Bainard's Castle" in London which Sir Robert Sidney rented from Lady Pembroke in 1594. *De L'Isle and Dudley,* II, 157.

13. Stephen Greenblatt, *Renaissance Self-fashioning* (Chicago, 1980), p. 166.

14. *De L'Isle and Dudley,* IV, 239; *Rutland,* IV, 493, 494.

15. Janice A. Radway, "Women Read the Romance: the Interaction of Text and Context," *Feminist Studies,* 9 (1983), 72.

men, I occasionally contrast *Urania* with the *Arcadia,* and with some of Shakespeare's plays. Where possible, I compare the action in *Urania* with seventeenth-century demographic studies and with my study of English family letters as well as the facts of Wroth's life.

I

Lady Mary Wroth's childhood probably encouraged her interest in romance as well as her sensitivity to unequal treatment of women. The daughter of Robert Sidney, Earl of Leicester, and Lady Barbara Gamage, Mary Sidney (born c. 1585) grew up, as did her heroine Pamphilia, with many brothers and sisters.[16] Letters in the Sidney papers reveal that her parents fostered her interest in books but catered to her brother's education. Sir Robert Sidney's agent Rowland Whyte wrote to him, "God bless her, she is very forward in her learning, writing, and other exercises, she is put to, as dauncing and the virginals."[17] Sir Robert secured books for her and encouraged her artistic talents, but he believed formal education important only for boys. He wrote his wife:

For the girls I kan not mislike the care you take of them: but for the boies you must resolve to let me have my wil. For I know better what belongs to a man than you do. Indeed I wil have him ly from his maide, for it is time, and now no more to bee in the nurcery among wemen. I wil not stick to give the schoolmaster whom you speak of 20 [pounds] a yeare, if I kan heare of his sufficiency. But then wil I have the boy delivered to his charge onely, and not to have him when he is to teach him, to be troubled with the women.

In contrast, Sir Robert was evidently satisfied to hear that Mary enjoyed reading and that she danced before the Queen.[18] This home must have ripened Wroth's awareness of the inequality of men and women even as it fostered her wide reading and her own romantic fantasies.

Urania draws heavily upon tradition although it alters traditional content and attitude. In accord with medieval romance conventions,[19] Wroth's heroines have perfect beauty, but she uses this stereotype to

16. Family letters clearly show the Gamage-Sidney marriage to have been a striking success. See also Lawrence Stone, *The Crisis of the Aristocracy, 1558–1641* (Oxford, 1965), p. 660, and Roberts in her Introduction to *The Poems.*

17. *De L'Isle and Dudley,* II, 176.

18. *De L'Isle and Dudley,* II, 269–70, 321, 618; III, 412, 464; IV, 44, 229, 234–35.

19. For a forceful, feminist summary of these conventions, see Adelaide Evans Harris, "The Heroine of Middle English Romances," *Western Reserve University Bulletin* (New Series), 31 (Aug. 1928) 2:2. Witten-Hannah (Chapter V) urges that Wroth's spectacular description of scene and costume derives from her interest in the masque rather than from the romance tradition.

reject masculine standards of female beauty and virtue. For example, Sidney creates ugly women as a source of brutal comedy: Misa is "so handsome a beldame, not onely her face and her splayfoote have made her accused for a witch" (*NA*, p. 21). Although such merciless descriptions may parody earlier stereotypes of female perfection,[20] he exploits such women. Thus the hero Pyrocles makes love to the infatuated Mopsa only in order to court Pamela (*NA*, p. 116) in a brutal comedy that pains this modern reader. In contrast, heroines in *Urania* are beautiful because Wroth finds in women a wit, courage, and spirit that create beauty. She alters the medieval stereotype of female perfection, however, by recognizing that women have faults equal to men's: women are "the children of men, and like them fault-full" (p. 36).

As in earlier romances, women in *Urania* rely on men for aid, yet Wroth changes the romance's stereotype of female passivity since her women characters sometimes venture forth alone. Leandrus wonders that Pamphilia will reject his courtship to "adventure without guard." She responds with some humor that she does not need him: "my person, my greatness, and these walls are sufficient warrants and guardians for my safety" (p. [178], printed p. 170). Her friend Antisia (Antissia) walks alone by the sea in humble dress in order to talk with travellers about their adventures (p. 267). The more venturesome Neriana "exercises the part of an adventurous lover" (p. 165), travelling unaccompanied into the woods.

Unlike other romances, however, Wroth's female characters have also developed unusual skills. One group of women actually fights (p. 108),[21] and a lady discourses "of martial things, being excellently learned in all the arts" (p. 154). In Sidney's *Arcadia* Basilius shares his hunting enthusiasm with Zelmane, the Amazon (*NA*, p. 67), but in *Urania* the lady takes the knight Dolorindus hawking (p. 154). In *Urania* as in *Arcadia* (*NA*, p. 96) women go fishing, a sport some seventeenth-century women in fact enjoyed,[22] although in *Urania* they evidently always hope to catch men as well as fish (pp. 240–41, 270). Pamphilia hunts deer with as much zest as she writes poetry, reads and pursues delicate conversations.[23]

20. Hamilton argues that Sidney responds to early male stereotypes when he debases his heroes (pp. 39–40).

21. Paloma, p. 63, discusses women warriors in Margaret Cavendish's work.

22. As in a letter by Elizabeth Knyvett to her son where she reports she is only catching eels and the fish she herself stocked; see the Bacon-Townsend Papers, L.d. 386, at the Folger Shakespeare Library. Letters in *Rutland*, I. 251, 423 likewise cite women interested in hunting.

23. Pp. 154, 299, 222, 181, 222.

Wroth's respect for women's capabilities probably grew from her own close friendships with other women. *The Countesse of Mountgomeries Urania* is named for her friend and cousin Susanna Herbert, the Countess of Montgomery, and her father's letters to her mother record "merry" meetings at Penshurst and in London between his "daughter Wroth" and "Lady Lucy," the Countess of Bedford, Lady Hoby, and Lady Arundel as well. In *Urania,* Wroth transforms the earlier romance pattern of heroine and confidante[24] into genuine friendship among women. Pamphilia and Antisia deeply mourn their impending separation, "lying together, and with sad but loving discourse passing those dark hours" (p. 123). Urania and Pamphilia loyally remain friends through two generations.

Wroth's understanding of intense female friendship helped her to treat the possibility of romantic love between women with more respect than her uncle did in *Arcadia.* Sidney dresses his hero as an Amazon because he views him as debased—rendered partly effeminate—by love for a woman. In *Urania,* by contrast, because Veralinda once loved Leonius when he dressed as a woman, she can see his virtues more clearly. "I am (my Lord) said shee, the woman that loves you as much, or more, if possible, then I did, having so many more bonds to tye me unto it" (p. 389). Their love is validated because he is really a man, but Veralinda asserts her love for Leonius' feminine self to be as great as for his masculine.

Although Wroth herself was bold enough as an author to write a sympathetic tale of a woman who thinks she loves another woman, the women in her romance are discreet, and whatever sexual acts they commit are euphemized. Lovers share "stolen and sweet delights" (p. 384). Evelina is "a woman free" who "freely offer[s]" herself in love (p. 252). "Honor" may be lost by a long courtship (p. 244). One pair of lovers "enjoy" each other after three years, "nor was ought denied." The few wicked women in *Urania* share the vice of "immoderate and ungovernable passions" (p. 43), while most women in *Urania* are temperate and speak decorously as Renaissance tracts on manners advised.[25]

However, Wroth's definition of decorous female speech differs from that in conventional romance. Whereas silence is one of Sidney's ideals for women (*NA,* p. 32), Wroth praises a woman's usual courtesy of

---

24. *De L'Isle and Dudley,* IV, 158, 234, 276, 282–83, 450; V, 409, 412, 414. Barbara Louise Magaw, *The Female Characters in Prose Chivalric Romance in England, 1475–1603* (Diss. University of Maryland, 1973). p. 23.

25. Pearl Hogrefe, *Tudor Women: Commoners and Queens* (Ames, Iowa, 1975), pp. 3–9.

silence only once, when she justifies Pamphilia's speaking without "respect" to an equally rude Amphilanthus (p. 50). "Sweet mildness" (p. 171) and "loveliness" (p. 255) are virtues in both men and women. As Wroth praises the "womanish part" in men (p. 255), she praises women whose "perfections are styled masculine" (p. 134). Thus in *Urania* women characters usually speak firmly and assertively. As a result, they articulate their pain at a society that values them only in courtly love affairs and in marriage.

II

Urania validates women but shows their limited spheres of action. With courage, Urania enters a cave in which she fearlessly examines the corpse of a knight who suddenly revives (pp. 2–3). That image of feminine courage describes the role of women in the society that Wroth creates in *Urania*. With bold hearts, they venture into the dark caves to find that society accepts them only, as the knight Steriamus later says, if they "comfort the souls of men" privately in romance and marriage (p. 159).

Wroth makes clear that a seventeenth-century woman was usually dependent on men for self-respect and survival, no matter what her talents or his failings. Consequently, the vibrant female fishers and hunters in *Urania* willingly become "prisoners" in the "House of Love," "fettered" (p. 242) "with linkes of gold enamelled with Roses" (p. 141). The image of men as prisoners of love is familiar in courtly literature.[26] Nevertheless, Wroth uniquely depicts the effects of obsessional love on women. In her image of gold-enamelled fetters, she recognizes that fantasy itself induces captivity to love, not the saintly but cruel mistress so often blamed in romances by men.

As a woman, Wroth knew that women can become enthralled in a love-game that may end in marriage to an overly possessive man or in an adulterous love affair that compensates for a miserable marriage. With venturesome spirits, women imagine the "sumptuous" House of Love to be "some magicall work," although they know that jealousy and grief usually ensue (p. 39). Men experience love's torments too; some are "fellow prisoners in the Castle of love" (p. 242), but others go on to new adventures. All the women in the towers of desire remain fettered by

---

26. See Geoffrey Chaucer, "The Romaunt of the Rose," *Complete Works*, ed. F. N. Robinson (Boston, 1957), l.5142.

what Wroth fittingly calls an "enemy within" (p. 395).

Even her virtue contributes to a woman's "ruine" in love (p. 395). Pamphilia grieves that she may "have a vertue, and loose all thereby" (p. 161) as her constancy traps her in love for an inconstant man. Trapped by her values, she ignores the ironic warnings of a romance she reads whose subject (like *Urania's*) was Love. "The story she then was reading, the affection of a Lady to a brave Gentileman, who equally loved, but being a man, it was necessary for him to exceede a woman in all things, so much as inconstansie was found fit for him to excell her in, hee left her for a new." Pamphilia throws the book away as disgracefully scoffing at love (p. 264), but Amphilanthus her lover, whose name means "lover of two," is away loving others.

To explain the hazards of love, Wroth generalizes male infidelity. Pamphilia's friend Limena tells her of a woman who learns that "mens words are only breath, their oathes wilde, and vows water" (p. 190). Musalena, the Queen of Bulgaria, warns that even "the best men, will and must change, not that he does it purposely, but tis their naturall infirmitie, and can not be helped" (p. 375). Musalena echoes the romance that Pamphilia previously had read: tradition calls women unfaithful, but men, "who excell us in all perfections, would not for their honours sake, let us surpass them in any one thing"—not even infidelity (p. 375).

This emphasis on male inconstancy is a main point of contrast between *Urania* and its predecessor, *Arcadia*. Sidney presents as a chivalric ideal the constant Argalus, who loves his wife even after she becomes scarred.[27] In *Urania* women's bodies always defeat them. One woman finds her lover "slighted her and told her she was growne old and her beauty altered; willed her to recover that [beauty] to regain him" (p. 248). Bellamira too loses her lover when she loses her youthful beauty (p. 335). Although even Sidney considers Argalus' Arcadian constancy unusual enough to cause Musidorus' delight (*NA,* p. 35), his protagonists, Pyrocles and Musidorus, also remain continually faithful to their women in startling contrast to the many fickle male lovers in *Urania.* Even if Wroth's greater stress on male infidelity is the result of Jacobean cynicism opposed to Sidney's Tudor idealism, she differs from those Jacobean writers we know best by insisting also that women are more constant than men (p. 159) and by stressing that their constancy to unfaithful lovers is painful and self-destructive.

27. Hamilton discusses Argalus as ideal (pp. 53–59).

Even Shakespeare, who recognized that Desdemona and Ophelia are destroyed by a husband's or lover's idealization, does not seriously recommend inconstancy. Emilia will make her husband a cuckold to win him a world, but her advice to Desdemona is comic in its dramatic effect. Urania's "excellent wit," in contrast, defines Pamphilia's constancy as a virtue "with limits." When Pamphilia boasts she would love Amphilanthus if he had never loved her or even if he had despised her, Urania does not respond, as we might expect, by praising her friend's faithfulness as a model for all women. She says, "'Tis pity . . . that ever that fruitlesse thing constancy was taught you as a vertue, . . . understand, this vertue hath limits . . . those . . . with whom it is broken are by the breech free to leave or choose again where more staidness may be found" (p. 400).

Such counsel to reject conventional virtue also occurs in Sidney's *Arcadia,* but when the evil Cecropia urges Pamela not to "love Virtue servillie," she is attempting a seduction (*NA,* p. 406). Urania, on the contrary, has offered Pamphilia a remarkable interpretation of feminine virtue as free of martyred loyalty. She explains that she herself has died to one love in order to "revive" (p. 160). Her imagery stresses that virtuous women must be inconstant to inconstant men in order to "revive" in self-respect.

Even in the last published book of *Urania,* Amphilanthus deserts Pamphilia again and returns to vow fidelity. In spite of Amphilanthus' clear perfidy in love, Pamphilia accepts him again from "pure love and"—as Wroth says very pointedly—"unfortunate subjection." He has used her so "vildly" that Perselina wonders why she will "endure him" (p. 452), and so do we when Pamphilia says, "can he smile on these wrinckles, and be loving in my decay? When hee told me I was altered for the worse and sleightly regarded me, I feared" (p. 482). Wroth excised Sidney's noble and faithful Argalus from her vision.

Hermione, the Queen in *The Winter's Tale,* remains faithful to her scoundrel King, and as a reward is accepted with her wrinkles at the play's conclusion. But Wroth makes clear, as Shakespeare never does, that she regrets her heroine's "unfortunate subjection" in this endless game of loving inconstant men. She also makes clear by ending her published narrative with the word "And," as if more were to follow, that Pamphilia's subjection is endless. Unlike Shakespeare's Leontes, Wroth's Amphilanthus will betray again and again. Even in the manuscript, Amphilanthus becomes faithful only after both he and Pamphilia marry others in despair. His faithfulness exists only within inconstancy.

III

In *Urania,* romantic love is a delusion, but marriage is a trap. Married women tell their own pain-filled stories to adventuring knights and ladies, who are only rarely able to rescue them. Wroth creates an exquisite symbol of marital misery early in her book in the story of Limena, whose cruel husband ties her to a pillar by her own hair (p. 68) in order to whip her and then pour salt in her wounds (p. 72). Just as Limena's own hair binds her to her torture, the female virtue of constancy binds women to painful romances, and the virtue of obedience renders them complicit in their marital misery.

Wroth's own marriage was evidently difficult. Her family protected her from marriage at age 13 when the guardians of the fifteen-year-old son of Sir Thomas Manxfild indifferently sought either Mary or her sister. But in an age when, according to Peter Laslett, the average woman married at 24, privileged women married earlier,[28] and Wroth's father arranged her marriage in 1604 when she was eighteen. Even this later marriage left much to be desired; her father's letters allude to Sir Robert Wroth's dissatisfaction a month after the wedding. Margaret Witten-Hannah conjectures that the marriage was at that time unconsummated.[29] Wroth's comments in *Urania* on marital misery, where husbands are jealous (p. 7) and only enjoy hunting (ms. II, 2c), suggest other sources of incompatibility. These sources are confirmed when we read Sir Robert Wroth's brief letters about hunting conditions and Ben Jonson's comment that Lady Wroth was "unworthily maried on a Jealous husband."[30]

Whatever the cause of her own marital problems, Wroth objected in *Urania* to the "cruel and tiranical power" that parents have to force marriages upon their children (p. 35). Virtuous daughters "esteem . . . obedience beyond all passions," and therefore "most dutifully though unwillingly . . . obey" (p. 5) even brutal fathers, who will use force if necessary, as they often did in life.[31] Like Egeus in *A Midsummer Night's Dream* and like Lord Capulet in *Romeo and Juliet,* Orilena's father forces

28. *De L'Isle and Dudley,* II, 412–13; Peter Laslett, *The World We Have Lost* (New York, 1965), pp. 82–83, 89. Stone says without qualification that "Marriage took place early" (p. 660).

29. P. 28; *De L'Isle and Dudley,* III, 127, 128, 140, 164.

30. *Marquis of Salisbury, Hatfield MSS.,* II, 397; V, 238; Ben Jonson's comments in *Works,* ed. C. H. Herford and Percy Simpson, I, p. 55n. See also Stone, *Crisis,* pp. 660.

31. Stone, *Crisis,* p. 596; see also his *The Family, Sex, and Marriage in England 1500–1800* (New York, 1977), p. 193.

upon her "a loathed match," which she says will cause her "destruction" (p. 169). The equally articulate Lisia also describes her own fate; her "tyrannous father" married her "before discretion appearing" to a "churlish" and "dull piece of flesh" (p. 474). In arranging marriages, fathers rarely considered a daughter's preferences. Therefore, Bellamira must ignore her contempt for Treborius' limited abilities; as his wife, she complains that she had to "commend his ordinary talke when hee praised rude sports, or told the plaine Jests of his Hunts-man" (p. 334). Many women, Lisia explains, endure their marriages by "hunting and other delights abroad, to take away trouble . . . at home" (p. 434).

Perhaps because Wroth writes from a woman's point of view, she presents families in *Urania* as more tyrannical than they are in Shakespeare or in Sidney. Amphilanthus learns from Sydelia how her brother, Terichillus, like the Duchess of Malfi's brothers, imprisoned and tortured her, ultimately hunting down and killing the husband of her choice (pp. 234–36). Liana too tells how her father "imprisons" her in his sister's home because she will not "breed" with the man of his choice (pp. 206–08). Another daughter explains that she was "shut up in a Towre." Her father instructed his sister to beat her brutally. Wroth comments that he "kept [in her] his choisest Treasure till the day of her marriage" (p. 36).

Wroth's use of the words "breed" and "Treasure" reveals her recognition that families used women as sources of new wealth.[32] Bellamira states explicitly that she married dull Treborius out of obedience to her parents who only saw "the goodness and greatness of his estate" (p. 330). Wroth also makes clear through her women characters that she condemns such parental brutality. In Shakespeare, when Kate's father colludes in her taming, we are expected to laugh; the beaten daughters in *Urania* recognize and describe their fathers' "cruel and tirannical power" (pp. 35, 439) and thus force us to acknowledge it. Yet Wroth recognized that if women married without family approval, they took enormous risks. For example, Dalinea would have been dishonored if Parselius, Pamphilia's own brother, had not acknowledged his marriage to her. Adventurous and courageous, she followed him to a distant country because "finding myselfe with child; then came the hazard of my honour in mind, the danger of my disgrace, the staine I might bring to my house: for few will believe us, poore women, in such extremity, but will rather increase our infamy" (p. 202).

32. Stone, *Crisis,* pp. 613, 617–18.

Lawrence Stone's statistics confirm Wroth's view that marriages arranged by families, common for "children of the rich," were often unhappy: one-third of the "older peers were estranged or actually separated from their wives . . . between 1595 and 1620." Stone conjectures that the extensive marital instability in the early seventeenth century resulted from "marriages deliberately designed to capture an heiress or to cement a political alliance, when the compulsion used may be supposed to have been particularly severe."[33] Wroth's narrative certainly makes clear that marriages advanced a family's interests more than a daughter's since married women often later became destitute widows. Wroth had herself experienced the humiliation of widowhood when Sir Robert Wroth's death in 1614 left his young wife with a £23,000 debt which she could never erase. The death of her only son, two-year-old James, two years later meant that much of her husband's estate reverted to his uncle.[34] Even the success of *Urania* would not have supplied her with wealth enough to discharge Sir Robert Wroth's debts since few seventeenth-century writers made more than forty pounds a year.[35] Wroth's indebtedness meant that remarriage was unlikely, even with her jointure of £1,200. Her own needs and the needs of the two illegitimate children that she later bore to William Herbert, Third Earl of Pembroke,[36] forced her to depend on the king's good will all her life. Every year after 1623, she obtained a royal order protecting her from creditors.[37] Naturally, then, she had to withdraw her book from sale in spite of her jaunty defense against Lord Denny's attack and the hours she had spent writing it. Marriage to an incompatible and jealous mate may have been limiting, but widowhood crippled her.

Nowhere in Shakespeare or Sidney is the widow's humiliating depen-

33. *Crisis,* pp. 662.
34. Roberts, "Biographical Problem," p. 45.
35. For accounts of the fortunes of English writers, see H. S. Bennett, *English Books and Readers, 1603–1640* (Cambridge, 1970), p. 230, and Douglas Bush, *English Literature in the Earlier Seventeenth Century,* 2d ed. (Oxford, 1962), p. 29.
36. Roberts, *Tulsa Studies in Women's Literature,* 45–46, discusses Wroth's illegitimate children. In *Crisis,* pp. 663–64, Stone writes that "Between 1560 and 1610, one marquis, eight earls, one viscount, and thirty-four barons are known to have fathered children by women other than their wives." However, illegitimate births were less common after the first decade of the seventeenth century when Wroth's children must have been born. See Keith Wrightson, "The Nadir of English Illegitimacy in the English Seventeenth Century," in *Bastardy and Its Comparative History,* ed. Peter Laslett, et al. (Cambridge, Mass., 1980), pp. 176–91.
37. *Acts of the Privy Council of England* (London, 1890–1960), 1621–23, pp. 431, 614; 1623–24, pp. 168, 232; 1625–26, p. 310; 1629–30, p. 1241.

dency defined as it is in *Urania*. Limena tells Pamphilia of a lady, "the mother to many, and delicate Children," who loses her fortune "with the losse of her Husband, (as many, wofully have with that felt their undoing)" (p. 237, p. 189, printed p. 199). But in spite of Wroth's bleak view of marriage, she still judges it to be a woman's main source of happiness. A prophet promises Pamphilia, "You might be happy had you power to wedd" (p. 160). When one woman marries, Wroth says she "now must change her name, and gaine the best, and blessed estate" (p. 297). Wroth comments explicitly, as Shakespeare does implicitly,[38] that there is a vast difference "betwixt servant love whose ends are love; and such, where only use and gaine attends desier" (p. 252). Even though the husband is "Lord" in all estates, marriage delights as partners show each other respect, "she to maintaine what she had gained, he to requite what she had given" (p. 296).

The contradiction between Wroth's images of marital torment and her praise of marriage as the "best and blessed estate" reflects her contradictory attitudes toward women. Like most books before the Victorian period, *Urania* makes marriage the only reward for women's merit and therefore desirable in spite of its pain. To be marriageable means to be attractive, to be successful. To be chaste, Wroth explains, is to be "dull" and to lack "affection" (p. 298).

In spite of its misery, the exaltation of marriage in *Urania* results in part from the impossible economic situation of unmarried women in the sixteenth and seventeenth centuries. A statute of 1563 stipulated that unmarried women between the ages of 12 and 40 could be forced to work at any job at any wage determined by municipal officials. Yet even the menial role of servant grew less available for women as households grew smaller. Family letters confirm that even in aristocratic and upper-middle class families unmarried daughters were burdens. Elizabeth Knyvett, for example, wrote to R. Townshend, on December 29, 1626, for aid to hasten her daughter's marriage. "I am suar it hath greatly afflicted me, these delayings. besides the daunger which may ensue my charge is lengthened out to the uttermost. Both in maintaining her, and also in calling in my monies."[39] Lack of paid employment for women,

38. Marianne Novy, "'And You Smile Not, He's Gagged': Mutuality in Shakespearean Comedy," *Philological Quarterly*, 55 (1976), 178–94.

39. Bernard I. Murstein, *Love, Sex, and Marriages through the Ages* (New York, 1974), p. 191. Richard Wall, "The Household: Demographic and Economic Change in England, 1650–1697)," in *Family Forms in Historic Europe* ed. Richard Wall, et al. (Cambridge, 1983), p. 496. Bacon-Townshend letters, L.d. 382, 386, Folger Shakespeare Library.

combined with the economic drain of their continued support, would naturally create a climate which favored women's marriage despite the evident misery that often resulted.

In *Urania,* Wroth envisages few alternatives. Women usually embrace chastity only when widowed or disappointed in love (p. 187). Melasinda retires to a monastery "to her own libertie" when her husband dies rather than remarry (MS II, fol. 29). Another woman serves as house-keeper in the home of a bachelor cousin (p. 321), but she can do that only because her age makes her unattractive in her society.

Yet some women characters dream of liberation from marriage. In the manuscript continuation of *Urania,* Wroth tells a story of a woman significantly named "Fancy," who thinks at the age of 14 that "a husband will cherish age" as he must become old himself. She imagines "hansome discourse with a reasonable husband, children to pass away the time." However, she also worries that she might have a jealous husband who restricts what she wears, "fearing other men's children calling him dad." She then says "therfore never will I marry . . . Libertie and good company are my chosen mates" (MS I, fol. 6c). Another woman, whose brother was an esteemed prince, "many sought for wife but shee knowing her perfections and greatnesse, was nice in accepting ay, nor indeed had shee much mind to marry, loving her libertie more than marriages bondage" (p. 243). These free women Wroth praises as recognizing their own self-worth; like Alarina, finally freed from her self-enslavement to obsessional love that made marriage seem desirable, they might say, "I love myself; my selfe now loveth me" (p. 107).

IV

Since some women value "libertie more than marriages bondage," we must wonder with Wroth why Pamphilia, a powerful queen, willingly remains painfully obsessed with the romantic possibility of marriage to Amphilanthus. Pamphilia herself wonders why (pp. 188, 191), but 600 pages later her passion endures. Unlike other women, she never needed "an increase, and sufficiency of estate . . . bought . . . with her marriage, and so grow subject to an Husband" (p. 448). Urania and Perselina are correct that Pamphilia's unnecessary choice to wait for the inconstant Amphilanthus is weakness in a woman whose discretion they otherwise admire.

The explanation, I think, lies in Wroth's presentation of a society that tends to destroy women. She makes clear that women receive an ambiguous message when marriage is their only validation, especially when marriage occurs to benefit fathers' and husbands' estates against the women's own desires. In presenting marriage as a reward while she also narrates tales of its accompanying misery, Wroth communicates an appalling awareness that women are worthy (that is, marriageable) only when they participate in a system that may victimize them. Since a woman's happiness is often irrelevant, the message is in part that they are worthy only when willing to be unhappy. While Wroth does not explicitly describe this process of female self-destruction, she repeatedly uses narratives in which a woman protests that in marriage she gained "so much libertie . . . as she had almost tyed herself" (p. 424). She also shows that male admiration may become the main form of female self-validation: "I was sought by many and beloved as they said by them. I was apt enough to believe them, having none the worst opinion of myself" (p. 268). As Wroth shows that a woman's self-worth may rest on the admiration of a man whom she may in many ways dislike, she also shows that this good opinion can therefore arise only when a woman rejects her own feelings, desires, and abilities. The resulting confusion renders true self-awareness impossible.[40]

Wroth's use of romance conventions reveals their destructive effects on women. The knights who aid some desperate ladies abuse others, and it is often questionable whether the women are rescued or simply degraded once again. The unfaithful Amphilanthus rescues Bellamira from lonely widowhood by returning her to the father who, in effect, sold her to her husband Treborius (p. 335). Limena is left tied by her hair to a pillar while Parselius and Perissus quarrel over which one had the right to rescue her and then over the proper respect owed her husband as he dies. Even though Perissus clearly puts protocol before Limena's health and safety, and even though her husband brutalized her, she obediently grants her husband's dying request that she marry Perissus (pp. 69–70).

Urania thus presents a rare, early female perspective on trapped and bewildered women. Shakespeare presents us with Hermia, who loses herself in love, but he views her plight as an amusing mortal foible; in *A Midsummer Night's Dream* he does not blame society for the destruction of

---

40. Wroth had no powerful queen like Elizabeth I upon which to build such a fantasy, nor even Margaret Beaufort, the Countess of Richmond, a justice from 1507–1509. See Hogrefe, pp. 34–39.

a woman's self-confidence. Shakespeare also presents us with a strong woman—Portia—who knows herself and is therefore confident enough to challenge injustice. But a woman judge in seventeenth-century England is a male fantasy. In *Urania,* no women can be as strong and accomplished as Portia because the world validates women by demeaning them. As Pamphilia reads the romance she discards, for example, she is confused about her own identity. She has been taught that constancy is crucial and that marriage would make her happy. Although her experience confirms the book's teaching about male infidelity, she cannot accept it. Pamphilia sits "in a delicate thick woods" as she reads (p. 252), woods not associated with the medieval woods of error which trap people in sin, but symbolize instead inner confusion.

Throughout *Urania,* venturesome women lose themselves. Philistella is "castaway," Selarina "stolen"; even the queenly Pamphilia is "lost" (p. 19). When Urania does not know her parentage, she grieves, "I am lost . . . not being able to know any more of myselfe: . . . now I am troubled to rule my owne thoughts" (p. 13). Nereana, the Queen of Stalamina, wanders in woods, "in amaze, and at last quite lost her self" (p. 165). But unlike Pamphilia, Nereana undermines society's restrictions as she pursues her beloved.[41]

This minor character, whose subplot intertwines with the main plot, trusts her own feelings and rejects romantic conventions. In the end she gains both power and confidence in a story that may be unique for women in early literature. Unlike Gynecia in Sidney's *Arcadia* or Webster's Duchess of Malfi, who similarly choose to pursue their own loves, Nereana chooses total autonomy. She prefers her own misery and mistakes to secure dependency. In her adventures Nereana finds she must cope with men's fantasies at odds with her own. She is seized and worshipped by Allanus: "That he might be sure of her stay, hee tied her to a tree" (p. 265). In a startling image Allanus strips Nereana so that she might better conform to his vision of the woman he loves, Liana, or to his vision of a goddess of the woods (p. 166). When she escapes, Nereana is then blamed for the tattered clothes that Allanus tore; Philarchos, Pamphilia's brother, from whom she seeks help, assumes her to be mad and rides off. In a comment that sounds remarkably modern, Wroth tells us that Nereana then decided to find security in "her own worth and deserts" (p. 167).

41. For other women whose disorder challenges society, see Natalie Zemon Davis, "Women on Top," *Society and Culture in Early Modern France* (Stanford, Calif., 1975), p. 131.

She sails back to her homeland "with resolution to exercise her just anger upon her people" (pp. 289–90). But her people are as fickle as her lovers. Nereana is "told still she was mad, and threatened to bee used accordingly, if she raved, accused of fury, and that made the cause to satisfie the people, who had sufficient cause to believe it, seeing her passions, which though naturall to her, yet appeared to their capacities meere lunaticke actions" (pp. 290–91). Finally, however, Wroth vindicates this woman accused of madness, and Nereana grows from her suffering. When a "noble man" aids her to regain her throne, "she by her poor living, and neglect being now invested in so staid an habitation of gravity, as she was fit for the honour they recalled her too" (p. 421). Nereana is restored to her throne because Wroth recognizes that Nereana is mad mainly in the eyes of an unreasonable world.

What a contrast to Shakespeare and Sidney! Shakespeare recognizes that Lady Macbeth's madness is more reasonable than her husband's barbarism and that Ophelia's sensitivity is more desirable than Laertes' well-adjusted opportunism. Even Sidney's *Arcadia* condemns rather than rewards the mad and jealous Gynecia, once she is overwhelmed by adulterous lust for Pyrocles as her husband is. In the *Arcadia,* as in *Macbeth* and *Hamlet,* a woman's disruption functions only to highlight the immoral masculine norm. In the story of Nereana, women are justly angry at being idolized as women and then rejected when they use the wisdom for which they are revered. For all his praise, for example, Allanus' worship tortures Nereana and drives her temporarily wild (p. 913).

In spite of her recognition that women may be justifiably angry at society, Wroth seems to suffer from a confusion that equals her characters'. When we read romances, we expect to be confounded by episodic narratives and multiple characters who fight, love, and recite verses through 600 pages. But conflicts arise in *Urania* between Wroth's empathy with society and her empathy with beleaguered women. She sympathizes fully with Urania "amazed" in thick woods; she understands Nereana's madness; and she is certainly aware that Pamphilia is lost when she is enchanted in the House of Love. She praises the "excellent wit" which causes Urania to advise Pamphilia to reject her unfaithful lover Amphilanthus. At the same time that Wroth's tales explore the consequences of ill-advised constancy, however, her narrator praises Pamphilia for remaining constant, "the true patterne of excellent affection, and affections truth" (p. 315). She even admires the passion that will allow a woman to bind herself to a dead lover's tomb (p. 305). These contradictory values prove that as author and as woman, Wroth herself still esteemed the conventions that she presents as exploitative.

Sidney openly disparages women when he presents love as effeminizing and debasing men who love them. Shakespeare in contrast fools us into believing that society values its Portias and Beatrices.[42] Wroth knew personally that her society rarely permitted women autonomy. Yet in *Urania* she sometimes validates social values that can destroy a woman's sense of self.

Stephen Greenblatt has shown that Renaissance "middle-class and aristocratic males . . . felt that they possessed . . . shaping power over their lives" (p. 256). By contrast, the contradictions in *Urania* show how limited the ability of Renaissance women was to fashion themselves as they wished. Evidently the independent Lady Mary Wroth was as much the victim of her age intellectually as she was financially. The same narrator who can call women and men "equally faultful" reveals her own acceptance of male superiority when she describes Pamphilia as having "soe great a spiritt, as might be called masculine" (p. 192). And the independent Urania uses the word "feminine" to mean "weak" when she questions why the obsessed Pamphilia will descend "below the poorest feminine in love?" (p. 398). Rather than be antagonized by a woman writer's acceptance of the word "masculine" as synonymous with "strong" and "feminine" with "weak," readers should recognize that Wroth's use of these verbal conventions reveals the power of language to alienate us from ourselves. Even in its contradictions, *Urania* reveals a feminine consciousness in conflict with societal values.[43]

42. See Clara Claiborne Park, "As We Like It: How a Girl Can be Smart and Still Popular," *The American Scholar,* 42 (Spring 1973), 262–78, rep. in *The Woman's Part: Feminist Criticism of Shakespeare,* ed. Carolyn Ruth Swift Lenz, Gayle Greene, and Carol Thomas Neely (Champaign, Ill., 1980), pp. 100–16.

43. This study was partially financed by the Rhode Island College Faculty Research Fund and by The Newberry Library. I especially wish to thank David L. Greene, Dean of Arts and Sciences, and John L. Salesses, Assistant Vice-President, Rhode Island College, for their encouragement and support.

JEAN C. CAVANAUGH

Lady Southwell's Defense of Poetry

ONE of the earliest known essays of literary criticism in English by a woman has recently been discovered in a seventeenth-century commonplace book belonging to Lady Anne Southwell. The essay, in the form of a letter, is a defense of poetry written in 1627 and addressed to Lady Southwell's friend Lady Ridgway, apparently in reply to her friend's stated preference for prose.

Little is actually known about Lady Southwell. She was born in Cornworthy, Devon, in 1574 and baptised there on August 22, the daughter of Sir Thomas Harris, a prosperous landowner and lawyer, and a sister of Sir Edward Harris, Third Justice of the King's Bench in Ireland. She married Sir Thomas Southwell of Spixworth, Norfolk, and seems to have gone with him to Ireland when he settled there as a planter in Munster. Shortly after the death of Sir Thomas in 1626, she married Sir Henry Sibthorpe, sergeant major and privy councillor in the Province of Munster. Memoranda in the commonplace book suggests that, at least after 1631, they lived in Clerkenwell and Acton.[1] Lady Southwell died in Acton on October 2, 1636.

If little survives about Lady Southwell's life, there is nevertheless ample evidence in her poems and letters that she had more than a merely polite interest in poetry. Nor was she just a theorist. She practiced writing poetry, experimenting with different kinds and sometimes making sweeping revisions of her own work, excising a whole page at a time. These poems were, for the most part, devotional, even those addressed to such contemporaries as the Countess of Somerset; Dr. Bernard Adams, bishop of Limerick; and the first Earl of Castlehaven.

Lady Ridgway, to whom she addressed the defense of poetry published here, was the wife of Sir Thomas Ridgway, Lord Treasurer of Ireland from 1606 to 1616. Before her marriage, Lady Ridgway was Cecily Macwilliam, sister of Henry Macwilliam of Ireland and like Lady Southwell a maid of honor to Elizabeth I. Barnabe Riche dedicated to her his *Catholicke Conference* (1612). She died in 1627. Lady Southwell's attachment to her is shown in a poem of 120 lines, "An Elegie written by the Lady A:S: to the Countesse of London Derrye supposyenge hir to be dead by hir longe silence" (fols. 19v–20), and by an elegy Lady Southwell wrote upon her death (fol. 21).

The present defense of poetry shows Lady Southwell's knowledge of Renaissance critical theory, particularly that of Sidney's *Apologie for Poetrie* (published 1595). She is primarily concerned with such problems as the form and function of poetry, truth and fiction, subject matter and the poet's intention, and the poet as a teacher, moral guide,

1. Her letters after 1626 are sent from Polynalong Castle, near Cork, or from Acton when she returned to England, sometime after 1631.

and transmitter of learning. Believing that the imagination prepares the way for reason, reality, and beauty as best exemplified in the Psalms of David, she argues primarily for the harmony of the created world, the "iust proportions [by which] all thinges are propagated" through the four elements perfectly balanced, which continually reveal a principle that is "poetically composed." Anyone who does not know and appreciate poetry, Lady Southwell writes, is not in harmony with the natural world. For her, good poetry provides patterns for directing one's life; hence it should not offend one's moral sense or waste time by being a "busye nothing" like Marlowe's *Hero and Leander*. Shakespeare's *Venus and Adonis* is likewise unacceptable to her because it also presents a wrong pattern for moral behavior. Although such arguments lean heavily on traditional ideas, Lady Southwell's presentation is not lacking in originality or charm. While her unusual use of architectural terms to explain the primacy of poetry among the arts may draw on a suggestion initially made by Sidney,[2] her own analogy of the string of pearls seems especially apt in a comment written by one member of the nobility for another.

The present text is a literal transcription of the manuscript now at the Folger Shakespeare Library (V.b.198, formerly Phillipps 8581). It is in a calf-bound folio titled *Lady Southwell's Works* and dated 1626. The letter, neither in Lady Southwell's nor Sibthorpe's hand, is on a sheet inserted into the book to form folio 3 and precedes another letter by Lady Southwell addressed to Lord Holland, Deputy of Ireland, dated 1628. Both letters—like a number of other manuscripts similarly pasted into the book—must have formed part of a gathering intended to complete Lady Southwell's writings, either put together by the author or by her husband after her death. The last pages of the folio contain Captain Sibthorpe's commendations and a biographical sketch of his wife as well as copies, in the Captain's hand, of the lady's inscriptions and epitaphs (fol. 73–74).

To my worthy Muse;

the Ladye Ridgway

that doth these lines infuse.

How falles it out (noble Ladye:) that you are become a sworne enemye to Poetrie; It being soe abstruse an art, as it is, that I may say, The other artes are but Bases & Pedestalles, vnto the wch this is the Capitall. The meere Herald of all Ideas; The worldes true vocall Harmonye, of wch all other artes are but partes, or rather, may I iustly say; It is the silke thredd that stringes your chayne of pearle; wch being broken, your iewells fall into the rushes; & tho more you seeke for it, the more it falles into the dust of obliuion. You say: you affect prose as your auncestors did; Error is not to bee affected for antiquitye. Therefore, (Noble & wittye Ladye:) giue mee your hand, I will leade you vpp the streame of all mankind. Your great great grandfather had a father, & soe the last, or rather the first father, was God; whose neuer enough to bee admired creation, was poetically confined to 4. generall genusses, Earth, Ayre, water & fire: The effectes wch giue life vnto his verse, were, Hott, Cold, Moist & Drye, wth produce

2. Sir Philip Sidney, *An Apologie for Poetrie* (1595), sigs. C4–D1.

Choller, melanchollye, Bloud & Flegme: By these iust proportions, all thinges are propagated. Now being thus poetically composed; How can you bee at unitye with your self, & at oddes wth your owne composition: It may bee, you will say, that Poesye is a fiction, & fiction is a lye: O but; Rahabs concealing the spyes,[3] was more to bee approued, then Doegs truth.[4] But heerein, Poesye seemes to doe more for nature, then shee is able to doe for her selfe, wherein, it doth but lay downe a patterne what man should bee; & shewes, that Imagination goes before Realitye. But hee is not worthy the name of a phisitian, but of an Emperick only, that giues one potion to all manner of diseases: for it is as great an error to giue purges to one in a consumption, as it is to giue cordialls to one in a Repletion. Therefore it is necessarye to knowe how the humor aboundes, that soe wee may the boldlyer applye. Then, since all are eyther fooles, or phisitians, to escape the former I will take vppon mee to knowe, what hath soe distasted / your palate against this banquett of soules, devine Poesye. some wanton venus or Adonis hath bene cast before your chast eares, whose euill attyre, disgracing this beautifull nimph, hath vnworthyed her in your opinion & will you, because you see a man madd, wish your self w^{th}out melancholye, wch humor is the hand of all the soules facultyes. All exorbitant thinges are monstrous; but bring them agayne to theyr orbicular forme & motion, & they will retayne theyr former beautyes. Our Reason ought to bee the stickler in this case: who would not skornefully laugh wth Micholl, to see the old Prophett dauñce, but when wee knowe hee daunced before the Arke, must wee not thinke the Host of heauen was in exaltation wth him, as well as that of Jerusalem:[5] To heare a Hero & Leander or some such other busye nothing, might bee a meanes to skandalize this art. But can a cloud disgrace the sunne: will you behold Poesye in perfect beautye: Then see the kingly Prophett, that sweete singer of Israell, explicating the glorye of our god, his power in creating; his mercye in redeeming, his wisedome in preseruing making these three, as it were the Coma, Colon, & Period to euery stanzae: who would not say, the musicall spheares did yeeld a cadencye to his songe, & in admiration crye out; Õ neuer enough to bee admired, deuine Poesye: It is the subiect, that coñends or condemmes the art. But noble Ladye, I will trouble you noe further, now; yett when I haue your honorable word of reconciliation I will then delineate out every liñe of her, & how shee is envelloped vpp wth the rest of the artes. In the meane time I rest more then thankfull for your noble louing letter, as the louer of your virtues.

(Signed)   Anne Southwell[6]

---

3. Cf. 2 Samuel 8:3–8.
4. Cf. 1 Samuel 21:7–9.
5. Michal; cf. 2 Samuel 6:16–20.
6. At the end of the page is a smudged erasure, apparently a note beginning "vera copie" but the remainder is indecipherable.

To my worthy Muse,   the Ladye Ridgway
that doth these lines infuse.

How falles it out (Noble Ladye) that you are become a sworne
enemye to Poetrie; It being soe abstruse an art, as it is, that I
may say, The other artes are but Bases & Pedestalles, vnto the wch
this is the Capitall. The meere Herald of all Ideas; The worldes
true vocall Harmonye, of wch all other artes are but partes, or
rather, may I iustly say, It is the silke thredd that stringes your
chayne of pearle; wch being broken, your iewells fall into the
rushes, & the more you seeke for it, the more it falles into the
Dust of obliuion. You say, you affect proze, as your auncestors
did. Error is not to bee affected for antiquitye. Therefore
(Noble & wittye Ladye) giue mee your hand, I will leade you
vpp the streame of all mankind. Your great great grandfather
had a father, & soe the last, or rather the first father, was God,
whose neuer enough to bee admired creation, was poetically
confined to 4 generall genuses, Earth, Ayre, water & fire.
The effectes wch giue life vnto his verse, were, Hott, Cold, moist
& Drye, wch produce Choller, melancolly, blaud & flegme.
By these iust proportions, all thinges are propagated. Now
being thus poetically composed; How can you bee at vnitye
wth your self, & at oddes wth your owne composition. It may
bee, you will say, that Poesye is a fiction, & fiction is a
lye. O but Rahabs concealing the spyes, was more to bee
approued, then Doegs truth. But heerein, Poesye seemes to
doe more for nature, then shee is able to doe for her selfe,
wherein, it doth but lay downe a patterne what man should
bee; & shewes, that Imagination goes before Realitye.
But hee is not worthy the name of a phisitian, but of an
Emperick only, that giues one potion to all manner of
diseases. for it is as great an error to giue purges to one
in a consumption, as it is to giue cordialls to one in a
Repletion. Therefore it is necessarye to knowe how the humor
aboundes, that soe wee may the boddyer applye. Then since
all are eyther fooles or phisitians, to escape the former
I will take vppon mee to knowe, what hath soe distasted

CLAUDIA LIMBERT

Two Poems and a Prose Receipt: The Unpublished Juvenilia of Katherine Philips (text)

 IN his brief biography of the Royalist poet Katherine Philips (1632–1664), known in her time as "The Matchless Orinda," John Aubrey (the cousin of Philips' lifelong friend and schoolmate, Mary Aubrey Montague) claims that, having been influenced as a small child by her grandmother Oxenbridge's interest in writing poetry, Katherine Philips had "Loved poetry at schoole, and made verses there."[1] While no poetry from these early school years seems to have survived, a hitherto unpublished manuscript in the uncatalogued Orielton Collection of the National Library of Wales[2] reveals Philips as a practicing poet, possibly as early as her fourteenth year.

The daughter of a prominent London merchant, John Fowler,[3] Philips was brought up in a family with strong Puritan connections.[4] A precocious child who could read the Bible at four and who "Took sermons down verbatim when she was but 10 years old,"

---

1. John Aubrey, *Aubrey's Brief Lives,* ed. Andrew Clark (Oxford, 1898), II, p. 153.

2. Orielton Collection, Parcel 24. National Library of Wales. Having found the manuscript under discussion, I discovered that I had been anticipated by two others: Ronald Lockley who gives excerpts in his *Orielton: The Human and Natural History of a Welsh Manor* (London, 1977), pp. 19–20, and Patrick Thomas who quotes the MS in full in "An Edition of the Poems and Letters of Katherine Philips," Diss. Univ. of Wales, 1982, III, pp. 129–30. However, Lockley confuses Anne Barlow with Anne Lewis Owen and does not identify "C. Fowler." Thomas, by the generic limitations imposed upon an edition, is unable to devote space to the implications of the manuscript. Additionally, since neither author's work is readily available, the Orielton MS is presented here for consideration.

3. John Fowler belonged to the Clothworkers' Guild, having paid his 29d. fee to join the guild on 18 July 1612. Between 1615–16, he became wealthy enough to set up his own workshop and to hire employees. By 1623, he had been elected as fourth of the four Wardens of the Yeomanry for 1624. He appears in annual lists of the Livery until his death in 1642. Joshua, his son by his first wife and Katherine's half-brother, became a member in 1645. (Letter received from D. E. Wickham, Archivist for the Clothworkers' Guild, 4 July 1984.)

4. An uncle, John Oxenbridge, became pastor of the First Church of Boston, Massachusetts. See *The Records of the First Church in Boston, 1630–1868,* ed. Richard D. Pierce (Boston, 1961), XXXIX, p. xxxiv. An aunt, Elizabeth Oxenbridge Cockcroft, in 1645 took as her second husband Oliver St. John, Cromwell's Chief Justice of the Common Pleas from 1648–60 who had been married formerly to Cromwell's cousin Elizabeth. See William Durrant Cooper, *The*

Philips was known to pray for an hour at a time and was, as a child, "much against the bishops, and prayed to God to take them to him."[5] At eight, she was enrolled at Mrs. Salmon's School in Hackney.[6] Obviously, the school climate was hospitable to Royalists as well as to Puritans, for Philips' two best friends at school—Mary Harvey (who later married Sir Edward Dering, a man devoted to the interests of the Crown) and Mary Aubrey—were both Royalists.

From the incomplete records available, it would seem that Orinda remained in London until she was approximately fourteen, when her widowed mother married Sir Richard Phillips [sic] of Picton Castle, Wales, and took her daughter along to her new home. At sixteen, Katherine married Colonel James Philips,[7] a prominent Puritan Parliamentarian and widower of fifty-four who had been married to Sir Richard's deceased daughter Frances by whom he had a small daughter. Orinda then moved to her new husband's home in Cardigan where James was active in politics, variously serving as a Commissioner of the Sequestration Committee, as a Commissioner of the Propagation of the Gospel Committee, and as High Sheriff, Justice of the Peace, councilman, and mayor.[8]

Shortly after her marriage, Philips' reputation as a poet began to grow; her poems were widely circulated by the friends who were also her poetic subject matter. In particular, Philips' best work may be her graceful Platonic friendship poems to and about her women friends whom she elevates to the status of goddesses with symbolic trappings of fire, water, and twinned spirits. There is no evidence that the women involved responded in kind.

Besides writing poetry, Philips translated Corneille's *Pompée*[9] which was enthusiastically received in 1663 at the new Theatre Royal in Dublin[10] before being published both

---

Oxenbridges of Brede Place, Sussex and Boston, Massachusetts (London, 1860), p. 6. Additionally, Katherine Philips' own mother lived to marry three times, her last husband being the famous Puritan military leader and writer of devotional books for his troops, Philip Skippon, Cromwell's major-general of London. See "The Will of Phillip Skippon, Major-General," Prob. 11/300, pr. 25 October 1660, by his son Phillip. Public Records Office, London.

5. Aubrey, II, p. 153.

6. Little is known of Mrs. Salmon's School and nothing of its curriculum. Indeed, its very existence can no longer be documented since none of the ratebooks for the period have survived. (Letter received from David Mander, Archivist for Library Services of Hackney, 15 January 1985.)

7. An intent to marry was filed in London 23 August 1648. See *Marriage License Allegations in the Registry of the Bishop of London, 1597–1648,* ed. Reginald M. Glencross (London, 1937), XXV, p. 256.

8. Basil Henning, *The History of Parliament: The House of Commons, 1660–1690* (London, 1983), III, p. 239.

9. The National Library of Wales has lately purchased another manuscript copy of *Pompey* (NLW 21867B—General Collection), their first copy being NLW 776B. The more recent acquisition is believed to date from the second half of the seventeenth century. It appears to have been originally part of a larger volume, coming to the library with the remains of raised bands and gold-tooled calf on its spine.

10. W. R. Chetwood, *A General History of the Stage* (London, 1749), p. 52 and Katherine Philips, *Letters from Orinda to Poliarchus* (London, 1705), letter no. xxvi, dated 8 April 1663, p. 124.

in Ireland[11] and in London.[12] It was at about this same time that a group of her poems fell into the hands of Richard Marriott, a London publisher, who filed to print a pirated edition on 25 November 1663.[13] While Philips was in London, partly to take care of business for her husband and partly to make certain that her friends had been successful in suppressing this pirated edition, she succumbed to smallpox on 22 June 1664. She left behind her a partial translation of Corneille's *Horace* (which was completed by Sir John Denham and which became a favorite with the court of Charles II)[14] as well as a considerable literary reputation. Her work was praised by Cowley, Tyrell, Flatman, and the Earls of Orrery and Roscommon in a posthumous edition of her poems,[15] and later by Keats.[16]

Philips' mature creative life is well documented by these commendatory poems and some contemporary accounts as well as by Philips' letters and poetry but, until recently, Aubrey's claim that Philips had written poetry while at school was the only evidence of any writing activity before her marriage. Now, however, the Orielton manuscript, composed of two poems and a short prose receipt that are relatively unformed and unpolished compared to her later work, yields a great deal of useful information about this poet's early years.

The envelope holding the manuscript bears the inscription "Emma Owen / Ode to her dog Sancho."[17] Just below, in a different ink, is written: "Also verses by C. Fowler"—Katherine Philips' maiden name. Folded within is the ode to the dead Sancho, plus a sheet of paper in another hand. On one side of this sheet is a poem beginning "No blooming youth shall ever make me erre." Under the poem appears "Humbly dedicated too Mrs Anne Barlow" and the poem is signed "C. Fowler." On the reverse is both a poem beginning "A marry^{d} state affords but little ease" and, in prose, "A receipt to cure a Love sick Person who can't obtain the Party desired."

The manuscript itself, written in a slightly less sure, more childish hand than Philips' later copybook,[18] can be fairly well dated. Since the poems concern marriage, they would have been written sometime after 1 December 1646, when Orinda's mother

---

11. *Letters,* p. 122.

12. *A Transcript of the Registers of the Worshipful Company of Stationers, 1640–1708 A. D.* (London, 1913; rpt. New York, 1950), p. 339.

13. *Stationer's Register,* p. 334. The edition concerned is *Poems By the Incomparable Mrs. K.P.* (London, 1664).

14. Records indicate one performance where Lady Castlemaine took a part, wearing the Crown Jewels taken from the Tower of London for the occasion. See *The London Stage, 1660–1800,* ed. William Van Lennep (Carbondale, Ill., 1965), I, pp. 128–29.

15. Katherine Philips, *Poems By the most deservedly Admired Mrs Katherine Philips, The Matchless Orinda To which is added Monsieur Corneille's Pompey and Horace, Tragedies* (London, 1667).

16. John Keats, *The Letters of John Keats,* ed. Maurice Buxton Forman, 3rd ed. (London, 1947), letter no. 22, dated 21 September 1817, p. 45.

17. Emma Owen, who lived during the early eighteenth century, was the eleventh of twelve children of Sir Arthur Owen and Emma Owen of Orielton. Dying childless, she was married to William Bowen of Williamston, Pembrokeshire, one of the Bowens of Upton Castle. Ronald Lockley documents this information and the existence of her dog Sancho whose grave he found in a little cemetery for three pets located just behind Orielton manor on the other side of a lily pond. See Lockley, pp. 23–24.

18. Katherine Philips, "Poems: Orinda," NLW 775B, National Library of Wales.

married Sir Richard, but before late August of 1648 when Orinda herself married. Thus, Philips was between fourteen and sixteen years of age.

It is not surprising to find such a manuscript among the materials from Orielton. Located three miles southwest of Pembroke, Wales, and now a nature study center,[19] Orielton was once the home of Anne Lewis Owen (called "Lucasia" by Philips), who was the object of Philips' most intense friendship. Besides Orielton, the Owen family also owned Llandshipping, just across the East Cleddau River and to the southeast of Picton Castle where Philips lived with her mother and step-father before her own marriage. The Anne Barlow of the manuscript can be identified as one of the Barlows living at the manor house of Slebech (pronounced Slebets),[20] less than two miles northeast of Picton Castle. Thus, all three young women lived within a short distance of one another.

Anne Barlow was one of nine children, two of her sisters becoming lady abbesses in France. Anne's first husband was Nicholas Lewis of Hean Castle and her second was Lewis Wogan of Wiston.[21] Genealogical information shows that she was approximately the same age as Philips and Owen. Anne's father John Barlow, a Royalist and "a church papist," is listed among the commanders captured in 1642 by Parliamentary forces at Fort Pill.[22] His extensive and personal estate was finally sequestered on 13 May, 1651.[23] Thus, the records would indicate that the Barlows most likely were at Slebech during the period before Philips' marriage in 1648.

As one reads the manuscript, it soon becomes clear that this is the earliest known evidence of Orinda's break from Puritanism and her subsequent commitment to the Royalist cause, a change most likely made while still at school. Here, Philips establishes herself as seeking an ideal Royalist husband: literate, of "good estate," and possessing beauty of mind. But Fate dealt Philips something quite different. James Philips, while instrumental in the formation of a local free school,[24] was never recorded as being a man

19. Letter received from J. D. Owen, Curator of the Ceredigion Museum, Cardiagan, Wales, 5 July 1984.

20. *Bartholomew Gazeteer of Britain,* comp. Oliver Mason (Edinburgh, 1977), p. 224. All mileages are drawn from a map in this volume on p. 22.

21. Francis Green, "The Barlows of Slebech" in *West Wales Historical Records* (Carmarthen, Wales, 1913), p. 144.

22. John Roland Phillips, *Memoirs of the Civil War in Wales and the Marches, 1642–1649* (London, 1874), II, p. 153.

23. Green, p. 142. John Barlow "of Slebitch" is also mentioned as one being investigated under "An Act concerning the Sequestration of South-Wales and County of Monmouth 23 Feb. 1648/9" in *Acts and Ordinances of the Interregnum, 1642–1660,* ed. C. H. Firth and R. S. Rait (London, 1911), II, p. 14. However, nothing seems to have been done until the date mentioned by Green. As Green states, Barlow's son John did not petition to regain one-fifth of the property for himself and the other children until 13 November 1651. Yet, when their request was granted, arrears were also awarded dating from 24 December 1649. This then would indicate an earlier sequestration date, but a date still well within the period considered here.

24. John Roland Phillips, *A List of the Sheriffs of Cardiganshire from A. D. 1539 to A. D. 1868 with Genealogical and Historical Notes* (Carmarthen, Wales, 1868), p. 17 and W. A. L. Vincent, *The State and School: Education, 1640–1660 in England and Wales* (London, 1950), p. 54.

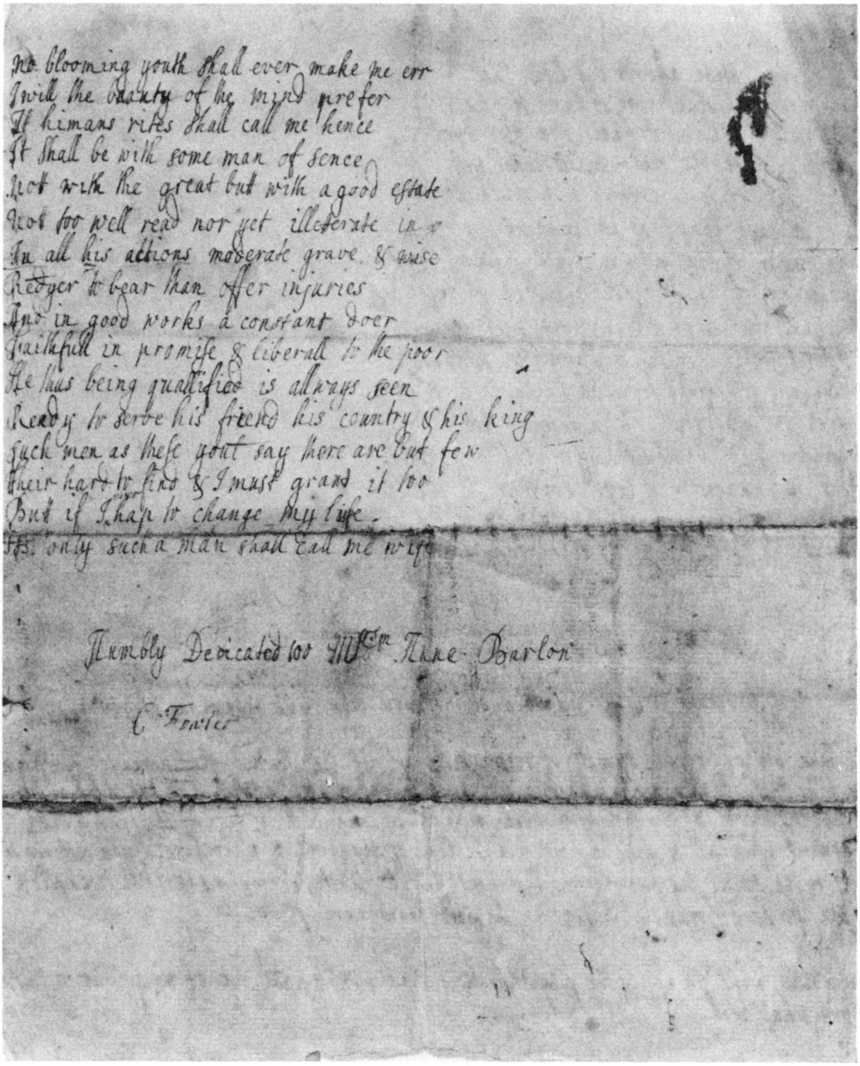

No blooming youth shall ever make me err
I will the beauty of his mind prefer
If himans rites shall call me hence
It shall be with some man of sence
Not with the great but with a good estate
Not too well read nor yet illeterate in &
In all his actions moderate grave, & wise
Redyer to bear than offer injuries
And in good works a constant doer
Faithfull in promise & liberall to the poor
He thus being qualified is always seen
Ready to serve his friends his country & his king
Such men as these yout say here are but few
Their hart to find & I must grant it too
But if I hap to change my life.
Tis only such a man shall call me wife

Humbly Dedicated too Mrs Anne Barlow

C. Fowler

PLATE I. Katherine Philips' holograph copy of "No blooming youth shall ever make me erre" followed by the inscription "Humbly dedicated too Mrs Anne Barlow." Reprinted from Orielton MS., parcel 34, with permission of the National Library of Wales.

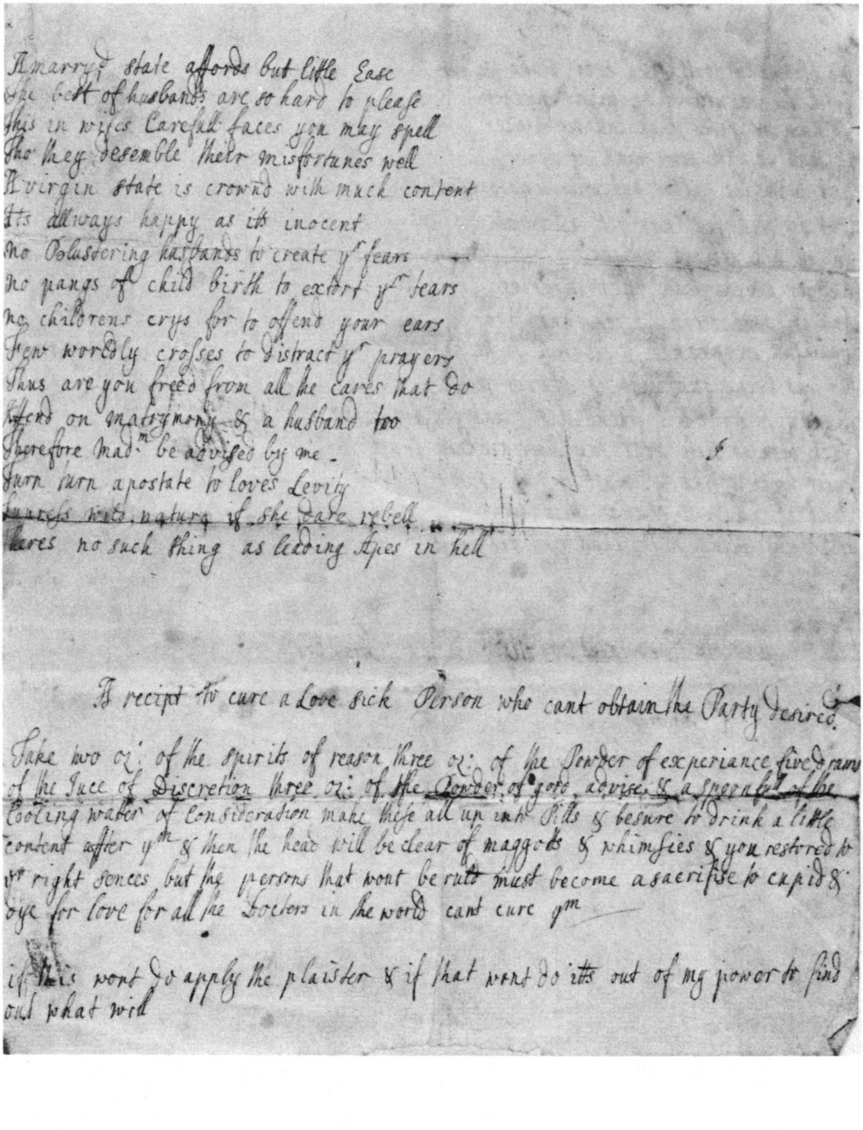

PLATE II. Katherine Philips' holograph copy of "A marry^d state affords but little Ease" and "A receipt to cure a Love sick Person who cant obtain the Party desired." Reprinted from Orielton MS., parcel 34, with permission of the National Library of Wales.

of books. He was recorded, however, as having made many enemies and was seen by some to be an enthusiastic sequestrator.[25]

Additionally, the manuscript provides a glimpse of Philips' early creative life, demonstrating that she was already familiar with the mechanics of composition and was approaching mastery of the heroic couplet. This manuscript also signals Philips' interest in communicating with other women through poetry, although the absence of her subsequent use of pseudonyms for her friends is noticeable since the work is dedicated directly to Anne Barlow. However, by at least 15 February 1651 / 2, Philips was employing pseudonyms, as in her "Philoclea's Parting."[26] Perhaps even more significant than the absence of a pseudonym for Barlow is the absence of the Orinda persona, so obvious later in her copybook.

Finally, in these pieces, Philips deals, as so many beginning poets do, with the topic of romance, but her voice is that of a pragmatic young woman of good humor voicing clearly anti-romantic expectations about love and marriage. The sentiments are hardly original, yet the perspective and voice are not so common in English literature. One thinks of Shakespeare's Beatrice or Congreve's Millamant, but the witty sophistication of such characters is very distant from Philips' tone. That distance might in some measure be related to the fact that Philips does not speak as a character imagined by a male author but as herself, a woman who would go on to transform herself into "the Matchless Orinda," the celebrator of the Platonic love of one woman for another.

[Text]

> No blooming youth shall ever make me err
> I will the beauty of the mind prefer
> If himans rites shall call me hence
> It shall be with some man of sence
> 5 Nott with the great butt with a good estate
> Nott too well read nor yet illetterate
> In all his actions moderate grave & wise
> Redyer to bear than offer injuries
> And in good works a constant doer
> 10 Faithfull in promise & liberall to the poor
> He thus being quallified is allways seen

25. W. R. Williams, *The Parliamentary History of the Principality of Wales, 1541–1895* (Brecknock, Wales, 1895), p. 30.

26. Philoclea, so far unidentified, can now be named by means of Philips' copybook, NLW 775B, p. 37, as being "Mrs. M. Stedman" who was probably Mallet Stedman of Strata Florida, Cardiganshire, less than forty miles northeast of Cardigan. Mallet was one of four children of John Stedman and Jane Vaughan. Mallet's eldest brother, James, married Margaret, daughter of Richard Owen of Rhiwsaeson, Montgomery. Upon James Stedman's death in 1672, Margaret married Hector Philips, the brother of James Philips. See Francis Green, "Stedman of Strata Florida" in *West Wales Historical Records* (Carmarthen, Wales, 1921), pp. 100–01.

Ready to serve his friend his country & his king
Such men as these yout say there are but few
Their hard to find & I must grant it too
15 Butt if I ^{ever} hap to change my life
Its only such a man shall call me wife.
             Humbly Dedicated too Mrs Anne Barlow
             C. Fowler

A marry^d state affords but little Ease
The best of husbands are so hard to please
This in wifes Carefull faces you may spell
Tho they desemble their misfortunes well
5 A virgin state is crownd with much content
Its allways happy as its inocent
No Blustering husbands to create y^r fears
No pangs of child birth to extort y^r tears
No childrens crys for to offend your ears
10 Few worldly crosses to distract y^r prayers
Thus are you freed from all the cares that do
Attend on matrymony & a husband too
Therefore Mad^m be advised by me
Turn turn apostate to loves Levity
15 Supress wild nature if she dare rebell
Theres no such thing as leading Apes in hell

A receipt to cure a Love sick Person who cant
obtain the Party desired

Take two oz: of the spirits of reason three oz:
of the Powder of experiance five drams of the Juce
of Discretion three oz: of the Powder of good advise
& a spoonfull of the Cooling watter of consideration
make these all up into Pills & besure to drink a
little content affter y^m & then the head will be
clear of maggotts & whimsies & you restored to y^r
right sences but the persons that wont be ruld must
become a sacrifise to cupid & dye for love for all
the Doctors in the world cant cure y^m

if this wont do apply the plaister & if that wont
do itts out of my power to find out what will

SYLVIA BOWERBANK

The Spider's Delight: Margaret Cavendish and the "Female" Imagination

> The world arose from an infinite spider
> who spun this whole complicated mass from
> his bowels.
>
> Brahmin Teaching
> (Cited by David Hume)

RECENTLY Margaret Cavendish, Duchess of Newcastle (1623–1673), was remembered in the popular *Book of Failures* as "the world's most ridiculous poet."[1] And for the past three hundred years—although Charles Lamb may have enjoyed the eccentricity of her person and prose—readers of her works have agreed that she failed as a philosopher and as a writer. In *A Room of One's Own,* Virginia Woolf goes searching for a seventeenth-century "Judith Shakespeare" and finds in Cavendish's writings "a vision of loneliness and riot . . . as if some giant cucumber had spread itself over all the roses and carnations in the garden and choked them to death."[2] In her study of seventeenth-century travel fantasies, *Voyages to the Moon,* Marjorie Nicolson refuses to describe Cavendish's *New Blazing World* because she cannot bear to reread that "ponderous tome" in order "to bring order out of . . . chaos."[3] But Cavendish herself confesses her shortcomings. In a typically disarming epistle to the reader she warns, "I shall not need to tell you, I

---

1. Stephen Pile, *The Incomplete Book of Failures* (New York, 1981), p. 94. This verdict is probably based on Samuel Pepys' comment on reading Cavendish's *Life* of her husband: "it shows her to be a mad, conceited, ridiculous woman, and he an asse to suffer [her] to write what she writes to him and of him." *The Diary of Samuel Pepys* (9 vols.), ed. Robert Latham and William Matthews (London, 1974), IX, 123.
2. Virginia Woolf, *A Room of One's Own,* 1st ed. 1929 (London, 1979), pp. 59–60.
3. Marjorie Nicolson, *Voyages to the Moon* (New York, 1948), p. 224.

had neither Learning nor Art to set forth these Conceptions, for that you will find yourself" (PO/63). Her naiveté of method can be and has been blamed on her lack of education and lack of access to learned and critical communities.[4] Yet anyone who has ventured to read ten pages of Cavendish's work knows that her method, or rather her defiance of method, is deliberate.

I. Cavendish's Conception of Herself as a True Wit

In most of her writings Cavendish celebrates, in theory and in practice, what she calls her "natural style." Her first book, *Poems and Fancies* (1653), announces the approach she exemplifies:

> Give Mee the Free, and Noble Stile,
> Which seems uncurb'd, though it be wild . . .
> Give me a Stile that Nature frames, not Art:
> For Art doth seem to take the Pedants part. (*PF,* p. 110)

She associates the writings of the learned with sterile artificiality and labored imitation. Cavendish's "true wit" is natural wit unrestrained. Occasionally in her writings she depicts playful confrontations between fancy and reason; for example, in *Philosophical Fancies* (1653), Reason cautions Thoughts to "walke in a Beaten Path" lest the world "think you mad." But Thoughts rebel: "we do goe those waies that please us best. / Nature doth give us liberty to run / Without check." For Cavendish, "Learning is Artificial, but Wit is Natural" (*OEP,* "To the Reader").

While Restoration comedy might be seen to share this perspective in spirit, if not in method, the prevailing literary opinion and practice of her age denied such a polarization between natural wit and learned judgment. As early as 1595, Philip Sidney's *Defence of Poesie* claimed that natural wit "reined with learned discretion" becomes true wit.[5] In *Timber,* Ben Jonson uses the same image (ultimately taken from Plato) of the rider-poet reining in his horse (spontaneous wit) with a bit (judgment). Like the bee—now known to scholars as "the neo-classic bee"— the true writer imitates; he is able "to draw forth out of the best, and

4. See Myra Reynolds' *The Learned Lady in England, 1650–1760* (Boston, Mass., 1920), pp. 46–49; Douglas Grant's *Margaret the First: A Biography of Margaret Cavendish, Duchess of Newcastle 1623–1673* (Toronto, 1957), pp. 37–38 and passim; Hilda Smith's *Reason's Disciples: Seventeenth-Century English Feminists* (Urbana, Ill., 1982), pp. 75–95. For the full titles of Cavendish's works, see the listing that follows this essay.

5. Philip Sidney, "An Apology for Poetry," in *Critical Theory since Plato,* ed. Hazard Adams (New York, 1971), pp. 158–59.

choicest flowers . . . and turn all into honey."[6] In *Epicoene,* Jonson creates the archetypal Truewit who has many descendants in Restoration comedy. In all his speeches Truewit seems to speak spontaneously; actually Jonson constructed his "instinctive" eloquence by means of a careful rejuvenation of classical sources.[7] For Jonson, study and imitation, rather than making wit artificial, purify it and make it more right and more natural. In later neoclassical writers, like Dryden, the trend to understand true wit in terms of judgment dominating fancy increased to the point of eliminating fancy altogether.[8]

It will be clear how estranged Cavendish was from the prevailing literary attitudes if we look at a passage from a writer of the next generation who excelled at anatomizing perversions of wit. Readers of *A Tale of a Tub* are familiar with Swift's masterly creation of the narrator who can be identified as "a mad modern." In a remarkable passage at the end of "A Digression concerning . . . Madness," Swift reveals the narrator's mentality by playfully applying the traditional horse/rider image: madness is the overthrow of reason by fancy; it is a "revolution" against the natural hierarchical order of the two faculties: "I myself, the author of these momentous truths, am a person, whose Imaginations are hard-mouthed, and exceedingly disposed to run away with his reason, which I have observed from long experience to be a very light rider, and easily shook off; upon which account my friends never trust me alone."[9]

What is mad for Swift is feminine for Cavendish. Reason may predominate in men, but fancy predominates in women. In *Poems and Fancies,* Cavendish reminds ladies of poetry as "belonging most properly to themselves." Female brains, she claims, "work usually in a Fantasticall motion" and therefore "go not so much by Rules and Methods as by choice" (*PF,* "To all Noble and Worthy Ladies"). Elsewhere she emphasizes that reason is enslaved by necessity while fancy is voluntary (*BW*/66, "To the Reader"). In "Poetesses hasty Resolution" prefacing *Poems and Fancies,* she describes how her self-love in its ambition for fame

---

6. Ben Jonson, "Timber or Discoveries," *The Complete Poems,* ed. George Parfitt (Harmondsworth, 1975), 11. 2146, 3068; pp. 426, 448. Also see James W. Johnson, "That Neo-classic Bee," *Journal of the History of Ideas,* 22 (1961), 262–66.

7. Jonas Barish, "Ovid, Juvenal and the Silent Woman," *PMLA,* 71 (1956), 213–24.

8. Dryden defined wit as merely "a propriety of thoughts and words"; see "Introduction," *Critical Essays of the Seventeenth Century* (3 vols.), ed. J. E. Spingarn (Oxford, 1980), I, xxxi.

9. Jonathan Swift, *A Tale of a Tub and other Satires,* ed. Kathleen Williams (London, 1975), p. 114.

overcame her judgment when she published her poems without revision. Reason is depicted as an authoritarian bully who would have told her how ill her poems were if she had not rushed them into print. In a later work she defends herself against a rude comment by a reader who said, "my wit seemed as if it would overpower my brain" by asserting that "my reason is as strong as the effeminate sex requires" (*TR*, p. 151).

She is claiming, for women at least, a freedom from "rules and method" denied writers by the seventeenth-century literary climate, dominated as it was by the opinions of Horace, whose satiric target in *Ars Poetica* is the Democritus who believes "that native talent is a greater boon than wretched art and shuts out from Helicon poets in their sober senses."[10] Cavendish was convinced that her originality was enough "ground" for "lasting fame."[11] Over and over again, she tells her readers that she has no time for studying other people's work because "our sex takes so much delight in dressing and adorning themselves." Besides, her ambition is not to be a lowly scholar but a great philosopher: "A Scholar is to be learned in other mens opinions, inventions and actions, and a philosopher is to teach other men his opinions of nature" (*PO/55*, "To the Reader"). This ambition led her to send her *Philosophical and Physical Opinions* (1655) to Oxford and Cambridge. Hoping this action is "not unnatural, though it is unusual for a woman," she asks the universities to house her book "for the good encouragement of our sex; lest in time we should grow irrational as idiots, by the dejectedness of our spirits, through the careless neglects and despisements of the masculine sex to the effeminate" (*PO/55*, "To the two Universities"). Besides, she does not see why her opinions should not be studied with other "probabilities" (such as Aristotle's teachings); after all, only the custom of teaching ancient authors prevents readers from a "right understanding" of "my newborn opinions" (*PO/55*, pp. 26–27).

As we have seen, Cavendish associates fancy unregulated by judgment with vanity, especially in women. Yet she expects readers to share her good-natured tolerance of this charming foible, "it being according to the Nature of our Sex" (*PL*, p. 1). At the same time, she presents literary labor as pedantry not becoming to noble persons like herself. Although this attitude was not uncommon among her contemporaries (at least

10. Horace, *Satires, Epistles and Ars Poetica*, trans. H. Rushton Fairclough, Loeb Classical Library (Cambridge, Mass., 1978), p. 475.

11. Grant, p. 192.

professedly), it led Cavendish to reject revision of her work as a task beneath her dignity and also unnatural to her as a woman. In her supposedly revised *Philosophical and Physical Opinions* (1663), she thinks it is enough that she is "very Studious in my own Thoughts and Contemplations" and that she records them in their natural and noble disorder: she had "neither Room nor Time for such *inferior Considerations* so that both Words and Chapters take their Places according as I writ them, *without any Mending or Correcting*" (*PO*/63, "Epistle to Reader," my italics). She goes on to hope that "Understanding Readers" will not reject the "Inward worth" of her philosophy "through a Dislike to the Outward Form." The truth is there somewhere, she claims, because she makes no attempt to censure "Nature," which gives her thoughts "which run wildly about, and if by chance they light on Truth, they do not know it for a Truth" (*PF*, "Epistle to Mistris Toppe").

Her justification for her lack of method is that she recreates pure nature. Although she cannot create a well-wrought urn, so to speak, she gives fresh thoughts: she asks, "Should we not believe those to be Fools, that had rather have foul Water out of a Golden Vessel, than pure wine out of Earthen or Wooden Pots?" (*ODS*, "To the Reader of My Works"). The natural trait she imitates is fecundity. Nature brings forth monsters, as well as well-proportioned offspring, and lets them die of their own deformity; in like manner, Cavendish claims, she "scribbles" down whatever comes to her and lets the reader sort it out (*TR*, pp. 185, 205, 206). Fecundity and originality are the gifts of the true wit. Cavendish is best understood, then, as a defender not of her sex, but of self and self-expression.

Hers is the mentality which is the target of Swift's *Battle of the Books* (1704). In the famous confrontation between the bee and the spider, the ancient and the modern respectively, Swift uses the bee to symbolize the principles and practices of neoclassicism. "By an universal Range, with long Search, much Study, true Judgment, and Distinction of Things," the bee-writer "brings home Honey and Wax."[12] The spider, on the other hand, is akin to Jonson's Littlewit, in *Bartholomew Fair,* who "like a silkworm" spins creations "out of myself."[13] Swelling up, Swift's spider boasts, "I am a domestick Animal, furnisht with a Native Stock within my self. This large Castle . . . is all built with my own Hands, and the

---

12. Swift, p. 149.
13. *Ben Jonson's Plays* (2 vols.), Everyman's Library (London, 1967), II, 183.

Materials extracted altogether out of my own Person." His character-istics—his stress on originality; his fondness for a domestic rather than a "universall" perspective; his aimless creativity which, although it creates a space for himself, gives nothing of use (honey and wax) to others—are so extreme that he is fittingly called a subjectivist. The neoclassical bee warns that the spider's perspective ("a lazy contemplation of four Inches round") and his method ("feeding and engendering on it self") turns "all into Excrement and Venom; producing nothing at last, but Fly-bane and a Cobweb."[14]

Yet with what exuberance did Cavendish embrace this subjectivist perspective and method as her own. With a curious aptness she favors imagery of silkworm, spider, and spinning for depicting literary creativ-ity, particularly hers. In *Poems and Fancies,* she writes that "all brains work naturally and incessantly" and goes on to call the writing of poetry "spinning with the brain." She intends to win fame as a writer "by spinning" a "Garment of Memory": "I cannot say the *Web* is strong, fine or evenly Spun, for it is a Course piece; yet I had rather my Name should go meanly clad, then dye with cold" (*PF,* "The Epistle Dedicatory"). I have italicized "web" to emphasize how naturally Cavendish could fuse the images of the spinner and the spider. Cavendish resorts to spinning imagery when excusing herself for encroaching on male prerogative: women have so much "waste time" that "our thoughts run wildly about," producing not only "unprofitable, but indiscreet Actions, wind-ing up the thread of our lives in snarles on unsound bottoms" (*PF,* "An Epistle to Mistris Toppe"). To describe "great masters of speech," she writes that they can speak "untangled"; they "can winde their words off their tongue" without a snarl or knot; they can work the "thread of sense into a flourishing discourse" (*TR,* p. 181). Yet Cavendish is aware of the commonplace implications of the imagery of silkworm and spider. In *Natures Pictures Drawn by Fancies Pencil* (1656), a collection of conflicting tales about life by various speakers usually identified by sex alone, she has "a Man" denigrate the creativity of spider and silkworm:

> The Silkworm and the Spider Houses make,
> All their Materials from their Bowels take . . .
> Yet they are Curious, built with Art and Care,
> Like Lovers, who build Castles in the Air,
> Which ev'ry puff of Wind is apt to break,
> As imaginations, when Reason's weak. (*NP,* p. 126)

14. Swift, pp. 149–50.

In her autobiography Cavendish presents a poignant picture of her life as an isolated duchess who would be a famous writer. Her one delight was her solitary creativity which she describes using her favorite imagery: "I had rather sit at home and write . . . I must say this on behalf of my thoughts, that I never found them idle; for if the senses bring no work in, they will work of themselves, like silkworms that spins [sic] out of their own bowels" (*TR,* p. 208).

II. No Room in Salomon's House

In his *New Atlantis,* Francis Bacon imagines Salomon's House, a patriarchal institution dedicated to enlarging "the bounds of Human Empire" over nature.[15] When the Royal Society was founded in 1662, it was based on the Baconian principle that the search for knowledge must be communal and experimental. Because the advancement of knowledge requires a mind "steadily fixed upon the facts of nature," Bacon was suspicious of the speculative mind which works "upon itself, as the spider worketh his web," and brings forth only "cobwebs of learning."[16] For Baconians, there could be no room in Salomon's House for natural philosophers who give out their "own imaginations for a pattern of the world."[17]

Margaret Cavendish's writings, as we shall see, attempted to provide an alternative perspective to the prevailing Baconian paradigm. Her lifelong ambition was to win public acceptance as Nature's true champion. In 1653, as R. H. Kargon points out, Cavendish "expounded an Epicurean atomism at once so extreme and so fanciful that she shocked the enemies of atomism and embarrassed its friends."[18] Everything could be explained by the motion of atoms, such as: what causes dropsy, how the brain works, and why the earth has attraction. And "the Cause why things do live and dye, / Is, as the mixed Atomes lye" (*PF,* p. 14). At times her descriptions of atoms are no less plausible than the descriptions of how the world works given in the learned texts of her more restrained contemporaries who were also fumbling around in search of a credible

15. Francis Bacon, *New Atlantis* in *A Selection of His Works,* ed. Sidney Warhaft (New York, 1965), p. 447.

16. Bacon, *The Proficience and Advancement of Learning,* in *Selections,* p. 225.

17. Bacon, *The Great Instauration,* in *Selections,* p. 323.

18. Robert Hugh Kargon, *Atomism in England from Hariot to Newton* (Oxford, 1966), p. 73.

mechanics—for example, Robert Boyle with his corpuscular universe.[19] At other times she is fancy-free and plays with her atoms, as when she imagines "A World in an Eare Ring": "Wherein a Sun goeth round, and we not see. / And Planets seven about that Sun may move." And her ultimate defense of her opinions is that, although they may or may not be true, they are natural. After all, "I do not applaud my self so much as to think that my works can be without errors, for Nature is not a Deity" (*OEP,* "To the Reader").

Her intuitive, if erratic, exposition and defense of Nature's ways continued after 1660, although, probably in response to the more restrictive intellectual climate of the Restoration, she abandoned atomism: if each atom were "absolute," there could never be "good government" in the universe (*PO*/63, "Another Epistle to the Reader"). This use of a political analogy suggests that her social perspective—that of a royalist duchess restored to her place in a regulated kingdom—had some influence on these later speculations about the natural order. In another work she repudiates atomism because in that philosophy every atom is "a kind of Deity" undermining the harmonious whole of Nature. In this typically entertaining passage she depicts rebellious democratic atoms: "Nature would be like a Beggars coat full of lice; Neither would she be able to rule those wandering and stragling atomes, because they are not parts of her body, but each is a single body by itself, having no dependance upon each other" (*OEP,* p. 142).

Yet she continued to present Nature as self-moving and perceptive. *Philosophical Letters* (1664) should be read as a vindication of the wisdom of nature and the "intelligence" of matter from what Cavendish considers the belittling attacks of Henry More, Hobbes and Descartes. She ridicules More for assuming the passivity of nature (*PL,* "Letter VIII"). She denies Hobbes' claim for human supremacy by means of language over the rest of creation. As everyone knows, she quips, "a talking man is not so wise as a contemplating one." Other creatures, she says, have their own reason: "For what man knows, whether Fish do not know more of the nature of water, and ebbing and flowing, and the Saltness of the Sea?" (*PL,* pp. 113, 40). She attacks Descartes' separation of mind from body and his reductionist attitude toward the body: "the Eye, Ear, Nose, Tongue, and all the Body, have knowledge as well as the Mind."

19. See Robert Boyle, *The Works* (6 vols.), ed. Thomas Birch (Hildesheim, 1966), I, 356; II, 43; Grant, pp. 193, 196.

The only difference is that the mind, rational matter, is not "encumbered with the grosser parts of matter to work upon" but the senses, sensitive matter, "works or moves only in its own substance" (*PL,* pp. 116, 127). Reason, as she tells us in another work, is "nothing but corporeal self-motion, or a particle of the purest, most subtil and active part of matter." This being the case, she asks why the human should "be the onely Creature that partakes of this soul of Nature," and why the rest of Creation "should be soulless or (which is all one) irrational." The natural soul of reason permeates nature: "I do not deny that a Stone has Reason" (*OEP,* pp. 45–46). Clearly these insights into nature's vital connectiveness resemble the ideas of Anne Conway and others.[20]

Her philosophy of nature is empathetic, subjective, and fragmentary. Sometimes she happens to create a startlingly beautiful analogy; for example, she likens animate matter to a spinner and inanimate matter to yarn: "Natural air seems to be made by such kinds of motions as spiders make cobwebs, for the animate matter's motions spin from a rare degree of inanimate matter."[21] But mostly her natural philosophy consists of passages excusing and flaunting her ignorance; for example, she writes about the anatomy of the body by confessing that she never read a book on the subject nor studied the body because "the modesty of my Sex would [not] permit me." In *Observations upon Experimental Philosophy* (1666), she presents a curious argument to show that speculation is a higher means toward knowledge than experiment is. Playing on the overlapping social and intellectual connotations of the word "mechanick," she writes that "experimental or mechanick Philosophy" should be subservient to speculative philosophy just as "the Artist or Mechanick is but a servant to the student" (*OEP,* p. 7). Her main target in *Observations* is the microscope, that "artificial informer" that "more deludes than informs." The year before, Robert Hooke published his influential *Micrographia* describing his experiments with the microscope. Cavendish thinks it "unnatural" to change the size of creatures so they "cannot be judged according to their natural figure." For illustration, she ridicules one of the experiments describing the 14,000 eyes on a fly. The microscope must be misleading us here or else, she asks, why doesn't a fly see a

---

20. In a chapter entitled "Women on Nature," Carolyn Merchant discusses Conway's vitalism, but does not note this strain in Cavendish's work. *The Death of Nature: Women, Ecology and the Scientific Revolution* (San Francisco, 1980), chapter 11.

21. *PO/63,* p. 183; Grant, pp. 199–200.

spider? She adds that these "eyes" might be "blisters or watery pimples" (*OEP,* pp. 24, 26–28).

This is the kind of speculation Joseph Glanvill, an apologist for the Royal Society, compliments in a letter to "your Grace" when he admires "the quickness and vigor of your conceptions." But he adds that hers is a pattern that men should not imitate. Glanvill denies that ratiocination is higher than "perfection of sense" by reasserting the Baconian paradigm. A natural philosopher must be willing "to tie down the mind in Physical things, to consider Nature as it is, to lay a Foundation in sensible collections, and from thence to proceed to general Propositions, and Discourses" (*Coll,* p. 99). Walter Charleton, another member of the Royal Society, also treats her with the tact required in writing to a duchess: he professes not to know "which of the two, Aristotle or your Grace, hath given us the best definition of the humane Soul." But he also warns her that all opinions, even hers, must be subjected to "skeptical Judgement" (*Coll,* pp. 111–12).

In another letter, Charleton tells her the use to which he puts her philosophy: "Whenever my own Reason is at a loss, how to investigate the Causes of some Natural Secret or other, I shall relieve the Company with some one pleasant and unheard of Conjecture of yours so that by reading your Philosophy, I have acquired thus much advantage: that where I cannot Satisfy, I shall be sure to Delight" (*Coll,* pp. 143–44). With her peculiar sense of humor and self-importance, Cavendish would have been pleased with this unusual tribute. There is no doubt that in small selected doses Cavendish delights us, as she intends to, with her fanciful conjectures and self-mockery. Charleton also teased her about her eccentric style: "You plant Fruit-trees in your Hedge-rows, and set Strawberries and Raspberries among your Roses and Lilies." Yet even for this "art" he flatters her: she has a fancy "too generous to be restrained" by "the laborious rule of Method" (*Coll,* pp. 143–44).

It was probably not any of her ideas—radical and eccentric as they may seem—that alienated her from the community of natural philosophers. After all, Charleton, a popularizer of Epicurean atomism of the type made respectable by Gassendi, was forgiven after he trimmed his work to the hostile winds of Restoration science.[22] As we have seen,

22. See Nina Rattner Gelbart, "The Intellectual Development of Walter Charleton," *Ambix,* 18 (Nov., 1971), 149–68; Howard Jones, *Pierre Gassendi 1592–1655: An Intellectual Biography* (Nieuwkoop, 1981), pp. 280–95.

Cavendish willingly discarded her politically dangerous atomism. And other writers, if more cautiously, were sympathetic to finding the life principle immanent in nature.[23] There were two main factors, then, contributing to her exclusion from the intellectual community: her sex and her untamed method. Lady Ranelagh is the only other contemporary Englishwoman who has a claim to being called "a scientific lady," and she was content to work through her brother, Robert Boyle.[24] To a limited extent Cavendish was able to overcome social restrictions because of her status as a duchess and as the wife of a patron of virtuosi: she corresponded with leading thinkers; she published her works; she got invited, albeit as a spectator, to the Royal Society in 1667. But mostly she was isolated. With good reason, then, she defends contemplation as the means, indeed her only means, to seek natural truths. The Royal Society, based as it was on the inductive method and the fraternal accumulation of knowledge, could provide no home for her person or her perspective.

Cavendish's response to her failure as a natural philosopher was to retreat into fantasy. In 1666 she created her own *New Blazing World*. As she tells us in "To all Noble and Worthy Ladies" of the 1668 edition, the opinions advanced in *New Blazing World* have "sympathy" and "coherence" with those expressed in *Observations*, to which it was originally appended in 1666. But in *New Blazing World*, she could be "Margaret the First" in a more congenial world; no one should begrudge her this pleasure "since it is in every ones power to do the like" (*BW/66*, "To the Reader").

The tedious chaos of the "plot" is an obvious feature of this work which has been attacked elsewhere.[25] The central character is an Empress of a newly found polar kingdom whose main interest is in ruling

23. Even the fathers of mechanics, Newton and Leibnitz, sought a vitalistic inner principle in nature because they were not satisfied with mechanistic explanations of biology. See Carolyn Merchant's chapter "Leibnitz and Newton," pp. 275–89. Descartes of course thought the machine metaphor was adequate to describe the life of bodies. See Philip R. Sloan, "Descartes, the Skeptics and the Rejection of Vitalism in Seventeenth-Century Physiology," *Studies in the History and Philosophy of Science*, 8 (1977), 1–28, p. 17.

24. For the close relationship between Boyle and Ranelagh, see Gilbert Burnet's "A Sermon at the Funeral of the Honourable Robert Boyle," *Select Sermons* (Glasgow, 1742). Brother and sister died within a week of each other; Burnet preached the sermon on January 7, 1692. See Charles Webster's attempt to establish Ranelagh's "membership" in the Invisible College, *The Great Instauration: Science Medicine and Reform 1625–1660* (London, 1975), pp. 62–63. For a general study, see Gerald Meyer, *The Scientific Lady in England 1650–1750: An Account of Her Rise, with Emphasis on the Major Roles of the Telescope and Microscope* (Berkeley, Cal., 1955).

25. See Nicolson's attack referred to at the beginning of this essay.

over the virtuosi: "the Bearmen were to be her Experimental Philosophers, the Bird-men her astronomers, the Flyworm- and Fish-men her
Natural Philosophers, the Ape-men her Chymists, the Satyrs her Galen-
ick Physicians," for example (*BW*/68, p. 15). The Empress becomes
angry at her virtuosi when the Bearmen observe celestial phenomena
through a telescope and begin to quarrel. The Empress condemns tele-
scopes as "false informers" which "delude" their senses. Obviously this is
the same opinion Cavendish advances in *Observations,* but in *New Blazing
World* the Empress has power to command them to smash their instru-
ments. She lets them keep their toys only when her experimental
philosophers admit that "we take more delight in Artificial delusions,
than in Natural truths" (*BW*/68, pp. 26–28).

In *New Blazing World,* Cavendish deliberately lets fancy take the reins
and creates a world which indulges her fondest wishes—even allowing
her some harmless retaliations against the Royal Society. Cavendish
imagined a situation, improbable even in the twentieth century, in which
a female leader dominates the scientific community. Her experimental
philosophers are hack workers on detail, servants who bring in their
observations so that the Empress can triumphantly speculate and create a
synthetic truth. But the independent, intelligent Empress gets lost in the
oblivion of Cavendish's prose.

What we remember instead is the eccentric duchess created in Pepys'
Diary, who made an infamous visit in 1667 to the Royal Society during
which leading scientists such as Robert Boyle and Robert Hooke did
experiments to provide what Marjorie Nicolson derisively calls "the
afternoon's entertainment."[26] According to Pepys' enduring version,
Cavendish did not "say anything that was worth hearing, but . . . was full
of admiration, all admiration."[27] What we remember, then, of the
seventeenth-century "scientific lady" of England is the image of woman
as audience and, at best, as patron of men's accomplishments.

To reinforce how fanciful, how "mad," how revolutionary, and
ultimately, how irrelevant Cavendish's vision of a female scientific
genius was to her contemporaries, we need only compare the relationship of the Empress to her virtuosi with the more famous depiction of the
relationship between an intelligent woman and a modern philosopher in

26. Marjorie Nicolson, "'Mad Madge' and 'The Wits'," *Pepys' Diary and the New Science*
(Charlottesville, Va., 1965), p. 113. For another account, see Samuel Mintz's "The Duchess of
Newcastle's Visit to the Royal Society," *Journal of English and Germanic Philology,* 51 (1952), 119–28.
27. Pepys, VIII, 243.

Bernard Fontenelle's *Plurality of Worlds. Entretiens sur la pluralité des mondes* (1686) was one of Fontenelle's most ingenious tactics in his life-long attempt to popularize the ideas of the new philosophy. There were 28 editions of *Entretiens* in Fontenelle's long lifetime (1657–1757).[28] The passages quoted in this essay are from the 1638 translation by Aphra Behn. The immense popularity of *Plurality of Worlds* can be explained, to a great extent, by Fontenelle's choice of format. As Behn's subtitle tells us, he uses "five nights conversation with Madam the Marchioness of***" in a garden in order to defend the mechanical philosophy and the theory that there are other inhabited worlds. We are to enjoy a pleasant and flirtatious dialogue between "Fontenelle" and Madam even as we learn the truths of the Cartesian universe: "we are always in the Humour of mixing some little Gallantries with our most serious Discourses."[29]

But what interests us here is the relationship between the two conversationalists: "Fontenelle" is the authority; he will teach the Copernican system. There are, for him, "no more unnecessary Difficulties" because he can reduce nature to a few easy laws. Because nature works like the contrivance of machines behind the scenes of an opera, he can "draw the Curtains and shew you the World." What room is there for dialogue when one party has all the answers? Well, this expert is a chivalrous servant to a noble and charming lady. Madam is an eager, intelligent, and pliable student. But she has her little rebellions—"just like a woman." When "Fontenelle" offers to demonstrate a point by drawing a zodiac in the sand, she stops him: "It would give a certain Mathematical Air to my Park, which I do not like." Although she admires the simplicity of the Copernican system, she objects to the insecurity of the earth in it. She teasingly claims to favor the Indian system in which the earth is supported by four elephants. If danger threatens these solid foundations, the Indians "would quickly double the number of their elephants." "Fontenelle" laughs "at her fancy"; this is reminiscent of Charleton's pleasure at Cavendish's wit. Late on the first night, Madam at last agrees to be reasonable and to be Copernican. Later when she holds back in attractive timidity from the implications of such a vast universe, he urges her on to intellectual courage.[30]

28. Leonard M. Marsak, "Introduction," *The Achievement of Bernard le Bouvier de Fontenelle* (New York, 1970), pp. xvi, xxvi.

29. "Monsieur Fontenelle's History of the Plurality of Worlds," in *Histories and Novels of Mrs. A. Behn* (2 vols.), (1718), II, 98. Behn's was the third English translation.

30. *Plurality of Worlds,* II, 7–9, 19, 22, 27, 95.

Thus although modernists like Fontenelle might eagerly debunk the traditional cosmic hierarchies of Aristotle and Aquinas, "Fontenelle" and Madam embark into the new universe with their respective sexual roles intact. He leads intellectually and she follows. Even though Behn might object to the inconsistency of Madam's superficial yet profound character, Fontenelle's book did teach women (and men) what was actually being debated in the science of the seventeenth century, and Behn approved of bringing women into intellectual circles. But Cavendish's *New Blazing World* offered no instruction and no access to or compromise with the outside world.

In her own world Cavendish can refuse to moderate her desires to accessible goals and can create her women free from the restrictions which hampered Cavendish in both the social and intellectual realms. Only in paradise, only in a state with people of many complexions— literally azure, purple and green—and only in a state ruled by an Emperor "extraordinary" like her husband in his easygoing, non-authoritarian character, only in fantasy, could Cavendish find a haven for the intellectually ambitious woman. But beyond making this crucial point, *New Blazing World* offers little reading satisfaction or intelligibility. A passage from Robert Boyle reiterating the contempt the new science felt for subjective truth illustrates why Cavendish failed as a natural philosopher in the age of reason. There was no room in Salomon's House for the spider who "taking notice only of those objects, that obtrude themselves upon her senses, lives ignorant of all the other rooms in the house, save that wherein she lurks."[31]

III. Margaret Cavendish and the Crabbed Reader

Cavendish was used to such complaints as mine. In *Orations of Divers Sorts* (1668), she ridicules her censorious critics: "those Faults or Imperfections I accuse my self of, in my Prefactory Epistles, they fling back with a double strength against my poor harmless Works; which shews their Malice and my Truth." She asks such "ill-natured" readers why they bother to accuse her plays of having no plots when she already acknowledges that. Such critics "prefer Plots before Wit." Then she states her most characteristic stance as a writer: "I write to please myself, rather than to please such Crabbed Readers."[32] Still there is a prolifera-

---

31. Boyle, "Of the Usefulness of Natural Philosophy," *Works*, II, 9.
32. "To the Readers of my Works," *ODS*; also see *TR*, p. 213.

tion of prefaces before her works in which she addresses readers, shares her problems as a writer and as a thinker, and tells us how to read her work. Yet for three hundred years, her readers have remained crabbed—except for her husband, Charleton perhaps, and Charles Lamb. Perhaps we have yet to understand the nature of the legacy she left to posterity.

Maybe her sense of humor eludes us. Maybe we are like her sour contemporary, Mary Evelyn, who on overhearing the friendly banter between Charleton and the Duchess to the effect that universities should be abolished if they didn't abandon Aristotle and teach Cavendish's new-found ideas, became so provoked by Cavendish's manner that she dismissed the Duchess as mad.[33] Maybe Cavendish intends us to laugh at the incongruous juxtaposition of her self-deprecation and self-dramatization. She not only ridicules herself and the foibles of her sex but also—and this is important—casts doubt upon serious claims to knowledge of nature's secrets. William Cavendish seems to have shared her skeptical and playful attitude in this passage inserted at the end of her *Philosophical and Physical Opinons* (1663): "Since now it is A-la-mode to Write of Natural Philosophy, and I know, no body Knows what is the Cause of any thing, and since they are all but Guessers, not Knowing, it gives every Man room to Think what he lists, and so I mean to Set up for my self, and play at this Philosophical Game as follows, without Patching or Stealing from any Body." Perhaps Margaret Cavendish developed her science of the fancy to restore the balance in an age of reason. Her work represents, in a whimsical way, a groping toward an alternative vision to Salomon's House with its pretence to finding certain and objective knowledge. And she does attempt a relationship with nature that runs counter to the exploitive mastery proposed by Bacon; her approach is sensitive and reverent as well as subjective.

By her own admission, she was vain, inconsistent and silly; yet she took herself and her philosophy seriously. She was incapable of sustained study and thinking, so she said; yet she wanted to be a famous philosopher and to join the scientific establishment. In the same work she expounds a vitalistic and a mechanistic universe. Her writing is muddled and indecisive; yet she expected posterity to admire it. The effect of letting contradictions stand is to undermine continually any authoritative stance

---

33. Mary Evelyn, "A Letter to Mr. Bohun," *Diary and Correspondence of John Evelyn* ed. William Bray (London, 1900), pp. 731–32.

she might be achieving. And yet at times this method gets at the complexity of psychological and social reality: for example, in *Orations of Divers Sorts,* she lets several female speakers describe the lot of women from conflicting perspectives. They claim everything from "we live like Batts, or Owls, labour like Beasts, and dye like Worms" to "what can we desire more, than to be Men's Tyrants, Destinies, and Goddesses?" (*ODS,* pp. 240–46). Since Cavendish makes no judgmental distinctions among her female orators, it would be a mistake to guess her viewpoint; perhaps she shared all their attitudes to some extent.[34] Contradiction is typical of her style. It is hard to say whether this is an intentional strategy or the unfortunate result of her refusal to revise and to edit her writing.

Cavendish's work is a defense of free fancy or subjective expression in principle and in practice. Some modern writers like Anaïs Nin advocate a revolution in style toward one that would reflect psychological reality: the new literary form would be "endlessly varied and fecundating as each crystal varies from the next."[35] Cavendish can be seen as a pioneer of such an approach. Even those of us who are attracted to her personality and ideas cannot help but wish she had been a more disciplined writer. It is also useful, then, to see Cavendish's place in literary history as a cautionary tale for those of us who would suggest that craftsmanship and order are masculine, and artlessness and chaos are feminine. Do we really want to create a literary ghetto called the "female imagination" and claim as its characteristic style of expression, anarchic formlessness? Style has no sex. After all, the real spider's web, although spun out of herself, is architectonically sound, even elegant.

ABBREVIATIONS:

The following abbreviations have been used in the text and notes:

BW/66: *The Description of a New Blazing World,* appended to *OEP.*
BW/68: *The Description of a New World, called the Blazing World.* London: A. Maxwell, 1668.
Life: *The Life of the First Duke of Newcastle.* First ed. 1667. Everyman Library #182. London: J. M. Dent, n.d.

34. Woolf takes the angry "we live like Batts" for Cavendish's own voice in *Room,* p. 59.
35. Anaïs Nin, *The Novel of the Future* (New York, 1976), p. 29.

NP: *Natures Pictures Drawn by Fancies Pencil to Life.* London: A. Maxwell, 1671.

OEP: *Observations upon Experimental Philosophy, to which is added, the Description of a New Blazing World.* London: A. Maxwell, 1666.

ODS: *Orations of Divers Sorts, Accommodated to Divers Places.* Second ed. London: A. Maxwell, 1668.

PF: *Poems and Fancies.* First ed. 1653. Facsimile, Scolar Press, 1972.

PL: *Philosophical Letters: or, Modest Reflections Upon some Opinions in Natural Philosophy, Maintained By several Famous and Learned Authors of this Age.* London, 1664.

PO/55: *The Philosophical and Physical Opinions.* London: J. Martin & J. Allestrye, 1655.

PO/63: *Philosophical and Physical Opinions,* London: William Wilson, 1663.

TR: *A True Relation of my Birth, Breeding and Life* appended to *Life.*

Coll: *A Collection of Letters and Poems: Written by several Persons of Honour and Learning, Upon divers Important Subjects, to the Late Duke and Dutchess of Newcastle.* London: Langly Curtis, 1678.

JACQUELINE DISALVO

Fear of Flying:
Milton on the Boundaries
Between Witchcraft and Inspiration

A Mask was written while England was embroiled over the acquittal of the Lancashire witches, *Paradise Lost* during one of the last of the seventeenth-century witch trials. We should not be surprised, therefore, if Milton's poems utilize the lore spread by such witch hunters as Matthew Hopkins who popularized a discourse drawn from Continental inquisition manuals. Dalila, literally a pagan, is given the "enchanted cup and warbling charms" of Circe, the archetypal witch, against whose "sorceries" Samson must learn "to fence [his] ear" (932, 937).¹ Comus (son of Circe and Bacchus) invites the Lady of Milton's *Mask* to enter a devilish association and join the lustful, woodland rites of his enchanted crew. And allusions to such lore in Eve's dream and the Fall it anticipates interpret her sin as a fall into witchcraft. While such references have been noted, they have not yet been given the full weight that they deserve. For when seen in relation to gender psychology, they can illuminate those paradoxical tensions and bridled energies in the viscera of Milton's poetry which render it so much richer than any account of its professed ideology alone could convey.

That energy bursts forth, like an eruption from the unconscious itself, as Satan breaks out of his infernal prison, "Puts on swift wings, and towards the Gates of Hell / Explores his solitary flight" (2.631–32). We sense that this flight is in the mind which is its own Hell as it culminates in the surreal, powerfully charged vision of Sin, her gaping womb in perpetual birth. Here we find embedded the poem's first reference to witchcraft in the flight of the "Night-Hag" to an orgy of "Lapland witches." The fact that Satan confronts Sin as she "sat / Fast by Hell Gate" reveals that she herself is the "hag" who guards the "bounds" (2.725, 644). Boundaries, however, can have inner meaning, and the

---

1. John Milton, *Complete Poems and Major Prose,* ed. Merritt Y. Hughes (New York, 1957); citations follow line numbers or page numbers in this edition.

emotional overtones of associations like these also allow one to examine the psychology underlying Milton's treatment of witchcraft. Moreover, since that witches' orgy will recur in the Invocation to Book 7 in the image of their traditional forbears, the maenads, tearing apart Orpheus, we can pursue the threat this psychology seems to pose to the poet himself. Hence, in tracing Milton's depiction of witchcraft, we can identify a state of consciousness associated with women that Milton condemned and feared as a danger to his identity as a man and a poet. We can then examine the possibility that the same fallen psychology, which Milton marginalizes in the intoxication and the nocturnal flights of witches, is paradoxically, not just the enemy, but the source of his own poetic inspiration.

Witch Lore in Milton

I am not particularly concerned with whether Milton believed that witches' powers actually existed, but a brief summary of John Steadman's treatment of this question will introduce some important background.[2] Steadman identifies two contending traditions cited equally by Milton's contemporaries. On the one hand, the *Malleus Maleficarum* (The Hammer of Witchcraft) of the Dominican Jacob Sprenger allowed Henry More, Joseph Glanville, Hopkins and the Presbyterian witch hunters to accept the existence of a demonically inspired sorcery.[3] Witches were believed to worship and have sex with the devil in a heretical sabbat in return for magical powers such as flight. On the other hand, an alternative approach, derived from the tenth-century *Canon Episcopi*, supported skeptics such as the sixteenth-century French Protestant, Johann Weyer, in seeing witchcraft rather as merely a delusion, although perhaps demonically inspired.[4] Identifying Milton with this skeptical tradition, Steadman rejects Trevor Davies' assumption that Milton "accepted the current beliefs of the witch-hunters of his day" and, instead, follows Howard Schultz in concluding that, while sparse evidence requires that Milton's views finally "remain largely a topic of conjecture," "we may guess with some confidence that he doubted the

2. Steadman, John. "Eve's Dream and the Conventions of Witchcraft," in *Milton's Biblical and Classical Mythology* (Pittsburg, Pa., 1984), pp. 160–66. See also Linda Draper Henson, "The Witch in Eve: Milton's Use of Witchcraft in *Paradise Lost*," in *Milton Reconsidered*, ed. John Karl Franson (Wolfeboro, N.H., 1976), pp. 122–34, and William B. Hunter, "Eve's Demonic Dream," *ELH* 13 (1946), 256–65.

3. J. Sprenger and H. Institutor, *Malleus Maleficarum, The Hammer of Witchcraft*, trans. Montague Summers (New York, 1971).

4. *The Canon Episcopi (Capitulum)* in Henry Charles Lea, *Materials Toward a History of Witchcraft*, ed. A. C. Howland (New York, 1957), pp. 178–80.

prevalence and just possibly the existence of sorcery in his own age."[5] Given my focus on psychological aspects of Milton's use of witch lore, Steadman's identification of him with those who alleged the experiences of witches to be only fantasy or dream underscores, rather than undermines, my argument.

Milton apparently accepts the belief in women's particular susceptibility to such delusion found in Weyer's linking of the devil's manipulation of witches to that of Eve, for "Chiefly that sly trickster seduces the female sex, which is temperamentally unstable, credulous, . . . weakminded . . . as it can control its emotions only with difficulty."[6] Thus, in his chapter on "How the Devil Corrupts Men's Phantasy and Seems to Prophesy According to Augustine's Opinion," Weyer writes, "Whence certain women devoted to Satan and seduced by demonic illusion and phantasms, believe and declare that they ride at night with the pagan goddess Diana or with Herodias or Minerva or a countless multitude of women . . . such phantasms are imposed . . . not by a divine but by an evil spirit. For Satan himself, who transforms himself into an angel of light, when he overcomes the mind of any woman and subjugates her to himself through infidelity . . . leads the captive mind astray deluding it with dreams."[7]

And indeed, in Book 5 Milton prefigures Eve's fall by such a devil-inspired dream, replete with the typical associations of witches' "fantasies." In Book 4 Satan is shown

> Squat like a Toad, close at the ear of *Eve*;
> Assaying by his Devilish art to reach
> The Organs of her Fancy, and with them forge
> Illusions as he list, Phantasms and Dreams. (4.800–03)

The toad is a common form of animal "familiar" through which evil spirits allegedly assisted witches, and Satan, as the *Canon* contends, is corrupting Eve's imagination. Associations with Weyer's "angel of light" are heightened when Eve anxiously reports to Adam the next morning how "Close at mine ear one call'd me forth to walk," who seems "One shap'd and wing'd like one of those from Heav'n / By us oft seen" (5.36, 55) in a scene where "reigns / Full Orb'd the Moon, and with more pleasing light / Shadowy sets off the face of things" (5.41–43). We

5. R. Trevor Davies, *Four Centuries of Witch Beliefs* (New York, 1957), pp. 170–72; Howard Schultz, *Milton and Forbidden Knowledge* (New York, 1955), pp. 46–47.

6. Johann Weyer. *De Praestigiis Daemonum et Incantationibus ac Veneficiis* (1568), cited by Steadman, p. 161.

7. Steadman, p. 162; Lea, pp. 490–98.

recognize the full moon of witches' nocturnal rites, but the "shadowy" ambience may also allude to Weyer's characterization of women's Satanic delusion: "When evil women resolve to put these wicked fictions into practice, they consecrate themselves with spells and ointments to the devil who . . . rules their phantasy, leading it to places where they desire to be. Nevertheless, their bodies remain without sensation, and the devil covers them with a shadow so that they are invisible and when he observes that their desires have been fulfilled in their imaginations, he restores them to their own motions and removes the shadow."[8]

The specific experience such commentators most sought to explain was witches' transportation across space in the "night-flying" by which they allegedly travelled outside of local settlements to distant or wild places. Weyer repeats the common identification of such women with the goddess Diana, who mythically roamed the forests with her tree nymphs and was associated with childbirth, with orgiastic dances, wild animals, outlaws and strangers. "Night-flying" was also identified with the "night–wandering" through which such "nocturnae" approached their infamous sabbats, secluded from official surveillance deep in the woods at night. The sixteenth-century Italian "Benandanti," studied in Carlo Ginzburg's *Night Battles,* confessed to a variant of these nocturnal cavalcades in which, after falling into a stupor, their souls would travel long distances where one participant reported "They fought, played, leaped about, and rode various animals . . . the women beat the men who were with them with sorghum stalks," and they did battle against witches threatening the crops. Ginzburg remarks that "it always seems to be closely connected to the myth of nocturnal travels by women led by Abundia-Satia-Diana-Perchta . . . Fraw Fenus(Venus)" and presumes all had roots in an older fertility rite.[9] He traces how these beliefs fused with those of the terrifying "Wild Hunt" of dead souls led by a vegetation goddess or the legendary "Wild Man" and also resembled nocturnal bands who allegedly turned into werewolves. Similarities can also be noted to the "festivals of misrule" throughout early modern Europe, studied by Natalie Zemon Davis, in which youths caroused in violation or deliberate reversal of the normal rules of society, religion, and even gender.[10]

Fertility cults had been prolific in archaic Greece and, as Jane Ellen

8. Steadman, pp. 162–63.
9. Carlo Ginzburg, *The Night Battles* (Baltimore, Md., 1984), pp. 1, 44.
10. Natalie Zemon Davis, "The Reasons of Misrule" and "Women on Top," *Society and Culture in Early Modern France* (Stanford, Cal., 1975).

Harrison has shown, had influenced later Greek mythology. Keith Thomas' *Religion and the Decline of Magic* records how widespread, if fragmentary, were the survivals of agrarian cults in the seasonal lore of peasant society.[11] Originally, therefore, the clergy had condemned various practices primarily as a reversion to paganism, citing particularly the female cults of Diana and of Bacchus with his maenad followers. Later persecution intensified when Inquisitors reinterpreted various phenomena as alleged convocations between witches and the devil, sometimes also denounced as demonically inspired reversions to ancient idolatry.[12] Similarly, Milton's learned classicism enabled him to weave various threads of myth and lore back into the whole cloth with which he costumes a reconstructed idolatrous cult flourishing in the English woods and fens to which the Lady and Eve are potential recruits.[13] This complex includes a journey into the wilderness by night-flying or wandering and seduction or temptation by a Pan-devil to a heretical rite including abandoned dancing, demonic lust, and magical food.

Comus, or course, led such a band of "night-travellers." After "Roving the Celtic and Iberian fields" (60), his "daily walks" now take him through "every alley green, / Dingle or bushy dell of this wild Wood" (311–12); we meet him leading his procession that "to the Moon in wavering Morris [dance] move" (116), calling his unruly band to "Hail the Goddess of Nocturnal Sport / Dark veil'd Cotytto" (128–29), patron of ancient orgiastic midnight rites, with "Midnight shout and revelry / Tipsy dance and Jollity" (103–04). In *Paradise Lost* such nocturnal gatherings in the wilderness are given associations both with delusion and with demonism when the suddenly dwarfed devils are compared to

> Faery Elves,
> Whose midnight Revels, by a Forest side
> Or Fountain some belated Peasant sees,
> Or dreams he sees, while over-head the Moon
> Sits Arbitress, and nearer to the Earth
> Wheels her pale course; they on their mirth and dance
> Intent with jocund Music charm his ear;
> At once with joy and fear his heart rebounds. (1.781–88)

11. Jane Ellen Harrison, *Prologomena to the Study of Ancient Greek Religion* (Cambridge, 1903); Keith Thomas, *Religion and the Decline of Magic* (New York, 1971); Margaret Murray's argument in *The Witch Cult in Western Europe* (Oxford, 1921) for a full pagan religion surviving underground has been discredited, however.

12. Peter Burke, *Popular Culture in Early Modern Europe* (New York, 1978).

13. See Richard Halpern, "Puritanism and Maenadism in *A Mask*" in *Re-Writing the Renaissance: The Discourses of Sexual Difference in Early Modern Europe,* ed. Margaret W. Ferguson, Maureen Quilligan, and Nancy J. Vickers (Chicago, 1986), pp. 88–105.

This rural observer is not directly accused of seeking out these rites, whereas Comus' "late Wassailers" had gone to the forest in order to join such peasant revels when "the sound / Of Riot and ill-manag'd Merriment / Such as the jocund Flute or gamesome Pipe / Stirs up among the loose unletter'd Hinds / When . . . / In wanton dance, they praise the bounteus *Pan*" (172–75).

In *A Mask,* moreover, Milton alludes to the strange roving fires, sometimes believed spirits, which were said to lure wanderers to the "obscured haunts of inmost bow'rs" where such "abhorred rites of Hecate" (536, 35) are performed, that

> evil thing that walks by night
> In fog or fire, by lake or moorish fen,
> Blue meager Hag or stubborn unlaid ghost
> That breaks his magic chains at curfew time. (431–35)

Thus Comus and his night-wandering forest crew of wanton revellers have sought to lure the Lady into the Bacchanalian rites of a full-blown black Sabbath. It is significant, therefore, that Milton similarly depicts Eve roaming with the serpent to her temptation after such a fire in an allusion which transforms her midday confrontation into a magical nocturnal one,

> as when a wand'ring Fire
> . . . .
> Which oft, they say, some evil Spirit attends,
> Hovering and blazing with delusive Light,
> Misleads th'amaz'd Night-wanderer from his way
> To Bogs and Mires. (9.634–41)

Eve was described, moreover, as having "Betook her to the Groves" "like a Wood-Nymph light . . . of Delia's [Diana's] Train" (9.338, 386–87). By linking Eve to the "Night-wanderer," Milton presents her being tempted, like the Lady, to witchcraft, as had been anticipated in her demonically inspired dream, when she first wandered to the interdicted Tree. Like the ointments and herbs said to make women susceptible to Satanic hallucinations, the "Fruit Divine" is presented by Satan as a magical potion which can bestow supernatural powers and participation in Godhead. He tempts Eve to the same demonic hubris for which Isaiah condemned the "Prince of the Air" ("I will ascend above the heights of the clouds: I will be like the most High," Is.11. 13–14):

> Taste this, and be henceforth among the Gods
> Thyself a Goddess, not to Earth confin'd,
> But sometimes in the Air, as wee, sometimes
> Ascend to Heav'n. (5.77–80)

This promise is immediately fulfilled, for upon tasting the fruit Eve begins "flying":

> Forthwith up to the Clouds
> With him I flew, and underneath beheld
> The Earth outstretcht immense, a prospect wide
> And various: wond'ring at my flight and change
> To this high exaltation. (5.86–90)

This "night-flying" is familiar to us in the commonest iconography of witch lore, the crone sailing upon her broom across a moonlit sky. Milton himself, as we have seen, had directed us to this emblem in the "Night-Hag" riding to orgiastic dances in the waste, a motif which also appears when Comus is said to "rid'st with *Hecat*" (135).

Of all the witches' alleged powers, flying was the most commonly ascribed delusion, for as George Gifford writes, "The devils make the witches in some place believe . . . that sometimes they flie or ride in the ayre, which thinges indeed are nothing so, but they strongly delude the fantasies of witches."[14] A materialist explanation for visions of flight was offered by Francis Bacon, who credits some ointment, remarking that "the greatest wonders which they tell of, carrying in the air . . . are still reported to be wrought . . . by ointments and anointing themselves all over" and are consequently "the effects of imagination." Bacon suggests "soporiferous medicines" as likely sources of inspiration.[15] Numerous reports alleged that witches anointed themselves or their brooms with salves. The convicted witch Ursula Kollarin testified in 1661 that "the old Wollwerkthin smeared them all with a black salve . . . soon their bodies became covered with feathers and forthwith they flew to Rohitsch Mountain like so many storks."[16] Galileo's colleague, Giovanni Battista della Porta, reports use of a nightshade ointment: "they anoint the body, having rubbed themselves very thoroughly before, so that they grow rosy. Thus, on some moonlight night they think they are carried off to banquets, music, dances and coupling with young men . . . So great is the force of the imagination." Andres Laguna, a sixteenth-century physician, described an unguent in a witches' jar made of "herbs cold and soporiferous in the ultimate degree," the same mentioned by Bacon,

---

14. George Gifford, *A Dialogue Concerning Witches and Witchcraftes* (1593), in G. L. Kittredge, *Witchcraft in Old and New England* (Cambridge, Mass., 1929), p. 248.

15. Francis Bacon, *Works* (London, 1870), p. 643.

16. Hans Peter Duerr, *Dreamtime: Concerning the Boundary Between Wilderness and Civilization*, trans. Felicitas Goodman (New York, 1985), p. 1.

"hemlock, nightshade, henbane, and mandrake."[17] The anthropologist Michael Harner points out that these plants have in common a psychotropic skin-penetrating alkaloid, atropine, present also in related nightshade plants used by the Jivaro Indians of Peru as hallucigens and speculates that brooms might have served as applicators to sensitive female membranes. Thus, in *Hallucigens and Shamanism* he concurs with early demonologists who treated witches' experiences as hallucinations and postulates that the night-flying, ecstatic dancing and the metamorphosis into animals reported by witches might involve a state of altered consciousness, induced at least sometimes by mind-altering drugs capable of creating visions.

In *Paradise Lost* aspects of the witch cult, clarified by parallels in *A Mask,* define Eve's temptation, although partly displaced to events before or after it. Thus Comus' charmed potion derived from the "Potent herbs and baleful drugs" culled by Circe, and the "Fruit Divine" of Eve's flying dream indicate that she too is tempted to an idolatrous banquet. After an ominous allusion to Circe ("more duteous at her call, / Than at *Circean* call the Herd disguis'd" (9.521–22), the serpent tempts Eve to seek transformation and illumination through magical food, a "Sacred, Wise, and Wisdom Giving Plant" which, as "Mother of Science" (679, 80), will open the doors of perception to a feminine wisdom of self-expansion: "opener mine Eyes / Dim erst, dilated Spirits, ampler Heart" (875–76). After tasting it, Eve falls into pagan tree worship, revering the "sciential sap" of "Nectar, drink of Gods" (837, 38) which might "op'n'st Wisdom's way, / And giv'st access" to "secret" knowledge (809–10). The intoxication grows, with Adam's participation as they enact the erotic "Great Rite" and experience sensations of flight and deification as "with new Wine intoxicated both / They swim in mirth, and fancy that they feel / Divinity within them breeding wings" (1008–10). This is the same Satanic delusion attributed to witches.

Boundary Crossing and Flight in *Paradise Lost*

Shortly thereafter Adam articulates a new desire to inhabit a barbaric wilderness and "In solitude live savage, in some glade / Obscur'd" of "highest Woods impenetrable" (1085–86), and they are compared to "th'*American* so girt / With feather'd Cincture, naked else and wild"

17. Giovanni Battista della Porta. *Magiae Naturalis,* (1561), in Michael Harner, "The Role of Hallucinogenic Plants in European Witchcraft," *Hallucigens and Shamanism* (New York, 1972), p. 138; Andres Laguna, *Materia Medica* (1555), iv, xxv, pp. 421–22, in Harner, p. 135; Bacon, p. 664.

(1116–17).[18] But as "heathens" inhabiting the "heath," witches were identified both with pagan savages and with the wilderness. Interestingly, the "hag" ("hagazussa") was the being that sat on the "hag," the hedge which separated village and woods. This fence was, moreover, sometimes seen as a barrier against demons. Again, "hagazussa" can literally mean "the one riding on the fence," the night-flyer, as implied in the medieval text that said "woman, I saw you riding on a fence switch . . . at that time when day and night were equal."[19]

But this threshold guarded by a frightening Hag can also be seen as the psychological boundary which must be crossed when entering certain psychic states. Like witch lore Milton seems to link the desire for an intoxicated state of consciousness, associated with "flying," to a physical retreat into the wilderness, a primitive site identified with barbaric emotions and practices. In *Paradise Lost* physical wandering materializes psychological flight with both involving a transgression of boundaries, a passage either over or beyond them. Furthermore, the maintenance of boundaries, distinctions, definitions and hierarchies are, as Regina Schwartz has insightfully demonstrated, the essence of the Miltonic world-view:

> In *Paradise Lost* Milton depicts the Creation as the act of delimiting, of setting bounds. . . . In contrast, Milton's chaos is virtually "defined" by its lack of definition, its limitlessness. . . . moral categories tend to assume physical shape. Boundaries take on far more than physical significance. . . . When the will is perceived not as the passive recipient of binding, but as the active force that binds, it replicates the divine creative act of separating, distinguishing, Miltonic choosing. . . . The primordial battle with chaos becomes symbolic of the human struggle with sin.[20]

In *Paradise Lost* all these images of flying, of wilderness and the crossing of boundaries are conjoined in association with the devil. Satan is a "night-flyer," a violator of boundaries, and a savage inhabitant of the wilderness. His perpetual flying overcomes the boundaries between hell and chaos, chaos and earth and finally Eden. We see him first as "with expanded wings he steers his flight / Aloft" (1.225–26) from the fiery lake of Hell; then as the "flying Fiend" approaches "Hell bounds" (2.643, 44); next passing through the "Illimitable Ocean without bound" (2.892) of chaos to limbo, the outer shell of the universe which "seems a

---

18. Jackie DiSalvo, "'In narrow circuit strait'n'd by a Foe': Puritans and Indians in *Paradise Lost*," in *Ringing the Bell Backwards,* ed. Ronald G. Shafer (Indiana, Pa., 1982).

19. Duerr, pp. 45, 243.

20. Regina Schwartz, "Milton's Hostile Chaos: '. . . And the Sea Was No More,'" *ELH* 52 (1985), 337–74.

boundless Continent / Dark, waste, and wild" (3.423–24); then as the one who has "o'erleapt these earthly bounds" (4.584); and finally, with all these themes converging, as he flies over the boundaries of an Eden, "Ill fenc't" (4.372) and

> At one slight bound high overleap'd all bound
> Of Hill or highest Wall, and sheer within
> Lights on his feet. As when a prowling Wolf
> Whom hunger drives to seek new haunt for prey,
> Watching where shepherds pen their Flocks at eve
> In hurdl'd Cotes amid the field secure,
> Leaps o'er the fence with ease into the Fold:
> . . . .
> Thence up he flew . . . on the Tree of Life. (4.181–95)

The language of flight ("soar," "ascend," "reascend," "Flight precipitant," "wandring flight," "bounds," "leaps") persistently confronts and overcomes a grid of successively nested boundaries ("chains," "bars," "bounds," "Iron Gates," the "restraint" of hell "prescrib'd," the "Frontiers" of chaos, the "enclosure green" with its "verdurous wall of Paradise," the "hurdle" and "fence" of its "cote," "pen," "fold," and "field secure," and the nuptial bower "fenc'd up" with its own "verdant wall").

Boundary Violation and Ego Dissolution

Hell has, however, been only "slightly barr'd," for although Gabriel is the "limitary Cherub" he admits, it is "hard . . . to exclude / Spiritual substance with corporeal bar" (4.967, 971, 584–85); spiritual or mental reality is less bounded than physical. As boundaries can refer not only to geographic but psychic terrain, the first lap of Satan's airborne journey from Hell hints at the psychological significance to Milton of witches' flight. In this unmitigated nightmare of masculine paranoia, Sin's children are "hourly conceiv'd / And hourly born" as "into the womb / That bred them they return" (2.796–98), perpetually enveloped in her vast, voluminous body:

> The one seem'd Woman to the waist, and fair,
> But ended foul in many a scaly fold
> Voluminous and vast, a Serpent arm'd
> With mortal sting: about her middle round
> A cry of Hell Hounds never ceasing bark'd
> With wide *Cerberean* mouths full loud, and rung
> A hideous Peal; yet, when they list, would creep,
> If aught disturb'd thir noise, into her womb,
> And kennel there. (2.650–57)

Feminist psychoanalysis has located the psychogenesis, and hence the problematics of masculinity, in the process of separation from a female mother. To the emphasis on infant bonding and differentiation from the "pre-oedipal" mother in the object-relations psychology of D. W. Winnicott and Margaret Mahler, feminists add the role played by gender formation.[21] Theorists like Nancy Chodorow see boys' formation as requiring an early and intensified "dis-identifying" with the mother in order to become "not-feminine."[22] As Milton's image so powerfully captures and as one male analyst of the process has poignantly observed, the result is an enduring terror of regression: "The whole process of becoming masculine is at risk in the little boy from the day of birth on; his still-to-be-created masculinity is endangered by the primary, profound, primeval oneness with the mother, a blissful experience that survives, buried but active, in the core of one's identity as a focus which can attract one to regress back to that primitive oneness. That is the threat latent in masculinity."[23] Sin's prime offspring, Death, "The other shape / If shape it might be call'd that shape had none / Distinguishable in member, joint or limb," actualizes such a complete loss of identity.

Significantly, this scene is also replete with allusions to witchcraft. Satan's flight gives way to witches' flight as we move by allusion from Sin waist-high in hounds to Scylla metamorphosized below the waist into dogs by Circe, to Circe's patroness, the "Night-Hag" Hecate, accompanied by her beasts to a witches' sabbat. In Milton's sequence of images Sin's monstrous children break out of that female engulfment only to enter another psychic subjection as the bestial familiars who are entranced and catapulted into flight in the train of witches:

> Nor uglier follow the Night-Hag, when call'd
> In secret, riding through the Air she comes
> Lur'd with the smell of infant blood, to dance
> With *Lapland* Witches, while the laboring Moon
> Eclipses at thir charms. . . . (2.662–66)

A connection between male psychology and female magic was originally perceived by Karen Horney who attributed to memories of appar-

---

21. Margaret Mahler, F. Pine, and A. Bergman, *The Psychological Birth of the Human Infant* (New York, 1975); D. W. Winnicott, *Collected Papers: Through Pediatrics to Psychoanalysis* (London, 1958); *The Maturational Processes and the Facilitating Environment* (New York, 1965).

22. Nancy Chodorow, *The Reproduction of Mothering: Psychoanalysis and the Society of Gender* (Berkeley, Cal., 1978).

23. Robert Stoller, "Facts and Fancies: An Examination of Freud's Concept of Bi-Sexuality," in *Women and Analysis,* ed. Jean Strouse (New York, 1974), p. 358.

ent maternal omnipotence a masculine "dread of women" which endows them with magical power that must be fended off with defensive hostility.[24] The allusions which link Circe, Sin, and the Hag join the psychological power of sorcery to the maternal entrapment Sin dramatizes. In addition, Circe's ability to reduce the men who succumbed to her charms to beasts had always expressed the danger of fear of women's psychological power. Also, we will see that such phylogenetic regression can mirror ontogenetic return to the womb. Finally, the passage culminates in the frightful unleashing of such feminine energies in the orgiastic dances of witches "Lur'd" by "infant blood" under a "laboring" moon in reverberations of infantile terror.

Other images of birth in Milton carry similar psychological implications. His Creation emphasizes a "birth" of the creature from the "great Mother" as a separation from an undifferentiated cosmic unity. In a sequence of parturitions, creatures emerge (un-merge) from the earth which had itself just been "form'd, but in the Womb as yet / Of Waters, Embryon, immature" (7.276–77). Similarly, it is intriguing that Satan's flight through chaos and transgression of boundaries was conflated with images of the dissolution of the boundaries of matter there, where all identity, still uncreated in the womb of nature, is reduced to its "embryon Atoms" in a "vast vacuity." Schwartz traces an analogy between Satan's loss of identity and the void of chaos. Satan's flight is identified with chaos itself and both with pre-natal existence, with womb and embryos. In this conjunction and in Satan's difficulty differentiating down from up, flying from falling, or flight from sailing in this "wasteful Deep" (2.961), Milton offers a particularly apt expression of the intra-uterine and symbiotic states preceding the consolidation of ego boundaries distinguishing self and other. Significantly, in Milton's vision of the Creation these images of birth also involve a breaking of bonds:

> The Earth obey'd and straight
> Op'ning her fertile Womb teem'd at a Birth
> Innumerous living Creatures . . .
> . . . out of the ground up rose
> . . . .
> The Tawny Lion, pawing to get free
> His hinder parts, then springs as broke from Bonds. (7.454–65)

These associations are reinforced for us by the puns of Milton's discourse which links the "bounding" of flight, to limiting "bounds" but

24. Karen Horney, "The Dread of Woman," *International Journal of Psychoanalysis* 13, 348–60.

also to the "bonds" of relationship and mental "bondage" of sin. As signifiers these words are closely allied; remove a single letter from the word "bound" and you have "bond," a morphological similarity for which there were some etymological links: the bonds or bounds that shackle and the bonds that connect (e.g., human beings in the "bonds of marriage") all derive from the Old English verb "binden" (to bind or constrict), with its past participle, "bounden" (the state of being so confined or fastened), related to the French "bander" (to tie). Although the bounds and boundaries that delimit and circumscribe derives from the Old French "bodne" (a limiting line), this signification seems to overlap the "bound" (bond, band) which restrains. Milton can therefore exploit multiple verbal paradoxes. In seeking boundless exaltation Eve must forge a bond with Satan that is simultaneously her bondage; Satan "at one slight bound high overleap't all bound" (4.181) in a "bound" (from the French "bondir"—to leap, bounce) which can evade boundaries and escape bonds.

Such verbal paradoxes can be used to reflect the psychological one in which the unbounded ego is the one most bonded to the other, its mother. Interestingly, the archaic "bounden" could mean either being "bound up" or "pregnant." Women have been seen as having more "malleable boundaries" than men, arising from the more intense, longer lasting bonds of the baby girl to a female mother who promotes such identification. Chodorow has viewed such feminine formation as preparation for a maternal role which requires a re-entry into symbiosis. The resulting tendency to emotional dependency has been summoned to explain women's obsessive need for romantic love.[25]

This psychology can explain the implication, so problematic for Milton criticism, that the poet identifies Adam's fall, in characteristic masculine emotional paranoia, with his excessive love for Eve. "Linkt," as Eve says, "in love so dear," they describe their relationship as complete merger, "One Heart, One soul . . . aught . . . shall separate us" (9.970, 965–970), with Adam falling because "I feel / The Link of Nature draw me" (913–14). "So forcible within my heart I feel / The Bond of Nature draw me to my own" (955–56). Admonishing him for such attachment, Raphael had urged enhancement of Adam's own ego and "self-esteem": "weigh her with thyself; / Then value" (8.572, 570–71).

---

25. Elizabeth J. Aries and Rose R. Oliver, "Sex Differences in the Development of a Separate Sense of Self During Infancy: Directions for Further Research," *Psychology of Women Quarterly* 9 (1985), 512–32; Chodorow, *Reproduction of Mothering;* Luise Eichenbaum and Susie Orbach, *What Do Women Want?* (New York, 1984).

He warns that the bonds which relate will become those that imprison. The Son condemns such attachment as "Subjection" and a violation of boundaries of gender in which Adam "didst resign thy Manhood" (10.153, 148), and Michael adds that men fall through women only by becoming feminine themselves, through "effeminate slackness" (11.634). Similar equations of excessive bonding, "foul effeminacy" (SA 410), and male catastrophe have been found in "Samson's Struggle With the Woman Within."[26] In the magical context of Adam and Eve's post-lapsarian erotic intoxication which, like the witches' lustful sabbat, recapitulates the intercourse of Satan and Sin, these bonds suggest a dangerous entrancement, and they fall into a "now fenceless World" (10.303).

Thus "effeminacy" seems to conjoin romantic and occult psychologies. Subjectively, the intense emotional bonding of symbiosis and romantic love share with "transcendent" experiences of flying beyond boundaries an immersion of the self in something larger, a dissolution of the self–limiting ego. Freud himself reached this conclusion after the poet Romain Rolland challenged him to account for the fact that beyond the religious beliefs which Freud had traced to neurotic illusions, there was a purely subjective feeling which was the source of religious energy, a "sensation of 'eternity,' a feeling as of something limitless, unbounded . . . oceanic." Freud attributed such feelings to the dissolution of boundaries between ego and outside and between ego and id through regression to a stage when the infant "does not yet distinguish his ego from the external world as the source of the sensations flowing in upon him." He postulated that for some this "primary ego feeling has persisted" as "an all embracing feeling which corresponded to a more intimate bond between the ego and the world about it" and remarks in passing that such regression through practices like yoga might explain mysticism, trances and ecstasies.[27]

While Freud simply seems to dismiss such experiences as "infantile," many others have appropriated his analysis for a materialist psychological defense of various kinds of extraordinary consciousness. Morris Berman writes that "[S]tudents of child development have largely agreed that the first three months of life constitute a period of "primary narcissism," or in Erich Neumann's terminology, the "cosmic-anony-

26. Jackie DiSalvo, "Intestine Thorn: Samson's Struggle With the Woman Within," in *Milton and the Idea of Woman,* ed. Julia Walker (Champaign, Ill., 1988), pp. 211–29.

27. Sigmund Freud, *Civilization and its Discontents,* trans. James Strachey (New York, 1961), pp. 14, 16.

mous phase." The infant is all Unconscious (primary process) . . . its life essentially a continuation of the intra-uterine period. It behaves as though it and its mother were *a dual unity, having a common boundary*."[28] Believing that adults can return to this awareness, Berman advocates the cultivation of "participating consciousness" as an antidote to alienation from nature, human relationship, and the unconscious. Finding that schizophrenics seemed to revert to a "de-differentiation" in which they could not distinguish themselves from things outside, Harold Searles began to view symbiosis as a state of "non-differentiation" from the non-human environment as well as from the mother. He also noted a related "phylogenetic regression" to animal states (comparable to the Circe myth and wolf cults). So long as one could return to ordinary consciousness, reversion to such states could, he believed, be therapeutic and liberating. After Ernst Kris defended such processes as "regression in service of the ego," the concept would be widely used to understand "altered consciousness."[29] Significantly, like the orthodox observers of female "delusion" and emotional instability, Berman and others often presume a particularly feminine quality in or capacity for such experiences. Following the poet Robert Graves in identifying the pursuit of such mental states with the archaic religion of a Mother-Goddess, another poet, Robert Bly, advocates "Mother-Consciousness."[30]

Anthropologist Hans Peter Duerr would explain myths like the "wild Hunt" and the flying of witches from a similar perspective. He maintains that "in archaic societies people . . . are trained to let their ordinary nature 'empty out' the way Indians put it, to bring about a 'lowering of the mental level' in the jargon of parapsychology; in other words, to surrender their boundaries." With regard to flying, he writes:

Let us compare our nature to an iceberg. What is ordinarily visible is merely a small . . . part of it above the water. . . . If anyone wants to see more of it, he needs to change into a diving bird the way Siberian shamans do. That which we include in our personalities will then expand to the extent as we, our everyday person, surrender our more or less firm boundaries. . . . The limits of our person now include matters we formerly saw as belonging to the "outside" world. . . . Our soul does not leave our body, but the limits of our person no longer coincide with the boundaries of our body. . . . It is not so much that we fly. It is that our ordinary "ego boundaries" evaporate and so we encounter ourselves at places where our "everyday body," whose boundaries are no longer

28. Morris Berman, *The Reenchantment of the World* (Ithaca, N.Y., 1981), p. 157.

29. Harold Searles, *The Non-Human Environment: In Normal Development and Schizophrenia* (New York, 1960); Ernst Kris, *Psychoanalytic Explorations in Art,* (New York, 1952), p. 294.

30. Robert Graves, *The White Goddess* (New York, 1948), pp. 422–41; Robert Bly, "I Came Out of the Mother Naked," *Sleepers Joining Hands* (New York, 1973), pp. 48–49.

identical with our person, is not to be found. Such an expansion of our person can easily be described as flying.[31]

But ego boundaries are in some ways also those of civilization. Wilhelm Reich analyzed the character structure as a defensive armor which was "the congealed sociological process of a given epoch."[32] In *Civilization and its Discontents* Freud depicts the ego as an adaptation to the frustrations of a "reality principle" whose repressions are required by labor and monogamous sexual mores. Interestingly, Duerr links the "Wild Hunt" and "night-flying" to "festivals of misrule" in these terms: "'Between the times' . . . normality was rescinded . . . order and chaos ceased to be opposites . . . they lost their normal, everyday reality and became beings of the 'other' reality . . . whether they turned into animals or hybrid creatures or . . . reversed their social roles. They might roam bodily through the land or only 'in spirit,' in ecstasy." Witches therefore could be seen as people wandering beyond the boundaries of their ordinary, civilized, repressed selves and in their intoxicated flights, dances, and other orgiastic practices "able to dissolve within themselves the boundary between civilization and wilderness."[33]

Milton, however, as Schwartz demonstrates, anxiously identifies the loss of boundaries with chaos. On the many levels here in which Eve's flying dream signifies access to either sub- or supra-rational realms, the experience is prohibited. Wandering has long been perceived as Milton's pervasive pun for human errancy; Adam and Eve fall into savagery, Satan into bestiality, and even Platonic mystics are relegated to limbo. Since flying is falling and the Hag who guards the boundaries is Sin at the borders of hell, crossing them only plunges one into a psychological inferno. For Satan "Which way I fly is Hell" (4.75).

Psychological Ambivalence in Miltonic Inspiration

Yet along with Satan and Eve, it is mostly the poet himself who flies, though with significant ambivalence. (Angels can fly, but their flight is

---

31. Duerr, p. 87.

32. Wilhelm Reich, *Character Analysis,* trans. Vincent R. Carfagno, 3rd ed. (New York, 1972), p. xxvi.

33. Duerr, pp. 37, 87.

34. Milton does allude to the incident in which Christ's was flown by Satan to the pinnacle (11.381–84) while Adam is ascending with Michael "In the Visions of God" (11.377). This was the most problematic Biblical story for those who denied the existence of magical flight and Satan's power to bestow it, and Milton's treatment of the passage merits more analysis. In *Paradise Regained* "Such power was given to him then" (3.251–52) in a divinely ordained exception. Christ's refusal to cast himself upon the air reinforces Milton's rejection of aspirations to flight, but in *Paradise Lost,* as Joseph Wittreich pointed out to me, the context is visionary.

neither fully dramatized nor subjectively described.)[34] Yet in the "Fifth Elegy" Milton had linked poetry to the shadowy "other side" of dreams, madness, and ecstasy (literally out of body) and to "night-wandering" and "night-flying":

[B]y night I am beside Pirene in my dreams. My breast is aflame with the excitement of its mysterious impulse and I am driven on by the madness and the divine sounds within me. . . . Already my mind is being borne up into the sheer liquid heights of the sky and, quit of the body, I go through the wandering clouds. I am carried through shadows and grottoes, the secret haunts of the poets; and the innermost shrines of the gods are open to me. My spirit surveys all that is done on Olympus and the unseen infernal world is not impervious to my eyes. What mighty song is my soul pouring from its full throat? What is to be the offspring of this madness and this sacred ecstasy? (38)

Although this is traditional rhetoric for poetic inspiration, Milton problematizes it in his epic. John Steadman shows that the motif of the flight of the soul to apotheosis becomes a negative one, a symbol of the vanity of creaturely conceit, as in limbo where contemplative spirits "upwhirl'd aloft / Fly o'er the backside of the World" (3.493–4).[35] So while Milton flies, he does so with considerable anxiety, as we see in the Invocations where these elements converge.

In the Invocation to Book 3, the poet, addressing the divine Celestial Light, also identifies inspiration with the night-flying and wandering of the "Elegy":

> Thee I revisit now with holder wing,
> Escap't the *Stygian* pool, though long detain'd
> In that obscure sojourn, while in my flight
> Through utter and through middle darkness borne
> . . . .
> Taught by the heav'nly Muse to venture down
> The dark descent and up to reascend,
> Though hard and rare: thee I revisit safe,
> And feel thy sovran vital Lamp; but thou
> Revisit'st not these eyes, that roll in vain
> To find thy piercing ray, and find no dawn;
> . . . .
> . . . Yet not the more
> Cease I to wander where the Muses haunt
> Clear Spring, or shady Grove, or Sunny Hill. (13–28)

It is, he insists, *"Sion"* that "Nightly I visit" (32), but this wandering and flight remains tinged with anxiety, for "up to reascend" is "hard and

---

35. Steadman, "*Paradise Lost* and the Apotheosis Tradition," *Milton's Biblical and Classical Mythology*, pp. 109–90.

rare" (20–21). In the Invocation to Book 7 to "soar / Above the flight of *Pegasean* wing" becomes even more terrifying:

> Lest from this flying Steed unrein'd (as once
> *Bellerophon,* though from a lower Clime)
> Dismounted, on the *Aleian* field I fall
> Erroneous there to wander and forlorn. (17–20)

For attempting to explore the heavenly mysteries on Pegasus, Bellerophon was thrown by Zeus down to earth to wander blind and mad till death. Milton disavows such aspiration and proclaims his own self-limited poetic sphere: diurnal, not nocturnal; narrowly earth bound, not heaven bound:

> narrower bound
> Within the visible Diurnal Sphere
> Standing on Earth, not rapt above the Pole,
> More safe I Sing with mortal voice. (21–24)

But the poet feels decidely unsafe, "in darkness, and with dangers compast round" (27). For this terror, he next conjures an image of the ancient prototypes of our night-wandering witches, those wild carousing women who destroyed Orpheus, Milton's poetic forbearer,

> Bacchus and his Revellers, the Race
> Of that wild Rout that tore the *Thracian* bard
> In *Rhodope,* where the Woods and Rocks had Ears
> To rapture, till the savage clamor drown'd
> Both Harp and Voice; nor could the Muse defend
> Her Son. (33–37)

But these women, who destroy Orpheus and the rapture he imparts, are themselves transported. Furthermore, before this "savage" path to ecstasy was suppressed, Bacchus was also mythically torn apart and rapturous like Orpheus, his analogue.[36] Milton perpetuates the distinction and repudiates being "rapt" in both its meanings, flying and the state of consciousness it represents.

As we move through these classical myths of terror, a desire to stand solidly on earth, definitely bounded, becomes a dread of dismemberment by ecstatic women, and the fear of flying becomes a fear of rapture as dissolution not inspiration. Stanley Fish recently noted in that reluctance to be "rapt above the Pole," where perceptions of the "visible Diurnal sphere" fade and are lost, an example of a recurrent image, accompanied

---

36. Robert Graves, *The Greek Myths* (Baltimore, Md., 1955), p. 114.

in Milton by desire and fear, of a world without or before differentiation. He also cited the Nativity Ode in which the world as yet "Hath took no print of the approaching light" (20).[37] Relevant too is William Kerrigan's observation of "the animism of a primitive ego" in the Invocation's orphic imagery, for the world of enraptured nature, where consciousness has seeped into the environment, is also one of non-differentiation.[38]

But in Book 3, alongside these images of night–flying and wandering, the dissolution to a "Universal blanc" occurs as a consequence not of mystical blanking out but of blindness:

> Thus with the Year
> Seasons return, but not to me returns
> Day, or the sweet approach of Ev'n or Morn,
> Or sight of vernal bloom, or Summer's Rose,
> Or flocks, or herds, or human face divine;
> But cloud instead, and ever–during dark
> Surrounds me, from the cheerful ways of men
> Cut off, and for the Book of knowledge fair
> Presented with a Universal blanc
> Of Nature's works to me expung'd and ras'd. (40–49)

In Book 7 blindness was also associated with dangers, among others, of solitary rapture:

> not rapt above the Pole
> More safe I Sing with mortal voice, unchang'd
> To hoarse or mute, though fall'n on evil days
> . . . .
> In darkness, and with dangers compast round,
> And solitude; yet not alone, while thou
> Visit'st my slumbers Nightly. (23–29)

The dangers of blindness and rapture then seem closely intertwined. The fact that the sun "Revisit'st not these eyes" (3.23) accompanies uncertainties regarding what Muse "Visit'st my slumbers Nightly" (7.29), and what spheres "Nightly I visit" (3.32). As blindness has erased the outer world, so in compensation might "Celestial Light / Shine inward" (3.51–52). As his precedent Milton calls up those ancient blind poet-prophets, "Blind *Thamyris* and blind *Maeonides,* / And *Tiresias* and *Phineus* Prophets old" (3.35–36), "those ancient bards and wise men,"

---

37. Stanley Fish, "How Not to Be Outstanding: Praise and Dispraise in Milton," Paper at MLA Convention, New York, 1986.

38. William Kerrigan, *The Sacred Complex: On the Psychogenesis of "Paradise Lost"* (Cambridge, Mass., 1983), pp. 177–80.

also cited in his *Second Defense,* "whose misfortune the gods, it is said, recompensed with far more potent gifts" (*Works* IV, 584). Tiresias' blind vision was the reward of a god as well as the punishment of a goddess and, and if inner vision is not just a compensation for loss of outer sight but its consequence, blindness itself is the gift. Flowing from an "unapproached" (3.4) divine Light of unbearable brillance, such inner light at its greatest intensity can overwhelm all other perception and become psychologically "blinding." When Michael pours drops into Adam's eyes which "pierc'd / Ev'n to the inmost seat of mental sight," he is "intranst" and then has visions (11.415-20). It becomes difficult to distinguish such visionary powers, identified by the Greeks with "divine madness" and by Milton with the poetic flight of Pegasus, from the terrible fate of Bellerophon, wandering blind and mad, except that Milton and the poets like "the wakeful Bird" who "Sings darkling" and "Tunes her nocturnal Note" (3.38-39) translated their fate into song.

The paradoxes and inconsistencies of Milton's use of these conventional symbols of inspiration invite speculation on its psychological dimension. Milton's obdurate insistence on rationality, order and self-identity might be read in two opposing ways: either an ego-bound Milton might be rejecting subjective experiences of which he was incapable, or, conversely, he may be expressing the fearfulness of states to which he was intensely prone. The first view sees Milton as maintaining the fences of the civilized psyche, well-barricaded in the masculine mode of separation. This is the Milton caricatured by Robert Graves, but echoed in feminist and other critics, as an egocentric patriarch of narrow psychological range aspiring to fame as prophet-propagandist for the stern deity of a repressive culture. In this case his condemnation of witches and maenads as women susceptible to demonic intoxicated states is a defensive construction which, by denigrating the more malleable boundaries he associates with the "feminine," reinforces and rationalizes his own ideology and pyschology. Although not the focus here, there are such ideological operations which give this portrait some truth. Some critics, however, think they have glimpsed another Milton. Kerrigan, for one, has tried to show through his Freudian lens a Miltonic psyche of greater richness and complexity.[39]

Milton's antagonism toward the mental state he associates with witchcraft might itself indicate a more expansive or ambiguous psychol-

---

39. Graves, *Wife to Mr. Milton* (Chicago, 1944). I am attempting to incorporate both an ideological critique and a psychological analysis in a book length study.

ogy. Arnold Ludwig has catalogued studies of over fifty routes to extraordinary consciousness.[40] One route in particular that has been found to induce the "de-differentiation" and dissolution of boundaries is sensory deprivation. "Ego diffusion," Kammerman writes, "appears to be a central aspect of the isolation experience."[41] Blindness has also been studied as a form of partial sensory deprivation eliciting abnormal mentalities.[42] Consequently, Milton's fearful association of blindness, dreams, flight and uninhibited female irrationality with threatening mental states might alternately suggest that the blind poet either actually found himself "fenceless" or at least felt very vulnerable to such a condition.

Romain Rolland's association of poetry with oceanic feeling and Kris' analysis in *The Psychoanalytic Function of Art* of "ego regression during the creative processes" imply that artistic imagination involves such a capacity to relax one's boundaries.[43] Moreover, new research, reported by Ernest Hartmann, on "The Psychology of Terrifying Dreams," finds a relationship between nightmares and creativity, with both occurring in people who have "thin boundaries" and "can let things through."[44] We have also noted that this tendency, which Virginia Woolf called "thin-skinnedness," has been particularly identified with women, who have been seen, in effect, as retaining the symbiotic capacities of a more

40. Articles on the psychology of altered consciousness in dreams, trance, hypnosis, etc. have been collected in books by Charles T. Tart, *Altered States of Consciousness* (Garden City, N.Y., 1969) and John White, *The Highest State of Consciousness* (Garden City, N.Y., 1972). For a research summary see Arnold Ludwig, "Altered States of Consciousness," in Tart, pp. 11–24; on regression see in White: Stanley Krippner, "Altered States of Consciousness," pp. 1–5; Roger W. Wescott, "States of Consciousness," pp. 17–33; R. D. Laing, "Transcendental Experience," pp. 104–13; Raymond Prince and Charles Savage, "Mystical States and the Concept of Regression," pp. 114–34; Edward Maupin, "Zen Buddhism: A Psychological Review," pp. 204–24; Abraham Maslow, "The 'Core-Religious' or 'Transcendent' Experience," pp. 352–64. See also M. Gill and M. Brenman, *Hypnosis and related states: psychoanalytic studies in regression* (New York, 1959).

41. Mark Kammerman, *Sensory Isolation and Personality Change* (Springfield, Ill., 1977); Peter Suedfeld, *Restricted Environmental Stimulation: Research and Clinical Applications* (New York, 1980); John Lilly, *The Deep Self* (New York, 1977).

42. J. Bartlett, "A case of organized visual hallucinations in an old man with cataract," *Brain* 74 (1951), 363–73; D. Boyd, and M. Norris, "Delirium associated with cataract extraction," *J. Indiana Medical Assn.* 34 (1941), 130–35. See Kerrigan's rich and subtle psychoanalytic reading for a different argument which also links Milton's blindness and his creativity, mostly through oedipal dynamics.

43. Kris, p. 312; see also Searles, pp. 128–31 and Winnicott, *Playing and Reality* (New York, 1971).

44. Ernest Hartmann, *The Nightmare: The Psychology and Biology of Terrifying Dreams* (New York, 1984).

diffuse ego. As we saw, what Milton seemed to fear in romantic bonding to a woman was the "slackness" of ego controls in an "effeminacy" consonant with just such an emotional merger. We should not be surprised, therefore, that his imagery conjoins femininity, ego dissolution, and poetic inspiration.

The image of Orpheus being dismembered by feminine forces, a favorite Miltonic motif, is particularly evocative of an ego dissolution closely wedded to poetic inspiration. Moreover, after seven books, still equivocating about her identity, Milton finally divulges the fact that his Muse, Urania, is feminine.[45] Since he calls upon his Muse "the mind through all *her* powers / [to] Irradiate" (52–53), he also presents his creative faculties as feminine. It is interesting, therefore, that he cites as his forbearer Tiresias, whose blindness and prophetic powers were related to his having lived both as a male and a female. Appropriately, after visiting what seems a feminine dimension within through his nocturnal reveries, Milton reported that in the morning he impatiently awaited his amanuensis because "he wanted to be milked" of his verses.

Kerrigan reminds us that Orpheus' Muse, Calliope, is also his mother and so by association is Milton's Muse; thus a regression to the preoedipal mother at the core of Milton's psyche is revealed as the source of his creativity.[46] But as Calliope cannot or will not "defend her Son" from physical dissolution, Milton's own muse is not so absolutely distinguished from the Bacchantes or the mental decomposition they symbolize. What he may be accurately recording here is the genuine frightfulness of such psychic encounters. For Robert Graves such terror and wonder are the same. The Muse-poet must undergo the sacrifice of his ordinary sense of self to the larger consciousness and energies represented by the Muse. Milton's conviction, explained by Schwartz, that moral chaos is the analogue of such psychological dissolution would probably have increased its fearfulness. Like Eve, Milton had inspired dreams which for several books took him flying between infernal, earthly, and heavenly spheres. On some level, he seems to realize that poetic flight is nearly indistinguishable from the risk of Bellerophon's free-falling state, so

45. For the feminine aspect of Milton's muse, see Stevie Davies, *The Feminine Reclaimed: The Idea of Woman in Spenser, Shakespeare and Milton* (Lexington, Ky., 1986), Noam Flinker, "Courting Urania: The Narrator of *Paradise Lost* Invokes His Muse," in Walker, and Virginia R. Mollenkott, "Some Implications of Milton's Androgynous Muse," *Bucknell Review* 24 (1978), i, 27–36.

46. Kerrigan, pp. 177–78; Jim Swan, in "Difference and Silence: John Milton and the Question of Gender," in *The (M)other Tongue: Essays in Feminist Psychoanalytic Interpretation,* ed. Shirley Nelson Garner, Claire Kahane, and Madelon Sprengnether (Ithaca, N.Y., 1985) observed the conflict between separation and regression in Milton's poetic.

exactly like Satan's in chaos.

Milton's repeated protestation of the divine source of his inspiration, coupled with the fact that his Muse's identity and gender keep changing could itself evince anxiety about his inspiration. Milton's Invocations attempt to metamorphose the classical Muse into a Christian one, but he may actually be torn between two Muses, the goddess a poet implores for the gift of flight, of altered consciousness, and the Spirit of the Father who will safeguard him from it or will "with like safety guided down / Return me to my Native Element" (7.16–17). Although he certainly eschewed the voluntary abandonment to intoxication of witches and maenads and committed himself to a diurnal stance and a poetic heart "upright . . . and pure" (1.18), blindness might have determined that Milton like Tiresias had more in common than he wished to admit with those ecstatic females who had dissolved the boundaries of the ordinary self. He may, in fact, have felt dismembered by his own "effeminate slackness." Since in Book 7 Milton's vision of Creation mirrors that of his own creativity, his nightly visitations also are to a realm whose cosmic equivalent would be described a few pages later as that vast, fertile, creative "Womb as yet / Of Waters." As the strenuousness of his Invocations suggests, it may have been a struggle to "reascend" from those depths (or descend from those heights) to the bounded ego with its rational controls. And the creative sphere may have been from "the loud misrule / Of Chaos far removed" (7.276–77,271–72) only by a defensive act of psychic denial and displacement. In her fine systematic account of Milton's conscious ideology in which chaos is the negation of creation or merely its negative motive, Schwartz can ignore the psychological motives of all this distinction–making, but such a reading then serves to reinforce Milton's own attempt to obliterate these significant instabilities of his discourse.

My focus here on potentially positive aspects of regression is not intended to deny the importance of the ego's ability to establish boundaries, or the dangers of boundary-dissolution which has, after all, been associated with schizophrenia. Another study might consider Milton's insights about the role of a strong ego or even the relationship between such strength and the capacity for fruitful regression. Here the intent is simply to recognize that just as regression under sensory deprivation, according to Kammerman, can be therapeutic in allowing the emergence of a healthier, more broadly reorganized self through the reintegration of repressed elements, so too such dissolution may be integral to Milton's process of artistic creation.[47] The blind poet may be wrestling with his own regression to a state prior to gender and ego and attempting "to build / In Chaos" following visitations to it in night-flying episodes analogous to Eve's. Finally, we cannot know whether he actually experienced such boundlessness or glimpsed it only in memory through the windows to the repressed opened in dreams or in imagination. What we can say is that Milton's depiction of this consciousness in the flight both of witches and poetic inspiration evidences profound psychological ambivalence.

In this poetic psychology Milton would have been, without knowing it, "a true poet and of the devil's party" as Blake proposed in *The Marriage of Heaven and Hell*. Blake's quarrel is with Milton's interpretation of his own creativity, which Blake traced to the same unconscious forces he believed Milton had unjustly and inaccurately maligned. Since Reason was only the "*bound* or outward circumference of Energy," Milton's Messiah, "call'd Reason," must have "formed a heaven of what he stole from the Abyss." In the drastic polarization of contemporary Milton criticism, he has been seen alternately as an archetypal misogynist or as a virtual feminist. Is part of the explanation that psychologically Milton was a poet with two Muses and of both parties, one of them the female party of Bacchus and Pan, enraptured followers of the savage ancient gods of the soul whose energies he had to strain to put at the service of his patriarchal God of Reason and Order? And might this creative tension partially explain the power of a poetry that speaks to us most movingly when paradoxically it speaks simultaneously both of patriarchal interdictions and of intuitive aspirations to something beyond them?

47. Kammerman, p. 283.

Recent Studies in Women Writers of the English Renaissance

As is usual with *ELR* "Recent Studies" essays, our goal in the following work is to combine a topical review of research with a reasonably complete bibliography of works published since 1945. Because the cost of resetting type prohibited incorporating new materials into the bibliographical essays we printed in the two special Women in the Renaissance issues published in 1984 and 1988, the following pages reprint "Recent Studies in Women Writers of Tudor England" from *ELR*, 14 (1984), 409–39, and "Recent Studies in Women Writers of the English Seventeenth Century" from *ELR*, 18 (1988), 138–67, each followed by a new essay summarizing more current articles, books, and (occasionally) dissertations. Items listed in our new work include combined entries from the most recent *PMLA*, *YWES*, and *MHRA* bibliographies, supplemented by other pieces we have been able to find as of April 1990. Journal abbreviations are those used by the MLA.

===

RECENT STUDIES IN WOMEN WRITERS OF TUDOR ENGLAND (1945–1984)

Part I: Women Writers, 1485–1603 Excluding Mary Sidney, Countess of Pembroke

ELIZABETH H. HAGEMAN

BACKGROUND STUDIES (Selected)

Bayne, Diane Valeri, "Richard Hyrde and the More Circle," *Moreana*, No. 45 (1975), 5–15.

Camden, Carroll. *The Elizabethan Woman* (1952).

Cannon, Mary Agnes. *The Education of Women During the Renaissance* (1916; rpt. 1981).

Dunn, Catherine M. "The Changing Image of Woman in Renaissance Society and Literature," in *What Manner of Woman: Essays on English and American Life and Literature*, ed. Marlene Springer (1977), pp. 15–38.

Dusinberre, Juliet. *Shakespeare and the Nature of Women* (1975).

Fitz, L. T. "'What Says the Married Woman?'": Marriage Theory and Feminism in the English Renaissance," *Mosaic*, 13 (1980), 1–22.

Gagen, Jean Elisabeth. "Early Learned Ladies," in her *The New Woman: Her Emergence in English Drama, 1600–1730* (1954), pp. 13–31.

Gardiner, Dorothy. *English Girlhood at School: A Study of Women's Education through twelve centuries* (1929).

Haller, William and Malleville. "The Puritan Art of Love," *HLQ*, 5 (1942), 235–72.

Henderson, Katherine Usher and Barbara F. McManus, ed. *Half Humankind: Contexts and Texts of the Controversy about Women in England, 1540–1640* (forthcoming).

Hogrefe, Pearl. *Tudor Women: Commoners and Queens* (1975).

————. *Women of Action in Tudor, England: Nine Biographical Sketches* (1977).

Hull, Suzanne W. *Chaste, Silent & Obedient: English Books for Women, 1475–1640* (1982).

Jardine, Lisa. *"Still Harping on Daughters": Women and Drama in the Age of Shakespeare* (1983).

Jordan, Constance. "Feminism and the Humanists: The Case of Sir Thomas Elyot's *Defence of Good Women*," *RQ*, 36 (1983), 181–201.

Kamm, Josephine. *Hope Deferred: Girls' Education in English History* (1965).

Kaufman, Gloria. "Juan Luis Vives on the Education of Women," *Signs*, 3 (1978), 891–96.

Kelly-Gadol, Joan. "Did Women Have a Renaissance?" in *Becoming Visible: Women in European History*, ed. Renate Bridenthal and Claudia Koonz (1977), 137–64.

Kelso, Ruth. *Doctrine for the Lady of the Renaissance* (1956; rpt. 1978).

Klein, Joan Larsen. "Women and Marriage in Renaissance England: Male Perspectives," *Topic: 36: The Elizabethan Woman* (1982), 20–37.

Maclean, Ian. *The Renaissance Notion of Woman: A Study in the Fortunes of Scholasticism and Medical Science in European Intellectual Life* (1980).

Masek, Rosemary. "Women in an Age of Transition, 1485–1714," in *The Women of England from Anglo-Saxon Times to the Present: Interpretative Bibliographical Essays*, ed. Barbara Kanner (1979), pp. 138–82.

Ong, Walter. "Latin Language Study as a Renaissance Puberty Rite," *SP*, 56 (1959), 103–24.

Powell, Chilton Latham. *English Domestic Relations, 1487–1653* (1917).

Reynolds, Myra. "Learned Ladies in England before 1650," in her *The Learned Lady in England, 1650–1760* (1920), pp. 1–45.

Rogers, Katherine M. *The Troublesome Helpmate: A History of Misogyny in Literature* (1966; rpt. 1973).

Stenton, Doris Mary. "The Renaissance and Reformation and their Consequences, 1400–1642," in her *The English Woman in History* (1957; rpt. 1977), pp. 120–51.

Stone, Lawrence. *The Family, Sex and Marriage in England, 1500–1800* (1977; abridged ed. 1979).

Thomas, Keith. "The Double Standard," *JHI*, 20 (1959), 195–216.

Utley, Francis Lee. *The Crooked Rib: An Analytical Index to the Argument about Women in English and Scots Literature to the End of the Year 1568* (1944; rpt. 1970).

Watson, Foster, ed. *Vives and the Renascence Education of Women* (1912).

Wellington, James E. "Renaissance Anti-feminism and the Classical Tradition," in *Sweet Smoke of Rhetoric: A Collection of Renaissance Essays*, ed. Natalie Grimes Lawrence and J. A. Reynolds (1964), pp. 1–17.

Woodbridge, Linda. *Women and the English Renaissance: Literature and the Nature of Womankind, 1540–1620* (1984).

Woolf, Virginia. *A Room of One's Own* (1929; rpt. 1967).

Wright, Louis B. *Middle-Class Culture in Elizabethan England* (1935; rpt. 1965).

————. "The Reading of Renaissance English Women," *SP*, 28 (1931), 671–88.

EDITIONS

Betty Travitsky, ed. *The Paradise of Women: Writings by Englishwomen of the Renaissance* (1981) prints excerpts from the Tudor, Stuart, and Caroline periods. Mary R. Mahl and Helene Koon, ed. *The Female Spectator: English Women Writers before 1800* (1977), include pieces by Catherine Parr; Elizabeth Tudor; Elizabeth Grymeston; and Mary Sidney, Countess of Pembroke. Editions of works by individual writers are noted below. Anthologies including writings by Tudor women are listed in the *See also* section.

I. GENERAL STUDIES

Ruth Willard Hughey's survey of printed works and unprinted manuscripts—including letters and diaries—in her "Cultural Interests of Women in England, from 1524–1640, Indicated in the Writings of the Women," Ph.D. dissertation, Cornell University, 1932, demonstrates that "Women in sixteenth-century England were disciples of the Reformation rather than of the Renaissance." Even while the example of Catherine Parr encouraged women to write and to publish religious devotions, "the religious tenets [of the period] contributed certainly toward the development of selfconscious humility among the women." Writings by women in Tudor England, Hughey shows, "reflect little concern for the gayer sides of the Renaissance." Charlotte Kohler, "The Elizabethan Woman of Letters: the Extent of Her Literary Activity," Ph.D. dissertation, University of Virginia, 1936, stresses the amount and variety of writing by women in sixteenth- and early seventeenth-century England. While "Opinions concerning the value of their contributions are bound to vary, according to the point of view of the commentator," Kohler argues, the fact is that "we find not fewer, but more feminine authors than conditions augured." Both Hughey and Kohler include chronological lists of women writers of the English Renaissance.

As she surveys the lives and works of Englishwomen in *Women of the English Renaissance and Reformation* (1983), Retha M. Warnicke traces "the English acceptance of classical training for women" through four generations, from the women of Thomas More's household to female scholars of the Jacobean period. In her Introduction to *Paradise of Women* (Editions, above), Betty Travitsky suggests that the increased numbers of written works by women in the Renaissance argues "the development of a new type of Renaissance Englishwoman." She notes similarities ("the goal of both groups was to produce sober, virtuous women") and differences (the humanists had a greater appreciation of intellectual activities) between Renaissance humanists and the Protestant reformers of the period, and she observes that their new learning led at least some Renaissance Englishwomen to question the ideals of their society. In her "The New Mother of the English Renaissance: Her Writings on Motherhood," in *The Lost Tradition: Mothers and Daughters in Literature,* ed. Cathy N. Davidson and E. M. Broner (1980), pp. 33–43, Travitsky outlines writings on motherhood by six Renaissance women to show how sixteenth-century humanists and religious reformers influenced women's perceptions of themselves "in a family-centered, religiously-oriented time." Among the eleven essays in *Silent but for the Word: Tudor Women as Patrons, Translators and Writers of Religious Works,* ed. Margaret P. Hanny (forthcoming), that treat authors included in this bibliographical essay are Valerie Wayne, "Some Sad Sentence: Vives' *Instruction of a Christian Woman,*" which stresses the limitations humanist and Protestant ideals imposed on Renaissance Englishwomen, and Gary F. Waller, "Marginalization and Silence: Women's Writing in the Discursive Structures of Renaissance Poetry," which argues that recent studies of Renaissance women writers affirm traditional, anti-feminist value systems; if future studies were to concentrate on the question "How do oppositional forces speak when the dominant language refuses them words? How are the voices of silence heard?" Waller writes, they could create a new and more valid literary history.

Patricia Gartenberg and Nena Thames Whittemore list works by some 56 women in "A Checklist of English Women in Print, 1475–1640," *Bulletin of Bibliography and Magazine Notes,* 34 (1977), 1–13. Merry E. Wiesner, "Women in the Sixteenth Century: A Bibliography," *Sixteenth Century Bibliography: 23* (1983), includes works by and about women of the Continental and English Renaissance.

II. STUDIES OF VARIOUS GENRES

A. *Diaries.* Rachel Weigall, "An Elizabethan Gentlewoman: The Journal of Lady Mildmay, circa 1570–1617 (unpublished)," *QR,* 215 (1911), 119–38, prints portions of Lady Mildmay's journal and of her books of prescriptions and recommendations; Weigall presents Lady Mildmay as a pious, capable household manager. In her Introduction to *The Diary of Lady Margaret Hoby, 1599–1605* (1930), Dorothy M. Meads stresses Lady Hoby's Puritanism and compares her life to Lady Mildmay's and Lady Anne Clifford's (1590–1676): all three Renaissance women "lived, for the greater part of their lives, in country districts in which their houses were the important centres of every aspect of life, economic, intellectual, physical and religious." Travitsky, *Paradise of Women,* pp. 84–86, prints excerpts from Lady Mildmay's and Lady Hoby's diaries.

B. *Letters.* James Gairdner's edition of *The Paston Letters, A.D. 1422–1509,* Vol. 6 (1904; rpt. 1965), includes letters to and from Tudor women. Muriel St. Clare Byrne's 6-volume edition of *The Lisle Letters* (1981) prints some 2,000 letters written between 1533 and 1540, many by Honor Greville Lisle. In her Introduction Byrne argues that the letters present a woman vastly different from theories about women articulated in most 16th-century treatises; Lady Lisle, she suggests, was rather like the independent Lady conceived by Castiglione in *The Courtier* and by Christine de Pisan in *The City of Ladies.* Bridget Boland's abridged edition of *The Lisle Letters* (1983) arranges 342 letters in topical rather than chronological order.

C. *Translation.* Mary Ellen Lamb, "The Cooke Sisters: Attitudes towards Learned Women in the Renaissance," in *Silent but for the Word* (I, above), suggests that women interested in religious issues turned to translation as "one of the few ways that they could contribute to a religious question of the time." She raises the issue of the extent to which Anne Cooke Bacon, Mildred Cooke Cecil, and Elizabeth Cooke Hoby were influenced by their husbands' interests in "their translations as contributions to a common cause"; notes that for women, translating religious works was "a way of justifying their education and character" against those men who felt threatened by women's assertions of their own viewpoints; and contrasts the "individual and energetic voices" of the Cooke sisters' letters with the impersonal tones of their translations.

III. STUDIES OF INDIVIDUAL AUTHORS

A. *Margaret Beaufort, Countess of Richmond and Derby (1443–1509).* Lady Margaret's translation of the fourth book of *De Imitatione Christi* is printed in *The Earliest English Translation of . . . De imitatione Christi,* ed. John K. Ingram for the Early English Text Society (1893; rpt. 1973), pp. 259–83.

Linda Simon, *Of Virtue Rare: Margaret Beaufort, Matriarch of the House of Tudor* (1982), is the most recent biography.

Pearl Hogrefe, *Women of Action in Tudor England* (Background Studies, above) pp. 136–53, describes Margaret Beaufort as "a literary woman. . . . a patron of printers, a translator from the French, a publisher of works she translated, and a reader of religious and secular books." In an unpublished essay, "The Mighty Pen: Margaret Beaufort, Literature and Power," Linda Simon suggests that work as patron and translator provided Beaufort "a way to transcend the strictures forced upon her by her status as a woman and by her peculiar political position."

B. *Margaret More Roper (1505–1544).* Richard L. DeMolen edits Margaret Roper's translation of Erasmus' *A Devout Treatise Upon the Pater Noster* (1524) in his *Erasmus of Rotterdam: A Quincentennial Symposium* (1971), pp. 93–124. The Latin *Treatise* is printed with Margaret Roper's translation on facing pages in *Moreana,* No. 7 (1965), 9–64; Roper's translation is transcribed in modern English and translated into French by Sr. Marie-Claire Robineau, O.P., in *Moreana,* No. 9 (1966), 65–91; No. 10 (1966), 91–109; and No. 11 (1966), 109–18.

Rita M. Verbrugge, "Margaret More Roper: Personal Expression in the *Devout Treatise Upon the Pater Noster,*" in *Silent but for the Word* (I, above), contrasts Margaret Roper's expert English style with Hyrde's awkward dedicatory letter and suggests that her skill matches that of her better-known countrymen from later in the century; in her translation, Verbrugge maintains, Margaret "can and does speak with her own mind and voice."

E. E. Reynolds, *Margaret Roper: Eldest Daughter of St. Thomas More* (1960), stresses Margaret Roper's learning, religious faith, independent mind, and (especially) her devotion to her father; Reynolds includes letters from Margaret to More. Letters to and from Margaret Roper are available in *The Correspondence of Sir Thomas More,* ed. Elizabeth Frances Rogers (1947; rpt. 1970). Letter number 206, from Margaret Roper to her sister Alice Alington, reports a dialogue between Margaret and her father which R. W. Chambers, *Thomas More* (1935), pp. 308–13, parallels with Plato's *Crito.* Chambers declines to make a definite attribution for the piece, but because he believes that "The Margaret speeches in the dialogue are pure Margaret, the More speeches pure More," he suggests that the dialogue may be a collaborative effort (p. 18). Walter M. Gordon, "Tragic Perspective in Thomas More's Dialogue with Margaret in the Tower," *Cithara,* 17:2 (1978), 3–12, elaborates Chambers' comments on the dramatic nature of the piece to focus on the tragic isolation of each participant in a dialogue that treats the conflicting demands of divine and secular love.

C. *Catherine Parr (1512–1548).* A facsimile edition of *The Prayers or Medytacions* (1545) has been published in the Scholars Facsimiles and Reprints Series (1977). *The Lamentacion, or*

Complaint of a Sinner (1547) is reprinted in *The Harleian Miscellany*, 1 (1808), 286–313. Travitsky, *The Paradise of Women*, includes excerpts from the *Prayers* and *Lamentacion*, pp. 37–41, and a letter from Catherine Parr to Mary Tudor, p. 78; Mahl and Koon, *The Female Spectator*, excerpt *Lamentation* and *Prayers*, pp. 35–43.

In "The Last Years of the Reign: The Role of Catherine Parr," Chapter 7 of his *English Humanists and Reformation Politics under Henry VIII and Edward VI* (1965), pp. 200–34, James Kelsey McConica argues the influence of a "group of distinguished humanists collected by Catherine Parr to provide instruction for the royal children, and for her own friends and associates, in learned pietism." Anthony Martienssen recounts Catherine's efforts to establish a "Humanist and Erasmian" Protestantism in England, describes her attempt to save Anne Askew's life, and credits her with the "conversion" of Henry VIII in 1546 in "The Queen's Ladies," Chapter 12 of his *Queen Katherine Parr* (1973), pp. 185–23. John N. King, "Patronage and Piety: The Influence of Catherine Parr," in *Silent but for the Word* (I, above), adds that the "patronage of devotional manuals and theological translations for the edification of a mixed audience of elite and ordinary readers" by women in Catherine Parr's circle led to the popularization of a particularly Protestant humanism.

Roland H. Bainton, "Catherine Parr," in his *Women of the Reformation in France and England* (1973; rpt. 1975), pp. 161–80, presents *The Lamentacion* as "one of the gems of Tudor devotional literature"—a work comparable to Marguerite of Navarre's *Chansons Spirituelles* or Vittoria Colonna's *Rime Religiose*. Conyers Read, *Mr. Secretary Cecil and Queen Elizabeth* (1955), argues that *Lamentacions* "came about as close to an endorsement of the position of the Reformers as the wife of Henry VIII could safely come." C. Fenno Hoffman, Jr., "Catherine Parr as a Woman of Letters," *HLQ*, 23 (1959), 349–67, notes that *Lamentacion* repudiates the earlier *Prayers*, for whereas the first volume is Roman Catholic in tone, the second is intensely personal and explicit in its rejection of Catholicism. William P. Haugaard, "Katherine Parr: the Religious Convictions of a Renaissance Queen," *RQ*, 22 (1969), 346–59, also contrasts the two works and presents *Lamentacion* as "the witness of one lay Christian, convinced she had awakened to an understanding of the profundity of her religion within the life of the Henrician church."

E. J. Devereux, "The Publication of the English *Paraphrases* of Erasmus," *BJRL*, 51 (1969), 348–67, describes the history of the compilation and publication of the *Paraphrases* but discounts the long-term significance of the work. Pearl Hogrefe, however, in "Catherine Parr," Chapter 8 of her *Women of Action in Tudor England* (Background Studies, above), pp. 181–206, judges *The First Tome . . . of the Paraphrase of Erasmus* (1548) Catherine Parr's "most ambitious project in publishing" and asserts that Catherine's patronage of the volume demonstrates "her zeal, her willingness to work for the religion she professed, and her ability to carry through a large plan with some success." Bainton (above) observes that the choice of translators for the *Paraphrases* reflects Catherine's "Protestant leanings with a spirit of catholicity."

D. *Anne Askew (1521–1546)*. *The Examinations of Anne Askew*, transcribed and edited by John Bale (1546, 1547), are reprinted in the Parker Society's *Select Works of John Bale . . . Containing the Examinations of Lord Cobham, William Thorpe, and Anne Askewe and the Image of Both Churches*, ed. Henry Christmas (1849), pp. 137–46. *The Examinations of Anne Askew* are also available in John Foxe, *Acts and Monuments of these latter and perilous days* (1563), ed.

George Townsend, Vol. 5 (1838; rpt. 1965), 537–50. Travitsky, *Paradise of Women,* pp. 167–86, prints excerpts from *The Examinations* and "The Balade Whych Anne Askewe Made and Sange When She Was in Newgate" with comments on Askew's "intellect, independence, and courage."

Anne Askew and her family's lives are among those Derek Wilson recreates from 16th-century printed and manuscript sources in *A Tudor Tapestry: Men, Women, and Society in Reformation England* (1972). Wilson portrays Anne Askew as a sincere and determined woman. In his discussion of Bale's creation of the genre of the Protestant saint's life which Foxe would later use in *Actes and Monuments,* Leslie P. Fairfield, "John Bale and the Development of Protestant Hagiography in England," *Journal of Ecclesiastical History,* 24 (1973), 145–60, expresses the opinion that while Bale's transcription of Anne Askew's words is generally accurate, his commentary emphasizes her courage and private faith to create an image of sainthood for Protestant England. John N. King, *English Reformation Literature: The Tudor Origins of the Protestant Tradition* (1982), *passim,* notes that while Bale treats Askew as an image of "the beleagered church in general as well as each individual Christian," Foxe presents her execution as the introduction to the "tranquil golden age" of the reign of Edward VI. Elaine V. Beilin, "Anne Askew's Self-Portrait in *The Examinations,*" in *Silent but for the Word* (I, above), contrasts John Bale's treatment of Askew as a weak woman inspired by God's strength with Askew's own portrait of herself as "neither 'dainty' or 'tender,' but rather, tough in mind and body, learned, and tenacious."

E. *Anne Cooke, Lady Bacon (1528–1610).* Lady Bacon's translation of John Jewell, *An Apology of the Church of England* (1564), is available in an edition prepared by J. E. Booty (1963). James Spedding, *The Works of Francis Bacon,* Vol. 8 (1862; rpt. 1968), includes letters from Lady Bacon to her sons; Spedding judges her to have been "an affectionate, vehement, fiery, grave, and religious soul . . . in creed a Calvinist, in morals a Puritan." Travitsky, *Paradise of Women,* prints a letter to Lady Anne's son Anthony, pp. 81–82, and a portion of the Preface to her translation of *Fouretene sermons of Bernadine Ochyne* (1550), p. 143.

Pearl Hogrefe, "Anne Cooke, Lady Bacon," in her *Women of Action in Tudor England* (Background Studies, above), pp. 39–56, presents Lady Bacon's life as devoted to "further[ing] Calvinistic Puritanism not only in her sons but in all England. She worked toward her aim with persistence, vigor, integrity, and intelligence supported by profound classical scholarship." Roland H. Bainton treats Lady Bacon and her three sisters (Katherine, Lady Killigrew; Elizabeth, Lady Hoby, and then Lady Russell; and Mildred, Lady Burghley) in "Feminine Piety in Tudor England," in *Christianity and Spirituality: Essays in Honour of Gordon Rapp,* ed. Peter Brooks (1975), pp. 183–220; after presenting Lady Bacon's translations of Ochino's sermons and Jewell's *Apology* as "entirely in line with the official forms of the [English] Reformation," Bainton notes a private letter in which "her Puritan leanings found expression."

F. *Elizabeth Cooke, Lady Hoby and then Lady Russell (1529–1609).* Travitsky, *Paradise of Women,* pp. 23–24, prints selections from Prefaces to Lady Hoby's translation of John Poynet's *Way of Reconciliation* (1605) and her elegy on the death of Lord Russell. Elizabeth Farber edits the 55 extant letters in "The Letters of Lady Elizabeth Russell

(1540–1609)," Ph.D. dissertation, Columbia University, 1977.

In the Introduction to the letters, Farber presents an optimistic view of Lady Russell's life, for she believes that the sixteenth century was "one of those very rare, brief periods in the history of the West" when at least some women were given education "equal to that of their brothers." Mary Ellen Lamb's questions about Thomas Hoby's support of his wife's work (II, C) raise, however, complementary questions about the degree of true intellectual independence that she enjoyed.

G. *Elizabeth I. (1533–1603).* Frances S. Teague has edited selected speeches and poems for *Renaissance Woman Writers,* ed. Katharina M. Wilson (forthcoming). Travitsky, *Paradise of Women, passim,* includes briefer excerpts, as do Mahl and Koon, *The Female Spectator,* pp. 44–51. More extensive editions of writing by Elizabeth I are listed below.

The standard biography remains J. E. Neale, *Queen Elizabeth I: A Biography* (1934; rpt. 1957). Among other recent biographies are Elizabeth Jenkins, *Elizabeth the Great* (1958; rpt. 1967); B. W. Beckingsale, *Elizabeth I* (1963); Mary M. Luke, *A Crown for Elizabeth* (1970); Alison Plowden, *The Young Elizabeth* (1971); Lacey Baldwin Smith, *Elizabeth Tudor: Portrait of a Queen* (1975); Paul Johnson, *Elizabeth I: A Biography* (1974; English ed. subtitled *A Study in Power and Intellect*); and Carolly Erickson, *The First Elizabeth* (1983). Larissa J. Taylor-Smither, "Elizabeth I: A Psychological Profile," *SCJ,* 15 (1984), 47–72, uses poetry and prose by Elizabeth to support her argument that "Elizabeth's handling of the sexual ambiguity inherent in her role as a female head of state and governor of the Church of England was not only a reflection of contemporary attitudes on gender roles but also a necessary result of her own psychological development."

1. *Poetry.* Leicester Bradner, ed. *The Poems of Queen Elizabeth I* (1964), prints six poems certainly by Elizabeth, ten possibly written by her, and six verse translations. *The Arundel Harington Manuscript of Tudor Poetry,* ed. Ruth Hughey, 2 vols. (1960), includes "The dread of future foes" and Elizabeth's translation of a part of Petrarch's *Triumph of Eternity*—the latter printed for the first time. *Queen Elizabeth's Englishings of Boethius "De Consolatione Philosophiae," A. D. 1593: Plutarch, "De Curiositate" [1598]; Horace, "De Arte Poetica" (part), A. D. 1598* was edited for the early English Text Society by Caroline Pemberton (1899; rpt. 1973).

Geoffrey B. Riddlehough, "Queen Elizabeth's Translation of Boethius' 'De Consolatione Philosophiae,'" *JEGP,* 45 (1946), 88–94, criticizes both Pemberton's edition and Elizabeth's translation; the latter, he says, is one by "an eager amateur who reveals, in a short burst of intellectual energy, capabilities that in a humbler station of life might have risen above mediocrity." Leonard Forster, "The Political Petrarchism of the Virgin Queen," in his *The Icy Fire: Five Studies in European Petrarchism* (1969), pp. 122–47, quotes "I grieve and dare not show discontent" to indicate Elizabeth's knowledge of what he calls "the Petrarchan stereotype": "I want," he says, "to suggest that throughout her life she was concerned to use the stereotype for her own purposes, by acting it herself and causing others to act in accordance with it." Other scholars who have treated the political, social, and literary ramifications of Elizabeth's image of herself as the virgin queen include Roy Strong, *The Cult of Elizabeth: Elizabethan Portraiture and Pagentry* (1977); Winfried Schleiner, "*Divina virago*: Queen Elizabeth as an Amazon," *SP,* 75 (1978), 163–80; Jonathan Goldberg, *Endless Worke: Spenser and the Structures of Discourse* (1981); and Louis Adrian Montrose, "'Shaping Fantasies': Figurations of

Gender and Power in Elizabethan Culture," *Representations*, 1 (1983), 61–94.

James E. Phillips, "Elizabeth I as a Latin Poet: An Epigram on Paul Melissus," *RN*, 16 (1963), 289–98, tentatively attributes "Reginae Responsum" from Melissus' *Mele sive Odae* (1580) to Elizabeth, and L. G. Black, "A Lost Poem by Queen Elizabeth I," *TLS*, 23 May, 1968, 535, prints the complete text of a poem quoted by George Puttenham in his *Arte of English Poesie* (1580) and the poem to which it responds, Ralegh's "Fortune hath taken the away my love." The two poems appear together—but without the attribution to Elizabeth—in Walter Oakeshott, *The Queen and the Poet* (1960), pp. 217–19.

2. *The Mirror of the Sinful Soul*. Percy W. Ames has edited a facsimile edition of Bodleian MS. Cherry 36, *The Mirror of the Sinful Soul: A Prose Translation from the French of a Poem by Queen Margaret of Navarre made in 1544 by the Princess (Afterwards Queen) Elizabeth, then eleven Years of Age* (1897), and Renja Salminen includes a transcription in *Marguerite de Navarre: Le Miroir de L'Ame Pecheresse: Edition critique et commentaire suivis de la traduction faite par la princesse Elisabeth future reine d'Angleterre: The Glasse of the Synnefull Soule* (1979).

Ruth Hughey, "A Note on Queen Elizabeth's 'Godly Meditation,'" *Library*, 15 (1934), 237–40, describes editions published by John Bale (1548) and James Cancellar (1568); Thomas Bentley prints Cancellar's text in his *Monument of Matrons* (1582). Joseph B. Collins, *"Le Miroir de L'ame Pecheresse*, and Queen Elizabeth's translation," in *Christian Mysticism in the Elizabethan Age: With its Background in Mystical Methodology* (1940), pp. 82–87, presents the piece as the first of a new literature "of mystical transcendence and spiritual fervor" in sixteenth-century England; its descendents include works by Robert Southwell, Nicholas Breton, and Edmund Spenser. Anne Lake Prescott, "The Pearl of the Valois and Elizabeth I: Marguerite de Navarre's *Miroir* and Tudor England," in *Silent but for the Word* (I, above) believes that Catherine Parr or some other adult suggested the project to Elizabeth, but by the time the translation was complete it was clear that the poem's content made it "a most unsuitable means of displaying Elizabeth's talents in Henry's court." Prescott contends that although the translation (which is probably from the 1539 Geneva edition) "is quite accurate, even dutiful," Elizabeth's departures from the French original are signs of "at best a confused anxiety and at worst a deep anger, particularly at her father."

3. *A Book of Devotions*. *A Book of Devotions Composed by Her Majesty Elizabeth R*, trans. Adam Fox and intro. J. P. Hodges (1970), provides modern transcriptions and translations of the six prayers.

In the Foreword to that edition and in "With Bended Knee," Chapter 7 of his *The Nature of the Lion: Elizabeth I and Our Anglican Heritage* (1962), pp. 126–41, Hodges presents the six prayers as evidence of the sincere "spiritual fervour with which she interpreted her responsibilities." In the latter piece, Hodges suggests that Elizabeth wrote the prayers "over more than a decade and [that they] were finally bound during the French marriage negotiations [in the late 1570s]." William P. Haugaard, "Elizabeth Tudor's *Book of Devotions*: a Neglected Clue to the Queen's Life and Character," *SCJ*, 12 (1981), 79–106, argues that in the *Devotions* Elizabeth presents herself as she "would have liked God to see her; as she, in such moments, esteemed herself to be; and, just possibly, as she would like future generations to see her." Haugaard hesitates to accept Hodges' dating of the prayers, but he agrees with his assessment of Elizabeth's orthodoxy and her sense of her "unique royal vocation."

4. *Speeches.* Twenty-one of Elizabeth's speeches are printed in George P. Rice, Jr., *The Public Speaking of Queen Elizabeth: Selections from Her Official Addresses* (1951; rpt. 1966). Sir J. E. Neale, *Elizabeth I and her Parliaments,* 2 vols. (1953–57), includes excerpts from the speeches and notes her polishing them for publication. Her speech to her last Parliament (the "golden speech" of 1601) is in *Elizabethan Backgrounds,* ed. Arthur F. Kinney (1975), pp. 327–35.

Using her own transcriptions of speeches by Elizabeth, Allison Heisch, "Queen Elizabeth I: Parliamentary Rhetoric and the Exercise of Power," *Signs,* 1 (1975), 31–55, examines her exploration and exercise of her power as monarch and the ways "in which rhetoric may become an instrument of power." In this article Heisch stresses Elizabeth's presentation of herself as England's "loving and yet virginal mother"; in "Queen Elizabeth I and the Persistence of Patriarchy," *Feminist Review,* 4 (1980), 45–56, she observes Elizabeth's manipulation of the humility *topos* to represent herself as "an exception to the Law of Nature"—refusing to follow the usual female pattern and become a wife, Elizabeth claimed the status of "honorary male." Louis Adrian Montrose, "'Eliza, Queene of shepheardes,' and the Pastoral of Power," *ELR,* 10 (1980), 153–82, argues Elizabeth's use of the rhetoric of pastoral "as a foil for the exersise of power, not as a rejection of aspiration but as an assertion of authority."

5. *Letters.* G. B. Harrison's edition of *The Letters of Queen Elizabeth I* (1935; rpt. 1968) offers a selection of personal and private letters. In the Introduction Harrison argues that they show Elizabeth's belief "in herself as absolute monarch, and God's Vicegerent on earth. . . . In her letters, as in her life, she was always the Queen of England." The *Letter from the Queens Maiestie to the Lord Maior of London* (1586) is printed in facsimile in the English Experience series (1969).

6. *Other Works.* Tucker Brooke, "Queen Elizabeth's Prayers," *HLQ,* 2 (1938), 69–77; rpt. in his *Essays on Shakespeare and Other Elizabethans* (1948), pp. 145–57, prints English prayers by the monarch. Margaret H. Swain, "A New Year's Gift from the Princess Elizabeth," *The Connoisseur,* 183 (1973), 258–66, describes Bodleian MS. Cherry 36 (see III, I, 2); Royal MSS.7.D.X., a collection of *Prayers and Meditations of Katherine Parr* now in the British Library; and MS.RH 13/78 in the Scottish Record Office. The last, entitled *How we ought to know God,* is a translation into French of the first book of Calvin's *Institutes.* Swain argues that *Prayers and Meditations* and *How we ought to know God* are a pair of New Year's gifts for Catherine Parr and Henry VIII, respectively, and that Elizabeth may have prepared four or even six such books for her parents—in addition to MS. Bod/1/6 made for Edward VI. Swain notes that Elizabeth may have helped embroider the covers of the books.

7. *Canon.* In "The Xenophon Translation Attributed to Elizabeth I," *JWCI,* 17 (1964), 324–26, L. Bradner disputes the assumption that MS Ff. 6.3 in the Cambridge University Library is by Elizabeth, and in "An Early English Metrical Psalm: Elizabeth's or John Bale's?" *N&Q,* 219 (1974), 404–05, David Scott Kastan demonstrates that the English version of Psalm 18 at the end of *A Godly Medytacyon* (1548) is by Bale. J. E. Neale, "The Sayings of Queen Elizabeth," in his *Essays in Elizabethan History* (1958), pp. 85–112, includes two pages (pp. 102–03) on "Christ was the Word," a quatrain some have thought to have been written by Elizabeth.

H. *Lady Jane or Joanna Lumley (1537?–1576/7).* Lady Lumley's translation of *Iphigenia at Aulis* was edited by Harold H. Child for the Malone Society in 1909.

David H. Greene's examination of the translation, "Lady Lumley and Greek Tragedy," *CJ,* 36 (1941), 537–47, concludes that she translated *Iphigenia* from a Greek original, with some help from Erasmus' Latin text, but Frank D. Crane, "Euripides, Erasmus, and Lady Lumley," *CJ,* 39 (1944), 223–28, maintains that her work is "a childish performance, derived directly and carelessly from Latin."

I. *Lady Jane Grey (1538–1554).* The writings of Lady Jane Grey are collected in John Foxe, *Acts and Monuments of these latter and perilous days* (1563), ed. George Townsend, Vol. 6 (1838; rpt. 1965), pp. 415–25, and in Nicholas Harris Nicolas, *The Literary Remains of Lady Jane Grey, with a Memoir of her Life* (1825; rpt. as *Memoirs and Literary Remains of Lady Jane Grey* [1832]). Travitsky, *Paradise of Women,* pp. 41–44 and pp. 78–81, presents excerpts.

Hester W. Chapman, *Lady Jane Grey* (1962), describes her as "the stuff of which the Puritan martyr is made: self-examining, fanatical, bitterly courageous, and utterly incapable of the art of compromise in which the Tudors specialized," and Carole Levin, "Lady Jane Grey: Protestant Queen and Martyr," in *Silent but for the Word* (I, above), argues that Lady Jane's "life and writings represented a rigid and uncompromising Protestantism that made her one of the best-known women of her age." David Mathew, *Lady Jane Grey: the Setting of the Reign* (1972), focuses on political forces that formed her place in English history, as does Barrett L. Beer, *Northumberland: The Political Career of John Dudley, Earl of Warwick and Duke of Northumberland* (1973).

J. *Mary Stuart (1542–1587).* The *Letters and Poems by Mary Stuart, Queen of Scots* have been modernized and (where necessary) translated by Clifford Bax (1947). Complete texts of the Casket Letters are also available in M. H. Armstrong Davison's defense of Mary, *The Casket Letters: A Solution to the Mystery of Mary, Queen of Scots, and the Murder of Lord Darnley* (1965). Travitsky, *Paradise of Women,* pp. 187–207, prints a number of poems, three letters, and a portion of *Essay of Adversity* (1580); in her notes, Travitsky supplies the French texts of the sonnets.

Antonia Fraser, *Mary Queen of Scots* (1969), uses manuscript and printed sources to correct false impressions of Mary inherited from such works as George Buchanan, *The Tyrannous Reign of Mary Stewart* (1571), trans. and ed. W. A. Gatherer (1958; rpt. 1978). In Chapter 20, "Her Privy Letters," pp. 385–408, Fraser explains her judgment that the authenticity of the Casket Letters is "highly dubious," and in an Appendix (pp. 556–68), she prints contemporary English and Scottish versions of the second letter. Mary Stuart is one of three "Exceptional Figures" (the others are Anne Askew and Elizabeth Cary [1585–1639])whom Travitsky treats in the latter part of *Paradise of Women;* Travitsky particularly admires the sonnets, which she discusses as successors of Ronsard and Du Bellay's work.

Samuel A. and Dorothy R. Tannenbaum include four pages on Mary's verse and prose in their *Marie Stuart in her Relation to the Arts (A Concise Bibliography),* Vol. 3 (1946), 31–34.

K. *Mary Sidney, Countess of Pembroke (1561–1621)*. See Part Two, below.

L. *Isabella Whitney (fl. 1567–1573)*. Whitney's two volumes of poems, *A Copy of a Letter* (1567?) and *A Sweet Nosgay* (1573), appear with Hugh Plat's *The Floures of Philosophie* (1572) in a facsimile edition edited by Richard J. Panofsky (1982). Betty Travitsky, "The 'Wyll and Testament' of Isabella Whitney," *ELR*, 10 (1980), 76–94, edits the final poem of the *Nosgay* volume; she also prints portions of Whitney's poems in *The Paradise of Women*, pp. 118–27.

Robert J. Fehrenbach, "Isabella Whitney (fl. 1565–75) and the Popular Miscellanies of Richard Jones," *CashiersE*, 19 (1981), 85–87, suggests that Whitney may have authored a few of the poems published in Jones' *Gorgeous Gallery of Gallant Inventions* (1578) and *A Handful of Pleasant Delights* (1584). In "Isabella Whitney, Sir Hugh Plat, Geoffrey Whitney, and 'Sister Eldershae,'" *ELN*, 21 (1983), 7–11, Fehrenbach demonstrates that the *Nosgay* volume is based on Plat's *Floures of Philosophie* and that Isabella and Geoffrey Whitney were sister and brother. Henry Green, *On the Emblems of Geffrey Whitney of Nantwich in the Sixteenth Century* (1845), pp. 15–16, indicates that Isabella Whitney is "Probably connected with or related to Geffrey Whitney," and, in a note, suggests that she contributed commendatory verses to Thomas Morley, *A Plaine and Easie Introduction to practicall Musicke* (1597), printed (as were her two volumes) by Richard Jones.

In "The Lady Doth Protest: Protest in the Popular Writings of Renaissance Englishwomen" in this issue of *ELR*, Betty Travitsky treats "A Letter . . . to her unconstant Lover" as the first published work in which an Englishwoman criticizes men.

M. *Margaret Tyler (fl. 1578)*. Travitsky, *Paradise of Women*, pp. 144–45, prints a portion of Tyler's Prefatory Letter to her translation of Diego Ortunez de Calahorra, *A mirrour of princely deedes and knighthood* (1578). Moira Ferguson, *The First Feminists: British Women Writers from 1578 to 1799* (forthcoming) will print the Dedication and Epistle to the Reader.

E. D. Mackerness, "Margaret Tyler: An Elizabethan Feminist," *N&Q*, 190 (1946), 112–23, notes Tyler's early defense of woman's equality in both reading and writing.

N. *Jane Anger (pseud.?) (fl. 1589)*. Excerpts from *Jane Anger, her protection for Women* (1589) appear in Travitsky, *Paradise of Women*, pp. 103–04, and in Joan Goulianos, ed., *"by a Woman writt": Literature from Six Centuries By and About Women* (1973; rpt. 1974), pp. 23–29. Henderson and McManus, *Half Humankind* (Background Studies, above), and Ferguson, *The First Feminists* (III, M), will print substantial excerpts.

Utley, *The Crooked Rib* (Background Studies, above), p. 314, suggests that Jane Anger is responding to "An old lover to a yong gentilwoman" in *Tottel's Miscellany* (1557). Helen Andrews Kahin, "Jane Anger and John Lyly," *MLQ*, 8 (1947), 31–35, connects Anger's work "directly or indirectly" with Lyly's *Euphues his Censure to Philautus* (1588) and contrasts Anger's sincerity and steadfastness with Lyly's "sophisticated insincerity." In "The Lady Doth Protest: Protest in the Popular Writings of Renaissance Englishwomen," (III, L) Betty Travitsky presents Jane Anger's piece as a response to the lost *Boke his Surfeyt in love* (1588); Anger, Travitsky believes, is a relatively moderate middle-class woman writing to other Englishwomen. Linda Woodbridge, *Women and the English Renaissance* (Background Studies, above), pp. 63–66, insists that "the material Anger refers to was the formal controversy's stock in trade" and that "Anger's enjoyment of her ingenuity in devising antimasculist insults argues aesthetic detachment" rather than a personal response to specific detractors against women.

Some historians believe "Jane Anger" was a pseudonym for a male writer (see Joan Kelly, "Early Feminist Theory and the *Querelle des Femmes*, 1400–1789," *Signs*, 8 [1982], 16, n. 26), but all of the scholars whose work is listed here believe Jane Anger was probably a woman.

O. *Elizabeth Grymeston (d. 1603).* The 1604 edition of *Miscelanea. Meditation. Memoratives* has been reprinted in facsimile for the English Experience Series (1979). B. Y. Fletcher and C. W. Sizemore, "Elizabeth Grymeston's *Miscelanea. Meditations. Memoratives:* Introduction and Selected Text," *LC,* 47 (1981), 53–83, print representative portions. Travitsky, *Paradise of Women,* pp. 51–55, includes briefer excerpts, as do Mahl and Koon, *The Female Spectator,* pp. 52–61. W. C. Hazlitt, ed. *Prefaces. Dedications. Epistles Selected from Early English Books, 1540–1701* (1874), pp. 195–200, prints the Introductory Letter in full.

Ruth Hughey and Philip Hereford, "Elizabeth Grymeston and her *Miscellanea,*" *Library,* 15 (1934), 61–91, describe the four editions of the book; point to quotations from Robert Southwell, Richard Rowlands, and *England's Parnassus* (1600) to show that Grymeston modified others' verses, rather than wrote her own; suggest that she used a compilation such as Hugh Platt, *Flores Patrum;* and argue that the book reveals "a mind well acquainted with contemporary and classic poetry and prose, and acquainted in such a way that the stuff of reading had become a part of the web and woof of itself." Fletcher and Sizemore (above) place the book in its historical context by suggesting Robert Southwell, *Epistle . . . unto His Father, Exhorting Him to the Perfect Forsaking of the World* (1595) as a likely model for Grymeston's work and note her "use of the meditation in her writing and . . . the metaphysical nature of her images."

IV. STATE OF CRITICISM

With the occasional exception of ground-breaking work by earlier scholars such as Myra Reynolds, Ruth Hughey, and Charlotte Kohler, most of the essays and books listed in this bibliography were published in the 1970s and early 1980s—the years of the burgeoning new scholarship on women. Although there is as yet no textbook of the period that includes substantial excerpts by women writers and no general literary history of Tudor England that allots appropriate space to them, recent scholars have edited enough of their works and examined them in enough detail to make it clear that women writers of Tudor England warrant careful study.

Many recent studies (Rita Verbrugge's of Margaret Roper and Elaine Beilin's of Anne Askew, for example) endeavor to see women writers on their own terms, rather than to examine them as their fathers' daughters or their biographers' subjects; others (Betty Travitsky on Mary Stuart's sonnets, Linda Woodbridge on Jane Anger, and B. Y. Fletcher and C. W. Sizemore on Elizabeth Grymeston, for instance) treat Tudor women's writing as consciously-crafted literary pieces—works whose authors are fully aware of their literary *milieu* and who work with the literary traditions of their age.

Until, however, editions of works by Tudor women are readily available for study by a larger group of readers and until more is known about the lives of individual women writers, it will not be possible to answer the question "Did women [in Tudor England] have a [literary] Renaissance?" with real accuracy or analytical subtlety. Critical issues that remain unresolved include questions concerning the extent to which women were "silenced" by the ideas of the Renaissance and Reformation and the extent to which women like Catherine Parr and Elizabeth Tudor (or lesser-known women like Elizabeth Grymeston) influenced the course and character of the English literary Renaissance; the degree to which Tudor women served as literary "models" for one another and/or their 17th-century female successors; and the amount and kinds of influence Tudor women writers exerted on their male counterparts.

See also

BACKGROUND STUDIES (Selected)

Bergeron, David M. "Women as Patrons of English Renaissance Drama," in *Patronage in the Renaissance*, ed. Guy Fitch Lytle and Stephen Orgel (1981), pp. 274–90.

Bradford, Gamaliel. *Elizabethan Women*, ed. Harold Ogden White (1936).

Bullough, Vern L. *The Subordinate Sex: A History of Attitudes Toward Women* (1973).

Cressy, David, ed. *Education in Tudor & Stuart England* (1975; rpt. 1976) [excerpts from Renaissance treatises].

————. "Literacy in pre-industrial England," *Societas*, 14 (1974), 229–40.

Davis, Natalie Zemon. "Woman on Top," in her *Society and Culture in Early Modern France: Eight Essays* (1975), pp. 124–51.

Hogrefe, Pearl. "Legal Rights of Tudor Women and the Circumvention by Men and Women," *SCJ*, 3 (1972), 97–105.

Holm, Janis Butler. "Toward a History of Women in Early Modern Europe," *Annals of Scholarship*, 2 (1981), 107–18.

Kaufman, Michael W. "Spare Ribs: The Conception of Women in the Middle Ages and the Renaissance," *Soundings*, 56 (1973), 139–63.

King, John N. "The Woman of Faith in Elizabethan Iconography," *RQ* (forthcoming).

Labalme, Patricia H., ed. *Beyond their Sex: Learned Women of the European Past* (1980).

Levin, Carole. "Women in *The Book of Martyrs* as Models of Behavior in Tudor England," *IJWS* 4 (1981), 196–207.

Notestein, Wallace. "The English Woman, 1580–1650," in *Studies in Social History: A Tribute to G. M. Trevelyan*, ed. John Harold Plumb (1955; rpt. 1969), pp. 69–107.

O'Faolain, Julia and Lauro Martines, ed. *Not in God's Image: Women in History from the Greeks to the Victorians* (1973).

Pearson, Lu Emily. *Elizabethans at Home* (1957; rpt. 1968).

Putnam, Maxine. "A Glimpse into the Lives of English Women During the Renaissance," *Florida State University Studies*, 5 (1952), 67–78.

Stone, Lawrence. *The Crisis of the Aristocracy, 1558–1641* (1965; abridged ed. 1967).

Todd, Margot. "Humanistic Puritans and the Spiritualized Household," *Church History*, 49 (1980), 18–34.

I. GENERAL STUDIES

Ballard, George. *Memoirs of British Ladies who have been Celebrated for their Writings or Skill in the Learned Languages, Arts and Sciences* (1775).

Buyze, Jean. *The Tenth Muse: Women Poets before 1806* (1980) [checklist].

Greco, Norma and Ronade Novotny. "Bibliography of Women in the English Renaissance," *University of Michigan Papers in Women's Studies,* 1 (1974), 30–57.

Travitsky, Betty S. "The New Mother of the English Renaissance (1489–1659): A Descriptive Catalogue," *BRH,* 82 (1979), 63–89.

Williams, Franklin B., Jr., "The Literary Patronesses of Renaissance England," *N&Q,* 207 (1962), 364–66.

Wyntjes, Sherrin Marshall. "Women in the Reformation Era," in *Becoming Visible: Women in European History,* ed. Renate Bridenthal and Claudia Koonz (1977), pp. 165–91.

II. STUDIES OF INDIVIDUAL WRITERS

A. *Margaret Beaufort, Countess of Richmond and Derby*

Axton, William E. A. "The Lady Margaret as a Lover of Literature," *Library,* 8 (1907), 34–41.

Jayne, Sears. *Library Catalogues of the English Renaissance* (1956).

Reynolds, E. E. "St. John Fisher and the Lady Margaret Beaufort," *Moreana,* No. 23 (1969), 32–33.

Routhe, E. M. G. *Lady Margaret: A Memoir of Lady Margaret Beaufort, Countess of Richmond & Derby, Mother of Henry VII* (1924).

Underwood, Malcolm G. "The Lady Margaret and her Cambridge Connections," *SCJ,* 13 (1982), 67–81.

Warnicke, Retha M. "The Lady Margaret, Countess of Richmond (d. 1509), as seen by Bishop Fisher and by Lord Morley," *Moreana,* No. 74 (1982), 47–55.

B. *Margaret More Roper*

Albin, Hugh O. "Opening of the Roper Vault in St. Dunstan's Canterbury and thoughts on the burial of William and Margaret Roper," *Moreana,* No. 63 (1979), 29–35.

Campbell, Mildred, ed. *The Utopia of Sir Thomas More including Roper's Life of More and Letters of More and his Daughter Margaret* (1947).

Gee, John Archer. "Margaret Roper's English Version of Erasmus' *Precatio Dominica* and the Apprenticeship behind Early Tudor Translation," *RES,* 13 (1937), 257–71.

Marie-Claire, Sr.; Sr. Gertrude-Joseph, E.E.R.; and F. Bierlaine. "Correspondence entre Erasme et Margaret Roper," *Moreana,* No. 12 (1966), 29–46.

Murray, Francis G. "Feminine Spirituality in the More Household," *Moreana,* No. 28 (1970), 92–102.

Plaidy, Jean [pseud. for Eleanor Hibbert]. *Meg Roper: Daughter of Sir Thomas More* (1964) [Children's novel].

Rogers, Elizabeth Frances, ed. *St. Thomas More: Selected Letters* (1961).

Routhe, E. M. G. *Sir Thomas More and his Friends, 1477–1535* (1934; rpt. 1963).

Stapleton, Thomas. "Margaret Roper, his Eldest Daughter," in his *The Life and Illustrious*

Martyrdom of Sir Thomas More (1588), trans. Philip E. Hallett (1928), ed. E. E. Reynolds (1966), pp. 103–09.

C. *Catherine Parr*

British Reformers. Vol. 3: Writings of Edward the Sixth, William Hugh, Queen Catherine Parr, Anne Askew, Lady Jane Grey, Hamilton, and Belnaves [n.d.].

Gordon, M. A. *Life of Queen Katherine Parr* (1951).

White, Helen C. *Tudor Books of Private Devotion* (1951).

D. *Anne Askew*

Bainton, Roland H. "John Foxe and the Women Martyrs," in his *Women of the Reformation in France and England* (1973; rpt. 1975), pp. 211–29.

British Reformers. Vol. 3: Writings of Edward the Sixth, William Hugh, Queen Catherine Parr, Anne Askew, Lady Jane Grey, Hamilton, and Belnaves [n.d.].

Macleod, Alison. *The Heretic* (1966) [novel].

E. *Anne Cooke, Lady Bacon*

Hughey, Ruth. "Lady Anne Bacon's Translations," *RES*, 19 (1934), 211.

Whiting, Mary Bradford. "Anne, Lady Bacon," *ContempR*, 122 (1922), 497–508.

————. "The Learned and Virtuous Lady Bacon," *Hibbert Journal*, 29 (1931), 270–83.

F. *Elizabeth I*

Coogan, Robert, C. F. G. "Petrarch's *Trionfi* and the English Renaissance," *SP*, 67 (1970), 306–07. [Brief comment on Elizabeth's translation of the *Triumph of Eternity*.]

Flügel, Ewald. "Die Gedichte der Königen Elisabeth," *Anglia*, 14 (1892), 346–61.

Hogrefe, Pearl. "Queen Elizabeth," in her *Women of Action in Tudor England: Nine Biographical Sketches* (1977), pp. 209–33.

Kouri, E. I. "Six Unpublished Letters from Elizabeth I of England to German and Skandinavian Princes," *ARG*, 73 (1982), 237–54.

Stenberg, Theodore. "Elizabeth as Euphuist before *Euphues*," University of Texas *Studies in English*, 8 (1928), 65–78.

————. "More about Queen Elizabeth's Euphuism," University of Texas *Studies in English*, 13 (1933), 64–77.

G. *Lady Jane Grey*

Bainton, Roland H. "Lady Jane Grey," in his *Women of the Reformation in France and England* (1973; rpt. 1975), pp. 181–90.

British Reformers: Vol. 3: Writings of Edward the Sixth, William Hugh, Queen Catherine Parr, Anne Askew, Lady Jane Grey, Hamilton and Belnaves [n.d.].

Mullally, Margaret. *A Crown in Darkness* [novel].

Nichols, John Gould, ed. *The Chronicle of Queen Jane . . . Written by a Resident in the Tower of London* (1850; rpt. 1968).

H. *Mary Stuart*

Arbuthnot, Mrs. P. Stewart-Mackenzie, ed. *Queen Mary's Book: A Collection of Poems and Essays by Mary Queen of Scots* (1907).

Black, John Bennett. *Andrew Lang and the Casket Letter Controversy* (1951).

Cowan, Ian B., comp. and ed. *The Enigma of Mary Stuart* (1971).

Diggle, H. F. *The Casket Letters of Mary Stuart: A Study in Fraud and Forgery: A Vindication of the Queen* (1960).

Donaldson, Gordon. *The First Trial of Mary, Queen of Scots* (1969).

————. *Mary, Queen of Scots* (1974).

King, Marian. *Young Mary Stuart, Queen of Scots* (1954).

Plaidy, Jean [pseud. for Eleanor Hibbert]. *Mary Queen of Scots: The Fair Devil of Scotland* (1975) [novel].

Read, Conyers. *Mr. Secretary Cecil and Queen Elizabeth* (1955), esp. pp. 374–415.

Sharmon, Julian. *The Library of Mary, Queen of Scots with an historical introduction and rare portrait of the Queen* (1889).

————. *The Poems of Mary, Queen of Scots* (1873).

Strickland, Agnes, ed. *Letters of Mary, Queen of Scots,* 2 vols., rev. ed. (1845).

Thomson, George Malcolm. *The Crime of Mary Stuart* (1967).

I. *Elizabeth Grymeston*

Bone, Gavin. "Jeremy Taylor and Elizabeth Grymeston," *Library,* 15 (1934), 247–28 [Taylor's use of a metaphor from Grymeston].

Krueger, Robert, "Manuscript Evidence for Dates of Two *Short-Title Catalogue* Books: George Wilkins's *Three Miseries of Barbary* and the Third Edition of Elizabeth Grymeston's *Miscelanea,*" *Library,* 16 (1961), 141–42.

III. ANTHOLOGIES INCLUDING WOMEN WRITERS OF TUDOR ENGLAND

Bernikow, Louise, ed. *The World Split Open: Four Centuries of Women Poets in England and America, 1552–1950* (1974) [Elizabeth I; Mary Sidney, Countess of Pembroke].

Bethune, George W., ed. *The British Female Poets with Biographical and Critical Notices* (1848; rpt. 1972) [Anne Boleyn; Catherine Parr; Lady Bergavenny; Countess of Arundel; Mary Queen of Scots; Elizabeth I; Mary Sidney, Countess of Pembroke].

Cosman, Carol, Joan Keefe, and Kathleen Weaver, ed. *The Penguin Book of Women Poets* (1978) [Elizabeth I; Mary Sidney, Countess of Pembroke].

Dyce, Alexander. *Specimens of British Poetesses: Selected and Chronologically Arranged* (1825; rpt. 1827) [Anne Boleyn; Anne Askew; Elizabeth Tudor; E. D.; Anne, Countess of Oxford].

Stanford, Ann, ed. *The Women Poets in English: An Anthology* (1972) [Elizabeth of York; Anne Boleyn; Anne Askew; Elizabeth I; Isabella Whitney; Anne Howard; Mary Sidney, Countess of Pembroke; Elizabeth Melvill].

I should like to thank the Central University Research Fund of the University of New Hampshire for financial support of this project.

Part II: Mary Sidney, Countess of Pembroke

JOSEPHINE A. ROBERTS

No standard edition of the collected works of Mary Sidney, Countess of Pembroke, is available. J. C. A. Rathmell edited *The Psalms of Sir Philip Sidney and the Countess of Pembroke* (1963), and G. F. Waller provided additional manuscript versions of the Countess' Psalms and occasional poems and of her translation of Petrarch's *Trionfo della Morte,* in *The Triumph of Death and Other Unpublished and Uncollected Poems by Mary Sidney, Countess of Pembroke (1561–1621).* Geoffrey Bullough, *Narrative and Dramatic Sources of Shakespeare,* Vol. 5 (1964), edited the Countess' verse translation of Garnier's play *Marc-Antoine,* and Diane Bornstein edited *The Countess of Pembroke's Translation of Philippe de Mornay's Discourse of Life and Death* (1983).

I. GENERAL

A. *Biographical.* Frances B. Young, *Mary Sidney, Countess of Pembroke* (1912), provides essential documentary material concerning the Countess' family background, education, marriage, and literary associations. In the first chapter of *Mary Sidney, Countess of Pembroke: A Critical Study of her Writings and Literary Milieu* (1979), Gary F. Waller corrects some of Young's errors, such as her use of the spurious genealogy of the Sidney family, and shows that the marriage to Henry Herbert, second Earl of Pembroke, was conventional by Elizabethan standards despite the couple's disparity of age. While regarding the Countess as the greatest woman writer of the Elizabethan era, Retha M. Warnicke, *Women of the English Renaissance and Reformation* (1983), questions whether there is any proof of her knowledge of Latin and argues that "because she was not skilled in classical languages, she cannot be identified as a humanist." (Yet see Kinnamon, "*Melle de petra,*" II, A). Margaret P. Hannay, "Unpublished Letters by Mary Sidney: A Preliminary Report," *SNew,* 4.2 (1983), 13, describes three newly discovered letters from the Countess to Sir Julius Caesar, the Earl of Shrewsbury, and Robert Devereux, Earl of Essex; Hannay's biography of the Countess is in progress.

Important evidence concerning the Countess' involvement in theatrical activities appears in Mary Edmond, "Pembroke's Men," *RES,* 25 (1974), 129–36, which contains a transcription of the will of an actor, Simon Jewell, who records a payment due from Lady Pembroke. Edmond believes that Jewell belonged to the original acting company, Pembroke's Men, but Karl P. Wentersdorf, "The Origin and Personnel of the Pembroke Company," *Theatre Research International,* 5 (1979–80), 45–68, maintains that the payment refers instead to a performance at the Countess' household in 1592. Sir Tresham Lever, *The Herberts of Wilton* (1967), suggests that a royal performance of Shakespeare's *As You Like It* was staged at Wilton in 1603 as part of the Countess' effort to secure a pardon for Ralegh from King James. In *The Age of Inigo Jones* (1953), James Lees-Milne states that Jones redesigned Houghton House in Bedfordshire for the Countess not long before her death in 1621.

The relationship between the Countess and Shakespeare has been the subject of speculation, ranging from George Bernard Shaw's Preface to *The Dark Lady of the*

Sonnets (1910), where he regards her as the model for the Countess of Rossillion in *All's Well That Ends Well*, to John Padel's *New Poems by Shakespeare: Order and Meaning Restored to the Sonnets* (1981), where she is seen as the prototype for the grief-stricken Olivia, excessively mourning the death of her brother, in *Twelfth Night*. Padel revives the hypothesis of Thomas Tyler, who edited Shakespeare's sonnets (1890), that the Countess commissioned Shakespeare to write the first seventeen poems as advice to her wayward son, William Herbert; he argues further that the Countess may have re-arranged and edited the 1609 quarto. Katherine Duncan-Jones, "Pyramus and Thisbe: Shakespeare's Debt to Moffett Cancelled," *RES*, 32 (1981), 296–301, writes that a poem dedicated to the Countess, Thomas Moffett's "The Silkewormes," is not a source for *A Midsummer Night's Dream* but rather a mock encomium interesting in its own right for allusions to the Countess' household at Wilton. E. K. Chambers, *William Shakespeare: A Study of Facts and Problems* (1930), II, 329, notes that a letter from the Countess to her son containing the phrase, "we have the man Shakespeare with us," was last mentioned as existing in 1865, but the letter (perhaps a forgery) has not been found.

Brief mention of the Countess' life appears in the major biographies of her eldest brother, Sir Philip Sidney: Malcolm W. Wallace, *The Life of Sir Philip Sidney* (1915); Mona Wilson, *Sir Philip Sidney* (1950); Roger Howell, *Sir Philip Sidney: The Shepherd Knight* (1968); James M. Osborn, *Young Philip Sidney, 1572–1577* (1972).

B. *General Studies.* T. S. Eliot's "Apology for the Countess of Pembroke," which first appeared in the *Harvard Graduates' Magazine,* 41 (1932), 63–75, follows the tendency of earlier critics to focus on the Countess' role as patron to the exclusion of her own writings. The essay, reprinted in *The Use of Poetry and the Use of Criticism* (1933), claims that despite the failure of the Countess' attempt to introduce a more classical form into drama, she succeeded in heightening a critical consciousness of poetic art: "The chief channel through which the Countess of Pembroke's circle may have affected the course of English poetry is the great civilising influence of Spenser." Gary Waller also presents the Countess as the leader of an important "crusade for the enrichment of Elizabethan life and culture" in *Mary Sidney* (I,A), the first book-length study devoted primarily to the Countess' written works. Waller believes that the Countess began composing verse shortly after Sir Philip Sidney's death by following his poetic models and then gradually gaining confidence in her own talents. He discusses *Antonie, The Triumph of Death, A Discourse,* and the occasional poems, devoting primary attention to the Countess' metrical imitations of the Psalms, which express a sophisticated combination of "courtliness and piety, Castiglione and Calvin" and anticipate the profoundly introspective religious poetry of the seventeenth century. In "'This Matching of Contraries': Bruno, Calvin and the Sidney Circle," *Neophil,* 56 (1972), 331–43, Waller sees the major works of both Sidney and his sister as characterized by a philosophical tension between the courtly-magical tradition of Bruno and the ethos of Calvinism.

John Buxton, *Sir Philip Sidney and the English Renaissance* (1954; 2nd ed. 1964), examines how the Countess of Pembroke continued the patronage of writers whom her brother had sponsored and sought other younger proteges, such as Daniel, to carry on the poetic tradition. Surveying the full range of dedications to her, Buxton concludes, "Myra,

Amaryllis, Urania, Clorinda, Miriam, Pandora, Pembrokiana, Poemenarcha—she is addressed by countless names, and addressed always as the living inspiration of the English Renaissance." David M. Bergeron discusses more specifically the impact of the Countess' well-defined set of classical principles on drama in "Women as Patrons of English Renaissance Drama," in *Patronage in the Renaissance,* ed. Guy Fitch Lytle and Stephen Orgel (1981), pp. 274–90. Pearl Hogrefe, "Mary Sidney Herbert, Countess of Pembroke," in her *Women of Action in Tudor England: Nine Biographical Sketches* (1977), pp. 105–35, traces the development of Wilton, the home of the Pembrokes, into an intellectual and literary center. According to Patricia Thomson, "The Literature of Patronage, 1580–1630," *EC,* 11 (1952), 267–84, members of the Countess of Pembroke's family served for over fifty years as some of the most influential patrons, with the Countess receiving dedications in works ranging in quality from the *Faerie Queene* to the execrable poetry of Nathaniel Baxter's *Ourania.* Franklin B. Williams Jr.'s statistical study of female patronage, "The Literary Patronesses of Renaissance England," *N&Q,* 207 (1962), 364–66, shows that Mary Sidney ranked second only to the Countess of Bedford in the number of books addressed to a woman not of royalty.

Mary Ellen Lamb, "The Countess of Pembroke's Patronage," *ELR,* 12 (1982), 162–79, contends that previous studies have exaggerated the nature and extent of the Countess' patronage by relying too heavily upon adulatory dedications that were often "the products of wish-fulfillment." Apart from those poets who had been sponsored originally by Sir Philip Sidney or claimed his friendship, Lamb believes that the predominant group of writers in residence at Wilton consisted of employees, such as Thomas Howell, Hugh Sanford, Thomas Moffett, and Samuel Daniel, who produced literature that was largely mediocre or trivial (with the notable exception of Daniel's *Cleopatra*). In a companion piece, "The Myth of the Countess of Pembroke: The Dramatic Circle," *YES,* 11 (1981), 194–202, Lamb also challenges the traditional view of the Countess as a leader of a coterie of playwrights dedicated to the reformation of the English stage after the French Senecan model. She shows that the only dramatists who explicitly acknowledged the influence of the Countess were Daniel and Fraunce, whose translation of Tasso's *Aminta* lacks any distinctively Senecan features.

Joan Rees, *Samuel Daniel: A Critical and Biographical Study* (1964), traces the changing relationship between the Countess and Daniel, who left Wilton in 1594, perhaps because he wished to free himself of her direction. Jean Robertson, ed., *Poems by Nicholas Breton not Hitherto Reprinted* (1952), examines Breton's temporary loss of the Countess of Pembroke's favor, and in "Drayton and the Countess of Pembroke," *RES,* 16 (1965), 49 she identifies Drayton's use of anagrams to refer to "Mari Sidnei" in "Idea's Mirror" and "Gaveston." According to A. Leigh DeNeef, "'The Ruins of Time': Spenser's Apology for Poetry," *SP,* 76 (1979), 262–71, Spenser pays tribute to both the Countess and Sir Philip in "The Ruins of Time" by applying the principles of Sidneian poetic theory.

The Countess' literary influence also extended to her other brother, Sir Robert Sidney, and her niece, Lady Mary Wroth. Peter J. Croft has edited Robert Sidney's poems (1984); selections are ed. Katherine Duncan-Jones in *ELR,* 9 (1979), 240–63. Hilton Kelliher and Duncan-Jones, "A Manuscript of Poems by Robert Sidney: Some Early Impressions," *BLJ,* 1 (1975), 107–44, analyze the nature and provenance of the collection. Josephine A. Roberts, *The Poems of Lady Mary Wroth* (1983), discusses how the Countess inspired the writing of Lady Mary Wroth, who presented a fictionalized portrait of her aunt in the pastoral play *Loves Victorie*.

In addition to the Countess' roles as writer and patron, her work as an editor is examined by Pearl Hogrefe, *Tudor Women: Commoners and Queens* (1975). In his edition of *The Poems of Sir Philip Sidney* (1962), William A. Ringler, Jr., provides an extensive analysis of the 1593 edition of the *Arcadia,* published under the direction of the Countess and her assistant Hugh Sanford, who "performed their editorial labours, if not with perfect accuracy and consistency, at least conservatively." Working from her own manuscript of the *Arcadia,* she preserved three poems and two passages of prose that otherwise would have been lost. In basic agreement with Ringler, Jean Robertson's edition of *The Countess of Pembroke's Arcadia (The Old Arcadia)* (1973) shows that the major changes in Books III–V of the *Old Arcadia* as printed in 1593 derive from Sidney's own instructions, rather than the Countess' bowdlerization. John Buxton, *Elizabethan Taste* (1963; rpt. 1983), believes that the Countess valued the original version of the *Arcadia* more highly than did Fulke Greville, who took great effort to publish Sidney's revised *Arcadia* (1590). Mona Wilson, *Sir Philip Sidney* (I,A), observes that the Countess' 1598 edition of *Astrophil and Stella* contains four poems that had not previously appeared, and that the authority of the text is "established by readings which are beyond the reach of the most brilliant emendator."

For illustration of the Countess' handwriting, see W. W. Greg, *English Literary Autographs* (1928). Both Waller (I, A) and Rathmell (II, A) contain bibliographies. For a list of the major bibliographies of Sir Philip Sidney that contain references to the Countess, see W. L. Godshalk, "Recent Studies in Sidney," *ELR,* 2 (1972), 148–64, and, updated by the same author and A. J. Colaianne for the period 1970–1977, *ELR,* 8 (1978), 212–23. *The Sidney Newsletter* includes an annotated bibliography for the Countess from 1977 to the present; see also *The New Cambridge Bibliography of English Literature,* ed. George Watson, 1 (1974), cols. 1115–16; 1468–69.

II. STUDIES OF INDIVIDUAL WORKS

A. *Psalms.* Critical interest in the Sidney-Pembroke Psalms was revived with the publication of J. C. A. Rathmell's edition (1963), the first to appear in nearly 150 years. Rathmell's Introduction emphasizes the key role of the Countess in revising the first forty-three Psalms composed by her brother and in completing the collection. Praising the Psalms for their subtle verbal play, energetic rhythms, and variety of stanzaic forms, Rathmell calls attention to the Countess' method of meditating on and re-creating the biblical text: "What is so striking about the Countess of Pembroke's versions is the way in which they convey, alive as it were, the impulse and force of the Hebrew originals." With emphasis on the sophisticated technique of the Sidney-Pembroke Psalter, Barbara Kiefer Lewalski, *Protestant Poetics and the Seventeenth-Century Religious Lyric* (1979), examines the poems in the larger context of the Protestant fascination with biblical poetics, in particular with the Psalms as "a compendium of lyric kinds." She contends that Sidney and the Countess created a new persona for the Psalmist by transfiguring him into "an Elizabethan poet, expressing a contemporary religious sensibility with rare and delicate artistry." In noting many anticipations of Donne and Herbert, Lewalski concludes that the Sidney-Pembroke Psalms provide "a secure bridge to the magnificent original seventeenth-century religious lyric in the biblical and psalmic mode." Although Louis L. Martz, *The Poetry of Meditation: A Study in English Religious Literature of the Seventeenth Century* (1954; rev. ed. 1962), does not refer specifically to the Countess' contributions to the Psalms, he cites the first forty-three as "the closest approximation to the poetry of Herbert's *Temple*" that can be found in earlier literature and admires their expression of "an intimate, personal cry of the soul to God."

G. F. Waller, "'This Matching of Contraries': Calvinism and Courtly Philosophy in the Sidney Psalms," *ES,* 55 (1974), 22–31, analyzes how Sidney and the Countess reinforced key Calvinist doctrines which they found explicitly in their sources [or which they discovered on their own as implicit in the text], but occasionally, he argues, their Psalms reveal a courtly philosophy glorifying man's creative autonomy (such as in the Countess' Psalms 45 and 81) that is contrary to the Calvinist view of man as a sinful and limited being. Waller, *The Triumph of Death and Other Unpublished and Uncollected Poems by Mary Sidney, Countess of Pembroke* (1977), shows that the Countess often produced several independent versions of the same Psalm, and demonstrates that the alternative texts offer insight into her methods of poetic composition. Waller believes that the Countess continued to revise the Psalms as late as 1611, but Michael Brennan, "The Date of the Countess of Pembroke's Translation of the Psalms," *RES,* 33 (1982), 434–36, argues that the Countess had finished at least a draft translation of the collection by 1593.

Examining the Sidney-Pembroke Psalms in relation to earlier metrical paraphrases, Coburn Freer, *Music for a King: George Herbert's Style and the Metrical Psalms* (1972), believes that Sidney's Psalms surpass his sister's in lyric grace, but commends the Countess' rigorous logic and keen eye for metaphor; the Countess' major failing, he says, is an obsession with metrical variety that sometimes leads her to use complex inversions for the sake of rhyme or to ignore more subtle rhythms. The final chapter of Chana Bloch's *Spelling the Word: George Herbert and the Bible* (forthcoming) provides background on the three main generic structures of the Psalms—hymns, complaints, thanksgivings—and the manner in which these forms were transmuted into Christian songs of praise. Hallett Smith, "English Metrical Psalms in the Sixteenth Century and their Literary Significance," *HLQ,* 9 (1946), 249–71, distinguishes the Sidney-Pembroke Psalms for their artful experimentation with a wide range of meters in correspondence with the changing moods of the individual poems; they serve as a "School of English Versification." In *Divine Poetry and Drama in Sixteenth-Century England* (1959), Lily B. Campbell regards the large number of metrical translations as part of "a concerted movement to displace the new love poetry and the newly popularized pagan literature by a poetry founded on the Bible." Three doctoral dissertations also examine the Sidney-Pembroke Psalter in the context of the genre of the metrical translation: Charles A. Huttar, "English Metrical Paraphrases of the Psalms, 1500–1640," *DAI,* 17 (1957), 631–32; Carl E. Calendar, "Metrical Translation of the Psalms in France and England: 1530–1650," *DAI,* 33 (1972), 6863A; and Ellen St. Sure Lifschutz, "David's Lyre and the Renaissance Lyric: A Critical Consideration of the Psalms of Wyatt, Surrey and the Sidneys," *DAI,* 41 (1981), 3118A.

According to Noel J. Kinnamon, "*Melle de petra:* The Sources and the Form of the Sidneian Psalms," *DAI,* 37 (1977), 5143–44A, both Sidney and the Countess consulted as major sources the Prayer Book Psalter, the Geneva Bible, and Beza's prose paraphrases of the Psalms (probably the original Latin, as well as an English version), but despite the strong influence of the French psalters of Marot and Beza, the Sidneys avoid direct translation and take greater care in shaping their Psalms than do their French predecessors. John Stevens, *Music and Poetry in the Early Tudor Court* (1961), emphasizes the debt both Sidneys owe to the courtly French versions of Marot, rather than to the native English tradition of Sternhold-Hopkins. Martha Winburn England, "Sir Philip Sidney and Francois Perrot de Messières: Their Verse Versions of the Psalms," *Papers of the New York Public Library,* 75 (1971), 30–54, 101–10, cites Perrot's Italian translations of the first seventy-five Psalms, published in 1581, as a possible influence.

Beth Wynne Fisken, "Mary Sidney's *Psalmes:* Education and Wisdom," in *Silent but for the Word,* ed. Margaret P. Hannay (forthcoming), considers the Countess' gradual achievement, through successive revisions of the Psalms, of an individual style stressing the immediacy of God's presence; she developed "original patterns of imagery, reflecting her public experiences as lady-in-waiting at court and manager of her husband's estate as well as her individual perceptions as a woman and a mother." In a summary of a paper delivered at Kalamazoo and summarized in *SNew,* 4.1 (1983), 32–33, Margaret P. Hannay, "'Princes you as men must dy': Advice to Monarchs in the Psalms of Mary Sidney and the Genevan Protestants," argues that Psalms 82, 83 and 101 contain "a subtle but highly charged political statement, giving advice to the monarch about the means necessary to maintain the one true faith," but the Countess' tone is less strident than that of Beza and the Genevan Bible.

Several scholars, in addition to Lewalski, Freer, and Waller, have analyzed the influence of the Sidney-Pembroke Psalms on later poets. J. C. A. Rathmell, "Explorations and Recoveries—Hopkins, Ruskin, and the *Sidney Psalter,*" *London Magazine,* 6 (1959), 51–66, examines the impact of the Psalms upon Victorian writers, especially Ruskin (who edited a selection under the title *Rock Honeycomb*) and Hopkins, who was interested in the Sidneys' strongly accented rhythms and may have borrowed from their translations in his "terrible sonnets." Arguing for the importance of the Psalms to critical theory, Rathmell concludes, "When recognition is accorded to the *Sidney Psalter* the history of the metaphysical revival of our own time will have to be rewritten." Joseph H. Summers, *George Herbert: His Religion and Art* (1954), shows that Sidney and the Countess anticipated the experiments of Herbert in their use of counterpoint, whereby the pattern of line lengths is independent of rhymes. In "Song and Speech in the Metrics of George Herbert," *PMLA,* 80 (1965), 62–68, Alicia Ostriker contends that the Sidney-Pembroke Psalms provided Herbert with an important precedent for composing religious poetry using the techniques of courtly song; she distinguishes between the "song" elements in Herbert's prosody that are supplied by the structure of stanzaic patterns (some borrowed from the Sidneys) and the "speech" elements created by internal rhythmic variation. Noel J. Kinnamon, "A Note on Herbert's 'Easter' and the Sidneian Psalms," *GHJ,* 1.2 (1978), 44–48, offers parallels between "Easter" and the Countess' early version of Psalm 108 as evidence of Herbert's probable familiarity with the collection. In "Notes on the Psalms in Herbert's *The Temple,*" *GHJ,* 4.2 (1981), 10–29, Kinnamon traces the pervasive influence of the Psalms in Herbert's verse, with attention to structures and allusions also found in the Countess' imitations. Contrasting Wyatt's paraphrase of Psalm 130 with the Countess' version, Patricia Thomson, "Wyatt and Surrey," in *English Poetry and Prose, 1540–1674* (1970), ed. Christopher Ricks, pp. 19–40, points to the vast difference between Wyatt's dramatic mode and the Countess' elegant lyricism.

As he analyzes the prosody of the Psalms, Derek Attridge, *Well-Weighed Syllables: Elizabethan Verse in Classical Metres* (1974), claims that the Countess' manuscripts contain ten translations in quantitative verse, two of which she apparently rejected. Attridge describes her alternative version of Psalm 89 as "the most successful Elizabethan attempt to naturalise the hexameter." Israel Baroway, "The Accentual Theory of Hebrew Prosody: A Further Study in Renaissance Interpretation of Biblical Form," *ELH*, 17 (1950), 115–35, surveys the controversy concerning the accentual nature of Hebrew versification and suggests that Sidney and the Countess may have begun translating the Psalms to demonstrate that accentual English verse was a proper counterpart to the original Hebrew. Theodore Spencer, "The Poetry of Sir Philip Sidney," *ELH*, 12 (1945), 251–78, theorizes that Sidney began translating the Psalms at the very beginning of his career as an experiment in vocabulary, metrics, and verse forms.

B. *Antonie.* Condemning the Countess' translation of Garnier's play as rough, harsh, and "at times so cryptic and condensed as to be almost unintelligible," Alexander MacLaren Witherspoon, *The Influence of Robert Garnier on Elizabethan Drama* (1924; rpt. 1968), views *Antonie* as part of a futile and misguided effort to halt the popularity of romantic tragedy. In disagreement, Virginia Wallcott Beauchamp, "Sidney's Sister as Translator of Garnier," *RN*, 10 (1957), 8–13, praises the Countess' *Antonie* as a prototype of the classical drama that Sidney championed in the *Apology for Poetry* and as a graceful tribute to his memory. In "Seneca in Elizabethan Translation," *Selected Essays* (1932), T. S. Eliot admits that the Countess and her followers may have had limited influence on the actual stage, but cautions against assuming too strict a division between the academic and popular playwrights. Mary Ellen Lamb (I,B) questions Witherspoon's assumption that the Countess served as leader of a dramatic coterie, and Russell E. Leavenworth, *Daniel's Cleopatra: A Critical Study* (1974), argues that the Countess intended not to reform the stage, but to encourage the writing of dramatic poems that might "add a new dimension to the existing narrative and monologue forms so exhaustively exemplified in the *Mirror for Magistrates.*"

In the Introduction to his edition of *Antonie* in *Narrative and Dramatic Sources of Shakespeare*, Vol. 5 (1964), Geoffrey Bullough asserts that the Countess' translation expresses the high moral tone and political theorizing of Garnier's play and is remarkable for its sympathetic treatment of Cleopatra. Although he detects verbal reminiscences of *Antonie* in *Antony and Cleopatra*, Bullough contends that Shakespeare probably read the Countess' translation many years before writing his own play and recalled from memory only isolated phrases and images. Bullough's text of *Antonie*, based on the 1595 edition, has largely replaced Alice Luce's edition (1897), whose text derives mainly from the 1592 version. Luce's work is still valuable for its detailed treatment of the source (the 1585 French reprint of Garnier), the analysis of the metrics of the choruses, and the discussion of influence.

Coburn Freer, *The Poetics of Jacobean Drama* (1981), examines the Countess' use of blank verse in *Antonie* to stress the heroic stance of the principal characters, in contrast to the elaborate and interlocking verse patterns of the choral speeches, where man is seen as a prisoner of fate. Freer observes, "While there were other poets at her time who were able to write more moving dramatic poetry, there were few with a surer grasp of the essential nature and pleasures of poetic drama." Mary Morrison, "Some Aspects of the Treatment of the Theme of Antony and Cleopatra in Tragedies of the Sixteenth Century," *JES*, 4 (1974), 113–25, considers *Antonie* in relation to eight other plays from France, Italy, and England; all of these dramas achieve a delicate balance between moral condemnation of excessive passion and sympathetic admiration for the lovers. J. Max Patrick, "The Cleopatra Theme in World Literature up to 1700," in *The Undoing of Babel: Watson Kirkconnell, the Man and His Work,* ed. James Russell Conway Perkin (1975), pp. 64–76, views the Countess' translation as part of an international movement that minimized dramatic action to focus on elegiac states of mind. C. S. Lewis, *English Literature in the Sixteenth Century Excluding Drama* (1954), points to the Countess' effective use of feminine rhyme in the chorus to the third act.

The extent of *Antonie*'s influence has stirred controversy. Ernest Schanzer, "Daniel's Revision of his *Cleopatra,*" *RES*, 8 (1957), 375–81, challenges the long-held assumption that Daniel revised his *Cleopatra* in 1607 after having seen a performance of Shakespeare's play and maintains that Daniel borrowed dramatic situations and speeches from the Countess' *Antonie* in adapting his closet drama for the stage. In a reply, Joan Rees, *RES*, 9 (1958), 294–95, points out that the Countess' version contains no reference to the specific devices used to hoist Antony's body—a pulley and rolls of taffeta— details that set Daniel's account apart from the Countess' description. Rees argues further in *Samuel Daniel: A Critical and Biographical Study* (I, B) that the revised *Cleopatra* represents a strong reaction against the Countess' classical principles. Cecil Seronsy, *Samuel Daniel* (1967), suggests that Daniel surpassed the Countess by achieving greater dramatic unity, more convincing motivation, and heightened poignancy in his figure of Cleopatra. The Introduction to Laurence Michel's edition of Daniel's *The Tragedy of Philotas* (1949) discusses the confused political ideas of Daniel's later play as a reflection of the conflicts between tyranny and insurrection originally found in *Antonie* and in dramas by Greville and Alexander.

J. Dover Wilson, in his Introduction to the text of *Antony and Cleopatra* (1950), lists five places where Shakespeare borrowed phrases from *Antonie*. Unlike Bullough, he believes that Shakespeare read *Antonie* in the winter of 1606–07 shortly before writing his own play. Ernest Schanzer, *The Problem Plays of Shakespeare* (1963), shows how Shakespeare developed a more ambivalent attitude toward the lovers than he found in *Antonie*, where the Countess' Cleopatra appears as truly devoted and faithful to a deeply flawed Antony. In "*Antony and Cleopatra* and the Countess of Pembroke's *Antonius,*" *N&Q*, 201 (1956), 152–54, Schanzer discusses Wilson's parallel passages and provides an additional five examples to support his case for Shakespeare's familiarity with the Countess' play. Kenneth Muir, *Shakespeare's Sources* (1957), also cites parallels of phrasing as evidence that Shakespeare consulted *Antonie*. On the other hand, Willard Farnham, *Shakespeare's Tragic Frontier: The World of his Final Tragedies* (1950), doubts the extent, if any, of *Antonie*'s impact on Shakespeare: "he found in it an idealized and sentimentalized pair of lovers that he was not disposed to use for his own dramatic purposes." Examining other areas of influence, Nancy Cotton, *Women Playwrights in England, c. 1363–1750* (1980), identifies the Countess' play as the first to be published by an Englishwoman and as the inspiration for Elizabeth Cary's closet drama, *Mariam.*

C. *The Triumph of Death.* Describing the Countess' translation as the finest English version of Petrarch's *Trionfo della Morte,* Robert Coogan, C. F. C., "Petrarch's *Trionfi* and the English Renaissance," *SP,* 57 (1970), 306–27, traces the rapid growth in popularity of the *Trionfi* beginning with the More circle about 1500; from the original collection of six poems, the Countess chose to translate the dream vision dealing most intensively with Petrarch's love for Laura. G. F. Waller, ed., *The Triumph of Death* (1977), offers a text that corrects many of the errors found in Frances Young's transcription of the sole surviving manuscript in the appendix to her biography (I, A) and in *PMLA,* 27 (1912), 47–75. In contrasting the Countess' translation with that of Henry Parker, Lord Morley, Waller points to her greater "rhythmical subtlety, concrete evocation, and technical mastery"; he sees the climax of the *Triumph,* Laura's farewell to the poet, as expressive of the Countess' own farewell to her brother. Identifying the Countess' translation as one of the very few to preserve the original terza rima, D. G. Rees, "Petrarch's 'Trionfo della Morte' in English," *IS,* 7 (1952), 82–96, demonstrates that she adheres closely (with occasional lapses) to the literal meaning of the text, yet at the same time enhances it through such stylistic devices as vigorous verbs and compound epithets. D. D. Carnicelli, ed., *Lord Morley's "Tryumphes of Fraunces Petrarcke": The First English Translation of the "Trionfi"* (1971), briefly mentions the metrical virtuosity of the Countess' translation, but provides thorough background on the widespread influence of the *Trionfi* on English iconography and literature.

D. *Discourse of Life and Death.* Diane Bornstein, ed., *The Countess of Pembroke's Translation of Philippe de Mornay's Discourse of Life and Death* (1983), offers a detailed stylistic analysis of the Countess' translation in her Introduction and notes to the text. Bornstein argues that although the Countess consulted the 1576 English version by Edward Aggas, she surpassed her predecessor in accuracy and conciseness; she not only preserved the rhetorical ornaments found in Mornay's treatise—"a somber, graceful meditation on the theme of death, steeped in Christian and stoic philosophy"—but also rendered the work more metaphorical. Bornstein's "The Style of the Countess of Pembroke's Translation of Philippe de Mornay's *Discours de la vie et de la mort,"* in *Silent but for the Word,* ed. Margaret P. Hannay (forthcoming), reprints selections from the Introduction to the edition. Katherine Duncan-Jones, "Stoicism in *Measure for Measure:* A New Source," *RES,* 28 (1977), 441–46, argues that the Countess' translation may have furnished Shakespeare with some of the arguments for the Duke's great philosophical speech against the fear of death in *Measure for Measure.* Also, Claudio's stoical reply to the Duke may derive from the Countess' final motto to the *Discourse:* "Die to live, Live to die."

E. *"A Dialogue Betweene Two Shepheards, Thenot and Piers, in Praise of Astrea."* Frances A. Yates, "Queen Elizabeth as Astraea," *JWCI,* 10 (1947), 27–82, later incorporated in *Astraea: The Imperial Theme in the Sixteenth Century* (1975), relates the

Countess' "Dialogue" to the extensive tradition identifying Queen Elizabeth as the righteous virgin of the golden age, associated with eternal spring. Gary Waller, "Mary Sidney's '. . . Two Shepherds,'" *AN&Q,* 9 (1971), 100–02, relates the poem to the potential split in the Sidneian ideal between courtly, neo-Platonic philosophy (represented by Thenot) and Calvinist doctrine (Piers); the last word is given to Piers, who insists upon "the inability of man's unaided mind to attain to genuine truth." Hallett Smith, *Elizabethan Poetry: A Study in Conventions, Meaning, and Expression* (1952, rpt. 1968) regards the Countess' "Dialogue" as part of the wealth of pastoral poetry inspired by the royal progress. Sallye J. Sheppeard, "Mary Herbert's 'A Dialogue Between Two Shepherdes': A Study in Renaissance Poetic Method," *Proceedings of the Conference of College Teachers of English of Texas,* 46 (1981), 17–21, interprets the poem as both flattery of Elizabeth and a "tongue-in-cheek repudiation of the conventional devices and conceits of Renaissance poetry."

F. *Dedicatory Poems.* From his privately owned manuscript of the Sidney-Pembroke Psalms, Bent Juel-Jensen, ed., *Two Poems by the Countess of Pembroke* (1962), presents the texts of a pair of the Countess' dedicatory poems: "To the Angell spirit of the most excellent Sir Phillip Sidney" and "To the thrise sacred Queen Elizabeth." William A. Ringler, Jr. also provides the text of "To the Angell spirit" in *The Poems of Sir Philip Sidney* (1962), where he points out that a slightly different version was erroneously assigned to Daniel in the posthumously published *Whole Workes of Samuel Daniel* (1623). Margaret P. Hannay, "'Do What Men May Sing': Mary Sidney and the Tradition of Admonitory Dedication," in *Silent but for the Word* (forthcoming), discusses the political implications of both poems, with one glorifying Sir Philip Sidney as a Protestant martyr and the other praising Elizabeth as England's David, in effect a veiled exhortation to the Queen for a stalwart defense of the Protestant faith.

G. *"The Dolefull Lay of Clorinda."* The question of authorship continues to dominate criticism on "The Dolefull Lay," which appeared with Spenser's "Astrophel" and other elegies by Ralegh, Royden, Dyer, and Bryskett in *Colin Clouts come home againe* (1595). Following Ernest de Selincourt, who first challenged the attribution of the poem to the Countess in his Oxford Standard Authors edition of Spenser (1908), much of the pre-1945 scholarship assigns the poem to Spenser on stylistic grounds (one exception is Walter G. Friedrich, "The Astrophel Elegies," Diss. Johns Hopkins, 1934). Gary Waller, *Mary Sidney* (I,A), argues that there is both external and internal evidence in favor of the Countess' authorship; he cites Spenser's ascription to the Countess in the introduction to the poem and in "The Ruins of Time," as well as vast differences in tone and quality between "Astrophel" and the "Lay." William Nelson, *The Poetry of Edmund Spenser* (1963), observes that Spenser deliberately avoids a personal tone in "Astrophel" in order to set his work apart from the Countess' more emotional lament. Michael O'Connell, "Astrophel: Spenser's Double Elegy," *SEL,* 11 (1971), 27–35, contends that Spenser, not the Countess, wrote "The Lay of Clorinda" because it is stylistically consistent with the rest of his "Astrophel" and makes use of the poem's most important symbol, the flower. In assigning the "Lay" to Spenser, Thomas P. Harrison, Jr., *The Pastoral Elegy: An Anthology* (1939; rpt. 1968), claims that "the device by which the poet attributed the piece to the Countess of Pembroke appears to be a means only of denoting the conclusion of the Astrophel-Adonis theme."

H. *State of Criticism.* Only in the past twenty years have critics begun to focus more on the Countess as a writer than as "Sidney's sister, Pembroke's mother." Her versions of the Psalms, regarded not simply as literal paraphrases, but as highly original meditations that express a rich diversity of tone and meaning, emerge as her major achievement. Although Lewalski and others have recognized the pivotal importance of the Countess' Psalms in the development of the seventeenth-century lyric, there is still need for further systematic study of their influence on Donne and Herbert. A comprehensive analysis, similar to Terence Cave's *Devotional Poetry in France, c. 1570–1613* (1969), would offer a fruitful context for understanding the Countess' work. To provide a sound basis for all these studies, a complete critical edition of the Psalms is urgently needed. *Antonie* has been discussed extensively for its influence on Shakespeare and Daniel, but has not received sufficient attention in its own right as poetic drama. The Countess' accomplishments, both as poet and patron, have yet to be examined in relation to those of Continental women writers, such as Marguerite de Navarre.

III. CANON AND TEXT

A. *Canon.* Gabriel Harvey's description in *Pierces Supererogation* of the Countess as a prolific author—"And what, if she can also publish more workes in a moneth then Nash hath published in his whole life"—has spurred scholars to search for additional writings. Thomas C. Izard, *George Whetstone: Mid-Elizabethan Gentleman of Letters* (1942), attributes to the Countess a dedicatory poem, "The mighty Jove beholding from above," which appeared before Whetstone's *The Heptameron of Civill Discourses* (1582). In *The Woman Poets in English: An Anthology* (1972), Ann Stanford also assigns to the Countess "If Ever Hapless Woman Had a Cause," a sister's lament over the death of a beloved brother. Gary Waller, *Mary Sidney* (I,A), disputes both attributions on the grounds of insufficient evidence. Jean Robertson, ed., *Poems by Nicholas Breton not Hitherto Reprinted* (1952), convincingly shows that a manuscript poem, "The Countesse of Penbrooks Passion" (Sloane MS 1303), is actually by Breton, who published the work in 1594 under the title "The Passions of the Spirit."

B. *Critique of the Standard Editions.* The Psalms pose a major editorial problem because they survive in seventeen manuscripts with extensive variants, including a number of alternative versions of whole poems. J. C. A. Rathmell's edition (1963) presents an emended text based on the Penshurst manuscript (MS A), but without scholarly apparatus. However, a table of variants derived from fourteen of the manuscripts does appear in Rathmell's Cambridge dissertation (1964). Gary Waller's edition (1977) includes early versions of 22 Psalms found in Bodleian MS. Rawlinson poet 25 (MS B), alternative versions of Psalms 89, 113, 122, 131, and the rhymed versions of Psalms 120–127, together with variants and commentary on the individual poems. Noel J. Kinnamon, "Emendations in G. F. Waller's Edition of the Countess of Pembroke's Psalms," *AN&Q* (forthcoming), cites a number of misreadings, misprintings, and twelve unnecessary emendations found in Waller's text. There is still great need for a definitive and fully annotated critical edition of the Psalms that would provide the variant readings for all of the poems, clarify the final state of the Countess' revisions, and explain the Countess' use of Biblical and interpretive sources.

C. *Textual Studies.* In establishing the text of Sidney's first forty-three Psalms, William A. Ringler Jr. provides a thorough account of fourteen of the manuscripts and their relationships to each other. Because Ringler wished to determine Sidney's original version, he used MS B as his copy-text, deleting all of the Countess' changes; nevertheless, he provides detailed commentary on the nature of the subsequent revisions. Cecil C. Seronsy, "Another Huntington Manuscript of the Sidney Psalms," *HLQ,* 29 (1965–66), 109–16, describes the fifteenth manuscript of the Psalms in the Huntington Library. G. F. Waller, "The Text and Manuscript Variants of the Countess of Pembroke's Psalms," *RES,* 26 (1975), 1–18, announces the existence of a sixteenth manuscript (MS G1) deposited at the Houghton Library and discusses the nature of the variants found in the surviving copies. Peter Beal, "Sir Philip Sidney," *The Index of English Literary Manuscripts, Vol. I, 1450–1625,* pt. 2 (1980), pp. 465–88, identifies the seventeenth manuscript of the Psalms, an eighteenth-century copy belonging to the National Library of Wales. Noel J. Kinnamon, "A Variant of the Countess of Pembroke's Psalm 85," *SNew,* 2.2 (1981), 9–12, furnishes the text, with variants and notes, of an early version of Psalm 85 found in MS B and omitted from Waller's collection. Describing his personal copy of the Psalms (MS J), Bent Juel-Jensen, "Contemporary Collectors XLIII," *BC,* 15 (1966), 152–74, includes an illustration of this beautiful calligraphic manuscript that was originally prepared for Queen Elizabeth I, and in "The Tixall Manuscript of Sir Philip Sidney's and the Countess of Pembroke's Paraphrase of the Psalms," *BC,* 18 (1969), 222–23, he traces its provenance to Sir Walter Aston, who may have acquired the Psalter as a gift from King James I.

See also

I. GENERAL

Bennett, H.S. *English Books and Readers, 1558–1603* (1965).
Bradbrook, Muriel C. *John Webster, Citizen and Dramatist* (1980).
Brown, Ivor. *The Women in Shakespeare's Life* (1968).
Greenfield, Thelma N. *The Eye of Judgment: Reading the New Arcadia* (1982) [The Countess as Urania in the *New Arcadia*].
Holzapfel, Rudolf. *Shakespeare's Secret* (1961) [The Countess as Shakespeare's Dark Lady].
Hope, A. D. "The Countess of Pembroke's Dream," *A Late Picking: Poems, 1965–74* (1975) [Poem based on John Aubrey's anecdotes concerning the Countess].
Hussey, Christopher. "Wilton House, Wiltshire," *Country Life,* 133 (1963), 1044–48; 1109–13; 1176–80.
Kohler, Charlotte, "The Elizabethan Woman of Letters: The Extent of her Literary Activities." Diss. University of Virginia, 1936.
Lamb, Mary Ellen. "The Countess of Pembroke's Patronage," *DAI,* 37 (1977), 6501A–02A.

Lewis, Janette. "'The Subject of All Verse': An Introduction to the Life and Work of Mary Sidney Herbert, the Countess of Pembroke," *DAI*, 37 (1977), 2199A–2200A.

Mohl, Ruth. "The Glosses concerning Spenser's Rosalinde," *Studies in Spenser, Milton, and The Theory of Monarchy* (1949; rpt. 1962), pp. 1–14 [The Countess as Spenser's Rosalinde in *Shepheardes Calender*].

Rowse, A. L., ed. *The Poems of Shakespeare's Dark Lady: Salve Deus Rex Judaeorum by Emilia Lanier* (1978).

Sasek, Lawrence, ed. *The Poems of William Smith* (1970).

Snare, Gerald, ed. *The Third Part of the Countesse of Pembrokes Yuychurch entitled Amintas Dale* (1975).

Thomson, Patricia. "The Patronage of Letters under Elizabeth and James I," *English*, 7 (1949), 278–82.

Williams, Franklin B., Jr. "Special Presentation Epistles before 1641: A Preliminary Check-list," *Library*, 5th ser. 7 (1952), 15–20.

Wilson, Christopher R. "*Astrophil and Stella*: A Tangled Editorial Web," *Library*, 6th ser. 1 (1979), 336–46.

Winchcombe, George and Bernard. *Shakespeare's Ghost Writers* (1968).

————. *Supplement to Shakespeare's Ghost Writers* (1971) [The Countess as Shakespeare's Dark Lady].

II. STUDIES OF INDIVIDUAL WORKS

A. *Psalms*

Collette, Carolyn P. "Milton's Psalm Translations: Petition and Praise," *ELR*, 2 (1972), 243–59 [Protestant attitudes toward the Psalms].

Prescott, Anne Lake. "The Reputation of Clément Marot in Renaissance England," *SRen*, 18 (1971), 173–202.

Waller, Gary F. "A 'Matching of Contraries': Ideological Ambiguity in the Sidney Psalms," *WascanaR*, 9 (1974), 124–33.

B. *Antonie*

Charlton, H. B. *The Senecan Tradition in Renaissance Tragedy* (1921; rpt. 1946).

Heinemann, Margot. *Puritanism and Theatre: Thomas Middleton and Opposition Drama under the Early Stuarts* (1980).

Leavenworth, Russell E. "Daniel's *Cleopatra*: A Critical Study," *Univ. of Colorado Studies*, 29.3 (1954), 26–27.

Williamson, Marilyn L. *Infinite Variety: Antony and Cleopatra in Renaissance Drama and Earlier Tradition* (1974).

Wilson, F. P. *The English Drama, 1485–1585* (1969).

III. CANON AND TEXTS

A. *Other Editions and Selections*

Barnstone, Aliki and Willis, ed. *A Book of Woman Poets from Antiquity to Now* (1980) [the Countess' Psalm 58].

Bernikow, Louise, ed. *The World Split Open: Four Centuries of Women Poets in England and America, 1552–1950* (1974) [excerpts from Psalms 52, 57, 59, 60, 67, 71, 72, and "The Dolefull Lay of Clorinda"].

Cosman, Carol, Joan Keefe, and Kathleen Weaver, ed. *The Penguin Book of Women Poets* (1978) [Psalm 62].

Hollander, John and Frank Kermode, ed. *The Literature of Renaissance England* (1973) [Psalm 137].

Hughey, Ruth, ed. *The Arundel Harington Manuscript of Tudor Poetry*, 2 vols. (1960) [Psalms 51, 69, 104, 112, 117, 120, 137 and a dedicatory poem probably addressed by Sir John Harington to the Countess].

Mahl, Mary R. and Helene Koon, ed. *The Female Spectator: English Women Writers Before 1800* (1977) ["To the Thrice Sacred Queen Elizabeth," Psalms 61, 100, 150].

Rollins, Hyder E. and Herschel Baker, ed. *The Renaissance in England: Non-dramatic Prose and Verse of the Sixteenth Century* (1954) ["A Dialogue Between Two Shepherds"].

Stanford, Ann, ed. *The Women Poets in English: An Anthology* (1972) ["If Ever Hapless Woman Had a Cause," Psalms 55, 58, 139].

Travitsky, Betty, ed. *The Paradise of Women: Writings by Englishwomen of the Renaissance* (1981) ["The Dolefull Lay of Clorinda" and "A Dialogue Between Two Shepherds"].

RECENT STUDIES IN WOMEN WRITERS OF TUDOR ENGLAND (1984–April 1990)

Part I: Women Writers, 1485–1603
Excluding Mary Sidney, Countess of Pembroke

ELIZABETH H. HAGEMAN

BACKGROUND STUDIES (Selected)

Amussen, Susan Dwyer. *An Ordered Society: Gender and Class in Early Modern England* (1988).

Cahn, Susan. *Industry of Devotion: The Transformation of Women's Work in England, 1500–1660* (1987).

Carlton, Charles. "The Widow's Tale: Male Myths and Female Reality in 16th and 17th Century England," *Albion*, 10 (1978), 118–29.

Emerson, Kathy Lynn, comp. *Wives and Daughters: The Women of Sixteenth Century England* (1984). [Brief biographical entries.]

Ferguson, Margaret W., Maureen Quilligan, and Nancy J. Vickers, ed. *Rewriting the Renaissance: The Discourses of Sexual Difference in Early Modern Europe* (1986).

Friedman, Alice T. *House and Household in Elizabethan England: Wollaton Hall and the Willoughby Family* (1989).

————. "The Influence of Humanism on the Education of Girls and Boys in Tudor England," *History of Education Quarterly*, 25 (1985), 57–70.

Holm, Janis Butler, ed. *A Critical Edition of Thomas Salter's "The Mirrhor of Modestie"* (1987).

Klaits, Joseph. *Servants of Satan: The Age of the Witch Hunts* (1985).

Klapisch-Zuber, Christiane. *Women, Family, and Ritual in Renaissance Italy*, trans. Lydia G. Cochrane (1985).

Larner, Christina. *Witchcraft and Religion: The Politics of Popular Belief*, ed. Alan Macfarlane (1984).

Levin, Carole. "Queens and Claimants: Political Insecurity in Sixteenth-Century England," in *Gender, Ideology, and Action: Historical Perspectives on Women's Public Lives*, ed. Janet Sharistanian (1986), pp. 41–66.

Levin, Carole and Jeanie Watson, ed. *Ambiguous Realities: Women in the Middle Ages and Renaissance* (1987).

Macek, Ellen. "The Emergence of a Feminine Spirituality in *The Book of Martyrs*," *SCJ*, 19 (1988), 63–80.

Marshall, Sherrin, ed. *Women in Reformation and Counter-Reformation Europe: Private and Public Worlds* (1989).

Prior, Mary, ed. *Women in English Society, 1500–1800* (1985).

Rose, Mary Beth. *The Expense of Spirit: Love and Sexuality in English Renaissance Drama* (1988).

————, ed. *Women in the Middle Ages and the Renaissance: Literary and Historical Perspectives* (1986).

Somerset, Anne. *Ladies in Waiting: From the Tudors to the Present Day* (1984).

Thickstun, Margaret Olofson. *Fictions of the Feminine: Puritan Doctrine and the Representation of Women* (1988).

Todd, Margo. *Christian Humanism and the Puritan Social Order* (1987).

Wayne, Valerie, ed. *"The Flower of Friendshippe": A Renaissance Discourse Contesting Marriage* (forthcoming).

Wiesner, Merry E. "Beyond Women and the Family: Towards a Gender Analysis of the Reformation," *SCJ*, 18 (1987), 311–21.

Willen, Diane. "Women and Religion in Early Modern England," in Marshall (above), pp. 140–65.

Williams, Robert. "A Moon to Their Sun: Writing Mistresses of the Sixteenth and Seventeenth Centuries," *Fine Print* (1985), 88–98.

EDITIONS

Betty Travitsky, *The Paradise of Women: Writings by Englishwomen of the Renaissance* (1981; rpt. with a new preface and updated notes, in a paperback edition, 1989), provides selections from women writers of the Tudor, Jacobean, and Caroline periods. *The Women Writers Project*, a computer project based at Brown University under the direction of Susanne Woods with the assistance of Patricia Caldwell, Stuart Curran, Margaret J. M. Ezell, Elizabeth H. Hageman, and Elizabeth D. Kirk, provides, for classroom and research use, copies of works by women who wrote in English from 1330 to 1830.

I. GENERAL STUDIES

The four books listed as forthcoming in my "Recent Studies in Women Writers of Tudor England," *ELR*, 14 (1984), 409–25, reprinted above, have been published: *Silent But for the Word: Tudor Women as Patrons, Translators, and Writers of Religious Works*, ed. Margaret P. Hannay (1985); *Half Humankind: Contexts and Texts of the Controversy about Women in England, 1540–1640* (1985), ed. Katherine Usher Henderson and Barbara F. McManus; *First Feminists: British Women Writers, 1578–1799* (1985), ed. Moira Ferguson; and *Women Writers of the Renaissance and Reformation*, ed. Katharina M. Wilson (1987).[1]

In 1987 Elaine V. Beilin published *Redeeming Eve: Women Writers of the English Renaissance*, a study of some thirty women who wrote between 1523 and 1623; Beilin's argument is that those women created a "tradition of women's writing" in which they defended women against male detractors and urged women to follow traditional Christian virtues. Ann Rosalind Jones' forthcoming *The Currency of Eros: Women's Love Lyric in Europe, 1540–1620* treats English, French, and Italian poets. In "Did Shakespeare Have Any Sisters? Editing Women Writers of the Renaissance," in *Editing Women Writers of the Renaissance: Papers Presented to the English Renaissance Text Society, 1987* (1988), Elizabeth H. Hageman argues that when women writers are included in Renaissance literary history, that history will be seen to be more complex and interesting than has been recognized. In the Introduction to *The Renaissance Englishwoman in Print: Counterbalancing the Canon,* ed. Anne M. Haselkorn and Betty S. Travitsky (1990), pp. 3–41, Betty S. Travitsky addresses the vexed question of "gendered assumptions of the English Renaissance" and argues that "at least some of these women did 'have' a Renaissance." Elaine V. Beilin, "Current Bibliography of English Women Writers, 1500–1640," pp. 347–60 in that volume, is a topical, annotated list of works by women. *British Women Writers: A Critical Reference Guide,* ed. Janet Todd (1989), includes entries on the lives and works of a number of Tudor women writers, as does *An Encyclopedia of British Women Writers,* ed. Paul Schlueter and June Schlueter (1988).

II. STUDIES OF INDIVIDUAL WRITERS

A. *Margaret More Roper (1505–1544).* Elizabeth McCutcheon edited selections from Margaret Roper's translation of Erasmus' *A Devout Treatise upon the "Pater Noster"* and from her letters for "Margaret More Roper: The Learned Woman in Tudor England," in Wilson (I, above), pp. 449–80. In "Life and Letters: Editing the Writing of Margaret Roper," in *Editing Women Writers of the Renaissance* (I, above), McCutcheon describes her work for Wilson's volume and argues that Roper is a significant "woman of letters [who] foreshadows the literary production of other Renaissance women." McCutcheon, "Margaret More Roper's Translation of Erasmus' *Precatio Dominica,*" in *Acta Conventus Neo-Latini Guelpherbytani,* ed. Stella P. Revard, Fidel Rädle, and Mario A. Di Cesare (1988), 659–66, shows her "erudition, piety, and literary sensitivity" in a volume that is "a prototype of the fruits of the new learning for women in sixteenth-century England."

---

1. In my 1984 survey of Tudor women writers reprinted above, I used Wilson's prepublication title, *Renaissance Women Writers.*

"Learning and Virtue: Margaret More Roper," the first chapter of Beilin's *Redeeming Eve* (I, above), outlines Renaissance humanist writing on women's education and then "reconsider[s] the nature of both her erudition and her goodness" to note that Margaret More Roper's accomplishments seemed "to be living proof that education made women more dedicated to feminine virtue." In "Absolute Margaret: Margaret More Roper and 'Well Learned' Men," *SCJ*, 20 (1989), 443–56, Peter Iver Kaufman studies Margaret Roper's voice in the 1534 letter to Alice Allington—"her persistence, her questions, qualifications, and rejoinders, which were less than defiant yet far more than decorative"—to qualify Beilin's view and to present Roper as an Erasmian humanist debating with her father.

B. *Catherine Parr (1512–1548)*. Janel Mueller, "A Tudor Queen Finds Voice: Katherine Parr's *Lamentation of a Sinner*," in *The Historical Renaissance: New Essays on Tudor and Stuart Literature and Culture*, ed. Heather Dubrow and Richard Strier (1988), pp. 15–47, contrasts Parr's "borrowed speech in translation (in the *Prayers*)" with her voice "as an author (in the *Lamentation*)." Mueller's argument is that Parr, influenced by Cranmer and Latimer, diverges from Erasmus—and that, because of her "precarious position as a Henrician queen," Parr is "both peculiarly powerful and peculiarly constrained in giving voice to her concerns for her own and England's godliness." In "Devotion as Difference: Intertextuality in Queen Katherine Parr's *Prayers or Meditations* (1545)," *HLQ*, 53 (1990), 171–97, Mueller demonstrates that in her abridgment of Richard Whitford's translation of the third book of *Imitatio Christi*, Parr boldly "reorient[ed] . . . the masterpiece of late medieval Catholic spirituality," degendering its voice in a manner appropriate to Tudor Protestantism and, more specifically, in accord with her own experience as a subject of her king and of God.

C. *Anne Askew (1521–1546)*. In "Anne Askew's Dialogue with Authority," forthcoming in *Contending Kingdoms: Historical, Psychological, and Feminist Approaches to the Literature of Sixteenth Century England and France*, ed. Peter Rudnytsky and Marie-Rose Logan, Elaine V. Beilin demonstrates Askew's use of the dialogue form to undermine the power of her male, Catholic judges and to establish her own authority as a reformer and a woman. Beilin's *Redeeming Eve* (I, above) includes "A Challenge to Authority: Anne Askew," pp. 29–47, which enlarges her "Anne Askew's Self Portrait in the *Examinations*," in Hannay (I, above), pp. 77–91, to stress Askew's creating "an alternate role for religious women." See also Macek (Background Studies, above).

D. *Elizabeth I (1533–1603)*. In "Two Private Prayers by Queen Elizabeth I," *N&Q*, 32 (1985), 26–28, Michael G. Brennan prints a prayer on the naval expedition to Cadiz in 1596 and, for the first time, a version now in the Cambridge University Library of a prayer composed while on a visit to Bristol in 1574. Allison Heisch's edition of Elizabeth's speeches is in progress.

In "Provenance and Propaganda as Editorial Stumbling Blocks," in *Editing Women Writers of the Renaissance* (I, above), Frances Teague addresses difficulties inherent in finding and analyzing texts by Renaissance women such as Elizabeth, and she argues that Renaissance women's writing demands "extraordinary care. We must always go back to our original sources and can accept nothing on faith. In particular, we must be cautious in examining the provenance of such women's texts and in considering how a contemporary audience might have understood them."

Jasper Ridley's recent biography, *Elizabeth I: The Shrewdness of Virtue* (1989), presents Elizabeth as "a convinced Protestant, determined to do her duty, as she saw it, to God and her people."

Mary Thomas Crane, " 'Video et Taceo': Elizabeth I and the Rhetoric of Counsel," *SEL*, 28 (1988), 1–15, examines Elizabeth's use of the "symbolic system" of "political counsel" in her speeches to assert and maintain control over national policy. Leah S. Marcus, "Erasing the Stigma of Daughterhood: Mary I, Elizabeth I, and Henry VIII," in *Daughters and Fathers*, ed. Lynda E. Boose and Betty S. Flowers (1989), pp. 400–17, distinguishes between Mary, who defied and rejected Henry, and Elizabeth, who "much more inscrutably, appeared submissive, professed devotion, subtly emphasized continuities between her father and herself, and used the relationship in remarkably creative ways to buttress her own power." Marcus, "Shakespeare's Comic Heroines, Elizabeth I, and the Political Uses of Androgyny," in Rose, *Women in the Middle Ages and the Renaissance* (Background Studies, above), pp. 135–53, suggests a parallel between the "sexually composite nature of Shakespeare's comic heroines" and Elizabeth's "anomalous rhetoric of masculinity." Parts of that essay are incorporated into "Elizabeth," the second chapter of Marcus' *Puzzling Shakespeare: Local Reading and Its Discontents* (1988), a more extensive argument about Shakespeare's response to a queen whose presentation of herself as an androgynous leader evoked "an upsurge of . . . fascination with, and horror of, [what was seen as] the Amazonian confusion of gender"; much of "Elizabeth" focuses on Shakespeare's Joan of Arc as "a distorted image" of the queen.

Constance Jordan, "Representing Political Androgyny: More on the Siena Portrait of Queen Elizabeth I," in Haselkorn and Travitsky (I, above), pp. 157–76, argues that the oxymoronic iconography of the Siena portrait portrays Elizabeth's virginity "includ[ing] the fiction of a male sexuality and the power it represented" in her culture. John N. King's chapter, "The 'Godly' Queens," in his *Tudor Royal Iconography: Literature and Art in the Age of Religious Crisis* (1989), pp. 182–266, revises and expands his article, "The Godly Woman in Elizabethan Iconography," *RenQ*, 38 (1985), 41–84, to focus on sixteenth-century Protestant transformations of Mariological iconography to define Elizabeth as a reformist heroine.

E. *Anne Locke (or Lok), later Anne Dering and Anne Prowse (early 1530s–after 1590). A Meditation of a Penitent Sinner* is available from the Brown University *Women Writers Project* (Editions, above) in a transcription by Roland Greene.

Patrick Collinson, "The Role of Women in the English Reformation Illustrated by the Life and Friendships of Anne Locke," *Studies in Church History*, 2 (1965), 258–72, focuses on Locke's relationships with her three husbands and, especially, with John Knox. Knox's letters to Locke are available in volumes 4 and 6 of *The Works of John Knox*, ed. David Laing (1854; rpt. 1966).

Roland H. Bainton, "Anne Locke," in his *Women of the Reformation: From Spain to Scandinavia* (1977), pp. 89–94, focuses on her translations of Calvin's sermon on King Hezekiah's song of thanksgiving published in 1560 and of J. Taffin's *The Markes of the Children of God*, published in 1590. Beilin, *Redeeming Eve* (I, above), p. 62, notes that Locke's 1560 dedication presents "her own sermon on the theme of spiritual sickness, a metaphor she sustains for eleven pages." Thomas P. Roche, Jr., *Petrarch and the English Sonnet Sequences* (1989), pp. 155–57, comments briefly on *Meditation of a Penitent Sinner* as the earliest known sonnet cycle in English.

F. *Joanna Lumley (c. 1537–1576/7)*. Beilin, *Redeeming Eve* (I, above), pp. 153–57, notes parallels between Lumley's translation of Erasmus' text of *Iphigenia* and her husband's earlier translation of Erasmus' *Education of a Christian Prince*.

G. *Lady Grace Mildmay (1553–1620)*. Retha M. Warnicke, "Lady Mildmay's Journal: A Study in Autobiography and Meditation in Reformation England," *SCJ*, 19 (1989), 55–68, describes the journal now at the Central Library, Northampton. A two-part manuscript—the first part, an Anglican autobiography; the second, a 900-page series of meditations—Lady Mildmay's journal reveals a woman whose "faith provided her with spiritual ammunition to use in confronting the gender discrimination of her society, as well as other tribulations."

H. *Anne Cecil de Vere, Countess of Oxford (1556–1588)*. Ellen Moody, "Six Elegiac Poems, Possibly by Anne Cecil de Vere, Countess of Oxford," *ELR*, 19 (1989), 152–70, prints poems attributed to the Countess in John Soowthern, *Pandora* (1584). *Pandora* is also available in a facsimile edition, ed. George B. Parks (1938).

I. *Joan Thynne (1558–1612) and Maria Thynne (c. 1578–c. 1611)*. Alison D. Wall has published *Two Elizabethan Women: Correspondence of Joan and Maria Thynne, 1575–1611* (1983).

J. *Mary Sidney, Countess of Pembroke (1561–1621)*. See Part Two, below.

K. *Isabella Whitney (fl. 1567–73)*. In "Nets and Bridles: Early Modern Conduct Books and Sixteenth-Century Women's Lyrics," in *The Ideology of Conduct: Essays on Literature and the History of Sexuality*, ed. Nancy Armstrong and Leonard Tennenhouse (1987), pp. 39–72, Ann Rosalind Jones contrasts the "public self-display [which] was the norm at court and in [Renaissance] urban coteries" with conduct literature in which "the bourgeois wife was enjoined to silence" and then shows how Whitney appropriates the language of conduct books "to write her way out of the discursive double bind that positioned loquacious women as whores . . . or . . . as exemplary tragic victims." Chapter 2 of Jones, *The Currency of Eros* (I, above), treats Whitney and Catherine des Roches as professional writers. Beilin, *Redeeming Eve* (I, above), pp. 88–101, sees Whitney as a middle-class Christian moralist and defender of women. Elizabeth H. Hageman, however, in "Isabella Whitney," in Todd (I, above), pp. 714–15, presents Whitney's work as lighthearted challenges to London poetic and social mores.

L. *Margaret Tyler (fl. 1578)*. Tina Krontiris, "Breaking Barriers of Genre and Gender: Margaret Tyler's Translation of *The Mirrour of Knighthood*," *ELR*, 18 (1988), 19–39 (reprinted in this volume), treats Tyler's defense of a woman translating a romance—a genre that many Renaissance writers consider immoral, in large part because the mores of courtly love challenge Renaissance definitions of married chastity. *The Mirrour*, Krontiris argues, is an oppositional book in that it "encourages both the heroine and the reader to abandon patriarchal standards," as, for example, when it "reiterates the chivalric rule that violence against women is a crime."

M. *Jane Anger (pseud.?) (fl. 1589)*. Simon Shepherd prints *Jane Anger her Protection for Women* in his *The Women's Sharp Revenge: Five Women's Pamphlets from the Renaissance* (1985).

In "*Jane Anger Her Protection, Boke His Surfeit,* and *The French Academie,*" *N&Q,* 36 (1989), 311–14, A. Lynne Magnusson notes similarities between passages from *Boke His Surfeit* embedded in Anger's work and passages from the 1586 English edition of Primaudaye's *The French Academy,* trans. T[homas] B[owes] to suggest that the author of *Boke His Surfeit* used *The French Academy* as a source of *exempla.*

III. STATE OF CRITICISM

As the brevity of this essay indicates, few women writers of the Tudor period have yet gained wide scholarly attention. Allison Heisch's edition of Queen Elizabeth's speeches will be a welcome addition to Renaissance studies, as are the various texts available through the Brown University *Women Writers Project.*

See also

Elizabeth I

Caldwell, Ellen M. "John Lyly's *Gallathea:* A New Rhetoric of Love for the Virgin Queen," *ELR,* 17 (1987), 22–40 (reprinted in this volume).

Greenhut, Deborah S. "*Persuade yourselves:* Women, Speech, and Sexual Politics in Tudor Society," *Proteus,* 3 (1986), 42–48.

Jackson, Gabriele Bernhard. "Topical Ideology: Witches, Amazons, and Shake-speare's Joan of Arc," *ELR,* 18 (1988), 40–65 (reprinted in this volume).

Montrose, Louis Adrian. "The Elizabethan Subject and the Spenserian Text," *Literary Theory/Renaissance Texts,* ed. Patricia Parker and David Quint (1986), 303–40.

Oakeshott, Walter and [Constance] Anson Jordan. "The Siena Portrait of Queen Elizabeth I," *Apollo,* 124 (1986), 306–09.

Strong, Roy. *Gloriana: The Portraits of Queen Elizabeth* (1987).

Part II: Mary Sidney, Countess of Pembroke

JOSEPHINE A. ROBERTS

A critical edition of the Countess' collected works is being prepared by Margaret P. Hannay and Noel Kinnamon.

I. GENERAL STUDIES

Margaret P. Hannay, *Philip's Phoenix: Mary Sidney, Countess of Pembroke* (1990) replaces Frances B. Young's 1912 biography by presenting the Countess as an eloquent, self-assertive woman, deeply committed to Protestant politics. In contrast to Young's portrait of the Countess as a modest, retiring figure, Hannay reconstructs a life of active involvement, with evidence derived from the Sidney and Pembroke account books, legal documents, letters, and diaries. Hannay traces the Countess' three-fold contribution—as writer, editor, and patron—to her brother's mythic stature in " 'This Moses and This Miriam': The Countess of Pembroke's Role in the Legend of Sir Philip Sidney," forthcoming in *Sir Philip Sidney: Quadricentennial Essays,* ed. Michael J. B. Allen, Arthur F. Kinney, and Dominic Baker-Smith. In "Unpublished Letters by Mary Sidney, Countess of Pembroke," *SSt,* 6 (1986), 165–90, Hannay provides the text of four previously unknown letters (reprinted in *Philip's Phoenix*), which shed light on the Countess' active role as an administrator of the castle and borough of Cardiff and on her "struggles with determined advocates of self rule, and with vandals, pirates, and murderers."

Gary F. Waller, "The Countess of Pembroke and Gendered Reading," in *The Renaissance Englishwoman in Print: Counterbalancing the Canon,* ed. Anne M. Haselkorn and Betty S. Travitsky (1990), pp. 327–45, demonstrates that the Countess' life and work are more contradictory than traditional hagiographical approaches suggest. In "Mother/Son, Father/Daughter, Brother/Sister, Cousins: The Sidney Family Romance," forthcoming in *MP,* Waller argues that a psychoanalytic reading of the incestuous substructure of the Sidney family sheds light on the relationship between the Countess and her brother Philip. The first chapter of Mary Ellen Lamb, *Gender and Authorship in the Sidney Circle* (forthcoming), analyzes the influence of gender on representations of the Countess. John Briley, "Mary Sidney—a 20th Century Reappraisal," in *Elizabethan and Modern Studies Presented to Professor Willem Schrickx on the Occasion of His Retirement,* ed. J. P. Vander Motten (1985), pp. 47–56, maintains that John Aubrey accurately recorded local gossip about the Countess' affairs. Jonathan Crewe argues in *Hidden Designs: The Critical Profession and Renaissance Literature* (1986), pp. 78–88, that Sir Philip Sidney sought "to forestall and even tactically reappropriate vulgar gossip" by creating Stella as a "screen woman," masking his incestuous longings for his sister and mother. In *Von Macht und Mäzenatentum: Leben und Werk William Herberts, des dritten Earls von Pembroke* (1987), Andreas Gebauer describes the influence of the Countess' literary circle at Wilton on her eldest son, William Herbert, third Earl of Pembroke. Margaret P. Hannay, "A Sidney Tho Unnamed," forthcoming in *Representing Alternatives: Lady Mary Wroth,* ed. Naomi Miller and Gary F. Waller, considers the relationship between the Countess of Pembroke and her niece, Lady Mary Wroth.

In *Literary Patronage in the English Renaissance: The Pembroke Family* (1988), Michael G. Brennan demonstrates that the Countess' influence as a patron was greatest in the 1580s and 1590s and that the literary works addressed to her after 1601 were generally mediocre. In "Nicholas Breton's *The Passions of the Spirit* and the Countess of Pembroke," *RES*, 38 (1987), 221–25, Brennan maintains that Breton lost favor with the Countess after 1592 when his work *The Passions of the Spirit* (which in manuscript bore the Countess' name) was published with a dedication to the lowly Mary Houghton, wife of one of the sheriffs of London. Brennan argues that the legend that Shakespeare was present at Wilton for a performance of *As You Like It* is "almost certainly a nineteenth-century fabrication" in " 'We have the man Shakespeare with us': Wilton House and *As You Like It*," *Wiltshire Archaeological Magazine*, 80 (1986), 225–27. Originally dedicated to the Countess, Thomas Moffet's *The Silkwormes and their Flies*, ed. Victor Houliston (1989), represents the first Vergilian georgic in English.

Clarifying the Countess' role in editing her brother's works, Victor Skretkowicz, "Building Sidney's Reputation: Texts and Editors of the *Arcadia*," in *Sir Philip Sidney: 1586 and the Creation of a Legend*, ed. Jan van Dorsten, Dominic Baker-Smith, and Arthur F. Kinney (1986), pp. 111–23, describes the differences in editorial policy between Fulke Greville, who sought to establish Sidney's reputation solely on the basis of his epic and religious writings, and the Countess, who wished to construct a monument to her brother that would preserve all his literary works. Skretkowicz explains in the Textual Introduction to his edition of *The New Arcadia* (1987) that Books I to III of the Countess' 1593 edition were printed from a copy of Greville's 1590 edition, with Books IV and V based on the same manuscript of Sidney's foul papers that Greville had used.

II. STUDIES OF INDIVIDUAL WORKS

A. *Psalms*. Elaine V. Beilin, "The Divine Poet: Mary Sidney, Countess of Pembroke," in her *Redeeming Eve: Women Writers of the English Renaissance* (1987), pp. 121–50, shows that although the Countess extended the range of women's literary accomplishments through her experiments with language and persona, she did not break with feminine literary decorum. Beilin regards the Psalms as "her greatest and most self-defining work." The final chapter of Rivkah Zim, *English Metrical Psalms: Poetry as Praise and Prayer, 1535–1601* (1987), pp. 185–202, considers how the Countess developed the potential of the figurative language in the Psalms by drawing upon imagery associated with the pagan, classical tradition and by improvising metaphorical details found in Calvin and Beza. Susanne Woods, *Natural Emphasis: English Versification from Chaucer to Dryden* (1984), pp. 169–75, describes the Countess as "the first known woman to have a solid and wide-ranging, though largely uncredited, impact on the development of English poetics." Woods analyzes how the Countess varies her stanza construction by use of feminine endings, counterpoint, internal rhyme, and strophic complexity; an appendix (pp. 287–302) lists verse forms in the Sidney-Pembroke Psalms. In " 'Princes you as men must dy': Genevan Advice to Monarchs in the *Psalmes* of Mary Sidney," *ELR*, 19 (1989), 22–41, Margaret P. Hannay examines Psalms 82, 83, and 101 (together with their French sources) for evidence of the Countess' sharpened political emphasis and argues that the Sidney

Psalter, dedicated to Elizabeth at the close of her long reign, "served as a reminder of the duties of the godly monarch." Gary F. Waller, *English Poetry of the Sixteenth Century* (1986), pp. 160–63, argues that the "metrical, stanzaic, and tonal variety of her Psalms is more a tribute to the inspiration of *Astrophil and Stella* than to earlier Psalters" and stresses the contradictory religious and political positions found in the verse. Beth Wynne Fisken, "'To the Angell Spirit': Mary Sidney's Entry into the World of Words," in Haselkorn and Travitsky (I, above), pp. 263–75, analyzes the tension between the Countess' imitation of her brother's verse and her own creativity as an artist. In "'The Art of Sacred Parody' in Mary Sidney's *Psalmes*," *TSWL*, 8 (1989), 223–39, Fisken considers how the Countess adopts the androgynous identity of the psalmist to explore "the emotive range of the love lyric without sacrificing the authorized respectability" of religious translation. Richard Todd, "'So Well Attyr'd Abroad': A Background to the Sidney-Pembroke Psalter and Its Implications for the Seventeenth-Century Religious Lyric," *TSLL*, 29 (1987), 74–93, believes that in addition to the Marot-Beza model, the Sidneian Psalms may have been influenced by a Dutch metrical psalter, remarkable for its stanzaic variety: the *Souterliedekens* (Little Psalter Songs), attributed to Jonkheer Willem van Zuylen van Nyevelt. Sallye Sheppeard, "Toward a Reassessment of the *Psalms of David* within Renaissance Poetry," *PMPA* (1988), 143–52, suggests that the Countess' poetic technique, as evidenced in her share of the Psalms, exercised greater influence on Renaissance verse than has generally been recognized.

Noel Kinnamon, "The Sidney Psalms: The Penshurst and Tixall Manuscripts," forthcoming in *English Manuscript Studies*, argues that a close relationship exists between the Penshurst manuscript (MS A), owned by Viscount De L'Isle, and the Tixall manuscript (MS J), now owned by Dr. Bent Juel-Jensen; both may have been copied by Sir John Davies. Michael G. Brennan, "Licensing the Sidney Psalms for the Press in the 1640s," *N&Q*, 229 (1984), 304–05, shows that a seventeenth-century manuscript of the Psalms at Trinity College, Cambridge, was approved for publication by the licenser John Langley at some date between 1643 and 1648, but that the manuscript was probably never delivered to a printer.

Two essays provide significant background for the Sidney-Pembroke Psalter, although they do not discuss the Countess' contribution: Roland Greene, "Sir Philip Sidney's *Psalms*, the Sixteenth-Century Psalter, and the Nature of Lyric," *SEL*, 30 (1990), 19–40, shows how Elizabethan poets understood the Psalter as a testing ground for "the nature and potentialities of lyric discourse"; Seth Weiner, "The Quantitative Poems and the Psalm Translations: The Place of Sidney's Experimental Verse in the Legend," in van Dorsten, Baker-Smith, and Kinney (I, above), pp. 193–220, shows that although Sidney knew no Hebrew, he belonged to a circle interested in the theory of Hebrew versification.

B. *Antonie*. Coburn Freer prints the text of *Antonie* (with the exception of Act IV, which he summarizes) in *Women Writers of the Renaissance and Reformation*, ed. Katharina M. Wilson (1987), pp. 481–521.

Mary Ellen Lamb, "The Countess of Pembroke and the Art of Dying," in *Women in the Middle Ages and the Renaissance: Literary and Historical Perspectives*, ed. Mary Beth Rose (1986), pp. 207–26, shows that the Countess' translations, *Antonie* and *The Triumph of Death*, reveal her struggle to apply the stoical insights of Philippe Du Plessis Mornay, whose *Ars moriendi* offered "a model of heroism that women might emulate without violating the dominant sexual ideology." An expanded version of this essay appears in her *Gender and Authorship in the Sidney Circle* (I, above), in which Lamb indicates how the Countess constructs her ideal of authorship as a version of the art of dying. Beilin (II, A), pp. 131–34, regards the Countess' creation of the language of "passionate, worldly women" in her translation *Antonie* as furnishing her with the resources for her poetic persona in the Psalms.

C. *"A Dialogue."* Mary C. Erler, "Davies' *Astraea* and Other Contexts of the Countess of Pembroke's 'A Dialogue,'" *SEL,* 30 (1990), 41–61, examines the formal and thematic resemblances between the Countess' poem to Elizabeth and Sir John Davies' *Hymnes of Astraea.* Both works, probably written in 1599 and set amid a background of anxiety and uncertainty over Elizabeth's approaching death, agree in celebrating the Queen's spring-bringing return.

D. *"The Dolefull Lay of Clorinda."* Debate continues on the question of authorship of "The Dolefull Lay." Hannay, *Philip's Phoenix* (I, above), pp. 63–67, argues that assumptions about gender—including doubt cast on the Countess' poetic abilities— have often led critics to assign the poem to Spenser; Hannay cites contemporary evidence in favor of the Countess' authorship, including the printer's layout of the 1595 edition. Beilin (II, A), pp. 137–39, believes that the similarities to Spenser derive from the Countess' ability "to harmonize with the style of other poets" and discusses the Christian symbolism of her guise as shepherdess. Brennan, *Literary Patronage* (I, above), p. 62, argues the probable author is Spenser, who had assigned earlier verse complaints to other persona, as in the case of Daphnaida. G. W. Pigman III, *Grief and English Renaissance Elegy* (1985), p. 152, regards Spenser as the author, citing the numerological argument that "The Dolefull Lay" contains 108 lines. Peter M. Sacks, *The English Elegy: Studies in the Genre from Spenser to Yeats* (1985), p. 54, considers "The Lay" as the second part of *Astrophil* without discussing the question of authorship.

III. State of Criticism

Recent studies of the Countess of Pembroke have identified the importance of her role as a model of intellectual self-assertion; in publishing her writings she set a precedent for literary women of the next generation. Criticism of the Countess' work has broadened to include attention to her role in relation to the Dudley–Sidney political alliance and to such wider cultural issues as gender construction and the difficulty of finding a legitimate individual voice within a publicly authorized discourse.

See also

Brennan, Michael G. "The Literary Patronage of the Herbert Family, Earls of Pembroke, 1500–1640," D. Phil., Oxford Univ., 1982.
——. "Sir Robert Sidney and Sir John Harington of Kelston," *N&Q,* 232 (1987), 232–37.

Hannay, Margaret P. "Countess of Pembroke (Mary Sidney)," in *British Women Writers,* ed. Janet Todd (1989), pp. 532–35.

———. "Mary Sidney, Countess of Pembroke," in *An Encyclopedia of British Women Writers,* ed. Paul Schlueter and June Schlueter (1988), pp. 412–13.

Hay, Millicent V. *The Life of Robert Sidney, Earl of Leicester (1563–1626)* (1984).

RECENT STUDIES IN WOMEN WRITERS OF THE ENGLISH SEVENTEENTH CENTURY, 1604–1674 (1945–1986)

ELIZABETH H. HAGEMAN

BACKGROUND STUDIES (Selected)

Amussen, S. D. "Gender, Family and the Social Order, 1560–1725," in *Order and Disorder in Early Modern England,* ed. Anthony Fletcher and John Stevenson (1985), pp. 196–217.

Camden, Carroll. *The Elizabethan Woman* (1952).

Cannon, Mary Agnes. *The Education of Women During the Renaissance* (1916; rpt. 1981).

Clark, Alice. *Working Life of Women in the Seventeenth Century* (1919; rpt. with Introduction by Miranda Chaytor and Jane Lewis, 1982).

Davis, Natalie Z. "Women's History in Transition: The European Case," *FSt,* 3 (1976), 83–103.

Ferguson, Margaret W., Maureen Quilligan, and Nancy J. Vickers, ed. *Rewriting the Renaissance: The Discourses of Sexual Difference in Early Modern Europe* (1986).

Fitz, Linda T. "'What Says the Married Woman?': Marriage Theory and Feminism in the English Renaissance," *Mosaic,* 13 (1980), 1–22.

Fraser, Antonia. *The Weaker Vessel: Woman's Lot in Seventeenth-Century England* (1984).

Gardiner, Dorothy. *English Girlhood at School: A Study of Women's Education through Twelve Centuries* (1929).

Haller, William and Malleville Haller. "The Puritan Art of Love," *HLQ,* 5 (1942), 235–72.

Houlbrooke, Ralph A. *The English Family, 1450–1700* (1984).

Hull, Suzanne W. *Chaste, Silent and Obedient: English Books for Women, 1475–1640* (1982).

Jardine, Lisa. *Still Harping on Daughters: Women and Drama in the Age of Shakespeare* (1983).

Kamm, Josephine. *Hope Deferred: Girls' Education in English History* (1965).

Kelly-Gadol, Joan. "Did Women Have a Renaissance?" in *Becoming Visible: Women in European History,* ed. Renate Bridenthal and Claudia Koonz (1977), pp. 137–64; rpt. in

Women, History, and Theory: The Essays of Joan Kelly (1984), pp. 19–64.

Kelso, Ruth. *Doctrine for the Lady of the Renaissance* (1956; rpt. with Foreword by Katharine M. Rogers, 1978).

Labalme, Patricia H., ed. *Beyond Their Sex: Learned Women of the European Past* (1980; rpt. 1984).

Latt, David J. "Praising Virtuous Ladies: The Literary Image and Historical Reality of Women in Seventeenth-century England," in *What Manner of Woman: Essays on English and American Life and Literature,* ed. Marlene Springer (1977), pp. 39–64.

Lougee, Carolyn C. *Le Paradis des Femmes: Women, Salons, and Social Stratification in Seventeenth-Century France* (1976).

Maclean, Ian. *The Renaissance Notion of Women: A Study in the Fortunes of Scholasticism and Medical Science in European Intellectual Life* (1980).

Masek, Rosemary. "Women in an Age of Transition, 1485–1714," in *The Women of England from Anglo-Saxon Times to the Present: Interpretive Bibliographical Essays,* ed. Barbara Kanner (1979), pp. 138–82.

Monter, E. William. "The Pedestal and the Stake: Courtly Love and Witchcraft," in *Becoming Visible: Women in European History,* ed. Renate Bridenthal and Claudia Koonz (1977), pp. 119–36.

Powell, Chilton Latham. *English Domestic Relations, 1487–1653* (1917).

Prior, Mary, ed. *Women in English Society, 1500–1800* (1985).

Reynolds, Myra. *The Learned Lady in England, 1650–1760* (1920; rpt. 1964).

Robinson, Lillian S. "Women Under Capitalism: The Renaissance Lady," in her *Sex, Class, and Culture* (1978; rpt. 1986), pp. 150–77.

Rose, Mary Beth, ed. *Women in the Middle Ages and the Renaissance: Literary and Historical Perspectives* (1986).

Schochet, Gordon J. *Patriarchalism in Political Thought: The Authoritarian Family and Political Speculation and Attitudes Especially in Seventeenth-Century England* (1975).

Schwoerer, Lois G. "Seventeenth-Century English Women Engraved in Stone?" *Albion,* 16 (1984), 389–403 [reviews Stone, *Family, Sex and Marriage*].

Shepherd, Simon. *Amazons and Warrior Women: Varieties of Feminism in Seventeenth-Century Drama* (1981).

Stenton, Doris Mary. *The English Woman in History* (1957; rpt. with Introduction by Louise A. Tilly, 1977).

Stone, Lawrence. *The Family, Sex and Marriage in England, 1500–1800* (1977).

Thomas, Keith. "The Double Standard," *JHI,* 20 (1959), 195–216.

Thompson, Roger. *Women in Stuart England and America: A Comparative Study* (1974; rpt. 1978).

Underdown, D. E. "The Taming of the Scold: The Enforcement of Patriarchal Authority in Early Modern England," in *Order and Disorder in Early Modern England,* ed. Anthony Fletcher and John Stevenson (1985), pp. 116–36.

Woodbridge, Linda. *Women and the English Renaissance: Literature and the Nature of Womankind, 1540–1620* (1984).

EDITIONS

Mary R. Mahl and Helene Koon, ed. *The Female Spectator: English Women Writers before 1800* (1977); Betty Travitsky, ed. *The Paradise of Women: Writings by Englishwomen of the*

Renaissance (1981); Angeline Goreau, ed. *The Whole Duty of a Woman: Female Writers in Seventeenth-Century England* (1985); and Moira Ferguson, ed. *First Feminists: British Women Writers, 1578–1799* (1985), print excerpts from writers in the period covered by this essay. Editions of works by individual writers are noted in Part III, below, and anthologies including briefer excerpts from seventeenth-century English women writers are listed in the *See also* section.

I. GENERAL STUDIES

Elaine V. Beilin, *Redeeming Eve: Women Writers of the English Renaissance* (1987), examines some thirty writers between 1524 and 1623 to argue that Renaissance Englishwomen created a "tradition of women's writing" in which, rather than redefine Renaissance ideas about proper female behavior, they defended women against their detractors and urged them to follow conventional Christian virtues. In *The Mental World of Stuart Women: Three Studies* (1987), Sara Heller Mendelson presents the lives and writings of Margaret Cavendish, Mary Rich, and Aphra Behn to suggest the "inconsistencies and ambiguities in the structure of the social order [of the seventeenth century] which occasionally blurred some of the sharp boundaries between the two sexes and cast doubt on the ubiquitous stereotype of the dependent wife."

In *Reason's Disciples: Seventeenth-Century English Feminists* (1982), Hilda L. Smith argues that (except for Katherine Philips and Aphra Behn) the women whose writing she examines were "the first group of modern 'feminists'—that is, individuals who viewed women as a sociological group whose social and political position linked them together more surely than their physical or psychological natures." Patricia Crawford, "Women's Published Writings, 1600–1700," in Prior (Background Studies, above), pp. 211–82, notes that many women writers of the seventeenth century express a sense of having been "forced to write for publication because they knew that their experiences as women were different from those of men." In "Women's Defense of Their Public Role," in Rose (Background Studies, above), pp. 1–27, Merry E. Wiesner analyzes the conditions under which Continental and English women defended their rights to public speech and action and concludes that the sharpening division between public and private spheres for men and women led many women to see that "any claim to a public role would have to be based on either a rejection of their female nature or on support for all women." In the Introduction to *First Feminists* (Editions, above), Ferguson demonstrates that seventeenth- and eighteenth-century women "thought creatively" about their society's discrimination against women. Throughout *The Whole Duty of a Woman* (Editions, above), Goreau uses texts by male and female writers to show the "intricate web of impediments, both external and self-imposed, that so often entangled a woman who aspired to write," but she finds "a surprising degree of feminist feeling" among those who did write. Two chapters of Margaret J. M. Ezell, *The Patriarch's Wife: Literary Evidence and the History of the Family* (1987), pp. 62–126, survey the range of printed and (especially) manuscript materials still extant to dispute the widely-held notion that there was a "lack of articulate, intellectually aggressive women in the seventeenth century"; unlike the authors treated above, Ezell argues against the notion that the women thought themselves limited by cultural constraints.

Ruth Willard Hughey, "Cultural Interests of Women in England from 1524 to 1640, Indicated in the Writings of the Women: A Survey," Ph.D. diss., Cornell Univ., 1932, surveys printed and manuscript materials (including letters and diaries) to show a "leveling of cultural interest among women. The sixteenth century contributed an ideal for the development of a highly educated women; the seventeenth century compromised with the ideal—lowering it and broadening it." Charlotte Kohler, "The Elizabethan Woman of Letters: The Extent of Her Literary Activities," Ph.D. diss., Univ. of Virginia, 1936, traces Englishwomen's writings to Anne Collins (fl. 1653) to demonstrate the extent and range of their work: "Throughout the era," she concludes, "the startling fact remains not the scarcity but the plentitude of women writers." She too notes an increasing number of middle-class women writing in the seventeenth century—and the increasing quality of their writing skills as educational opportunities increased. In the concluding chapter, "The Jacobean Generation," in her *Women of the English Renaissance and Reformation* (1983), pp. 186–204, Retha M. Warnicke surveys the literary accomplishments of learned women of the period; her interest in "the English acceptance of classical training for women" determines the shape and content of the study. Six of the essays scheduled for publication in a volume tentatively entitled *The Englishwoman of the Renaissance, 1500–1640*, ed. Anne M. Haselkorn and Betty S. Travitsky, treat women authors listed below. Gary F. Waller, "Struggling into Discourse: The Emergence of Renaissance Women's Writing," in *Silent But for the Word: Tudor Women as Patrons, Translators, and Writers of Religious Works*, ed. Margaret Patterson Hannay (1985), pp. 238–56, opines that studies of Renaissance women in literature should focus not on the recovery and explication of writings by and about women, but on the questions "how do oppositional forces speak when the dominant language refuses them words? How are the voices of silence heard?"

Hughey, Kohler, and Beilin, and Crawford (above) provide lists of women's writing in the periods covered by their studies. Patricia Gartenberg and Nena Thames Wittemore list works by some fifty-six women in "A Checklist of English Women in Print, 1475–1640," *Bulletin of Bibliography and Magazine Notes*, 34 (1977), 1–13.

II. STUDIES OF INDIVIDUAL GENRES

A. *Defenses of Women.* In *The Women's Sharp Revenge: Five Women's Pamphlets from the Renaissance* (1985), Simon Shepherd edits Jane Anger's *Protection for Women* (1589), Rachel Speght's *A Mouzell for Melastomus* (1617), Ester Sowernam's *Ester hath hang'd Haman* (1617), Constantia Munda's *The Worming of a Mad Dogge* (1617), and Mary Tattlewell and Joan Hit-him-home's *The Women's Sharpe Revenge* (1640). The first half of Katherine Usher Henderson and Barbara F. McManus, *Half Humankind: Contexts and Texts of the Controversy about Women in England, 1540–1640* (1985), outlines the history of the debate about woman's worth since classical antiquity, the social contexts within which the Renaissance debate flourished, and images of women in literature by writers such as Sidney, Shakespeare, Spenser, Donne, and Jonson. The second half of the volume provides extensive excerpts from ten attacks and defenses of womankind and six eulogies and condemnations of individual women. Three of the defenses are by seventeenth-century women: Ester Sowernam, Constantia Munda, and Mary Tattlewell and Joan Hit-him-home. In a "Selected Bibliography of Pamphlets from the Controversy," Henderson and McManus list forty-seven works published between 1540 and 1640. Travitsky, *Paradise of Women*, pp. 104–10, prints excerpts from Speght, Sowernam, and Munda.

Louis B. Wright, "The Popular Controversy over Women" in his *Middle-Class Culture in Elizabethan England* (1935; rpt. 1965), pp. 465–507, outlines the debate as a bourgeois phenomenon which included a "trend of middle-class opinion [arising] to defend woman against her traducers." In "Books about the Controversy," in her *Chaste, Silent and Obedient: English Books for Women, 1475–1640* (Background Studies, above), pp. 106–26, Suzanne W. Hull notes women's participation—as readers and writers—in the debate over woman's worth. In response to Francis Lee Utley's comment that anti-feminist jest is "the civilized veneer for sex antagonism" (*The Crooked Rib: An Analytical Index to the Argument about Women in English and Scots Literature to the End of the Year 1568* [1944; rpt. 1970]), Hull suggests that in a society in which women had few rights, "henpecking, carping, or complaining were perhaps the only real retaliations or options the law allowed" them. Joan Kelly, "Early Feminist Theory and the *Querelle des Femmes, 1400–1789*," *Signs*, 8 (1982), 4–28; rpt. in *Women, History, and Theory: The Essays of Joan Kelly* (1984), pp. 65–109, presents Speght, Sowernam, and Munda as "outraged by a mounting wave of misogyny streaming from 'the scribbling pens of savage and uncouth Monsters,'" and Goreau, *The Whole Duty of A Woman* (I, above), argues that in the Renaissance "The repeated attacks on women . . . provided a great source of anger that pushed women to answer in print." Betty Travitsky, "The Lady Doth Protest: Protest in the Popular Writings of Renaissance Englishwomen," *ELR*, 14 (1984), 255–83, believes that women's contributions to the controversy are generally "characterized by reasoned defense rather than by theoretically motivated, generalized, hyperbolic attack." Linda Woodbridge, "The Jacobean Controversy to 1620," Chapter 4 of her *Women and the English Renaissance* (Background Studies, above), pp. 74–113, treats Speght, Sowernam, and Munda as particpants in a debate which is "at heart a literary exercise"; but Beilin (I, above), pp. 247–66 argues that they exploit a genre hitherto the province of male writers to "[vindicate] women's Christian virtue." Beilin's view is that as they "set out . . . to redeem Eve by argument . . . they discovered both a new verbal power and a new source of anxiety in the clash of language with decorum." Ann Rosalind Jones, "Counter-Attacks on 'the Bayter of Women': Three Pamphlets of the Early Seventeenth Century," forthcoming in *Englishwoman of the Renaissance* (I, above), analyzes Speght's, Sowernam's, and Munda's responses to Swetnam's *Arraignment of Lewd, Idle, Froward and Unconstant Women* in terms of their posing new questions about misogyny: "Rachel Speght caught him out in his misuse of the Bible; Esther Sowernam diagnosed the processes through which the misogynist projects his own sins onto women; Constantia Munda pointed out the opportunitism of the writer who manipulates the woman question for his own profit." Jones' argument is that these defenders of women moved the debate about women onto new, proto-feminist ground.

B. *Autobiography*. Estelle C. Jelinek, "The Seventeenth Century: Psychological Beginnings," Chapter 2 of her *The Tradition of Women's Autobiography: From Antiquity to the Present* (1986), pp. 23–32, surveys the wide range of women's autobiographies in this century to argue that they "improved the genre of autobiography by freely adapting the conventional narrative forms practiced by men. . . . They inaugurated psychological self-analysis and the fictional shaping of autobiographies, anticipating those by contemporary women." Paul Delany, "Female Autobiographers," in his *British Autobiography in the Seventeenth Century* (1969), pp. 158–66, argues that seventeenth-century women tend to be more interested in "intimate feelings" than are their male counterparts; beginning, as a rule, by writing about their husbands, the women developed keen skills at self-analysis. Working from the premise that autobiography derives from an obsession with the self coupled with a desire to escape that obsession, Mary G. Mason, "The Other Voice: Autobiographies of Women Writers," in *Autobiography: Essays Theoretical and Critical,* ed. James Olney (1980), pp. 207–35, presents Dame Julian of Norwich, Margery Kempe, Margaret Cavendish, and Anne Bradstreet as representative women who "record and dramatize self-realization and self-transcendence through the recognition of another." Sandra Findley and Elaine Hobby, "Seventeenth Century Women's Autobiography," in *1642: Literature and Power in the Seventeenth Century,* ed. Francis Barker, et al. (1981), pp. 11–36, treat autobiographies by Anne Halkett, Mary Rich, Ann Fanshawe, Lucy Hutchinson, and Margaret Cavendish as "different attempts to negotiate the boundaries of femininity" at a time when upper and middle class women were increasingly confined to the private sphere of family life. Mary Beth Rose, "Gender, Genre, and History: Seventeenth-Century English Women and the Art of Autobiography," in her *Women in the Middle Ages and the Renaissance* (Background Studies), pp. 245–78, argues that Margaret Cavendish, Anne Halkett, Ann Fanshawe, and Alice Thornton found in the new genre of autobiography a "literary opportunity to assert themselves as social personalities."

C. *Biography.* In "Biography," Chapter 3 of her *Women Writers* (II, G, below), pp. 70–121, B. G. MacCarthy argues that biographies by Anne Clifford, Lucy Hutchinson, Margaret Cavendish, and Ann Fanshawe are significant antecedents of the English novel in their "mastery of narrative form and . . . expression of inner being." Gloria Italiano, "Two Parallel Biographers of the Seventeenth Century: Margaret Newcastle and Lucy Hutchinson," in *Critical Dimensions: English, German and Comparative Literature Essays in Honour of Aurelio Zanco,* ed. Mario Curreli and Alberto Martino (1978), pp. 241–51, shows that, taken together, *The Life of William Cavendish* and *Memoirs of the Life of Colonel Hutchinson* provide "a penetrating analysis of the English Civil War." Both authors "gave an epic patina to their husband's deeds," but it is Cavendish whose skillful presentation of "her hero" creates a true "literary classic." Patricia A. Sullivan, "Female Writing Beside the Rhetorical Tradition: Seventeenth Century British Biography and a Female Tradition in Rhetoric," *IJWS,* 3 (1980), 143–60, uses Cavendish's *Life of William Cavendish* and Thomas Sprat's "Life of Cowley" to argue a difference between male and female biographers which can be traced to the distinction between seventeenth-century women's "practical educations" and men's training in formal rhetoric.

D. *Letters.* The *Private Correspondence of Jane Lady Cornwallis, 1613–1644, from the Originals in the Possession of the Family* (1842), prints letters from Lucy, Countess of Bedford, and other seventeenth-century English women. *The Oxinden Letters, 1607–1642, Being the Correspondence of Henry Oxinden of Barnham and His Circle* (1933) and *The Oxinden and Peyton Letters, 1642–1670, Being the Correspondence of Henry Oxinden of Barnham, Sir Thomas Peyton of Knowlton and Their Circle* (1937)—both edited by Dorothy Gardiner—include letters by and about seventeenth-century women. Other letters are listed below under the names of their writers.

In "Dorothy Osborne's 'Letters,'" in her *The Second Common Reader* (1932; rpt. 1956), pp. 59–67, Virginia Woolf asserts that in the seventeenth century letter writing was a literary activity: "Had she been born in 1827, Dorothy Osborne would have written novels; had she been born in 1527, she would never have written at all. But she was born in 1627, and at that date though writing books was ridiculous for a woman there was nothing unseemly about writing a letter." Johnye C. Stuchen, "The Letters of Lydia Dugard: A Seventeenth-Century Rural English Gentlewoman," *PMPA*, 3 (1978), treats thirty-three manuscript letters in the Folger Shakespeare Library as documents chronicling "the concerns of a middle-class family in rural England." Hughey (I, above) cites letters from women of the gentry and middling classes to show the increased writing skills of women of those classes.

E. *Diaries.* In a study of twenty-three diaries by Stuart women of the upper and middling classes, Sara Heller Mendelson, "Stuart Women's Diaries and Occasional Memoirs," in Prior (Background Studies), pp. 181–210, notes that many women's diaries of this period are in the form of spiritual journals or records of God's mercies and that for those women, "gender was apparently more important than class in shaping the basic pattern of their lives."

F. *Prophetic Writing and Preaching.* Phyllis Mack, "Women as Prophets During the English Civil War," *FSt,* 8 (1982), 19–45, examines "the cage of symbols and stereotypes that conditioned the liberty of women prophets during the English Civil War," noting, for example, that radical Protestants "chose to interpret the receptivity of the female prophet as a positive political emblem"—even in spite of their insistence that women not serve as preachers or theologians.

G. *Prose Fiction.* In "The Pastoral Romance," Chapter 2 of her *Women Writers: Their Contribution to the English Novel, 1621–1744* (1944; rpt. 1948), pp. 47–70, B. G. MacCarthy presents Mary Wroth's *Urania* and Anne Weamys' *Continuation of Sir Philip Sidney's Arcadia* as early examples of writing in "the realistic vein." She also presents chapters on seventeenth-century biography and on Margaret Cavendish in her account of English-women's contribution to the novel. Similarly, Dale Spender, *Mothers of the Novel: 100 Good Women Writers before Jane Austen* (1986), begins by contrasting Mary Wroth, whose *Urania* was written "for a public audience and for profit" (and whose "realistic" stories laid "foundation stones" for women's fiction) and Katherine Philips, whose preference for anonymity is more characteristic of seventeenth-century women; she argues that in "blurr[ing] some of the distinctions between fact and fantasy," four seventeenth-century biographers—Anne Clifford, Lucy Hutchinson, Ann Fanshawe, and Margaret Cavendish—"helped to launch new literary traditions" that led to the novel. Jane Spencer, *The Rise of the Woman Novelist: From Aphra Behn to Jane Austen* (1986), includes a section entitled "Writers as Heroines: Foundations for Women's Literary Authority in the Seventeenth Century," pp. 22–40, in which she argues that women like Katherine Philips and Margaret Cavendish evoked interest in women writers "as heroines to celebrate and examples to emulate."

H. *Mothers' Advice Books.* Betty S. Travitsky, "The New Mother of the English Renaissance: Her Writings on Motherhood," in *The Lost Tradition: Mothers and Daughters in Literature,* ed. Cathy N. Davidson and E. M. Broner (1980), pp. 33–43, sees "natural maternal feeling" combined with the teachings of Renaissance humanists and religious reformers in "a family-centered, religiously-oriented time." Christine W. Sizemore, "Early Seventeenth-Century Advice Books: The Female Viewpoint," *SAB*, 41:1 (1976), 41–48, notes significant differences in seventeenth-century women's points of view but stresses Leigh's, Joceline's, and Grymeston's shared goal of educating their children in their religious faith. Beilin (I, above), pp. 266–85, argues that because the women whose advice books were published in the seventeenth century were aware of the conflict between the conservative ideology expressed in their books and the fact that writing "brings [them] public notice," they present themselves as "impelled by their calling as Christian women into the role of writer."

III. STUDIES OF INDIVIDUAL WRITERS

A. *Aemilia Lanier (1570?–1645)*. A. L. Rowse prints Lanier's poetry as *The Poems of Shakespeare's Dark Lady: Salve Deus Rex Judaeorum by Emilia Lanier* (1978). Travitsky, *Paradise of Women*, pp. 97–103, and Mahl and Koon, *Female Spectator*, pp. 73–87, provide excerpts.

Lanier's life is outlined in the Introduction to Rowse's edition. His identification of Lanier as the dark lady of Shakespeare's sonnets appeared in the mid-seventies in his *Shakespeare the Man* (1973); *Shakespeare's Sonnets: The Problems Solved: A Modern Edition, with Prose Versions, Introduction and Notes* (2nd ed. 1973); and *Simon Forman: Sex and Society in Shakespeare's Age*—English edition, *Sex and Society in Shakespeare's Age* (1974). That attribution, however, is not accepted by literary scholars; see, for example, S. Schoenbaum, "Shakespeare, Dr. Forman, and Dr. Rowse," in his *Shakespeare and Others* (1985), pp. 54–79.

Barbara K. Lewalski, "Of God and Good Women," in *Silent But for the Word* (I, above), pp. 203–24, examines the dedicatory poems, the prose "Epistle to the Virtuous Reader," the long poem on Christ's Passion, and "The Description of Cookeham" to show that the volume "is set forth as a comprehensive Book of Good Women, fusing religious devotion and feminism so as to assert the essential harmony of those two impulses." In "The Feminization of Praise: Aemilia Lanyer," Beilin, in *Redeeming Eve* (I, above), pp. 177–207, contrasts Lanier's praise of women with that by poets like Donne and Jonson to show that her concern is to present "her sex as the heroic protectors of the Christian spirit." Beilin's argument is that Lanier is "a millenarian advocating the establishment on earth of God's will through the particular agency of women."

B. *Esther Inglis (1571–1624)*. Travitsky, *Paradise of Women*, pp. 151 and 24–25, prints the Dedicatory Letter and three eight-line stanzas from *Octonaries upon the Vanitie and Inconstancie of the World*.

Dorothy Judd Jackson, *Esther Inglis: Calligrapher, 1571–1624* (1937), adds thirteen manuscript books by Inglis to the list of twenty eight compiled by David Laing, "Notes Relating to Mrs. Esther (Langois or)Inglis," *Proceedings of the Society of Antiquaries of Scotland,* 6 (1865). Inglis is one of six women whose work Robert Williams describes in "A Moon to Their Sun: Writing Mistresses of the Sixteenth and Seventeenth Centuries," *Fine Print* (1985), 88–98. Williams adds three books to Jackson's list.

C. *Elizabeth Clinton, Countess of Lincoln (1574–1630?)*. *The Countess of Lincolnes Nurserie* appears in an English Experience Series facsimile (1975). Travitsky, *Paradise of Women,* pp. 57–60, and Mahl and Koon, *Female Spectator,* pp. 88–98, print excerpts.

Beilin (I, above), pp. 280–85, notes that Clinton, who did not nurse her own eighteen children, composed her exhortation to other women to expiate her own guilt; thus she expressed a "concern for her sex that had previously been more implicit than explicit in women's writing."

D. *Lady Anne Southwell (1574–1626).* In *ELR,* 14 (1984), n.p., Jean C Cavenaugh transcribes a letter in which Lady Southwell defends poetry.

In "The Library of Lady Southwell and Captain Sibthorpe," *SB,* 20 (1967), 243–54, Cavenaugh prints the list of 110 books Lady Southwell left to her husband when she died.

E. *Arbella Stuart (1575–1615).* Elizabeth Cooper published *The Life and Letters of Lady Arabella Stuart. Including Numerous Original and Unpublished Documents,* 2 vols. in 1866; E. T. Bradley, *Life of the Lady Arabella Stuart,* 2 vols. (1889) also includes transcriptions of Stuart's letters.

David N. Durant, *Arbella Stuart: A Rival to the Queen* (1978), uses contemporary documents to chronicle the life of "an eccentric whom even the Jacobeans could not explain." P[hyllis] M[argaret] Handover, *Arbella Stuart: Royal Lady of Hardwick and Cousin to King James* (1957), presents Stuart's life as molded by her grandmother, Bess of Hardwick.

Sara Jayne Steen, "Fashioning an Acceptable Self: Arbella Stuart," in this issue of *ELR,* studies drafts of Stuart's letters to show "a verbally talented woman giv[ing] rhetorical shape to a self she thought would be more acceptable to a misogynistic king and his court than her unreformed one ever could be."

F. *Lady Katherine Paston (1578–1628/9).* Ruth Hughey's edition of *The Correspondence of Lady Katherine Paston, 1603–1627* (1941) includes a petition from Lady Katherine to the Lord Chancellor, Francis Bacon, and three additional documents relating to a chancery suit of 1618.

In "Katherine, the Lady Paston, A Seventeenth-Century Portrait," a chapter in her "Cultural Interests of Women in England, from 1524–1640" (I, above), pp. 199–259, Hughey uses the letters to outline Lady Katherine's life as "a careful secretary and accountant, a competent manager, a far-sighted and fearless champion, an intelligent person, neither masculine nor feminine, if we assume that in either parent the motivating force is the future protection of the family."

G. *Elizabeth Cary, Viscountess Falkland (1586–1639). The Tragedie of Mariam, Faire Queene of Jewry* (1613) is edited for the Malone Society by A. C. Dunstan and W. W. Greg (1914). Excerpts appear in Travitsky, *Paradise of Women,* pp. 220–33, Mahl and Koon, *Female Spectator,* pp. 99–114, and Goreau, *Whole Duty,* pp. 13–14. *The History of the Most Unfortunate Prince, King Edward the Second* is printed in *Harleian Miscellany,* 1 (1808), 67–95, and excerpted by Travitsky, *Paradise of Women,* pp. 216–19. Travitsky, *Paradise of Women,* pp. 219–20, also prints the Dedication to Queen Henrietta Maria and the Epistle to the Reader from Lady Falkland's translation of Cardinal Perron's *Reply to The Attack on His Work by King James* (1630).

In 1861 Richard Simpson published an edition of *The Lady Falkland: Her Life: from a MS in the Imperial Archives at Lille* written by one of her daughters. Cary is one of three "Exceptional Women" with whom Travitsky, *Paradise of Women,* pp. 209–33, closes her volume. She presents Cary as a translator of religious works and as a writer of "original literature which, if not actually religious, is certainly of a serious, almost philosphical cast."

1. *The Tragedie of Mariam.* Sandra K. Fischer, "Elizabeth Cary and Tyranny, Domestic and Religious," in Hannay (I, above), pp. 225–37, argues that Cary uses a marginal genre, Senecan tragedy, to represent the difficult "dilemma of a woman of independent thought who also believes unerringly in the Catholic ideals." Nancy Cotton Pearse, "Elizabeth Cary, Renaissance Playwright," *TSLL,* 18 (1977), 601–08; rpt. with minor revisions in "Renaissance Noblewomen," the first chapter of Nancy Cotton, *Women Playwrights in England, 1363–1750* (1980), pp. 27–54, parallels elements of Lady Falkland's life with *Mariam* to suggest that Mariam and Salome represent the author's own conflict between an idealized notion of proper wifely behavior and "an even more impossible ideal of an independent, even rebellious, intellectual life." She argues that *Mariam* emulates Senecan dramas by the Countess of Pembroke and members of the Countess' circle and speculates that its publication in 1613 was incited by a poem published in 1612 by Sir John Davies. Noting the play's focus on the issue of wifely obedience and the transformation of *Mariam* into a type of Christ at the end of the drama, Elaine Beilin, "Elizabeth Cary and *The Tragedie of Mariam,"PLL,* 16 (1980), 45–64, speculates that the piece justifies Lady Cary's own life. The play, she argues, shows an acute awareness of the "difficulties of dutiful obedience in the authoritarian structure of marriage," and Mariam's final triumph may be "Cary's way of superseding male authority" without relinquishing her religious piety. Beilin expands her analysis in *Redeeming Eve* (I, above), to suggest that the play is "a psychomachia" that affirms Christian values: in the drama, if not in her life, Cary was able to create a "resolution for her [personal] dilemmas and a triumph for her highest ideals." In "The *Feme Covert* in Elizabeth Cary's *Mariam,"* in *Ambiguous Realities: Women in the Middle Ages and Renaissance,* ed. Carole Levin and Jeanie Watson (1987), pp. 184–96, Travitsky expands her comments in *Paradise of Women* (above) to present *Mariam* as a play which analyzes both a husband's jealousy and a wife's "stirring of personhood." Noting the negative imagery with which Cary presents insubordinate women, however, Travitsky believes she is "ambivalent" toward Mariam's actions.

2. *The History of the Most Unfortunate Prince, King Edward the Second.* Donald A. Stauffer, "A Deep and Sad Passion," in *Essays in Dramatic Literature: Parrott Presentation Volume,* ed. Hardin Craig (1935; rpt. 1967), pp. 289–314, assigns the piece to Elizabeth Cary and uses it to show the "deep influence of drama on historical biography" of the Renaissance. Tina Krontiris, "Style and Gender in Elizabeth Cary's *Edward II,"* forthcoming in *Englishwoman of the Renaissance* (I, above), sees the work as a rewriting of history from Isabel's point of view; although Cary continues to accept some of her culture's negative ideas about womanhood, this play demonstrates her increased confidence as a writer.

H. *Lucy, Countess of Bedford (1581–1627).* W. Milgate prints "Death, be not proud," possibly by the Countess of Beford, in Appendix B of his edition of *John Donne: The Epithalamions, Anniversaries, and Epicedes* (1978), pp. 235–37—as does Barbara K. Lewalski, "Lucy, Countess of Bedford: Images of A Jacobean Courtier and Patroness," in *Politics of Discourse: The Literature and History of Seventeenth-Century England,* ed. Kevin Sharpe and Steven N. Zwicker (1987), pp. 52–77.

Herbert J. C. Grierson, *The Poems of John Donne: Edited from the Old Editions and Numerous Manuscripts with Introduction and Commentary,* Vol. 2 (1912; rpt. 1951), cxliii–clxv, first suggested that Lady Bedford may have authored the poem; Helen Gardner, ed. *John Donne: The Divine Poems,* 2nd ed. (1978), pp. xlvii–xlviii, agrees that "someone else in [Donne's] circle, possibly the Countess herself, rebuk[ed] him with words out of his own mouth."

Lewalski's essay (above) examines the Countess of Bedford's success in "elicit[ing] and creat[ing] various idealized images of herself in literature and in art, making the role of courtier-patroness into something of a cultural myth."

I. *Lady Mary Wroth (1586?–1640).* Travitsky, *Paradise of Women,* pp. 135–39, prints brief excerpts from *Urania* and *Pamphilia to Amphilanthus.* Josephine A. Roberts' edition of *The Poems of Lady Mary Wroth* (1983) is based on the holograph at the Folger Shakespeare Library, with additional poems from the 1621 *Urania,* the Newberry manuscript of the second part of the *Urania,* and the Huntington manuscript of *Loves Victorie;* in an appendix, Roberts prints Lady Mary's correspondence. *Pamphilia to Amphilanthus by Lady Mary Wroth* (1977), ed. G. F. Waller, is based on the 1621 edition. Margaret Patterson Hannay edited twenty poems from the cycle for *Women Writers of the Renaissance and Reformation,* ed. Katharina M. Wilson (1987), pp. 548–65.

1. *The Countess of Montgomery's Urania.* The three pieces cited in II, G, above, treat the *Urania.* Naomi J. Miller, "Strange Labyrinth: Pattern as Process in Sir Philip Sidney's *Arcadia* and Lady Mary Wroth's *Urania,*" Ph. D. Diss., Harvard Univ, 1987, presents the *Urania* in terms of its Sidneian, Spenserian, and Shakespearean antecedents but emphasizes that it is shaped by Wroth's own perspective as a Renaissance woman writer. Margaret A. Witten-Hannah, "Lady Mary Wroth's Urania: The Work and the Tradition," Ph.D. Diss., Univ. of Auckland, 1978, argues that the *Urania* is a mannerist work combining "social allegory" based on Lady Mary's own experience in Renaissance England and the traditional elements of literary romance—the latter often influenced by Lady Mary's knowledge of court masques.

John J. O'Connor, "James Hay and The Countess of Montgomerie's Urania," *N&Q,* 200 (1955), 150–52, and Paul Salzman, "Contemporary References in Mary Wroth's *Urania,*" *RES,* 29 (1978), 178–81, note Wroth's references to James Hay, his wife Honora Denny, and his father-in-law Lord Denny in her story of Sirelius. Josephine A. Roberts, "An Unpublished Literary Quarrel Concerning the Suppression of Mary Wroth's *Urania* (1621)," *N&Q,* 222 (1977), 532–35, chronicles the protests leading to Lady Mary's withdrawing her book from sale; she prints Edward Denny's "To Pamphilia from the father-in-law of Seralius" and Lady Mary's "Railing Rimes returned upon the Author by Mistress Mary Wrothe."

Carolyn Ruth Swift, "Feminine Identity in Lady Mary Wroth's Romance *Urania,*" *ELR,* 14 (1984), 328–46, focuses on Wroth's representation of a world in which women are "trapped and bewildered" yet argues that in *Urania* "Wroth sometimes validates social values that can destroy a woman's sense of self." In "Radigund Revisited: Perspectives on Women Rulers in Lady Mary Wroth's *Urania,*" in Hazelkorn and Travitsky's forthcoming *Englishwoman of the Renaissance* (I, above), Josephine A. Roberts places *Urania* beside *The Faerie Queene* to argue that Wroth "offers a highly ambivalent view of female rule" in Parts One and Two of her prose romance.

Paul Salzman, "*Urania* and the Tyranny of Love," in his *English Prose Fiction, 1558-1700: A Critical History* (1985; rpt. 1986), pp. 138–44, follows MacCarthy (II, G) in crediting the *Urania* with "represent[ing] a new engagement with the minutiae of contemporary life, which makes it possible for the later political romances to encompass the events of the Civil War in detail rather than to look at political issues in a more abstract way, as Sidney did in the *Arcadia,*" and he agrees with Swift (above) that Wroth reveals an awareness of "the disappointment in store for women who believe in the heroic stories which men tell."

2. *Pamphilia to Amphilanthus*. Josephine A. Roberts, "The Biographical Problem of *Pamphilia to Amphilanthus,*" *TSWL*, 1 (1982), 43–53, argues that the cycle is loosely based on Wroth's relationship with William Herbert, third Earl of Pembroke (1580–1630). In "Lady Mary Wroth's Sonnets: A Labyrinth of the Mind," *JWSL*, 1 (1979), 319–29, Roberts treats her "effort to dramatize the conflict between passionate surrender and self-affirmation." Elaine V. Beilin, "'The Only Perfect Vertue': Constancy in Mary Wroth's *Pamphilia to Amphilanthus,*" *SSt*, 2 (1981), 229–45, argues that the cycle, especially the crown of sonnets at its center, celebrates female constancy. In *Redeeming Eve* (I, above), she expands that argument to say that in both *Urania* and *Pamphilia to Amphilanthus,* Wroth presents Constancy as "the heroic virtue capable of transforming a lovelorn woman into a great queen, a poet, and finally, a transcendent image of divine love." May Nelson Paulissen, "Forgotten Love Sonnets of the Court of King James: The Sonnets of Mary Wroth," *PMPA*, 3 (1978), 24–31, presents the cycle as four sequences moving "through the stages of physical love, Neo-Platonic love, to a higher spiritual plane where love is viewed with reason and maturity." Noting Wroth's success in the seventeenth century, Paulissen suggests twentieth-century readers "welcome her sonnets into the mainstream of English poetry." Naomi Miller, "Ancient Fictions and True Forms: The Role of the Lady in Mary Wroth's *Pamphilia to Amphilanthus,*" forthcoming in *Englishwoman of the Renaissance* (I, above), argues that Wroth rewrites the role of the lady in the sonnet tradition.

3. *Loves Victorie*. In "The Huntington Manuscript of Lady Mary Wroth's Play, *Loves Victorie,*" *HLQ*, 46 (1983), 156–74, Roberts demonstrates that HN 100 is a holograph of most of a pastoral drama written by Lady Mary, probably in the 1620s. (Another holograph of the play is in private hands in England.)

Noting probable influences of Ben Jonson's masques, a "graceful tribute to Sir Philip Sidney," and the play's development of the theme of love's various effects, Roberts sees the drama as evidence of Lady Mary's literary skill. Margaret Anne McLaren, "*Loves Victorie*: A Forgotten Manuscript from the Court of James I," forthcoming in *Englishwoman of the Renaissance* (I, above), stresses "the language of avoidance" of a Jacobean woman writer.

J. *Anne Clifford, Countess of Dorset, Pembroke, and Montgomery (1590–1676)*. Travitsky, *Paradise of Women*, pp. 87–88 reprints excerpts from V. Sackville-West's edition of *The Diary of the Lady Anne Clifford with an Introductory Note* (1923). Appended to A. G. Dickens' edition of the *Clifford Letters of the Sixteenth Century* (1962) is the portion of British Museum, Harley MS 6177 in which Anne Clifford summarizes the lives of her ancestors the Veteriponts, Cliffords, and the Earls of Cumberland. The remaining portion of the manuscript, Clifford's account of her own life, is in *Lives of Lady Anne*

Clifford, Countess of Dorset, Pembroke, and Montgomery (1590–1676) Summarized by Herself, Printed From the Harley MS. 6177 (1916). In 1922 George C. Williamson compiled *Lady Anne Clifford, Countess of Dorset, Pembroke, and Montgomery, 1590–1676. Her Life, Letters and Work Extracted from All the Original Documents Available, Many of Which are Here Printed for the First Time* (2nd ed. 1967).

Wallace Notestein, *Four Worthies: John Chamberlain, Anne Clifford, John Taylor, Oliver Heywood* (1957), and Martin Holmes, *Proud Northern Lady: Lady Anne Clifford, 1590–1676* (1975), base their biographies on Lady Anne's accounts of her life.

K. *Lady Eleanor Davies, later Lady Eleanor Douglas (c. 1590–1652).* Travitsky, *Paradise of Women,* pp. 156–57, prints a portion of *A Warning to the Dragon and All His Angels* (1625).

In "Lady Elinor Davies: The Prophet as Publisher," *Women's Studies International Forum,* 8 (1985), 403–09, Beth Nelson demonstrates that Davies "appropriate[d] the printing press for the public expression of her vision of herself" as a prophet of the apocalypse. Esther S. Cope, "'Dame Eleanor Davies Never Soe Mad a Ladie'?" *HLQ,* 50 (1987), 133–44, uses Davies' pamphlets and other seventeenth-century documents to reconstruct Lady Eleanor's difficult life; whether or not she was mad, Cope proposes, the extent to which Lady Eleanor threatened her contemporaries' ideas of "order in the church and commonwealth" teaches us a great deal about the age in which she lived.

C. J. Hindle provides "A Bibliography of the Printed Pamphlets and Broadsides of Lady Eleanor Douglas, the Seventeenth-Century Prophetess," in *Edinburgh Bibliographical Society Transactions,* 1 (1935–36), 65–75. A "Summary Report on the Hastings Manuscripts," *Huntington Library Bulletin,* 5 (1934), 14, indicates that there are twelve manuscript letters in the Huntington collection from Lady Douglas to her daughter.

L. *Elizabeth Joceline (1595–1622).* Excerpts from *The Mothers Legacie to her Unborne Childe* (1624) appear in Travitsky, *Paradise of Women,* pp. 60–63. R. Lee edited the third impression (1625) in 1852; Randall T. Roffen, the sixth impression (1632) in 1894.

Sizemore (II, H) describes Joceline's work as a tender, moderate presentation of advice against social temptations, particularly against extravagant dress. Beilin (I, above) stresses her ambivalence about woman's abilities and virtues, and Travitsky (above) suggests that Joceline's desire that a daughter may not be educated may be an attempt "to protect her unborn daughter from a potentially difficult and uncomfortable way of life."

M. *Lady Brilliana Harley (1600–1643). Letters of the Lady Brilliana Harley, Wife of Sir Robert Harley, of Brampton Tryan, Knight of the Bath* were edited for the Camden Society by Thomas Taylor Lewis in 1854. Lewis' Introduction notes the "practical piety" informing all 205 of the letters. Travitsky, *Paradise of Women,* pp. 82–83, prints a letter in which Lady Harley's postscript cautions her son not to tell her husband she has written.

N. *Bathsua Makin (c. 1610–1682). An Essay to Revive the Antient Education of Gentlewomen, in Religion, Manners, Arts & Tongues: with an Answer to the Objections against this Way of Education* (1673) is edited by Paula L. Barbour (1980) and excerpted in Mahl and Koon, *Female Spectator,* pp. 126–35, Ferguson, *First Feminists,* pp. 128–42, and in a chapter on Makin by Frances Teague in *Women Writers of the Seventeenth Century,* ed. Katharina M.

Wilson (forthcoming). *The Malady . . . and Remedy of Vexations and Unjust Arrests and Actions* and a manuscript poem, "Upon the much lamented death of the Right Honourable, the Lady Elizabeth Langham," are printed in Mahl and Koon, *Female Spectator,* pp. 118–25.

Teague's outline of Makin's life and works (above) presents Makin as an exemplary woman whose witty arguments anticipate twentieth-century views on the value of education for women. In "New Light on Bathsua Makin," *SCN,* 49 (1986), 16, Teague establishes that Makin was teaching Princess Elizabeth by 1640—perhaps as early as 1639.

Mitzi Myers, "Domesticating Minerva: Bathsua Makin's 'Curious Argument' for Women's Education," in *SECC,* 14 (1984), pp. 173–92, demonstrates the essay's "rich sense of possibilities, its ardent purpose, and its argumentative vitality." J. R. Brink, "Bathsua Makin: Scholar and Educator of the Seventeenth Century," *IJWS,* 1 (1978), 417–26; rpt. with minor changes as "Bathsua Makin: Educator and Linguist (1608?–1675?)," in *Female Scholars: A Tradition of Learned Women before 1800,* ed. J. R. Brink (1980), pp. 86–100, compares Makin's theories with Milton's and notes that she transcends the Christian humanists' practical views on education for women by arguing that learning provides "a glymps of that glory we afterwards expect."

O. *Margaret Fell (1614–1702).* The second edition of *Women's Speaking Justified* (1667) was edited by David J. Latt for the Augustan Reprint Society (1979). Ferguson, *First Feminists,* pp. 114–27, prints excerpts.

The standard biography remains Isabel Ross, *Margaret Fell: Mother of Quakerism* (1949).

P.   *Lucy Hutchinson (b. 1620).* In his edition of *The Memoirs of the Life of Colonel Hutchinson with the Fragment of an Autobiography of Mrs. Hutchinson* (1973), James Sutherland uses the holograph of the *Life* now in Nottingham Castle Museum; for the autobiographical piece, he relies on Julius Hutchinson, ed. *Memoirs of the Life of Colonel Hutchinson . . . To Which is Prefix'd The Life of Mrs. Hutchinson, Written by Herself, a Fragment* (1806). Julius Hutchinson also edited *On the Principles of the Christian Religion, Addressed to her Daughter; And On Theology* (1817).

In his Introduction, Sutherland focuses on Hutchinson's intelligent appraisal of a man who was "intelligently attractive and socially repellent . . . an entirely credible and deeply interesting personality." D. A. Hobman, "A Puritan Lady," *ContempR,* 176 (1949), 115–18, quotes portions of the *Memoirs* to show that Lucy Hutchinson was "a humane, cultivated, and Liberal-minded English gentlewoman." The Everyman edition of the *Memoirs of the Life of Colonel, Hutchinson Written by his Widow Lucy* (n.d.) includes an Introduction by François P. G. Guizot who values the piece for its presentation of "living pictures" of an important historical period. At the end of the volume are two pages of "Verses by Mrs. Hutchinson." MacCarthy (II, G) contrasts Hutchinson's "intelligent and systematic mind" with the Duchess of Newcastle's "erratic genius" to argue against A. H. Upham's belief, "Lucy Hutchinson and the Duchess of Newcastle," *Anglia,* 36 (1912), 200–20, that Hutchinson's autobiography is indebted to the Duchess' *True Relation* and her *Memoirs* to *The Life of William Cavendish.*

Samuel A. Weiss, "Dating Mrs. Hutchinson's Translation of Lucretius," *N&Q,* 200 (1955), 109, suggests the translation was done in the late 1640s or the 1650s.

Q. *Anne, Lady Halkett (1623–1699).* John Loftis edited *The Memoirs of Anne, Lady Halkett and Ann, Lady Fanshawe* (1979).

Loftis dates Lady Halkett's birth 4 January 1623. He notes her "fluent prose, the expression of a high intelligence fully engaged in what she is saying," and presents her Memoirs as "above all a study in personal relationships." Margaret Bottrall, "A Kind of Picture Left Behind Me . . . ," Chapter 7 of her *Every Man a Phoenix: Studies in Seventeenth-Century Autobiography* (1958), pp. 141–64, presents the work as "a thoroughly feminine document. . . . concerned with persons and actions, not with ideas." Agreeing with Delany (II, B) that Lady Halkett's was "one of the most perceptive and skillful stylists among British autobiographers of her time," Jelinek (II, B) focuses on the "romance, excitement, and suspense" that mark her talent as "a psychological novelist." Rose's view (II, B) is that the Lady Halkett's work is remarkable in its portrayal of the narrator's choice "to undertake, rather than to deny, ignore, or submerge [a] struggle with authority"—in Halkett's case with her mother. Her narrative strategy, Rose sees, is to present her life in terms that would in the next century form the basis of the English novel: this female protagonist "struggle[s] toward creating a desirable position for herself in the mainstream of society."

R. *Margaret Cavendish, Duchess of Newcastle (1623–1673).* Two of Cavendish's works— *Sociable Letters, 1644* (1969) and *Poems and Fancies, 1653* (1972)—appear in facsimile editions. The most recent edition of *The Life of William Cavendish Duke of Newcastle to Which is Added the True Relations of my Birth Breeding and Life* is by C. H. Firth (1886; 2nd ed. [1906]). In 1956 Douglas Grant published *The Phanseys of William Cavendish Marquis of Newcastle Addressed to Margaret Lucas and Her Letters in Reply.*

Moira Ferguson excerpts a number of Cavendish's works in *Women Writers of the Seventeenth Century,* ed. Katharina M. Wilson (forthcoming). Mary Grimley Mason and Carol Hurd Green print excerpts of *A True Relation, The Life of William Cavendish,* and *The Blazing World* in their *Journeys: Autobiographical Writings by Women* (1979), pp. 41–55; Mahl and Koon, *Female Spectator,* pp. 136–53, excerpt *Nature's Pictures*; and Ferguson, *First Feminists,* pp. 84–101, prints "To the Two Most Famous Universities of England" from *Philosophical and Physical Opinions* and portions of *The Convent of Pleasure.*

Douglas Grant, *Margaret the First: A Biography of Margaret Cavendish, Duchess of Newcastle, 1623–1673* (1957), is a sympathetic presentation of Cavendish's life, but Grant downplays her significance as a writer. Sara Heller Mendelson, "Margaret Cavendish, Duchess of Newcastle," in *The Mental World of Stuart Women* (I, above), pp. 12–61, accounts for Cavendish's work by noting her haphazard education and the social conventions that limited the scope of seventeenth-century women's lives: "in fiction Margaret could concoct incredible circumstances to satisfy her ambitions, whereas in the real world those urges were limited." Cavendish, she believes, was unable to decide "about the exact gender role, or blend of roles, that she wished to emulate," but noting her influence on other seventeenth-century writers, Mendelson suggests that her "effrontery in challenging certain barriers which sustained the polarity of the two sexes" may have worked towards "broadening women's ideas of what constituted conceivable behaviour." Jean Gagen, "Honor and Fame in the Works of the Duchess of Newcastle," *SP,* 56 (1959), 519–38, examines Cavendish's use of ideas of honor and fame throughout her works to show that "even though she was a woman she set out to gain for herself the applause which is the just reward of those who dare and do greatly." In

"Margaret Cavendish: Defining the Female Self," *WS,* 7 (1980), 55–66, Dolores Paloma points to "Cavendish's largely unconscious sense of the distinction between the masculine and the feminine" and argues that, particularly in her plays, she seeks "to enlarge the definition of woman." Hilda M. Smith, *Reason's Disciples* (I, above), pp. 75–95, notes how many of the topics and "emphases" Cavendish introduces are explored by later feminists. "Her greatest contribution to feminist thought," Smith argues, "was the degree to which questions of sex division dominated her work"; even the contradictions within her writing address the "central [and disturbing] fact of her life . . . that she was a woman determined to act in what was considered a male sphere."

MacCarthy (II, G) treats Cavendish in her chapters on biography, on the epistolary form prior to Richardson's *Pamela,* and in a separate chapter, "Living Restoration Trends" (pp. 122–38); her contention is that by "avoiding the decadent, and by showing in many forms her adherence to the living trend in story-telling" Cavendish contributed to the development of the English novel.

1. *Scientific writing.* In "A Science Turned Upside Down: Feminism and the Natural Philosophy of Margaret Cavendish," *HLQ,* 47 (1984), 289–307, Lisa T. Sarasohn places Cavendish's work beginning with *Poems and Fancies* (1653) in the context of seventeenth-century science to chronicle her use of "the skeptical methodology of the new science" to write a feminist critique of the new learning. Noting, however, Cavendish's own deep ambivalence toward womanhood, Sarasohn explicates *The Blazing World* (1666) as a fantasy of a "world upside down, where Cavendish could fulfill her wishes on the grand scale." Robert Kargon, *Atomism in English from Hariot to Newton* (1966), passim, argues that the atheistic implications of Cavendish's and Thomas Hobbes' atomism provoked writers like Walter Charleton, John Evelyn, and Robert Boyle to defend their own work against charges of impiety. Sylvia Bowerbank, "The Spider's Delight," *ELR,* 14 (1984), 392–408, argues that Cavendish's goal was "to win public acceptance as Nature's true champion," to defend "free fancy or subjective expression in principle and in practice." Although Cavendish's vision of Nature was different from that of many of her contemporaries, Bowerbank argues that it was not philosophic differences but "her sex and her untamed method" that led to her exclusion from the scientific community of her day. Gerald Dennis Meyer devotes the first chapter of his *The Scientific Lady in England, 1650–1760: An Account of Her Rise, with Emphasis on the Major Roles of the Telescope and Microscope* (1955), pp. 1–15, to "The Fantastic Duchess of Cavendish," whom he sees as important not for the excellence of her scientific work—for she was "too extravagant" to be a first-rate scientist, but for her insistence that the sciences be made "intelligible, and therefore accessible, to 'those of meaner capabilities'—the ladies." In raising key questions about women's abilities and their rights to participation in the intellectual life, Meyer maintains, Cavendish "[set] an example and [established] a precedent for talented but timorous English authoresses of the future to follow." Although he believes that Cavendish's scientific work was "written from an erroneous point of view," he notes that her anti-Baconian beliefs were shared by "many thoughtful persons of her day."

2. *Autobiographical writing.* Mason (II, B) presents Cavendish as the "archetype of the double-focus writer; that is, she was the one who established the pattern according to which many subsequent women would imagine their lives and literary careers and would structure their autobiographies." Findley and Hobby (II, B) argue that Cavendish's autobiography is written, in part, to defend her reputation for chastity.

Rose (II, B) describes *A True Relation* as the record of a woman as "unable to commit herself to the self-effacement required by socially defined female behavior as she is to the more fully human challenge of individualism."

3. *Drama.* Jacqueline Pearson, "'Women may discourse . . . as well as men': Speaking and Silent Women in the Plays of Margaret Cavendish," *TSWL,* 4 (1985), 33–45, argues that Cavendish shares with other seventeenth-century women writers a deep ambivalence about women. Of all her plays, *Love's Adventures,* which is "about speech and silence," is "the most affirmative in its treatment of the condition of women [and] her most mocking in its treatment of men."

S. *Jane Lead (1624–1704).* Two excerpts from *A Fountain of Gardens* are printed in *The Norton Anthology of Literature by Women: The Tradition in English,* ed. Sandra M. Gilbert and Susan Gubar (1985), pp. 76–80.

In "The English Philadelphians: (I) Mrs Lead," in his *The Decline of Hell: Seventeenth-Century Discussions of Eternal Torment* (1964), pp. 218–30, D. P. Walker outlines Lead's published work and explains her position as leader of the Philadelphia Society. Catherine F. Smith, "Jane Lead: Mysticism and the Woman Cloathed with the Sun," in *Shakespeare's Sisters: Feminist Essays on Woman Poets,* ed. Sandra M. Gilbert and Susan Gubar (1979), pp. 3–18, surveys Lead's life and work to show her construction of "a language of feeling, particularly female feeling, that speaks from the bound, radiant matrix of female experience"; Smith's suggestion is that "the connection of ecstacy and feminism (as affirmation of the female) may be very old." In "Jane Lead: The Feminist Mind and Art of a Seventeenth-Century Protestant Mystic," in *Women of Spirit: Female Leadership in the Jewish and Christian Traditions,* ed. Rosemary Ruether and Eleanor McLaughlin (1979), pp. 184–203, Smith treats Lead as a representative woman mystic whose work has been an unappreciated but important "form of women's protest and self-affirmation within patriarchal culture." In "Jane Lead's Wisdom: Women and Prophesy in Seventeenth-Century England," in *Poetic Prophesy in Western Literature,* ed. Jan Wojcik and Raymond-Jean Frontain (1984), pp. 55–63, Smith suggests that Lead's work mirrors a recognition of the financial realities of women's lives in the seventeenth century, and she notes the significance to literary history of Lead's perception of Wisdom as "a coherent mental and emotional grasp of paradoxical reality in which a feminine ideal might be bride of Christ while a female person might be essentially powerless." In "*Three Guineas:* Virginia Woolf's Prophecy," in *Virginia Woolf and Bloomsbury: A Centenary Celebration* (1985), ed. Jane Marcus, Smith placed Lead at the beginning of a tradition of women writers extending to Woolf's prophetic *Three Guineas.*

T. *Mary Boyle, Countess of Warwick (1624–1678).* In 1847 the Religious Tract Society published a *Memoir of Lady Warwick: Also Her Diary, From A. D. 1666 to 1672 . . . [and] Extracts From Her Other Writings;* in 1848 T. Crofton Croker edited the *Autobiography of Mary Countess of Warwick* for the Percy Society.

In "Mary Rich, Countess of Warwick" Mendelson (I, above), pp. 62–115, presents Rich as "a pious lay saint" who found in religion consolation for "disappointments and demographic accidents of married life." Mendelson establishes 1624 as Rich's birthdate.

U. *Ann, Lady Fanshawe (1625–1680).* John Loftis has edited *The Memoirs of Anne, Lady Halkett and Ann, Lady Fanshawe* (1979).

In his Introduction, Loftis presents Lady Fanshawe's detailed record of her own and her husband's families as a valuable document of "the depth of the social upheaval among persons of her rank" during the Civil War. MacCarthy (II, B), who admires Lady Fanshawe's energy, courage, and spontaneity, praises the *Memoirs* for its narrative power and "complete realism." Rose (II, B) notes that it was the war that freed the conventional Lady Fanshawe from her position as her husband's "silent partner": "her marriage provides her with a motive and cue for action during the revolution without requiring her to question prevailing sexual assumptions."

V. *Elizabeth Egerton, Countess of Bridgewater (1626–1663)*. In "The 'Loose Papers' of Elizabeth Egerton," forthcoming in *The Englishwoman of the Renaissance* (I, above), Betty S. Travitsky describes Egerton's prayers, meditations, and brief essays as writings by a woman who had been impressed with Renaissance religious reformers' ideas about womanhood.

W. *Alice Thornton (1626/7–1706/7)*. In his edition of *The Autobiography of Mrs. Alice Thornton, of East Newton, Co. York* (1875), Charles Jackson omits passages he sees as repetitive and transposes others to maintain chronological order. Additional material about Thornton's life is in documents appended to Jackson's edition of *The Autobiography* and in *The Autobiographies and Letters of Thomas Comber* [Thornton's son-in-law], ed. C. E. Whiting, 2 vols. (1946–1947).

In his Preface, Jackson presents Thornton's *Autobiography* as an attempt by a pious and loving daughter, wife, and mother, "to rebut slander and vindicate her own good name." Rose (II, B) stresses Thornton's emphasis on her bodily experiences, especially in marriage and childbirth, as a way of asserting spiritual heroism; and she observes an unresolved conflict between "the angry and subversive subtext" of the *Autobiography* and the "negative self-assertion" of her story of a successful life.

X. *Dorothy Osborne (1627–1695)*. Kenneth Parker, ed. *Letters to Sir William Osborne* (1987), supersedes G. C. Moore Smith, ed. *The Letters of Dorothy Osborne to William Temple, 1652–1654* (1928; rpt. 1959).

Lord David Cecil, *Two Quiet Lives: Dorothy Osborne, Thomas Gray* (1948; rpt. 1965), follows Moore Smith (above) in reading Osborne's letters to create a sentimental tale of love, but Parker (above) presents the letters in their political and social contexts and suggests that Osborne "intended the letters to be discourses concerning philosophies— arguments not only with W[illiam] T[emple] but also with herself." Virginia Woolf, "Dorothy Osborne's 'Letters,'" (II, D), presents Osborne as a gifted writer; and Genie S. Lerch-Davis, "Rebellion Against Public Prose: The Letters of Dorothy Osborne to William Temple," *TSLL*, 20 (1978), 386–415, demonstrates Osborne's use of a range of styles and a private voice to convey a sense of "immediacy and intimacy."

Y. *Anne Finch, Viscountess Conway (1631–1679)*. Peter Loptson prints the Latin and English texts of *The Principles of the Most Ancient and Modern Philosophy* (1982). Except for one passage discussing More's view of Descartes, Marjorie Hope Nicolson edited all of Conway's letters for her *Conway Letters: The Correspondence of Anne, Viscountess Conway, Henry More, and Their Friends, 1624–1684, Collected from Manuscript Sources and Edited with a Biographical Account* (1930; rpt. 1979).

Nicolson's declared purpose is the presentation of Conway not as "the most brilliant of the brilliant women of her generation," but as "the most appealing personality with whom they [her male contemporaries]—scholars and churchmen alike—had come in contact." Loptson's Introduction indicates that the published versions of Conway's work are "edited—it is difficult to say how much" from her philosophical notebook by More and/or van Helmont.

In "The Vitalism of Anne Conway: Its Impact on Leibniz's Concept of the Monad," *Journal of the History of Philosophy*, 17 (1979), 255–69; rpt. with minor revisions in her "Women on Nature: Anne Conway and Other Philosophical Feminists," Chapter 11 of her *The Death of Nature: Women, Ecology, and the Scientific Revolution* (1980; rpt. 1983), pp. 253–74, Carolyn Merchant traces Conway's influence on Francis Mercury van Helmont (whom she credits with editing Conway's work) and on Leibniz; reading van Helmont and Conway helped Leibniz "to confirm and buttress his vitalistic view of nature and to stimulate the coalescence of his ideas into a 'monadology.'" In the Prologue to *Hypatia's Heritage: A History of Women in Science from Antiquity through the Nineteenth Century* (1986), Margaret Alic notes that Conway was one of the first to dispute Descartes' philosophy and that because her work dealt with the most significant issue of the seventeenth-century scientific revolution—the nature and relationship of matter and motion—it should be remembered.

Z. *Katherine Philips (1631/2–1664)*. George Saintsbury edited Philips' poems from the 1678 edition for his *Minor Poets of the Caroline Period*, 1 (1905; rpt. 1968), 485–612. Elizabeth H. Hageman's selection of poems (all but one from the 1667 edition) appears in *Women Writers of the Renaissance and Reformation*, ed. Katharina M. Wilson (1987), pp. 566–608. Mahl and Koon, *Female Spectator*, pp. 154–64; Goreau, *Whole Duty*, pp. 193–205; and Ferguson, *First Feminists*, pp. 102–13, include selections from the poems.

Philip Webster Souers, *The Matchless Orinda* (1931; rpt. 1968), establishes the principal biographical details. Having examined her writing, however, he concludes that "little enthusiasm is possible." In "Gleanings from the Orinda Holograph," *AN&Q*, 23 (1985), 100–02, Lucy Brashear presents details from poem titles in National Library of Wales MS 175 to date poems and identify persons to whom they are addressed. Patrick Thomas, "Orinda, Vaughan, and Watkyns: Anglo-Welsh Literary Relationships During the Interregnum," *AWR*, 62 (1976), 96–102, demonstrates Philips' connections with London literary circles.

1. *Poetry*. In her Introductory essay on Philips' life and works, Hageman (above) stresses Philips' creative use of literary conventions of her age. Lucy Brashear, "The Forgotten Legacy of the 'Matchless Orinda,'" *AWR*, 65 (1979), 68–79, argues that although Philips' image as a "reluctant poetess" inhibited later women poets, what should be remembered is her real success as a writer.

W. G. Hiscock's publication of "*Friendship*: Francis Finch's Discourse and the Circle of the Matchless Orinda," *RES*, 15 (1939), 466–68, establishes that is was Finch to whom Philips addressed "To the Noble Palaemon, on his incomparable Discourse of Friendship." Identifying the addressee of "To my dear Sister Mrs. C. P. on her Marriage" as Erasmus Philips' wife Catherine Darcy, Lucy Brashear, "The 'Matchless Orinda's' Missing Sister: Mrs. C. P.," *Restoration*, 10 (1986), 76–81, reads the poem as "a confidential message . . . acknowledging a bond between them forged by their shared unhappiness that an event so sacred as marriage has become an occasion for profane revelry." (For a different reading of the poem, see Hageman, above.)

Paul Elmen, "Some Manuscript Poems by the Matchless Orinda," *PQ,* 30 (1951), 53–57, discusses ten poems from MS 776 in the National Library of Wales to show that Philips' poems should be reedited. Margaret Crum, *First-line Index of English Poetry, 1500–1800, in Manuscripts of the Bodleian Library, Oxford,* 2 vols. (1969), tentatively attributes three poems to Philips. Catherine Cole Mambretti, "'Fugitive Papers': A New Orinda Poem and Problems in her Canon," *PBSA,* 71 (1977), 443–52, rejects two of Crum's attributions but accepts "On the Coronation" as Philips'; she also accepts "To The Right Honorable the Lady Mary Boteler on her Marriage to My Lord Cavendish" in NLW 776 as Philips' and argues that NLW 776 "derives from Charles Cotterell, Orinda's literary adviser and editor." As Patrick Hungerford Thomas, "An Edition of the Poems and Letters of Katherine Philips, 1624–1664," Ph.D. diss., Univ. College of Wales, 1982, edits the poems and letters from (where available) manuscript sources, he adds three poems in Cardiff MS 1053 and two early poems and a paragraph of prose in the National Library of Wales to the canon. Claudia Limbert, "Two Poems and a Prose Receipt: The Unpublished Juvenalia of Katherine Philips," *ELR,* 16 (1986), 383–90, transcribes the NLW manuscript Thomas had added to the canon. Mahl and Koon, *Female Spectator,* pp. 157–59, print "To Rosania and Lucasia, Articles of Friendship," an hitherto unpublished poem from H. E. Huntington MS HM 183, no. 17a.

Cyrus Lawrence Day and Eleanor Boswell Murrie, *English Song-Books, 1651–1702: A Bibliography with a First-Line Index of Songs* (1940), index Philips' poems that were set to music by Henry Lawes and others. Allan Pritchard, "Marvell's 'The Garden': A Restoration Poem?" *SEL,* 23 (1983), 371–88, demonstrates Marvell's debt to Philips and Cowley.

2. *Translations of Corneille's "Pompey" and "Horace."* Catherine Cole Mambretti, "Orinda on the Restoration Stage," *CL,* 37 (1985), uses Philips' letters to show that her *Pompey* "is the first clearly documented production of heroic drama in English heroic couplets." Cotton, *Women Playwrights in England* (III, Q), includes Philips in her chapter entitled "Renaissance Noblewomen," pp. 27–54, "because the pattern of her life and work was so much like theirs." In her last chapter, "Astrea and Orinda," pp. 194–212, Cotton argues that later women playwrights chose either Aphra Behn or Philips as their model: while in Behn they found a "female adventuress," in Philips they saw a "lady writer"—both unfortunate stereotypes.

AA. *Lady Elizabeth Delaval (1649–1717).* In the Introduction to *The Meditations of Lady Elizabeth Delaval, Written between 1662 and 1671* edited for the Surtees Society (1975), Douglas G. Green presents Lady Elizabeth as strong-willed and self-centered—as "too much an individual to submit contentedly to the dictates of a society which judged her primarily in her roles as a daughter and a wife."

BB. *Dorothy Leigh (fl. 1616).* The *Mothers Blessing* is excerpted in Travitsky, *Paradise of Women,* pp. 56–57.

Beilin (I, above) argues that Leigh "recognized the conflicts in her role as a writing mother, but attempted to resolve them by redefining the mother's role to include an authorized public voice." For other comments on Leigh, see II, H.

CC. *Rachel Speght (fl. 1617–1621)*. Simon Shepherd prints *A Mouzell for Melastomus* in *The Women's Sharp Revenge* (II, A), pp. 57–83. Travitsky, *Paradise of Women*, pp. 31–33, 105–07, and 152–53, excerpts *Mouzell* and *Moralities Memorandum, with a Dreame Prefixed*.

Beilin (I, above), pp. 110–17 and 253–75, contrasts Speght's use of conventional arguments in the prose work with the revisionary vision of the later poem: "'The Dream' firmly includes women in the poetic search for salvation." For other comments on Speght, see II, A.

DD. *Esther Sowernam (pseud.) (fl. 1617)*. *Ester hath hang'd Haman* is printed in Shepherd, *The Women's Sharp Revenge* (II, A), pp. 85–124. Travitsky, *Paradise of Women*, pp. 107–08 and 153–55, Ferguson, *First Feminists*, pp. 74–79; Goreau, *Whole Duty*, pp. 75–80; and Henderson and McManus, *Half Humankind*, pp. 217–43, provide excerpts.

Beilin (I, above) argues that Sowernam's voice is that of a Christian teacher and preacher who aims "to strengthen women and correct men." Smith (I, above) suggests that Joseph Swetnam wrote Sowernam's response to his *Arraignment of Women*, but the writers cited in II, A above believe Sowernam to have been female.

EE. *Joane Sharp (pseud.) (fl. 1617)*. "A Defense of Women" is printed in Goreau, *Whole Duty*, pp. 81–84, and Ferguson, *First Feminists*, pp. 80–83.

See also II, A.

FF. *Constantia Munda (pseud.) (fl. 1617)*. Shepherd, *The Women's Sharp Revenge* (II, A), pp. 125–57, prints *The Worming of a Mad Dogge*. Travitsky, *Paradise of Women*, pp. 109–10, and Henderson and McManus, *Half Humankind*, pp. 244–63, provide excerpts.

Shepherd and Jones (II, A) suggest that Constantia Munda is a pseudonym for a male writer.

Beilin (I, above), pp. 263–66, accounts for Munda's vigorous, even undecorous response to *The Arraignment of Women* by recalling "The Christian tradition of righteous anger in the cause of good against evil." For other comments on Munda, see II, A.

GG. *M. R. (fl. 1624)*. Travitsky, *Paradise of Women*, pp. 66–68, prints excerpts of *The Mothers Counsell*.

Crawford (I, above), p. 278, n. 87, believes M. R. to have been a man. But Beilin (I, above), pp. 282–85, treats M. R. as an index to the extent to which women writers may be influenced by male ideas that they should be humble and chaste.

HH. *Jane Owen (d. before 1634)*. A facsimile edition of *An Antidote against Purgatory, 1634* appears in the series of English Recusant Literature published by the Scolar Press (1973). Travitsky, *Paradise of Women*, pp. 158–59, excerpts the Prefatory Letter.

II. *Mary Tattlewell and Joan Hit-him-home (pseud.) (fl. 1640)*. Shepherd, *The Women's Sharp Revenge* (II, A), pp. 159–93, prints *The Women's Sharpe Revenge*. Goreau, *Whole Duty*, pp. 103–07, and Henderson and McManus, *Half Humankind*, pp. 305–25, print excerpts. Travitsky, *Paradise of Women*, pp. 162–63, excerpts the Prefatory Letter.

Ferguson, *First Feminists* (Editions, above) and Shepherd (above) raise the possibility that John Taylor wrote *The Women's Sharpe Revenge* as a response to his own *Juniper Lecture* of 1639. The 2nd edition of the *STC*, rev. and enlarged by W. A. Jackson, F. S. Ferguson, and Katherine F. Pantzer (1976), makes the same suggestion, as do S. Halkett and J. Laing, *A Dictionary of Anonymous and Pseudonymous Publications in the English Language, 1475–1640,* 3rd edition ed. John Horden (1980); Crawford (I, above), p. 281, n. 166, argues for female authorship.

JJ. *Anne Weamys (fl. 1651).* In her chapter "The Pastoral Romance" in *Women Writers* (II, G, above), MacCarthy praises Weamys' *A Continuation of Sir Philip Sidney's Arcadia* for its "clear, straightforward and economical" style. See II, G for other brief comments on Weamys.

KK. *Anne Collins (fl. 1653).* In 1961 Stanley N. Stewart published a facsimile edition of selections from *An. Collins: Divine Songs and Meditacions (1653).*

LL. *Sarah Jinner (fl. 1658).* Brief mentions of Jinner in Bernard Capp, *English Almanacs, 1500–1800: Astrology and the Popular Press* (1979), present her almanacs as "combining a spirited defense of women with medical notes, social comment and a vigorous political commentary."

IV. State of Criticism

Much recent work on seventeenth-century women has questioned the extent to which women's writing in our period was influenced by Renaissance notions of proper female behavior; the place women's writing plays in the literary, religious, and political history of the period; whether women's writing belongs to a distinguishable women's literary tradition; and—perhaps inevitably (if prejudicially)—the question of the artistic merit of work by women in early modern England. Scholarship on the women whose work is treated in this essay demonstrates that the relationship between women's writing and Renaissance culture is complex and multifaceted; that women's writing is important in the history of a number of genres—among them, biography, autobiography, prose fiction, the sonnet, even drama—and in religious and political (and scientific) history as well; that many Renaissance women thought of themselves as writing to and for women; and that the writing of Renaissance women is well worth careful attention. Perhaps most surprising to many scholars are the revelations that so many of the women writers recently rediscovered were read—in printed books and in manuscript—and admired by their contemporaries, both male and female, and that Renaissance women wrote so many different kinds of literature.

Works by some seventeenth-century Englishwomen—Ann Halkett, Anne Fanshawe, and Mary Wroth, for example—are available in superb editions by scholars such as John Loftis and Josephine Roberts; we are in urgent need of similar texts of other women writers—most notably Elizabeth Cary, Margaret Cavendish, and Katherine Philips. Although several anthologies present helpful selections of women's writing of the seventeenth century, there is no so-called "standard" anthology or literary history of the period that pays ample attention to women writers.

See also

Background Studies (Selected)

Ashley, Maurice. "Love and Marriage in Seventeenth-Century England," *History Today,* 8 (1958), 667–75.

Bergeron, David M. "Women as Patrons of English Renaissance Drama," in *Patronage in the Renaissance,* ed. Guy Fitch Lytle and Stephen Orgel (1981), pp. 274–90.

Bradford, Gamaliel. *Elizabethan Women,* ed. Harold Ogden White (1936).

Bullough, Vern L. *The Subordinate Sex: A History of Attitudes toward Women* (1974).

Cressy, David. *Literacy and the Social Order: Reading and Writing in Tudor and Stuart England* (1980).

Davis, Natalie Zemon. *Society and Culture in Early Modern France: Eight Essays* (1965; rpt. 1985).

Frye, Roland Mushat. "The Teaching of Classical Puritanism on Conjugal Love," *SR,* 2 (1955), 148–59.

Gagen, Jean Elisabeth. *The New Woman: Her Emergence in English Drama, 1600–1730* (1954).

Hageman, Elizabeth H. "Recent Studies in Women Writers of Tudor England, Part I: 1485–1603, Excluding Mary Sidney, Countess of Pembroke," *ELR,* 14 (1984), 409–25.

Hanawalt, Barbara A., ed. *Women and Work in Preindustrial Europe* (1986).

Hill, Christopher. "Base, Impudent Kisses," in his *The World Upside Down: Radical Ideas During the English Revolution* (1972; rpt. 1984), pp. 306–23.

Hole, Christina. *The English Housewife in the Seventeenth Century* (1953).

Horowitz, Maryanne Cline. "The Woman Question in Renaissance Texts," *History of European Ideas,* 8 (1987), 587–95 [review essay].

Hufton, Olwen. "Women in History. Part I. Early Modern Europe," *Past and Present,* 101 (1983), 125–41 [survey of recent work].

Illick, Joseph E. "Child-Rearing in Seventeenth-Century New England and America," in *The History of Childhood,* ed. Lloyd de Mause (1974), pp. 303–50.

Kinney, Arthur, ed. "Women in the Renaissance," *ELR,* 14 (1984) [a special issue].

Koehler, Lyle. *A Search for Power: The "Weaker Sex" in Seventeenth-Century New England* (1980).

Lazlett, Peter. *Family Life and Illicit Love in Earlier Generations* (1977).

——————. *The World We Have Lost: England Before the Industrial Age* (1965).

Martin, Wendy. "Anne Bradstreet's Poetry: A Study of Subversive Piety," in *Shakespeare's Sisters: Feminist Essays on Women Poets,* ed. Sandra M. Gilbert and Susan Gubar (1979), pp. 19–31.

Notestein, Wallace. "The English Woman, 1580–1650," in *Studies in Social History: A Tribute to G. M. Trevelyan,* ed. John Harold Plumb (1955; rpt. 1969), pp. 69–107.

O'Faolain, Julia, and Lauro Martines. *Not in God's Image: Women in History from the Greeks to the Victorians* (1973).

Rogers, Katharine M. *The Troublesome Helpmate: A History of Misogyny in Literature* (1966; rpt. 1973).

Shücking, Levin L. *The Puritan Family: A Social Study from Literary Sources,* trans. Brian Battershaw (1969).

Slater, Miriam. *Family Life in the Seventeenth Century: The Verneys of Claydon House* (1984).

——————. "The Weightest Business: Marriage in an Upper-Gentry Family in Seventeeth-Century England," *Past and Present,* 72 (1976), 25–54.

Smith, Hilda. "Gynecology and Ideology in Seventeenth-Century England," in *Liberating Women's History: Theoretical and Critical Essays,* ed. Bernice A. Carroll (1976), pp. 97–114.

Spring, Eileen. "Law and the Theory of the Affective Family," *Albion,* 16 (1984), 1–20.

Spufford, Margaret. "First Steps in Literacy: The Reading and Writing Experiences of the Humblest Seventeenth-Century Spiritual Autobiographers," *Social History,* 4 (1979), 407–35 ["Additional Note on the Influence of 'Literate' Women," pp. 434–35].

Stock, Phyllis. *Better than Rubies: A History of Women's Education* (1978).

Stone, Lawrence. *The Crisis of the Aristocracy, 1558–1641* (1965; abr. ed. 1967).

Thomas, Keith. *Religion and the Decline of Magic: Studies in Popular Belief in Sixteenth and Seventeenth Century England* (1971).

Todd, Margo. "Humanists, Puritans and Spiritualized Household," *Church History,* 49 (1980), 18–34.

Williams, Franklin B., Jr. "The Literary Patronesses of Renaissance England," *N&Q,* 207 (1962), 364–66.

I. General Studies

Ballard, George. *Memoirs of Several Ladies of Great Britain Who Have Been Celebrated for Their Writings or Skill in the Learned Languages, Arts and Sciences* (1752; rpt. ed. Ruth Perry, 1985).

Bowerbank, Sylvia Lorraine. "'By What Authority': Women Writing in the Seventeenth Century," Ph.D. diss., McMaster Univ., 1985.

Costello, Louisa Stuart. *Memoirs of Eminent Englishwomen,* 2 vols. (1844).

Hale, Sarah Josepha. *Women's Record: or, Sketches of all Distinguished Women . . . with Selections from Authoresses of Each Era* (1853; rpt. 1970).

Waller, Jennifer R. "'My Hand a Needle Better Fits': Anne Bradstreet and Women Poets in the Renaissance," *DR,* 54 (1974), 436–50.

Williams, Jane. *The Literary Women of England, Including a Biographical Epitome of all the Most Eminent to the Year 1700 . . . with Extracts from Their Works, and Critical Remarks* (1861).

II. Studies of Individual Genres

A. *Defenses of Women*

Camden, Carroll. "Certain Controversies over Women," in his *The Elizabethan Woman* (1952), pp. 239–71.

Crandall, Coryl. "The Cultural Implications of the Swetnam Anti-Feminist Controversy in the 17th Century," *JPC,* 2 (1968), 136–48; rpt. with minor changes in his *Swetnam the Woman-hater: The Controversy and the Play, A Critical Edition with Introduction and Notes* (1969).

de Bruyn, Jan. "The Ideal Lady and the Rise of Feminism in Seventeenth-Century England," *Mosaic,* 17 (1984), 19–28.

Nadelhaft, Jerome. "The Englishwoman's Sexual Civil War: Feminist Attitudes towards Men, Women, and Marriage, 1650–1740," *JHI,* 43 (1982), 555–79.

Naess, Eli Lindtner. "Mad Madge and Other 'Lost' Women. The Situation of the Woman Writer in Seventeenth Century England," *Edda,* 4 (1979), 197–209 [focus on Margaret Cavendish].

Rowbotham, Sheila. "Impudent Lasses," in her *Women, Resistance and Revolution* (1972), pp. 15–35.

Shepherd, Simon. "Beating Up Men," in his *Amazons and Warrior Women: Varieties of Feminism in Seventeenth-Century Drama* (1981), pp. 203–17.

B. *Autobiography*

Bowerbank, Sylvia Lorraine. "By What Authority" (I, above).
Coleman, Linda S. "Public Self, Private Self: Women's Life-Writing in England, 1570–1720," *DAI,* 48 (1987), 130A.
Mitra, Anuradha Mookerjee. "Images of the Self: A Study of Seventeenth-Century Women's Autobiography," *DAI,* 47 (1987), 4398–99A.
Pomerleau, Cynthia S. "The Emergence of Women's Autobiography in England," in *Women's Autobiography: Essays in Criticism,* ed. Estelle C. Jelinek (1980), pp. 21–38.

C. *Biography*

Stauffer, Donald A. *English Biography before 1700* (1930), esp. pp. 148–50 and 206–14.

D. *Letters*

Sister Mary Humiliata. "Standards of Taste Advocated for Feminine Letter Writing, 1640–1797," *HLQ,* 13 (1950), 261–77.

E. *Preaching and Prophetic Writing*

Berg, Christine and Philippa Berry. "'Spiritual Whoredom': An Essay on Female Prophets in the Seventeenth Century," in *1642: Literature and Power in the Seventeenth Century,* ed. Francis Barker, et al. (1981), pp. 37–54.
Bowerbank, Sylvia Lorraine. "By What Authority" (I, above).
Burrage, Champlin. "Anna Trapnel's Prophecies," *English Historical Review,* 26 (1911), 526–35.
Gentles, Ian. "London Levellers in the English Revolution: the Chidleys and Their Circle," *Journal of Ecclesiastical History,* 29 (1978), 281–309 [Katherine Chidley].
Higgins, Patricia. "The Reactions of Women, with Special Reference to Women Petitioners," in *Politics, Religion, and the English Civil War,* ed. Brian Manning (1973), pp. 177–222.
Ludlow, Dorothy Paula. "'Arise and Be Doing,' English 'Preaching' Women, 1640–1660," *DAI,* 39 (1978), 5664A.
Nuttall, Geoffrey F. *Visible Saints: The Congregational Way, 1640–1660* (1957).
Thomas, Keith. "Women and the Civil War Sects," *Past and Present,* 13 (1958), 42–62; rpt. in *Crisis in Europe, 1560–1660: Essays from "Past and Present,"* ed. Trevor Aston (1965), pp. 317–40.
Williams, Ethyn Morgan. "Women Preachers in the Civil War," *JMH,* 1 (1929), 561–69 [Catherine Chidley, Mistress Attaway, the "mayor's wife" of Old Bailey, and Elizabeth Warren].

F. *Mothers' Advice Books*

Klein, Joan Larsen. "Women and Marriage in Renaissance England: Male Perspectives," *Topic: 36,* The Elizabethan Women" (1982), 20–37 [includes woman writers].
Schnucker, R. V. "The English Puritans and Pregnancy, Delivery and Breast Feeding," *History of Childhood Quarterly,* 1 (1973–74), 637–58 [cites Joceline, Clinton, and a number of male writers].

Travitsky, Betty S. "The New Mother of the English Renaissance (1489–1659): A Descriptive Catalogue," *BHR,* 82 (1979), 63–89.

III. STUDIES OF INDIVIDUAL WRITERS

A. *Aemilia Lanier*

Barnstone, Aliki. "Women and the Garden: Andrew Marvell, Emelia Lanier, and Emily Dickinson," *W&L,* NS 2 (1981), 147–67.

B. *Arbella Stuart*

McInnes, Ian. *Arbella: The Life and Times of Lady Arabella Seymour, 1575–1615* (1968).

C. *Elizabeth Cary*

Belsey, Catherine. *The Subject of Tragedy: Identity and Difference in Renaissance Drama* (1985), esp. pp. 171–75.

Dunston, A. C. *Examination of Two English Dramas: "The Tragedy of Mariam" by Elizabeth Carew; and "The True Tragedy of Herod and Antipater: with the Death of faire Marriam" by Gervase Markham and William Sampson* (1908).

Fullerton, Lady Georgiana. *The Life of Elizabeth Lady Falkland, 1585–1639* (1883).

Goreau, Angeline. "Two English Women in the Seventeenth Century: Notes for an Anatomy of Feminine Desire," in *Western Sexuality: Practice and Precept in Past and Present Times,* ed. Philippe Aries and Andre Bejin (1985), pp. 103–113 [Cary and Aphra Behn].

Lawson, Mildred Smoot. "Elizabeth Tanfield Cary and 'The Tragedie of Mariam,'" *DAI,* 45 (1985), 2886A.

Levin, Richard. "A Possible Source of *A Fair Quarrel, N&Q,* 228 (1983), 152–53 [episode in *Mariam* as source for scene in Middleton and Rowley's play].

Lunn, David. "Elizabeth Cary, Lady Falkland (1586/7–1639)," *Royal Stuart Papers,* 11 (1977).

Murdock, Kenneth B. *The Sun at Noon: Three Biographical Sketches: Elizabeth Cary, Viscountess Falkland, 1585–1639; Lucius Cary, Viscount Falkland, 1610–1643; John Wilmot, Earl of Rochester, 1647–1680* (1939).

Shapiro, Arlene Iris. "Elizabeth Cary: Her Life, Letters, and Art," *DAI,* 45 (1984), 1762A.

Valency, Maurice J. *The Tragedies of Herod and Mariamne* (1940; rpt. 1966), esp. pp. 87–91.

Witherspoon, Alexander Maclaren. *The Influence of Robert Garnier on Elizabethan Drama* (1924; rpt. 1968).

D. *Lucy, Countess of Bedford*

Thomson, P[atricia]. "John Donne and the Countess of Bedford," *MLR,* 44 (1949), 329–38.

E. *Lady Mary Wroth*

Croft, P. J. "Echoes of Robert's Sequence in his Daughter Mary Wroth's Verse," in *The Poems of Robert Sidney* (1984), pp. 342–45.

Duncan-Jones, Katherine. "'Rosis and Lysa': Selections from the Poems of Sir Robert Sidney," *ELR*, 9 (1979), 240–63.

Kelleher, Hilton, and Katherine Duncan-Jones. "A Manuscript of Poems by Sir Robert Sidney: Some Early Impressions," *BLJ*, 1 (1975), 107–44.

Maxwell, C. H. J., ed. "Loves Victorie," Master's Thesis, Stanford Univ., 1933.

Parry, Graham. "Lady Mary Wroth's *Urania*," *PLPLS-LHS*, 16 (1975), 51–60.

Paulissen, May Nelson. *The Love Sonnets of Lady Mary Wroth: A Critical Introduction* (1982).

Roberts, Josephine A. "Recent Studies in Mary Sidney, Countess of Pembroke," *ELR*, 14 (1984), 426–39.

Waller, W. C. "An Extinct Country Family: Wroth of Loughton Hall," *Transactions of the Essex Archeological Society*, 8 (1903), 145–81.

F. *Anne Clifford*

Sackville-West, V. "Knole in the Reign of James I: Richard Sackville, 3rd Earl of Dorset and Lady Anne Clifford," in her *Knole and the Sackvilles* (1922), pp. 48–81.

Spence, R. T. "Lady Clifford, Countess of Dorset, Pembroke and Montgomery (1590–1676): A Reappraisal," *Northern History*, 15 (1979), 43–65.

G. *Bathsua Makin*

Watson, Fostor. "Mrs. Bathsua Makin and the Education of Gentlewomen," *Atalanta*, 8 (1895), 634–37.

H. *Eleanor Davies*

Spenser, Theodore. "The History of an Unfortunate Lady," *Harvard Studies and Notes on Philology and Literature*, 29 (1936), 43–59.

Wright, S. G. "Dougle Fooleries," *Bodleian Quarterly Record*, 7 (1932), 95–98.

I. *Margaret Fell*

Barbour, Hugh. "Quaker Prophetesses and Mothers in Israel," in *Essays in Quaker History, in Honor of Edwin B. Bronner*, ed. J. M. Frost and J. M. Moore (1986), pp. 41–60.

Huber, Elaine C. "A Woman Must Not Speak: Quaker Women in the English Left Wing," in *Women of Spirit: Female Leadership in the Jewish and Christian Traditions*, ed. Rosemary Ruether and Eleanor McLaughlin (1979), pp. 153–81.

Speizman, Milton D. and Jane C. Kronick, ed. "A Seventeenth-Century Quaker Women's Declaration," *Signs*, 1 (1975), 231–45 [perhaps by Sarah Fell].

J. *Lucy Hutchinson*

Braund, Elizabeth. "Mrs. Hutchinson and her Teaching," *Evangelical Quarterly*, 31 (1959), 72–81 [on *On the Principles of the Christian Religion* and *Of Theology*].

Meynell, Alice. "The Seventeenth Century," in her *Essays*, ed. Francis Meynell (1947), pp. 195–200.

Sutherland, James. "Down Chancery Lane," in *Evidence in Literary Scholarship: Essays in Memory of James Marshall Osborn*, ed. René Wellek and Alvaro Ribeiro (1979), pp. 165–78 [on the discovery of the holograph of the *Memoirs*].

K. *Margaret Cavendish*

Alic, Margaret. "The Rise of the Scientific Lady," in her *Hypatia's Heritage: A History of Women in Science from Antiquity through the Nineteenth Century* (1986), pp. 77–94.

Blaydes, Sophia. "The Duchess' Dilemma," *BWVACET,* 4 (1977), 44–52.

_____. "The Poetry of the Duchess of Newcastle: A Pyramid of Praise," *BWVACET,* 6 (1981), 26–31.

Bordinat, Philip. "The Duchess of Newcastle as a Literary Critic," *BWVACET,* 5 (1979), 6–12.

Davis, Natalie Zemon. "Gender and Genre: Women as Historical Writers, 1400–1820,"in *Beyond Their Sex: Learned Women of the European Past,* ed. Patricia H. Labalme (1984), pp. 153–82.

McGuire, Mary Ann. "Margaret Cavendish, Duchess of Newcastle, On the Nature and Status of Women," *IJWS,* 1 (1978), 193–206.

Merchant, Carolyn. *The Death of Nature: Women, Ecology, and the Scientific Revolution* (1980; rpt. 1983), esp. 270–72.

Mintz, Samuel I. "The Duchess of Newcastle's Visit to the Royal Society," *JEGP,* 51 (1952), 168–76.

Nicolson, Marjorie Hope. *Pepys' "Diary" and the New Science* (1965), esp. pp. 104–14.

_____. *Voyages to the Moon* (1948), esp. pp. 220–24 [*The Blazing World*].

Perry, Henry Ten Eyck. *The First Duchess of Newcastle and her Husband as Figures in Literary History* (1918).

Prasad, Kashi. "Margaret Cavendish's *Blazing World:* A Seventeenth-Century Utopia," in *Essays Presented to Amy G. Stock,* ed. R. K. Kaul (1965), pp. 58–65.

Spacks, Patricia Meyer. *The Female Imagination* (1975), esp. pp. 190–96.

Woolf, Virginia. "The Duchess of Newcastle," in her *The Common Reader* (1925), pp. 101–12.

L. *Jane Lead*

Bailey, Margaret Lewis. *Milton and Jakob Boehm: A Study of German Mysticism in Seventeenth-Century England* (1914), esp. pp. 106–08.

Bowerbank, Sylvia Lorraine. "By What Authority" (I, above).

Hirst, Désirée. *Hidden Riches: Traditional Symbolism from the Renaissance to Blake* (1964).

Smith, Catherine F. "A Note on Jane Lead, With Selections from her Writings," *SMy,* 3 (1980), 79–82.

Sperle, Joanne Magnami. "God's Healing Angel: A Biography of Jane Ward Lead," *DAI,* 46 (1985), 1289A.

M. *Mary Boyle, Countess of Warwick*

Palgrave, Mary E. *Mary Rich, Countess of Warwick (1625–1678)* (1901).

Smith, Charlotte Fell. *Mary Rich, Countess of Warwick (1625–1678): Her Family and Friends* (1901).

N. *Dorothy Osborne*

Wade, Rosalind. "Dorothy Osborne (Lady Temple) 1626–1695: The Missing Years," *ContempR,* 248 (1986), 98–104.

O. *Anne Conway*

Bowerbank, Sylvia Lorraine. "By What Authority" (I, above).

Colie, Rosalie L. *Light and Enlightenment: A Study of the Cambridge Platonists and the Dutch Arminians* (1957), passim.

Coudert, Allison. "A Cambridge Platonist's Kabbalist Nightmare," *JHI*, 36 (1975), 633–52.

Walker, D. P. "Lady Conway and van Helmont," in his *The Decline of Hell: Seventeenth-Century Discussions of Eternal Torment* (1974), pp. 137–46.

P. *Katherine Philips*

Clark, William Smith. *The Early Irish Stage: The Beginnings to 1720* (1955).

Evans, G. Blakemore, ed. *The Plays and Poems of William Cartwright* (1951).

Evans, Willa McClung. *Henry Lawes: Musician and Friend of Poets* (1941).

Faderman, Lillian. *Surpassing the Love of Men: Romantic Friendship and Love between Women from the Renaissance to the Present* (1981), esp. pp. 68–71.

Hageman, Elizabeth. "Katherine Philips: The Matchless Orinda," Matrologia Latina Series: Draft Research Papers (1986).

Latt, David Jay. "The Progress of Friendship: The *Topoi* for Society and the Ideal Experience in the Poetry and Prose of Seventeenth-Century England," *DAI*, 32 (1972), 4616–17A.

Lennep, William van, ed. *The London Stage, 1660–1800, Part I: 1660–1700* (1965).

Libertin, Mary. "Female Friendship in Women's Verse: Toward a New Theory of Female Poetics," *WS*, 9 (1982), 291–308.

Longe, Julia G., ed. *Martha, Lady Giffard: Her Life and Correspondence (1664–1722), A Sequel to the Letters of Dorothy Osborne* (1911), esp. pp. 37–46.

Mambretti, Catherine Cole. "A Critical Edition of the Poetry of Katherine Philips," Ph.D. Diss., Univ. of Chicago, 1979.

Miner, Earl. *The Cavalier Mode from Jonson to Cotton* (1975), esp. pp. 300–02.

Morgan, Fidelis. "Katherine Philips—The Matchless Orinda," in her *The Female Wits: Women Playwrights of the Restoration* (1981), pp. 3–11.

Price, Curtis A. "The Songs for Katherine Philips' *Pompey* (1663)," *TN*, 33 (1979), 61–66.

Roberts, William. "The Dating of Orinda's French Translations," *PQ*, 49 (1970), 56–67.

_____. "Saint-Amant, Orinda and Dryden's Miscellany," *ELN*, 1 (1964), 191–96.

_____. "Sir William Temple on Orinda: Neglected Publications," *PBSA*, 57 (1963), 328–36.

Røstvig, Maren-Sofie. *The Happy Man: Studies on the Metamorphoses of a Classical Ideal, 1600–1700* (1954), esp. pp. 348–59.

Turner, James. *The Politics of Landscape: Rural Scenery and Society in English Poetry, 1630–1660* (1979), passim.

IV. ANTHOLOGIES INCLUDING WOMEN WRITERS OF THE SEVENTEENTH CENTURY

Abrams, M. H., et al., eds. *The Norton Anthology of English Literature,* 5th ed., Vol. 1 (1986) [Mary Wroth, Aemilia Lanier, Anne Halkett, Dorothy Osborne].

Barnstone, Aliki, and Willis Barnstone, ed. *A Book of Women Poets from Antiquity to Now* (1980) [Aemilia Lanier, Katherine Philips].

Bernikow, Louise, ed. *The World Split Open: Four Centuries of Women Poets in England and America, 1552-1950* (1974) [Katherine Philips, Anne Collins].

Bethune, George W., ed. *The British Female Poets with Biographical and Critical Notices* (1849; rpt. 1972) [Elizabeth Carew (Cary), Katherine Philips, Margaret Cavendish].

Broadbent, John, ed. *Poets of the 17th Century,* Vol. 2 (1974) [Anne Collins, Margaret Cavendish, Lady Katherine Dyer, Katherine Philips].

Cosman, Carol, Joan Keefe, and Kathleen Weaver, ed. *The Penguin Book of Woman Poets* (1978; rpt. 1979) [Margaret Cavendish, Katherine Philips].

Dyce, Alexander, ed. *Specimens of British Poetesses, Selected and Chronologically Arranged* 91827) [Elizabeth Melvill; Elizabeth Carew (Cary); Mary Wroth; Anne, Countess of Arundel; Diana Primrose; Mary Fage; Anna Hume; Anne Collins; Mary Morpeth; Elizabeth Stuart; Katherine Philips; Frances Boothby; Margaret Cavendish].

Gilbert, Sandra M. and Susan Gubar, ed. *The Norton Anthology of Literature by Women: The Tradition in English* (1985) [Aemilia Lanier, Margaret Cavendish, Jane Lead, Katherine Philips].

Goulianos, Joan, ed. *by a Women writt: Literature from Six Centuries by and about Women* (1973; rpt. 1974) [Alice Thornton, Margaret Cavendish].

Rogers, Katherine M. and William McCarthy, ed. *The Meridian Anthology of Early Women Writers: British Literary Women from Aphra Behn to Maria Edgeworth, 1660-1800* (1987) [Katherine Philips].

Rowton, Frederic, ed. *The Female Poets of Great Britain: Chronologically Arranged with Copious Selections and Critical Remarks* (1848; facsimile of 1853 text ed. Marilyn L. Williamson, 1981) [Elizabeth Carew (Cary); Mary Wroth; Anne, Countess of Arundel; Diana Primrose; Mary Fage; Anna Hume; Ann Collins; Mary Morpeth; Katherine Philips, Princess Elizabeth; Frances Boothby; Margaret Cavendish].

Stanford, Ann, ed. *The Women Poets in English: An Anthology* (1972) [Lucy Harington, Elizabeth Cary, Mary Wroth, Rachel Specht, Lady Diana Primrose, Anne Finch, Margaret Cavendish, Katherine Philips].

I should like to thank the College of Liberal Arts Summer Faculty Fellowship Fund for financial support of this project.

======

RECENT STUDIES IN WOMEN WRITERS OF THE ENGLISH SEVENTEENTH CENTURY, 1604–1674
(1987–April 1990)

ELIZABETH H. HAGEMAN

BACKGROUND STUDIES (Selected)

Bonfield, Lloyd. *Marriage Settlements, 1601–1740: The Adoption of the Strict Settlement* (1983).

Carlton, Charles. "The Widow's Tale: Male Myths and Female Reality in 16th and 17th Century England," *Albion,* 10 (1978), 118–29.

Davidson, Caroline. *A Woman's Work Is Never Done: A History of Housework in the British Isles, 1650–1950* (1982).

Fleming, Juliet. "*The French Garden:* An Introduction to Women's French," *ELH,* 56 (1989), 19–51.

Hamill, Frances. "Some Unconventional Women before 1800: Printers, Booksellers, and Collectors," *PBSA,* 49 (1955), 300–16.

Jordan, Constance. "Gender and Justice in *Swetnam the Woman-Hater,*" *RenD,* 18 (1987), 149–69.

Leites, Edmund. *The Puritan Conscience and Modern Sexuality* (1986).

Lipking, Joanna. "Fair Originals: Women Poets in Male Commendatory Poems," *ECLife,* 12 (1988), 58–72.

Morgan, Paul. "Frances Wolfreston and 'Hor Bouks': A Seventeenth-Century Woman Book Collector," in *Shakespeare: Text, Language, Criticism: Essays in Honour of Marvin Spevack,* ed. Bernhard Fabian and Kurt Tetzeli von Rosador (1987), pp. 193–211; rev. and expanded in *Library,* 11 (1989), 13–19.

Mulvihill, Maureen E. "Feminism and the Rare-Book Market," *Scriblerian,* 22 (1989), 1–5.

Somerset, Anne. *Ladies in Waiting: From the Tudors to the Present Day* (1984).

Welles, Theodore de. "Sex and Sexual Attitudes in Seventeenth-Century England: The Evidence from Puritan Diaries," *Ren&R,* 24 (1988), 45–64.

EDITIONS

Her Own Life: Autobiographical Writings by Seventeenth-Century Englishwomen, ed. Elspeth Graham, Hilary Hinds, Elaine Hobby, and Helen Wilcox (1989), provides selections from twelve seventeenth-century Englishwomen. *Kissing the Rod: An Anthology of Seventeenth-Century Women's Verse,* ed. Germaine Greer, Susan Hastings, Jeslyn Medoff, and Melinda Sansone (1988), prints poetry by some fifty women who are described in Greer's Introduction as "*guerrilleras,* untrained, ill-equipped, isolated and vulnerable." Some of the authors excerpted in *Her Own Life* and *Kissing the Rod* are listed individually in Section II, below.

Betty Travitsky, *The Paradise of Women: Writings by Englishwomen of the Renaissance*

(1981; rpt. with a new preface and updated notes in a paperback edition, 1989), prints excerpts from women poets and prose writers of the Tudor, Stuart, and Caroline periods. Copies of writings by pre-Victorian women writers are available for classroom and research use from *The Women Writers Project,* a computer project based at Brown University under the directorship of Susanne Woods, with the assistance of Patricia Caldwell, Stuart Curran, Margaret J. M. Ezell, Elizabeth H. Hageman, and Elizabeth D. Kirk.

I. GENERAL STUDIES

In *Virtue of Necessity: English Women's Writing, 1649–88* (1989), Elaine Hobby treats some two hundred women writers in chapters entitled "Prophets and Prophecies," "Religious Poetry, Meditations and Conversion Narratives," "Autobiographies and Biographies of Husbands," "Romantic Love—Prose Fiction," "Romantic Love—Plays," "Romantic Love—Poetry," "Skills Books—Housewifery, Medicine, Midwifery," and "Education." The book is "a guide to women's writing in that period of social upheaval and change, and an analysis of the strategies they were bound to use to have their voices heard." Hobby's bibliography includes a sixteen-page list of Englishwomen's works published between 1649 and 1688. Marilyn L. Williamson, *Raising Their Voices: British Women Writers, 1650–1750* (1990), traces women's literary traditions from the mid-seventeenth century into the eighteenth century, demonstrates the continuity of "feminist commentary about the condition of women" since the seventeenth century, and argues that in about 1640 in England "a definite female voice begins to be heard: women take female pseudonyms, turn discourse to their needs, create distinctive themes and conventions."

Elaine V. Beilin, *Redeeming Eve: Women Writers of the English Renaissance* (1987), remains the only recent book-length study focusing on early seventeenth-century Englishwoman writers. Betty S. Travitsky, "Introduction: Placing Women in the English Renaissance," in *The Renaissance Englishwoman in Print: Counterbalancing the Canon,* ed. Anne M. Haselkorn and Betty S. Travitsky (1990), pp. 3–41, addresses the vexed question of "gendered assumptions of the English Renaissance" to show that "an examination of the writings of Renaissance Englishwomen suggests that at least some of these women did 'have' a Renaissance and that the experience of the Renaissance for women has not yet been as fully evaluated as possible."[1] Ann Rosalind Jones' forthcoming *The Currency of Eros: Women's Love Lyric, 1520–1640* treats English, French, and Italian women poets.

Brief notes on the lives and works of some seventeenth-century women are included in *An Encyclopedia of British Women Writers,* ed. Paul Schlueter and June Schlueter (1988); *British Women Writers: A Critical Reference Guide,* ed. Janet Todd (1989); and *A Dictionary of British and American Women Writers, 1660–1800,* ed. Janet Todd (1985). Elaine V. Beilin, "Current Bibliography of English Women Writers, 1500–1640," in Haselkorn and Travitsky (above), pp. 347–60, includes works by a number of early seventeenth-century women; the annotated bibliographies follow-

---

1. Some of the essays in Haselkorn and Travitsky's volume are summarized in my 1988 survey of seventeenth-century women under the book's prepublication title, *The Englishwoman of the Renaissance, 1500–1640.*

ing each of the essays in Haselkorn and Travitsky are also useful. Maureen E. Mulvihill, "Essential Studies of Restoration Women Writers: Reclaiming a Heritage, 1913–1986," *Restoration*, 11 (1987), 122–31, surveys scholarship on later seventeenth-century women writers. Hilda L. Smith and Susan Cardinale's *Women and the Literature of the Seventeenth Century: An Annotated Bibliography Based on Wing's Short Title Catalogue* (1990) has just appeared.

II. STUDIES OF INDIVIDUAL WRITERS

A. *Aemelia Lanier (1570?–1645)*. "The Description of Cooke-ham" is printed in *Kissing the Rod* (Editions, above). *Salve Deux Rex Judaeorum* is available from the Brown University *Women Writers Project* (Editions, above).

Barbara K. Lewalski, "The Lady of the Country-House Poem," in *The Fashioning and Functioning of the British Country House*, ed. Gervase Jackson-Stops, Gordon J. Schochet, Lena Cowen Orlin, and Elisabeth Blair MacDougall (1989), pp. 261–75, treats "The Description of Cooke-ham" with country-house poems by Ben Jonson, Richard Lovelace, and Andrew Marvell. Lewalski's "Rewriting Patriarchy and Patronage: Margaret Clifford, Anne Clifford, and Aemelia Lanyer" is forthcoming in volume 21 of *YES*.

B. *Elizabeth Cary, Viscountess Falkland (1586–1639)*. "To the Queenes most Excellent Majestie," is attributed to Cary in *Kissing the Rod* (Editions, above), and in Arlene Iris Shapiro, "Elizabeth Cary: Her Life, Letters and Art," Ph.D. diss., SUNY-Stony Brook 1984. R. Valerie Lucas has announced a forthcoming edition of *Mariam*.

Nancy A. Gutierrez, "Valuing *Mariam*: Genre Study and Feminist Analysis," forthcoming in *TSWL*, treats *Mariam* as a highly sophisticated literary piece in which Cary transforms closet drama and the sonnet.

Tina Krontiris, "Style and Gender in Elizabeth Cary's *Edward II*," in Haselkorn and Travitsky (I, above), pp. 137–86, adds internal evidence to Donald Stauffer's argument, "A Deep and Sad Passion," in *The Parrott Presentation Volume* (1935; rpt. 1967), that *Edward II* is by Elizabeth Cary, not by her husband as has traditionally been thought. Krontiris goes on to note how Cary defends Edward's wife, Queen Isabel, and she compares *Mariam* and *Edward II* to show that the latter is more assertive—perhaps because "religious dissidence [was] a liberating catalyst for Viscountess Falkland as it was for many other Renaissance women." D. R. Woolf, "The True Date and Authorship of Henry, Viscount Falkland's *History of the Life, Reign and Death of King Edward II*," *BLR*, 12 (1988), 440–52, argues, however, that the piece is not a Caroline work at all, but a response to the Exclusion Crisis of 1679–81.

C. *Lady Mary Wroth (1586–1640)*.[2] The text of the first part of *The Urania*, the printed 1621 edition, is available in a transcription of the Folger Library copy, through the Brown University *Women Writers Project* (Editions, above). Josephine A. Roberts is preparing an annotated, critical edition of the complete *Urania*, including the unpublished Newberry Library manuscript of the second part. Michael G. Brennan has edited *Lady Mary Wroth's "Love's Victory": The Penshurst Manuscript* (1989).

---

2. I am indebted to Josephine A. Roberts for providing most of the material on Lady Mary Wroth. I remain, of course, responsible for any errors here or elsewhere in this essay.

Margaret P. Hannay, *Philip's Phoenix: Mary Sidney, Countess of Pembroke* (1990), pp. 143–46, 208–10, believes that there was a close relationship between Lady Mary Wroth and her aunt, the Countess of Pembroke; she demonstrates that in 1588, at the height of the Armada invasion, Wroth remained under the protection of the Countess. In "A Sidney Tho Unnamed," forthcoming in *Representing Alternatives: Lady Mary Wroth,* ed. Naomi Miller and Gary Waller, Hannay explores Wroth's biographical heritage, including the influence of her aunt. Gary Waller, "Gender Construction in Early Modern England: Mary Wroth and the Sidney Family Romance," forthcoming in Miller and Waller (above), argues that in their lives and writings Wroth and her first cousin, William Herbert, third Earl of Pembroke, reveal how they were "constructed as gendered subjects in a period seemingly highly repressive but actually unusually fluid and contradictory in its gender assignments." In "Mother/Son, Father/Daughter, Brother/Sister, Cousins: The Sidney Family Romance," forthcoming in *MP,* Waller argues that an incestuous substructure existing within the entire Sidney family finds expression particularly within Wroth's *Urania,* with its "projection of conscious autobiography, wish fulfilment fantasy, and deeper demands of the culturally produced unconscious upon a fantasy landscape."

Michael G. Brennan, *Literary Patronage in the English Renaissance: The Pembroke Family* (1988), pp. 156–57, notes that the names of Wroth's two children by Pembroke are recorded in an early version of Sir Thomas Herbert's manuscript history, now located in the Wilton House Archive Room. Brennan also provides a brief biography of Wroth as part of the Introduction to his edition of *Love's Victory* (above). David Norbrook, *Poetry and Politics in the English Renaissance* (1984), pp. 190–92, considers Ben Jonson's relationships to various members of the Sidney-Pembroke family; he believes that Jonson's "To Robert Wroth" constitutes a tactful reminder that Wroth "could derive more real satisfaction from a traditional rural existence than from frenzied gambling on court favor."

1. *The Countess of Montgomery's Urania.* Maureen Quilligan, "Lady Mary Wroth: Female Authority and the Family Romance," in *Unfolded Tales: Essays on Renaissance Romance,* ed. George M. Logan and Gordon Teskey (1989), pp. 257–80, discusses Wroth's recasting her uncle's *Arcadia* and Spenser's *Faerie Queene* to provide a critique of the patriarchal traffic in women. Quilligan contrasts Wroth's treatment of Urania with that of Pamphilia, "who wins a space for her writing at the cost of all social movement." Naomi J. Miller, " 'Not much to be marked': Narrative of the Woman's Part in Lady Mary Wroth's *Urania,*" *SEL,* 29 (1989), 121–37, treats Wroth's revising romance conventions according to a female perspective to create "models of affirmation who transcend the literary and historical stereotypes of the period." Mary Ellen Lamb, "Women Readers in Wroth's *Urania,*" forthcoming in Miller and Waller (above), traces a development, in the women readers in *Urania,* from the sexual woman reader who is passive in the face of male desires and codes to the intellectual woman reader who achieves autonomy for both herself and her audience. In her forthcoming *Gender and Authorship in the Sidney Circle,* Lamb discusses the effects of gender constraints of the narrator and of authorship on the work. In "Feminine Endings: The Sexual Politics of Sidney's and Spenser's Rhyming," in Haselkorn and Travitsky (I, above), pp. 311–26, Maureen Quilligan briefly analyzes how Wroth's use of feminine rhyme "reemphasizes the gender reversals she points to directly in

other parts of her text." Quilligan also deals with the poetry embedded within the romance in "The Constant Subject: Instability and Female Authority in Wroth's *Urania* Poems," forthcoming in *Seventeenth-Century Poetry,* ed. Katharine Maus and Elizabeth Harvey.

Discussing theatricality in *The Urania,* Heather Weidemann, "Mary Wroth and the Court Masque Tradition," forthcoming in Miller and Waller, considers the impact that the Jacobean court masques, with their contradictory ideologies of the female role, exerted on Wroth's career and work. Michael Shapiro, "Lady Mary Wroth Describes a 'Boy Actress,'" *MRDE,* 4 (1987), 187–94, examines the "esthetic sophistication" of Wroth's two major allusions to the depiction on stage of female characters by young boys. Naomi Miller, "Engendering Discourse: Women's Voices in Wroth's *Urania* and Shakespeare's Plays," forthcoming in Miller and Waller, suggests how Wroth adapts the discourse of Shakespeare's female protagonists, especially in the late plays, to portray women discovering their own voices.

Renée M. Pigeon discusses Wroth's revisions of chivalric romance to emphasize the dangers—"passivity, masochism, and the self-hatred of internalized misogyny"—posed by the idealization of love in "The Re-vision of Romance: Lady Mary Wroth's *The Countess of Montgomery's Urania,*" the third chapter of "Prose Fiction Adaptations of Sidney's *Arcadia,*" Ph.D. diss., UCLA 1988, pp. 116–59. Josephine A. Roberts, "'The Knott Never to Bee Untide': The Controversy Regarding Marriage in Lady Mary Wroth's *Urania,*" forthcoming in Miller and Waller, contrasts Wroth's depiction of arranged marriage with her treatment of secret unions initiated by the partners themselves. Josephine A. Roberts and James F. Gaines, "Amatory Landscapes in Lady Mary Wroth's *Urania* and Mlle. de Scudery's *Clélia,*" forthcoming in *Sexuality and Gender in Early Modern Europe: Institutions, Texts, Images,* ed. James Grantham Turner, offer a comparative analysis of the allegorical landscapes in *The Urania* and *Clélie* and their treatment of gender differences. Roberts discusses the publication history of the romance in "Lady Mary Wroth's *Urania:* A Response to Jacobean Censorship," in *Editing Women Writers of the Renaissance: Papers Presented to the English Renaissance Text Society, 1987* (1988).

2. *Pamphilia to Amphilanthus.* Gary Waller, *English Poetry of the Sixteenth Century* (1986), pp. 266–68, argues that the "all-encompassing melancholy of Wroth's poems seems to grow from wider cultural disillusion than the Petrarchan convention affords" and finds signs of her alienation from public discourse in her "jagged, disruptive text." In "Designing Women: Visual and Verbal Portraits in Veronica Franco's *Rime* and Mary Wroth's *Pamphilia to Amphilanthus,*" forthcoming in Miller and Waller (above), Ann Rosalind Jones relates Wroth's verse to the tradition of lyric poetry by European women, particularly that of the Italian courtesan poet Franco. Chapter 4, "Feminine Pastoral as Heroic Martyrdom," forthcoming in Jones (I, above) treats Mary Wroth and Gaspara Stampa as pastoral poets. Nona Fienberg, "Fair Shows and Secret Cabinets: Mary Wroth's Career in the Jacobean Court," forthcoming in Miller and Waller, argues that Wroth's verse explores the distinction between a private world of female subjectivity and a public world of heroic values. Jeff Masten, "'Shall I then turne blabbe': Mary Wroth's Private Space and the Emergence of Women's Subjectivity," forthcoming in Miller and Waller, believes that in *Pamphilia to Amphilanthus* Wroth writes against Petrarchan discourse and gives evidence of a new sense of

heightened female subjectivity, which will become fully articulated in the eighteenth century. In "'A Sydney, Though Un-Named': Lady Mary Wroth and Her Poetical Progenitors," *ESC*, 15 (1989), 12–20, Janet MacArthur notes in *Pamphilia to Amphilanthus* "a tension between feminine difference and Lady Wroth's desire to emulate the poetic models of her uncle and her father." MacArthur's argument is that Wroth "tries to write within [the tradition of her uncle and her father], but because of her gender necessarily writes outside and against it."

3. *Love's Victory*. Brennan's edition of the play (above) provides a photographic facsimile of the manuscript and a transcription on facing pages, with a list of textual variants from the Huntington Library's manuscript copy. In a discussion of the provenance of the manuscripts, Brennan argues that the Huntington copy is identical with the Plymouth manuscript described in 1853 by James O. Halliwell.

Barbara K. Lewalski, "Lady Mary Wroth's *Love's Victory* and the Tradition of Dramatic Pastoral," forthcoming in Miller and Waller (above), situates Wroth's play in the genre of pastoral tragicomedy, as developed by Tasso, Guarini, Daniel, and Fletcher. Carolyn Ruth Swift, "Feminine Self-Definition in Lady Mary Wroth's *Love's Victorie* (c. 1621)," *ELR*, 19 (1989), 171–88, discusses the play as a feminine dreamworld, in which Wroth draws her protagonists from *Astrophil and Stella*, but rewrites the story so that her characters "may control their own fortunes if they are determined enough to love strongly and live freely."

D. *Anne Clifford (1590–1676)*. A portion of Clifford's diary is reprinted in *Her Own Life* (Editions, above) with a reproduction of her other "autobiography": the "Great Picture" Clifford commissioned in 1646. Harriet Blodgett, *Centuries of Female Days: Englishwomen's Private Diaries* (1988), also prints excerpts from the diary in an Appendix, pp. 249–57.

Barbara K. Lewalski, "Rewriting Patriarchy and Patronage: Margaret Clifford, Anne Clifford, and Aemelia Lanier," is forthcoming in volume 21 of *YES*.

E. *Lucy Hutchinson (1620–80?)*. In "The Source for Lucy Hutchinson's *On Theology*," *N&Q*, 36 (1989), 40–41, Katherine Narveson notes that *On Theology* is a translation of the first two books of John Owen's *Theologoumena Pantodapa* (London, 1661).

F. *Margaret Cavendish, Duchess of Newcastle (1623–73)*. *The Blazing World* is available from the Brown University *Women Writers Project* (Editions, above). A selection of *A True Relation of my Birth, Breeding and Life* is printed in *Her Own Life* (Editions, above), pp. 87–100.

Kathleen Jones, *A Glorious Fame: The Life of Margaret Cavendish, Duchess of Newcastle, 1623–1673* (1988), uses Cavendish's own writings to help reconstruct her life.

In "Embracing the Absolute: The Politics of the Female Subject in Seventeenth-Century England," *Genders*, 1 (1988), 24–39, Catherine Gallagher discusses Margaret Cavendish and Mary Astell (1666–1730) to argue that in the seventeenth century "Toryism and feminism converge because the ideology of absolute monarchy provides, in particular historical situations, a transition to an ideology of the absolute self." Williamson (I, above) begins with a chapter (pp. 37–63) arguing that self-contradictory attitudes in the writing of "Margaret the First" arise from uncertainties inherent in her having been "the first Englishwoman to write a substantial body of literature intentionally for publication." Janet Todd, " 'Were I Empress of the World': The 'German Princess' and the Duchess of Newcastle," in her *The Sign of Angellica: Women, Writing, and Fiction, 1660–1800* (1989), pp. 52–68, distinguishes between the Duchess' public self and "the unique private self scrutinized by Puritan diarists" of the period, and she quotes Pepys' assertion that "The whole story of this Lady is a romance . . . and all she does is romantic" as she makes the point that the Duchess "*was* the first to use published fiction to create a fantastic, wish-fulfilling, compensatory world." Sophia B. Blaydes, "Nature Is a Woman: The Duchess of Newcastle and Seventeenth-Century Philosophy," in *Man, God, and Nature in the Enlightenment*, ed. Donald C. Mell, Jr., Theodore E. D. Braun, and Lucia M. Palmer (1988), pp. 51–64, outlines the development of the Duchess' thought in the seven philosophical works she published between 1653 and 1668. Noting her ability "to argue with some of the more prominent figures of her day," Blaydes also observes that the Duchess was aware that her position as a seventeenth-century woman prohibited her from participating fully in the scientific world into which she "dared to trespass." Hobby (I, above), presents Cavendish in a sympathetic, respectful light, emphasizing her plays, in which "Freed from the authorial voice of lyric poetry or narrative, the texts can be left open-ended, if not unweighted," pp. 105–11. In the plays, Hobby argues, Cavendish "can give [women] a medium through which to learn about the world."

G. *Margaret Fell Fox (1614–1702)*. *The Papers of William Penn*, 5 vols. (1981–82), ed. Mary Maples Dunn and Richard S. Dunn, includes letters to and from Margaret Fell Fox.

Bonnelyn Young Kunze, "Religious Authority and Social Status in Seventeenth-Century England: The Friendship of Margaret Fell, George Fox, and William Penn," *Church History*, 57 (1988), 170–86, notes the significance of social class in the Fell, Fox, Penn friendships and argues that Margaret Fell's "role in relation to Fox and Penn constituted a new construction of gender and class." See also *Anne Conway* (J, below).

H. *Lady Jane Cavendish (c. 1621–1669) and Lady Elizabeth Brackley (c. 1623–1663)*. Nathan Comfort Starr, "*The Concealed Fansyes*: A Play by Lady Jane Cavendish and Lady Elizabeth Brackley," *PMLA*, 46 (1931), 802–38, transcribes the play from Bodleian Library, MS Rawl. Poet. 16; his brief biographical introduction dates the play between 1642 and 1649. Excerpts are printed in *Kissing the Rod* (Editions, above)—as is one poem by each of the sisters.

Margaret J. M. Ezell, " 'To Be Your Daughter in Your Pen': The Social Functions of Literature in the Writings of Lady Elizabeth Brackley and Lady Jane Cavendish," *HLQ*, 51 (1988), 281–96, treats the manuscript volume from which the play comes as a sophisticated, profeminist "collaborative production, designed to please a reasonably extensive audience." Ezell argues that anything but private, "closet" verse, the 45 pages of poems present "a public proclamation of patterns of behavior"; the poems and the two dramas in the handsome volume testify to the Cavendish sisters' efforts "to confirm threatened social values and relationships" during England's Civil War years.

For other writing by Elizabeth Brackley, see *Elizabeth Egerton, Countess of Bridgewater* in my 1988 survey of seventeenth-century women writers, reprinted in this volume.

I. *Jane Lead (1624–1704).* See *Anne Conway* (J, below).

J. *Anne Conway (1631–1679).* The seven essays in "Perspectives on the Seventeenth-Century World of Viscountess Anne Conway," the Spring 1986 issue of the *Guilford [College] Review,* treat Conway and her contemporaries, including Margaret Fell Fox and Jean Lead. Carol Stoneburner, "Comparison of Margaret Fell Fox and Anne Conway," pp. 64–70, notes that Quakers such as Fell and Conway altered seventeenth-century roles of both women and the home by combining public and private activities: "The home became almost as important a space in Quakerism as the Meeting House, and the family was a crucial extension of the Meeting." Elizabeth Keiser, "Jane Lead and the Philadelphia Society: Connections with Anne Conway and the Quakers," pp. 71–89, describes the power of Lead's publications to gain support for the Philadelphians. Observing similarities but also significant differences between the Philadelphians and seventeenth-century Quakers, Keiser records a number of connections between Lead and Conway's circle, and she notes that members of a prominent Quaker family of printers, the Sowles, printed some of Lead's books.

K. *Katherine Philips (1631/2–1664).* Harriet Andreadis has announced a forthcoming facsimile edition of Philips' poetry.

Gerald M. MacLean, "What Is a Restoration Poem? Editing a Discourse, Not an Author," *Text,* 3 (1987), 319–46, explicates "Upon his Majesties most happy restauration, to his Royall Throne in Brittaine," ascribed to Philips in a manuscript at the Bodleian Library, to show that "Editing a discourse involves principles of multiplicity different from those employed in editing an author": when one edits the poem as a piece celebrating the Restoration, one sees, for example, the poem's lines "express[ing] their historical moment precisely by celebrating female subordination as though it were general liberation."

In "Katherine Philips' Friend Regina Collyer," *Restoration,* 13 (1989), 62–67, and "Katherine Philips: Another Step-Father and Another Sibling, 'Mrs C: P.,' and 'Polex:r,'" *Restoration,* 13 (1989), 2–6, Claudia A. Limbert presents biographical evidence about Philips' friends and relatives to help in reading some of the poems.

Harriette Andreadis, "The Sapphic-Platonics of Katherine Philips, 1632–1664," *Signs,* 15 (1989), 34–60, argues that by using familiar seventeenth-century literary forms to present "a desexualized—though passionate and eroticized—version of platonic love in the form of same-sex friendship," Philips "sanctioned her unconventional subject and, in fact, made it a novelty in her time." Noting that Philips' letters confirm the passion of her friendships and also the absence of passion as she writes about her husband or her children, Andreadis argues that "her manipulations of the conventions of male poetic discourse constitute a form of lesbian writing." In "Orinda and Female Intimacy," Hobby (I, above), pp. 128–42, notes how well known Philips was in her own day, argues that "Orinda" is a carefully constructed "feminine" persona, and demonstrates Philips' use of courtly love conventions in her friendship poems.

Philips is one of two authors (the other is Aphra Behn) who Williamson (I, above) sees providing models for later women writers. While Behn and her "daughters" used seventeenth-century "libertine ideology," Orinda used "the retirement discourse, which evolves from the *beatus vir,* the Horatian tradition of the Happy Man," to create a politically conservative "set of terms to critique the public world from a woman's perspective." Lipking (Background Studies, above), treats male writers' commendations of Orinda's poetry.

Curtain Calls: American and British Women in the Theater, 1670–1820, ed. Cecilia Machiski and Mary Anne Schofield (forthcoming), includes an essay by Maureen E. Mulvihill, "A Feminist Link in the Old Boys' Network: The Cosseting of Katherine Philips," which appraises Philips' dramatic career with focus on her privileged management by several influential networks in London, Wales, and Dublin.

L. *Mary Carleton (c. 1635–1673).* An excerpt from *The Case of Madam Mary Carleton* (1663) is printed in *Her Own Life* (Editions, above), pp. 131–46.

Hobby (I, above), pp. 92–96, treats Carleton as "a great manipulator of romance, both in her life, and in the works in which she embroidered upon her exploits." Todd (F, above) contrasts Carleton's appeal to men such as Pepys with Margaret Cavendish's seventeenth-century reputation for eccentricity. Todd focuses on the 1663 *The Case of Mary Carleton* as a titillating narrative of a "heroic Restoration woman." In Chapter 6, "Stories of Virtue," pp. 212–70, in his *The Origins of the English Novel, 1600–1740* (1987), Michael McKeon includes a comment on "Carleton's autobiography [as] an extraordinary instance of progressive plotting most of all at the boundary between her real and her constructed lives." C. F. Main, "The German Princess, or Mary Carleton in Fact and Fiction," *HLB,* 10 (1956), 166–85, presumes that John Carleton wrote "merely to set the record straight" against a woman who "sought to advertise herself." "There is no truth in her," Main writes, "though there are several potential novels." After recounting her "scandalous" life, Main presents an Appendix listing seventeenth-century works devoted to Carleton.

M. *Rachel Speght (fl. 1617).* Cis van Heertum, "A Hostile Annotation of Rachel Speght's *A Mouzell for Melastomus* (1617)," *ES,* 68 (1987), 490–96, summarizes the sometimes scurrilous annotations by a seventeenth-century misogynist who wrote in what is now the Beinecke Library copy of *A Mouzell for Melastomus.*

N. *Frances Boothby (fl. 1669).* Two excerpts from *Marcelia: or, the Treacherous Friend* are printed in *Kissing the Rod* (Editions, above).

Hobby (I, above), pp. 111–13, notes that *Marcelia,* whose Preface defines the author's "daring female invasion of male territory," presents marriages as "dire arrangements."

O. *Elizabeth Polwhele (fl. 1671).* Judith Milhous and Robert D. Hume have edited *The Frolicks: or The Lawyer Cheated (1671)* from the manuscript in the Cornell University Library (1977).

In "Two Plays by Elizabeth Polwhele: *The Faithfull Virgins* and *The Frolicks,*" *PBSA,* 71 (1977), 1–9, Milhous and Hume announce the rediscovery of the manuscript from which they printed their edition of *The Frolicks* (above) and attribute *The Faithfull Virgins* (MS. Rawl. Poet 195, ff. 49–78) to Polwhele. They propose a performance date of 1669 or 1670 for *The Faithfull Virgins* and note that "*The Frolicks*—whether actually performed or not—is the *first* comedy written by a woman for professional production." Milhous and Hume list *The Frolicks* in their "Lost English Plays, 1660–1700," *HLB,* 25 (1977), 5–33.

P. *Jane Sharp (fl. 1671).* A facsimile edition of *The Midwives Book* (1671) has been published by the Garland Press (1985).

Hobby (I, above), pp. 185–87, notes the "intricate effects" that arise from Sharp's determination to teach anatomy to women who are excluded from universities and apprenticeships.

III. STATE OF CRITICISM

In treating later seventeenth-century writing, Elaine Hobby's *Virtue of Necessity* and Marilyn L. Williamson's *Raising Their Voices* nicely complement Elaine V. Beilin's earlier *Redeeming Eve,* which closes with the year 1623. Ann Rosalind Jones' forthcoming *The Currency of Eros* will provide helpful cross-cultural perspectives. Although a number of women treated in this survey of scholarship have been explored with increasing depth and appreciation (even Margaret Cavendish is now seen as far more than an amusing eccentric), the writings of Lady Mary Wroth have attracted the greatest number of critical approaches: feminist, psychoanalytic, new (and old) historicist, cultural materialist, comparative, and new critical. The focus of scholarly attention on *The Urania* is due not simply to the fact that it is the first work of original fiction in English by a woman, but rather to the fact that the tensions, disruption, and contradictions of the text appear to reveal the gender constraints under which Wroth was writing. Now that the complete text of her play is available, further study can be devoted to *Love's Victory* and to the related question of Wroth's treatment of pastoral, of the masque, and of theatricality and role-playing throughout her works. While we wait for full-scale critical editions of other works by seventeenth-century women, computer copies available from the Brown University *Women Writers Project* of many of their works serve a real need—as do anthologies such as *Her Own Life* and *Kissing the Rod.*

See also

BACKGROUND STUDIES (Selected)

Fogle, French R. " 'Such a Rural Queen': The Countess Dowager of Derby as Patron," in French R. Fogel and Louis A. Knafla, *Patronage in Late Renaissance England: Papers Read at a Clark Library Seminar 14 May 1977* (1983).
Gardner, Judith E. "Women in the book trade, 1641–1700: A preliminary survey," *GJ* (1978), 343–46.
Staves, Susan. *Players' Scepters: Fictions of Authority in the Restoration* (1979), esp. Chapter 3: "Sovereignty in the Family," pp. 111–89.

I. STUDIES OF INDIVIDUAL WRITERS

A. *Mary Wroth*
Kennedy, Gwynne. "Feminine Subjectivity in the English Renaissance: The Writings of Elizabeth Cary, Lady Falkland, and Lady Mary Wroth," Ph.D. diss., Univ. of Penn. 1989.
"Noted with Pleasure," *New York Times Book Review,* 28 May 1989, p. 27 [reprints "Griefe, killing griefe" from *Pamphilia to Amphilanthus*].
Waller, Gary. "Five Poems on a Seventeenth Century Romance," forthcoming in his

Other Flights, Always. [A sequence of poems dealing with the relationship between Wroth and William Herbert, third Earl of Pembroke.]

Zurcher, Amelia. " 'Dauncing a Net': Representation in Lady Mary Wroth's *Urania*," M.Phil. thesis, Oxford Univ. 1989.

B. *Dorothy Osborne*

Fitzmaurice, James and Mattine Rey. "Letters by Women in English, the French Romance, and Dorothy Osborne," in *The Politics of Gender in Early Modern Europe*, ed. Jean R. Brink, Allison P. Coudert, and Maryanne C. Horowitz, Sixteenth Century Essays and Studies, Vol. 16 (1989), 149–60.

C. *Margaret Cavendish*

Hampsten, Elizabeth. "Petticoat Authors: 1660–1720," *WS*, 7 (1980), 21–38.

Perry, Ruth. *The Celebrated Mary Astell: An Early English Feminist* (1986).

D. *Katherine Philips*

Limbert, Claudia. "Woman to Woman: The Female Friendship Poems of Katherine Philips," *DAI*, 49 (1988), 1463A–1464A.

Lund, Roger D. "*Bibliotecha* and 'the British Dames': An Early Critique of the Female Wits of the Restoration," *Restoration*, 12 (1988), 96–105.

Moody, Ellen. "Orinda, Rosania, Lucasia *et aliae:* Towards a New Edition of the Works of Katherine Philips," *PQ*, 66 (1987), 325–54.

Perry, Ruth. *The Celebrated Mary Astell: An Early English Feminist* (1986) [Philips' reputation].

Thomas, Patrick. *Katherine Philips ('Orinda')* (1988).

E. *Margaret Fell and Other Quaker Women*

Bacon, Margaret Hope. *Mothers of Feminism: The Story of Quaker Women in America* (1986), esp. Chapters 1 and 2: "Quaker Women in Puritan England" and "The Traveling Women Ministers, 1650–1800," pp. 5–23, 24–41.

Blecki, Catherine La Lourreye. "Alice Hayes and Mary Pennington: Personal Identity within the Tradition of Quaker Spiritual Autobiography," *Quaker History*, 65 (1976), 19–31.

Dailey, Barbara Ritter. "The Husbands of Margaret Fell: An Essay on Religious Metaphor and Social Change," *SCen*, 2 (1987), 55–71.

Evans, Katharine and Sarah Cheevers. *A Short Relation of Cruel Sufferings*, excerpted in *Her Own Life* (Editions, above), pp. 116–30.

Kunze, Bonnelyn Young. "The Family, Social and Religious Life of Margaret Fell," Ph.D. diss., Univ. of Rochester 1987.

Schofield, Mary Anne. " 'Women's Speaking Justified': The Feminine Quaker Voice, 1662–1797," *TSWL*, 6 (1987), 61–77.

F. *Mary Carleton*

Bernbaum, Ernest. *The Mary Carleton Narratives, 1663–1673: A Missing Chapter in the History of the English Novel* (1914).

Singleton, Robert R. "English Criminal Biography, 1651–1722," *HLB*, 18 (1970), 63–83.

Todd, Janet. "Marketing the Self," *Studies in Voltaire*, 217 (1983).

Notes on Contributors

SYLVIA BOWERBANK teaches seventeenth-century literature at McMaster University. In addition to doing research on Margaret Cavendish, she has written on Mary Shelley (*ELH*, 1979), Gertrude More (*Studia Mystica*, 1986), and twelve writers for *A Dictionary of British and American Women Writers 1660–1800* (1985). She is presently editing a book on women and early modern nature philosophy.

ELLEN M. CALDWELL teaches courses on medieval and Renaissance literature and Shakespeare as an assistant professor of English at Kalamazoo College. She has published on the emblem in literature, the rhetoric of fourteenth-century mystics, and the meditative paradigm in *The Winter's Tale*. She is currently working on marriage anti-masques, Hecate and Proserpine in Renaissance drama, and the cloister of chastity metaphor in early Renaissance prose by women.

JEAN C. CAVANAUGH has taught at Loretto Heights College and Webster College and is now Professor of English at Fairmont State College in West Virginia. Her work on Lady Anne Southwell was conducted while holding a Folger Shakespeare Library Fellowship.

JACQUELINE DISALVO is Associate Professor of English at Baruch College, City University of New York. She has published an ideological study of Milton, *War of Titans: Blake's Critique of Milton and the Politics of Religion*, and is working on a book-length feminist reading of Milton. Her essays on Milton have appeared in *Milton Studies, Milton Quarterly, ELR,* and several anthologies.

KIRBY FARRELL, Professor of English at the University of Massachusetts at Amherst, has been an editor of *English Literary Renaissance* since 1978. He is the author of *Shakespeare's Creation* and *Play, Death, and Heroism in Shakespeare*.

R. J. FEHRENBACH, Professor of English at the College of William and Mary, has written widely on English Renaissance literature, particularly the drama, with an emphasis on the historical and the bibliographical; he has published as well on black American literature. He is general editor of *Private Libraries in Renaissance England*, a collection and catalogue of Tudor and early Stuart book-lists.

SUZANNE GOSSETT is Professor of English at Loyola University Chicago. She writes on women in Renaissance English literature as well as in American literature. She is the coauthor, with Barbara Bardes, of *Declarations of Independence: Women and Political Power in Nineteenth-Century American Fiction* (1990). Together with Thomas L. Berger she recently published Malone Society *Collections XIV: Jacobean Academic Plays*. She currently is working on a study of the plays of Beaumont and Fletcher.

ELIZABETH H. HAGEMAN, Professor of English at the University of New Hampshire, has edited "Recent Studies in Renaissance Literature" for *English Literary Renaissance* since 1973. She has written on a number of Renaissance works—most recently on Katherine Philips' poems and (as part of a collaborative editorial project) on Juan Luis Vives' *Instruction of a Christian Woman*.

GABRIELE BERNHARD JACKSON, Professor of English at Temple University, is the author of *Vision and Judgment in Ben Jonson's Drama* and editor of *Every Man in His Humor* in the Yale Ben Jonson series. Currently she is completing an illustrated project that documents and interrogates visual representation of viragos in Renaissance England. Also in progress are a book on eighteenth-century poetry and philosophy and a collection of essays on Shakespeare.

ARTHUR F. KINNEY, founding editor of *English Literary Renaissance*, is Thomas W. Copeland Professor of Literary History at the University of Massachusetts at Amherst. His most recent books include *John Skelton: Priest as Poet, Humanist Poetics*, and *Continental Humanist Poetics*, with an extended analysis of the *contes* of Marguerite of Navarre.

TINA KRONTIRIS took her doctorate at the University of Sussex and now teaches in Athens, Greece.

CLAUDIA LIMBERT, Assistant Professor of English at Penn State University (Shenango Campus), has published and lectured widely on Katherine Philips. She is now completing *I Am Not Thine but Thee: The Biography of Katherine Philips*.

WILLIAM A. RINGLER, JR. (1912–1987) was Professor of English at the University of Chicago (1962–1979) and upon retirement became Senior Research Associate at The Huntington Library (1979–1987). He devoted much of his life to establishing definitive texts for both well-known and lesser-known Renaissance works. Among the lesser-known texts he championed are "The Nutbrown Maid," "A Quatrain Version of the Trental of St. Gregory," William Baldwin's *Beware the Cat*, and the epic poem "Capystranus" (*New Hungarian Quarterly*, 27 [1986]).

JOSEPHINE A. ROBERTS is Professor of English at Louisiana State University. Her publications include a book on Sir Philip Sidney's *Arcadia* (1978), an edition of the poems of Lady Mary Wroth (1983), a two-volume bibliography of Shakespeare's *Richard II* (1988), and essays on Renaissance poets in such journals as *ELR, Huntington Library Quarterly*, and *Comparative Literature*. She is presently preparing a two-volume edition of Lady Mary Wroth's *Urania* for the Renaissance English Text Society.

SARA JAYNE STEEN, Professor of English at Montana State University, is the author of *Thomas Middleton: A Reference Guide* and the editor of Richard Brome's *The English Moore; or, The Mock-Mariage*. She has published on pedagogy and bibliography as well as on English Renaissance drama and women writers. Currently, she is editing the letters of Arbella Stuart.

CAROLYN RUTH SWIFT, Professor of English and Women's Studies at Rhode Island College, coedited *The Woman's Part: Feminist Criticism of Shakespeare* (1980). She is presently studying the writings of women in the Renaissance.

Index

Titled persons are listed by title and cross-referenced by family name. Significant critical terms are indexed, as are major scholars and critics cited in this volume; any works cited appear under the author's name. Only anonymous works are indexed by title. Generally characters are not indexed nor is any portion of "Recent Studies."